D1553972

Dreams for a Decade

POWER, POLITICS, AND THE WORLD

Series editors: Christopher R. W. Dietrich,
Jennifer Mittelstadt, and Russell Rickford

Power, Politics, and the World showcases new stories
in the fields of the history of U.S. foreign relations,
international history, and transnational history. The
series is motivated by a desire to pose innovative
questions of power and hierarchy to the history of
the United States and the world. Books published in
the series examine a wide range of actors on local,
national, and global scales, exploring how they
imagined, enacted, or resisted political, cultural,
social, economic, legal, and military authority.

A complete list of books in the series
is available from the publisher.

DREAMS FOR A DECADE

International Nuclear Abolitionism
and the End of the Cold War

Stephanie L. Freeman

PENN

UNIVERSITY OF PENNSYLVANIA PRESS

PHILADELPHIA

Published by
University of Pennsylvania Press
Philadelphia, Pennsylvania 19104-4112
www.upenn.edu/pennpress

Printed in the United States of America on acid-free paper
10 9 8 7 6 5 4 3 2 1

Hardcover ISBN: 978-1-5128-2422-3
eBook ISBN: 978-1-5128-2423-0

A Cataloging-in-Publication record is
available from the Library of Congress

For Lynn and Patrick Freeman and
in memory of Susan Parham

CONTENTS

ABBREVIATIONS

ABM	Anti-Ballistic Missile
ACDA	Arms Control and Disarmament Agency
AFSC	American Friends Service Committee
AGDF	Action Committee Service for Peace
ASF	Action Reconciliation Service for Peace
CALC	Clergy and Laity Concerned
CDU	Christian Democratic Union
CMEA	Council for Mutual Economic Assistance
CND	Campaign for Nuclear Disarmament
CODENE	Comité pour le Désarmement Nucléaire en Europe
CPSU	Communist Party of the Soviet Union
CSCE	Conference on Security and Cooperation in Europe
EEC	European Economic Community
END	European Nuclear Disarmament
FDP	Free Democratic Party
FOR	Fellowship of Reconciliation
FRG	Federal Republic of Germany
GDR	German Democratic Republic
GE	General Electric
ICBM	Intercontinental Ballistic Missile
IDDS	Institute for Defense and Disarmament Studies
IKV	Interchurch Peace Council
INF	Intermediate-Range Nuclear Forces
IPCC	International Peace Communication and Coordination Center
KAL 007	Korean Airlines Flight 007
KOS	Committee for Social Resistance
LRTNF	Long-Range Theater Nuclear Forces
MAD	Mutual Assured Destruction

MFS	Mobilization for Survival
MIRV	Multiple Independently Targetable Reentry Vehicle
MP	Member of Parliament
NATO	North Atlantic Treaty Organization
NMS	Independent Peace Association-Initiative for the Demilitarization of Society
NSC	National Security Council
NSDD	National Security Decision Directive
OMB	Office of Management and Budget
PAC	Political Action Committee
SAG	Screen Actors Guild
SALT	Strategic Arms Limitation Talks (also Strategic Arms Limitation Treaty)
SANE	Committee for a Sane Nuclear Policy
SCG	Special Consultative Group
SDI	Strategic Defense Initiative
SED	Socialist Unity Party
SIPRI	Stockholm International Peace Research Institute
SLBM	Submarine-Launched Ballistic Missile
SPD	Social Democratic Party
START	Strategic Arms Reduction Talks (also Strategic Arms Reduction Treaty)
TNF	Theater Nuclear Forces
UCS	Union of Concerned Scientists
UN	United Nations
WILPF	Women's International League for Peace and Freedom
WiP	Freedom and Peace

Introduction

In April 1980, four American organizations published a four-page document that would spark a nationwide grassroots movement to end the nuclear arms race. Issued by the Institute for Defense and Disarmament Studies, the American Friends Service Committee, Clergy and Laity Concerned, and Fellowship of Reconciliation, *The Call to Halt the Nuclear Arms Race* had a simple message.[1] The United States and the Soviet Union "should adopt a mutual freeze on the testing, production and deployment of nuclear weapons and of missiles and new aircraft designed primarily to deliver nuclear weapons." The freeze was envisioned as an "essential, verifiable first step" toward averting the danger of nuclear war, sharply reducing or eliminating nuclear weapons, and preventing nuclear proliferation.[2] As détente between the United States and the Soviet Union collapsed and the superpowers escalated the nuclear arms race, millions of Americans flocked to the nuclear freeze movement. They voted for local and state freeze resolutions, marched for an end to the nuclear arms race, campaigned for anti-nuclear candidates, and urged members of Congress to pass a national freeze resolution and withhold funding for new nuclear systems.

Across the Atlantic Ocean, a movement against nuclear weapons was also taking shape in Europe. On April 28, 1980, a group of anti-nuclear activists and British members of Parliament presented an appeal for European nuclear disarmament during a press conference at the House of Commons. Written primarily by the renowned British historian E. P. Thompson, the appeal was unveiled simultaneously in Paris, Berlin, Oslo, and Lisbon.[3] Contending that officials in both the East and West bore responsibility for the nuclear arms race, the "Appeal for European Nuclear Disarmament" (or END Appeal) called on ordinary Europeans to "act together to free the entire territory of Europe, from Poland to Portugal, from nuclear weapons, air and submarine bases, and from all institutions engaged in research into or manufacture of nuclear weapons." It also urged "the two superpowers to withdraw all nuclear weapons from European territory. In particular, we ask the Soviet Union to halt production of the SS-20 medium range missile and we ask the United States not to implement the decision to develop cruise missiles and Pershing II missiles for deployment in Europe." While the denuclearization of Europe was the main aim of the appeal, it also called for "effective negotiations on general and complete disarmament."[4]

Signed by individuals from twenty-five different countries in just five months' time, the END Appeal launched both a British organization known as European Nuclear Disarmament (END) and the annual END Conventions, which were organized by the transnational Liaison Committee to bring together anti-nuclear activists and politicians from across Europe.[5] The END Convention Liaison Committee consisted of British END and other signatories of the END Appeal. Sharing END's opposition to Soviet and U.S. deployments of intermediate-range nuclear forces (INF) in Europe, millions took to the streets across Western Europe to demonstrate against the "Euromissiles" in the early 1980s. They urged European leaders to refuse to host INF.

Yet grassroots activists were not the only ones calling for the reduction and elimination of nuclear weapons in early 1980. In the same month that *The Call to Halt the Nuclear Arms Race* was published in the United States and the END Appeal was launched in Europe, Republican presidential candidate Ronald Reagan privately expressed his desire for an agreement that would reduce U.S. and Soviet nuclear weapons. In an April 8 letter to Charles Burton Marshall, Reagan advocated telling the Soviets that "we would be willing to sit at the table as long as it took to negotiate a legitimate reduction of nuclear weapons on both sides to the point that neither country represented a threat to the other." Though Reagan doubted that the Soviets would agree to such talks, he noted that a U.S. offer of arms reduction negotiations would "prove to the world which nation truly wants peace."[6] Reagan would shift from advocating nuclear arms reduction to nuclear abolition during the first year of his presidency. In November 1981, he told his advisors that he hoped that the U.S. zero option proposal to eliminate land-based INF missiles would be a gateway to dramatic reductions in other categories of nuclear weapons.[7] After learning from the Pentagon on December 3 that 150 million Americans would die in a nuclear war with the Soviet Union, Reagan became convinced that the best way to prevent a nuclear conflict would be to abolish nuclear weapons altogether.[8] He pursued this goal of a nuclear-free world for the remainder of his presidency.[9]

Reagan's strategy for reducing and eliminating nuclear weapons contrasted sharply with the approaches advocated by grassroots anti-nuclear activists. Believing that the Soviets maintained a decided advantage in the nuclear arms race, Reagan contended that the United States needed to modernize its nuclear forces before pursuing arms control talks in order to give the Soviets an incentive to engage in meaningful reductions. In his April 8 letter to Marshall, Reagan alluded to this strategy of "peace through strength," writing, "I am deeply concerned about our precarious position at present and believe that we should be looking for the most likely deterrent and the one we could get on line the fastest before the window of opportunity becomes any wider for them [the Soviets]."[10] Their different disarmament strategies led Reagan and grassroots anti-nuclear activists to dislike and mistrust one another. Nevertheless, their shared interest in nuclear abolition reshaped U.S. arms control policies during Reagan's first term.

Although Mikhail Gorbachev was only the Central Committee secretary for agriculture and a candidate member of the Politburo in April 1980, he too would pursue nuclear abolition after coming to power in the Soviet Union in March 1985. Even before he assumed leadership in the Kremlin, Gorbachev expressed moral opposition to nuclear weapons due to the horrific consequences that would result from their use. During a conversation with British prime minister Margaret Thatcher on December 16, 1984, Gorbachev produced a diagram representing the superpowers' nuclear arsenals and declared that "only a fraction of this would be needed to bring about nuclear winter." He feared that "if both sides continued to pile up weapons in ever increasing quantities it could lead to accidents or unforeseen circumstances."[11] In a speech to the House of Commons Select Committee on Foreign Affairs two days later, Gorbachev endorsed "the most radical reduction in nuclear armaments—with a view to eventually dismantling them completely."[12]

The 1980s was a unique decade during which the radical goal of nuclear abolition enjoyed support from both grassroots movements across the globe and the leaders of the two superpowers, Reagan and Gorbachev. During most of the Cold War, the superpowers had built a broad consensus among their publics that a nuclear arsenal provided essential security by deterring the actions of hostile states. Yet in the 1980s, millions of ordinary individuals around the world mobilized in support of nuclear disarmament. In the West, veterans of the earlier ban-the-bomb campaign and the anti–Vietnam War movement joined with individuals who had never engaged in political activism to advocate an end to the nuclear arms race. In Eastern Europe and the

Soviet Union, dissidents who sought human rights protections, freedom, and democracy also began pushing for nuclear disarmament. Although Reagan and Gorbachev were not part of these grassroots movements, they too wanted to eliminate nuclear weapons. Nuclear abolitionism took hold across the political landscape in the 1980s. During this period, nuclear abolitionism was not a single, unified vision but rather a broad spectrum of ideas, sometimes overlapping and oftentimes conflicting. Nuclear abolitionism brought together surprising coalitions of grassroots protesters and government leaders who shared the aim of a nuclear-free world but disagreed on many issues, including the best strategy for eliminating nuclear weapons. It is therefore a mistake to view "nuclear abolitionist" as simply a synonym for "grassroots anti-nuclear activist."

This book examines nuclear abolitionists' influence on the trajectory of the Cold War's last decade. It begins in 1979, as the collapse of détente and the escalation of the nuclear arms race led ordinary individuals around the world to fear the outbreak of nuclear war. It concludes with the December 1989 Malta summit, during which Gorbachev and President George H. W. Bush declared the Cold War over. During this period, nuclear abolitionism was an international phenomenon that existed on a spectrum. Nuclear abolitionism included individuals who sought the elimination of nuclear weapons as a long-term aim, like U.S. nuclear freeze activists, as well as groups that linked peace and disarmament with human rights, like Charter 77, the Committee for Social Resistance (KOS), and Freedom and Peace (WiP). It encompassed not only grassroots activists, but also government leaders committed to nuclear disarmament, most significantly Reagan and Gorbachev. Although these individuals and organizations had different strategies and timetables for eliminating nuclear weapons, their shared goal of a nuclear-free world made them all nuclear abolitionists. Recognizing that nuclear abolitionism was a diverse and global force in the 1980s, this book is an international history that interweaves the efforts of grassroots anti-nuclear activists and government officials committed to nuclear disarmament. It considers the views of grassroots and government nuclear abolitionists, the interactions between these grassroots and government actors, and the ways in which their ideas and contacts transformed U.S. and Soviet foreign policy during the 1980s.

The central argument of this book is that nuclear abolitionists played a significant role in ending the Cold War. During the 1980s, grassroots and government nuclear abolitionists shifted U.S. and Soviet nuclear arms control paradigms from arms limitation to arms reduction. This new emphasis on nuclear arms reduction paved the way for the reversal of the superpower nuclear arms race, which began with the landmark 1987 INF Treaty. European peace activists also influenced Gorbachev's "common European home" initiative and support for freedom of choice in Europe, which prevented the Soviet leader from intervening to stop the 1989 East European revolutions. These revolutions ripped the fabric of the Iron Curtain, which had divided Europe for more than four decades.

Throughout the 1980s, there were two different visions of how to end the Cold War, both of which had roots in the nuclear abolitionist movement. One school of thought held that undertaking global nuclear disarmament was the way to overcome Cold War tensions. U.S. nuclear freeze activists and Reagan maintained and pursued this vision throughout the decade, as did Gorbachev in 1985 and 1986. Although this vision was not triumphant, Reagan's support for it was crucial to the Cold War's endgame. It inspired his eagerness to engage with Soviet leaders and pursue nuclear arms reduction agreements like the INF Treaty. The second view focused only on Europe, where the Cold War began. It openly embraced not only the elimination of nuclear weapons in Europe, but also the dissolution of the blocs and the achievement of greater European autonomy, which the denuclearization of Europe would facilitate. It also called for the extension of human rights protections throughout Europe. East European dissidents and West European peace activists advanced this second vision and convinced Gorbachev of its merits by 1987. In doing so, these European activists influenced some of the key Soviet policies that precipitated the end of the Cold War, such as Gorbachev's agreement to eliminate land-based INF missiles, his advocacy of a "common European home," his support for all Europeans' right to choose their form of government, and his unwillingness to use force to halt the 1989 East European revolutions.

By demonstrating nuclear abolitionists' vital role in ending the Cold War, this book helps reshape the explanation of the Cold War's end. Although scholars have been debating why the Cold War ended since its conclusion in 1989, they have largely ignored nuclear abolitionism in their analyses. Instead, they have typically advanced one of four major interpretations. Triumphalists contend that the Reagan administration successfully pursued a grand strategy to win the Cold War. Rejecting containment, Reagan pursued a more aggressive strategy to undercut Soviet power at home and abroad by embarking on a military buildup, launching the Strategic Defense Initiative (SDI), engaging in economic warfare against the Soviet Union, and providing support to forces fighting communism across the globe.[13] By contrast, other scholars argue that Gorbachev was the central figure in the Cold War's endgame. In their view, Gorbachev's personality and embrace of "new thinking" led him to alter Soviet foreign policy in a way that ended the Cold War.[14] Another major interpretation highlights the importance of the 1975 Helsinki Final Act in undermining communist regimes in Eastern Europe and the Soviet Union and ending the Cold War.[15] Finally, some scholars attribute the end of the Cold War to changes in the global economy that advantaged the West and prompted Gorbachev to pursue reforms.[16]

Each of these interpretations, however, has shortcomings. Triumphalists ignore Gorbachev's central role in ending the Cold War as well as anti-nuclear and peace activists' influence on the Soviet and American policies that led to the Cold War's demise. They fail to recognize that the staunch anti-communist Reagan contributed to the Cold War's endgame by engaging Soviet officials and pursuing nuclear arms reduction agreements in an effort to realize his radical dream of a nuclear-free world. Triumphalists claim that SDI pressured Soviet leaders to shift their foreign policy in a conciliatory direction, but SDI actually hindered U.S.-Soviet nuclear arms reduction negotiations, most notably at the Reykjavik summit. In the summit's final session, Reagan and Gorbachev's discussion of a ten-year plan for eliminating nuclear weapons broke down due to the leaders' disagreement over the nature and purpose of SDI.[17] As this book will demonstrate, Reagan and Gorbachev concluded the landmark INF Treaty only after peace activists convinced Gorbachev to pursue an INF agreement separately from accords on strategic arms reduction (START) and strategic defenses.

The other three major interpretations of the end of the Cold War reveal only part of the story. Scholars who credit Gorbachev with ending the Cold War generally acknowledge his abhorrence of nuclear weapons. Yet they ignore the profound influence that grassroots anti-nuclear and peace movements had on the substance and timing of the Soviet nuclear arms control initiatives and policies toward Europe that ended the Cold War. Similarly, the Helsinki Final Act played a role in the Cold War's endgame, but it was not sufficient on its own to end the Cold War. Gorbachev did present his "common European home" initiative as an extension of the Helsinki process, but only after four years of exposure to European peace activists' argument that revitalizing the Helsinki process could help overcome the division of Europe. Also, the Helsinki Final Act did galvanize East European dissidents who advocated respect for human rights. Many of these dissidents, however, believed in the indivisibility of peace and human rights and worked with West European anti-nuclear activists to promote the denuclearization and reunification of an autonomous and free Europe. This partnership was critical to East Europeans' ability to influence the Soviet policies that ended the Cold War. West European activists lent a powerful voice to the arguments of East European and Soviet dissidents, who were persecuted in their home countries.

The structural interpretation rightly notes that economic woes contributed to Gorbachev's determination to reform Soviet foreign policy in a way that would precipitate the Cold War's demise. Gorbachev recognized that the end of the Cold War would enable him to redirect Soviet economic resources from the defense sector to domestic needs. But Gorbachev also came to power with a moral abhorrence of nuclear weapons that led him to seek an end to the Cold War so that he could reduce the risk of nuclear war. Even without Soviet economic troubles, Gorbachev likely would have sought to end the Cold War in order to avert nuclear war. Economic constraints also did not dictate the specific policies that Gorbachev pursued in his efforts to end the Cold War. Rather, Gorbachev's nuclear abolitionism and the arguments set forth by European peace activists shaped the content of his nuclear arms reduction proposals and "common European home" initiative, which were crucial in bringing the Cold War to a peaceful end.

Those scholars who do highlight nuclear abolitionism in their analyses of the end of the Cold War either do not consider its international scope or neglect to examine both the grassroots activists and government officials who advocated the elimination of nuclear weapons. Thus, they overlook some of the important ways in which nuclear abolitionists hastened the end of the Cold War and discount some of the key actors who deserve credit for bringing the Cold War to a close. In other words, they essentially underplay nuclear abolitionism's importance in the Cold War's endgame. Political scientist Matthew Evangelista has made the important case that transnational peace activists played the key role in ending the Cold War by influencing Soviet policies on nuclear testing, missile defense, and conventional forces.[18] Yet Evangelista does not consider activists' influence on Gorbachev's nuclear arms reduction proposals, "common European home" initiative, and support for freedom of choice in Europe, which were even more important in winding down the Cold War. In addition, he does not examine the ways in which Reagan and anti-nuclear activists' shared interest in nuclear disarmament contributed to the reversal of the U.S.-Soviet nuclear arms race and the end of the Cold War.

Other scholars consider Reagan and Gorbachev's nuclear abolitionism but neglect grassroots anti-nuclear activists in their accounts of the Cold

War's end. They argue that Reagan and Gorbachev's shared nuclear abolition-ism enabled the two leaders to develop a strong sense of trust and persuaded Gorbachev that Reagan would not launch a nuclear attack against the Soviet Union. This reinforced Gorbachev's desire to pursue the dramatic reforms that ended the Cold War.[19] Yet these scholars overlook the important influ-ence that anti-nuclear activists had on the substance and timing of the U.S. and Soviet policies that precipitated the Cold War's demise.

This book contends that grassroots anti-nuclear activists, Reagan, and Gorbachev all played critical roles in the Cold War's endgame. If any of these nuclear abolitionists had not been present during the 1980s, the Cold War would not have ended when and how it did. On the U.S. side, both Reagan and grassroots anti-nuclear activists played essential roles in shifting the U.S. nuclear arms control paradigm from arms limitation to arms reduction. This was the first step toward reversing the superpower nuclear arms race and ending the Cold War. Reagan entered the White House with an abhorrence of nuclear weapons that prompted him to announce his intention to pursue nuclear arms reduction, rather than mere arms limitation. Within the first six weeks of his presidency, he professed support for strategic nuclear arms reduction and the arms control track of the 1979 NATO dual-track decision.[20] These statements came months before U.S. and West European anti-nuclear movements began attracting widespread attention, and they reflected Rea-gan's personal belief that the best way to avert nuclear war was through the dramatic reduction and eventual elimination of nuclear weapons.

Reagan's budding nuclear abolitionism, however, was not sufficient to shift the U.S. nuclear arms control paradigm. Upon taking office, Reagan was surrounded by advisors who did not share his enthusiasm for nuclear disar-mament and actively stymied his pursuit of this goal. Averse to personal con-frontation, Reagan was reluctant to challenge or fire aides.[21] Pressure from U.S. and West European anti-nuclear activists proved crucial in prompting Reagan's advisors to support the opening of talks aimed at dramatically reducing INF and strategic nuclear weapons. Anti-nuclear activists therefore were able to accomplish a critical task that Reagan could not: garner the sup-port of the president's advisors for INF and START negotiations.

Pressure from anti-nuclear activists also accelerated the Reagan adminis-tration's timetable for pursuing INF and START talks with the Soviets. Believ-ing that U.S. nuclear modernization was a necessary incentive for the Soviets to engage in meaningful arms reduction, Reagan initially wanted to wait to pursue START negotiations until after his administration had completed a strategic modernization program.[22] In addition, he originally offered only general promises to undertake INF negotiations and did not provide a specific time frame for initiating these talks.[23] The growing popularity of U.S. and West European anti-nuclear movements, however, led Reagan to change his policy. He feared that anti-nuclear activists' disarmament strategies would endanger U.S. national security and impede nuclear arms reduction. Eager to prove that his "peace through strength" disarmament strategy could yield results, Reagan decided to begin INF negotiations in November 1981. He also embarked on START talks while the modernization of U.S. strategic nuclear forces was taking place. START negotiations opened in June 1982, years before Reagan's strategic modernization plan would be implemented.

The INF and START proposals that Reagan set forth in these accelerated talks had a major influence on the final agreements that U.S. and Soviet officials concluded. Reagan's zero option proposal, which called for the elimination of U.S. and Soviet land-based INF missiles, formed the basis of the INF Treaty that Reagan and Gorbachev signed in December 1987.[24] Reagan's opening START proposal insisted on significant reductions in both strategic missiles and strategic warheads, which was an idea that framed the rest of the START debate. The final START Treaty signed by Gorbachev and Bush in July 1991 incorporated deep cuts in both strategic missiles and strategic warheads.[25]

Yet it would be wrong to assume that Reagan's nuclear abolitionism was superfluous or that grassroots anti-nuclear activists could have persuaded any American president to pursue the reversal of the superpower nuclear arms race. Not only did Reagan advocate nuclear arms reduction before U.S. and West European anti-nuclear movements garnered significant attention, but he crucially continued to pursue nuclear disarmament after these movements began to lose steam or reevaluate their aims in 1984. These efforts were driven by Reagan's sincere desire to rid the world of nuclear weapons. In fact, it is difficult to envision a president pursuing a radical agreement to eliminate U.S. nuclear weapons in ten years, which Reagan did at the October 1986 Reykjavik summit, if he did not personally want a nuclear-free world.[26]

Gorbachev, however, played an indispensable role in the Cold War's endgame by altering long-standing Soviet approaches to arms control and Eastern Europe. Gorbachev's nuclear abolitionism initially led him to seek to end the Cold War by concluding nuclear disarmament treaties.[27] In an effort to jumpstart this process, he quickly began offering nuclear arms reduction proposals that provided for significant cuts in Soviet weapons and even global nuclear abolition.[28] Soviet arms control initiatives contained major concessions that enabled Reagan and Gorbachev to sign the INF Treaty and agree on a general outline for a START agreement. Gorbachev also called for a nuclear-free and reunified Europe.[29] He made this "common European home" initiative a priority in 1987, as it became clear that he and Reagan were unlikely to sign a treaty abolishing their nuclear weapons. Gorbachev's commitment to this "common European home" concept, which precluded the use of force against other European states, prevented him from deploying Soviet troops to halt the East European revolutions in 1989. In the face of protests and liberalization in Eastern Europe, Gorbachev would not take the approach that his predecessors had in the German Democratic Republic (GDR) in 1953, Hungary in 1956, and Czechoslovakia in 1968.[30]

Peace activists, however, had an important effect on Gorbachev's nuclear arms reduction and "common European home" initiatives, enhancing their impact on the Cold War's endgame. Gorbachev may have offered a host of concessions on arms control at the October 1986 Reykjavik summit, but his insistence on linking INF and START agreements with restrictions on SDI hindered the conclusion of any offensive arms reduction treaty.[31] Anti-nuclear activists, however, influenced Gorbachev's February 1987 decision to pursue an INF treaty separately from agreements on START and strategic defenses. This was a crucial decision that removed the major obstacle blocking the INF Treaty.

As Gorbachev developed his "common European home" initiative between 1985 and 1989, European peace activists' appeals for a denuclearized, reunified, and free Europe were influential. They shaped Gorbachev's vision of a nuclear-free "common European home," which he ultimately thought would include pan-European security structures, economic integration, and cooperation on environmental and humanitarian issues. Gorbachev also adopted European activists' proposals for how to overcome the division of Europe, embracing in particular their appeals for the revitalization of the Helsinki process. By 1989, Gorbachev believed that the "common European home" promised vital security and environmental benefits for Europe and the superpowers, as well as economic benefits for the Soviet Union and Eastern Europe. Understanding that the use of force in Eastern Europe would undermine his "common European home" proposal, Gorbachev refused to intervene to stop the revolutions of 1989. He hoped in vain that the "common European home" would provide a framework for a stable and peaceful post–Cold War order.

Given the dramatic alterations in Soviet foreign policy brought about by Gorbachev and peace activists, did Reagan truly matter in the Cold War's endgame? Would not any American president have welcomed Gorbachev's initiatives and moved the Cold War toward its conclusion? While less significant than Gorbachev, Reagan's nuclear abolitionism enabled him to play a key part in reversing the nuclear arms race and ending the Cold War. His desire for a nuclear-free world led him to engage Soviet officials and work for bold, equitable, and verifiable nuclear arms reduction agreements. Since Reagan's nuclear abolitionism was not shared by other conservatives, it cannot be assumed that another Republican president would have signed the INF Treaty or agreed to an outline for a sweeping START agreement with Gorbachev. In fact, President George H. W. Bush, who had served as Reagan's vice president but did not share his nuclear abolitionism, rebuffed Gorbachev's nuclear arms reduction proposals throughout 1989.[32] Contrary to recent works that praise Bush's deft handling of the end of the Cold War, this book contends that Bush bears the primary responsibility for the missed opportunity to achieve more dramatic nuclear arms reduction as the Cold War drew to a close in 1989.[33]

In examining Reagan's and grassroots anti-nuclear activists' contributions to the Cold War's endgame, this book also challenges prevailing interpretations of the Reagan administration's arms control policy. These arguments tend to be one-sided, privileging either anti-nuclear activists or Reagan's nuclear abolitionism as the driving force behind U.S. policy in the early 1980s. One school of thought holds that the Reagan administration was unserious about nuclear arms control for most or all of its first term and pursued negotiations with the Soviets due to pressure from anti-nuclear activists.[34] By contrast, a second school contends that Reagan became a nuclear abolitionist in the late 1940s and his anti-nuclearism was the most important factor shaping U.S. arms control policy.[35] This book demonstrates that both Reagan and grassroots anti-nuclear activists played essential roles in shifting the U.S. nuclear arms control paradigm from arms limitation to arms reduction. Neither Reagan nor the activists could have started reversing the nuclear arms race without the other.

This book also illuminates the agency and importance of East European dissidents within the transnational European peace movement. East Europeans exerted a significant influence on the agenda of the European peace movement, which scholars have not fully appreciated.[36] Residing in countries without protections for basic freedoms and frequently facing government repression, independent East European peace and human rights activists did not form mass movements like their West European counterparts. Yet Czechoslovak, Polish, East German, and Hungarian activists still developed relationships with Westerners through correspondence and meetings in Eastern Europe. Through these contacts, East European dissidents helped West European activists appreciate the interconnections among nuclear disarmament, the elimination of the blocs, European autonomy, and human rights.

East European activists argued that the reduction of U.S. and Soviet nuclear weapons in Europe would facilitate the dissolution of the military blocs by reducing tensions in Europe. Since the existence of the military blocs provided the underlying rationale for the continuation of the nuclear arms race, the elimination of the blocs in turn would make possible the abolition of nuclear weapons. Nuclear disarmament would also enable European countries to achieve greater autonomy from the superpowers. Freed from the threat of nuclear blackmail and the ties of alliance nuclear strategy, European states would be able to act more independently and work for the reunification of Europe. The dissolution of the blocs would help Eastern Europe attain even more autonomy from the Soviet Union, which used NATO's existence to justify its interventions in East European affairs. East European activists also believed in the indivisibility of peace and human rights, contending that only a government that respected the rights of its citizens would promote nuclear disarmament and peace in the international arena. Government officials who infringed on the rights of their own citizens would not honor the rights of other states. Everyone should have the right to work for peace and disarmament.

After increased contact with East Europeans, West European activists began seeking to end the Cold War through the denuclearization and reunification of an autonomous and free Europe. Despite numbering far fewer than their West European counterparts and confronting government persecution in their home countries, East European dissidents shifted the agenda of the broader European peace movement in the mid-1980s to include the reunification of Europe, European autonomy from the superpowers, and human rights, in addition to traditional nuclear disarmament issues. This new agenda enhanced European activists' influence on Gorbachev's policies. Their calls for a denuclearized, reunified, and free Europe shaped Gorbachev's concept of a "common European home" and his proposals for how to achieve this new Europe. Gorbachev's dedication to the idea of a "common European home" prevented him from intervening to stop the revolutions that toppled communist regimes across Eastern Europe in 1989.

As an international history of grassroots and government nuclear abolitionists' influence on the Cold War's last decade, this book relies on a range of sources produced by nonstate and government actors. These include newly available U.S., European, and Soviet government documents; the personal writings of Reagan and Gorbachev and their top advisors; and the papers of American, European, and Soviet anti-nuclear and peace organizations. These sources reveal that Reagan's and Gorbachev's radical ideas about nuclear weapons dramatically reshaped U.S. and Soviet security policy, as did the grassroots anti-nuclear and peace activism of ordinary individuals across the globe. Together, grassroots and government nuclear abolitionists altered Soviet and American approaches to nuclear arms control and Europe in a way that brought the Cold War to a peaceful conclusion. In this book, the story of nuclear abolitionists' role in ending the Cold War develops over the course of seven chronological chapters. Each chapter interweaves analysis of grassroots anti-nuclear activists and government officials committed to nuclear disarmament.

Following the Reykjavik summit, during which Reagan and Gorbachev nearly agreed to a plan to abolish their nuclear weapons by 1996, Gorbachev told the press that the meeting was a "breakthrough" that enabled the two nations to "look over the horizon" to a world without nuclear weapons.[37] Although grassroots and government nuclear abolitionists have yet to eliminate nuclear weapons, this book shows that they deserve credit for playing a pivotal role in ending the Cold War struggle that dominated international affairs for nearly half a century. Nuclear abolitionists helped all nations to "look over the horizon" to a world without the Cold War.

CHAPTER 1

"We Are in Position of Resistance"

In January 1981, the *Bulletin of the Atomic Scientists'* famous Doomsday Clock struck four minutes to midnight. In explaining the decision to move the clock hands "another step toward doomsday," physicist Bernard T. Feld highlighted the dangerous state of the U.S.-Soviet nuclear arms race. In light of President Jimmy Carter's withdrawal of the second Strategic Arms Limitation Treaty (SALT II) from Senate consideration after the Soviet invasion of Afghanistan, the treaty seemed "to be out the window." Meanwhile, the Soviets were deploying SS-20 missiles aimed at targets in Western Europe, and NATO was preparing to deploy U.S. Pershing II and ground-launched cruise missiles in five West European countries in 1983. Both superpowers were developing new weapons with counterforce or "nuclear war-fighting" capabilities, meaning that they were designed to attack an adversary's nuclear forces in a first strike, rather than provide a second-strike deterrence capability. Neither side would agree to a no-first-use policy for nuclear weapons. Feld lamented that "as the year 1980 drew to a close, the world seemed to be moving unevenly but inexorably closer to nuclear disaster."[1]

Yet Feld found comfort in the incoming Reagan administration's professed desire to curb the nuclear arms race and ordinary citizens' growing concerns about the prospect of nuclear war. "Our immediate task is to find means of taking hold of this concern and converting it into an international accord to eliminate the threat of global nuclear suicide," he declared. "The seemingly inevitable advance of the warning hand to midnight can and must be reversed in the months to come."[2]

This chapter contends that Ronald Reagan and grassroots anti-nuclear activists advocated starkly different strategies for realizing their shared goal of nuclear disarmament. U.S. nuclear freeze activists thought that a bilateral superpower freeze on the testing, production, and deployment of new nuclear weapons must precede arms reduction negotiations on existing systems in order to prevent the negotiations from becoming obsolete. European anti-nuclear activists sought the withdrawal of nuclear weapons from Europe as a precursor to talks on complete nuclear disarmament. Reagan, on the other hand, wanted to modernize U.S. nuclear forces in order to give the Soviets, who he believed were winning the arms race, an incentive to engage in meaningful arms reduction negotiations. These different strategies for eliminating nuclear weapons emerged from contrasting views on the utility of military strength in negotiations and the threshold of danger in the nuclear age. Reagan and grassroots anti-nuclear activists loathed and mistrusted one another due to their disagreements on these issues. Nevertheless, as future chapters in this book will show, their shared interest in nuclear disarmament ultimately reshaped U.S. arms control policies during Reagan's first term.

∗   ∗   ∗

As the 1980s began, grassroots anti-nuclear activism was on the rise across the globe. The collapse of détente and the escalation of the nuclear arms race led millions to worry that the United States and the Soviet Union were headed for a nuclear confrontation. Concerned about the prospect of nuclear war, individuals around the world engaged in activism to try to convince leaders to retreat from the nuclear precipice. These activists, however, touted a variety of nuclear disarmament strategies. Most Americans argued that a nuclear freeze should precede sweeping nuclear arms reduction, while West Europeans generally sought the elimination of nuclear weapons in Europe as the first step toward disarmament.

The nuclear freeze proposal, which was at the heart of American activists' disarmament strategy, energized members of existing peace and anti-nuclear weapons organizations. It also started attracting the support of individuals who had not previously advocated nuclear disarmament. The U.S. anti-nuclear movement had been small and divided for much of the 1970s. During the early part of the decade, activists prioritized opposition to the Vietnam War at the expense of nuclear weapons issues. After the war ended, activists' disagreements over aims and tactics left the anti-nuclear movement fragmented. One faction of the movement consisted of traditional pacifist and peace groups like the American Friends Service Committee (AFSC), Fellowship of Reconciliation (FOR), Women's International League for Peace and Freedom (WILPF), and Clergy and Laity Concerned (CALC). These organizations sought nuclear disarmament as part of broader campaigns for peace and social justice, and they were willing to use radical tactics in pursuit of their aims. More moderate organizations advocating nuclear arms control comprised the other faction of the anti-nuclear movement. This faction included groups like the Committee for a Sane Nuclear Policy (SANE), the Council for a Livable World, and the Union of Concerned Scientists (UCS).[3]

For most of the 1970s, there was no central issue around which these two factions could unite and build a nationwide movement against nuclear weapons. Anti-nuclear activists spent the decade engaging in a variety of campaigns against single nuclear weapons systems and nuclear power. For example, AFSC led a coalition of anti-nuclear, environmental, and religious groups in opposition to the B-1 bomber. The Stop the B-1 Bomber campaign lobbied Congress and the Carter administration to abandon this expensive weapons program. Anti-B-1 activists also held vigils and demonstrations across the United States. In June 1977, Carter cancelled the B-1 program but began equipping existing B-52 bombers with long-range air-launched cruise missiles. Believing that their campaign had ended in victory, activists proudly took credit for Carter's decision to scrap the B-1.[4]

Other anti-nuclear activists worked with environmentalists to mount local campaigns against nuclear power plants. They highlighted the threats that these plants posed to public health and safety and the environment. Many of these activists engaged in nonviolent direct action, occupying nuclear power plant sites like the one in Seabrook, New Hampshire. In the wake of the accident at the Three Mile Island nuclear power plant on March 28, 1979, the anti-nuclear power movement garnered increased public support and media coverage.[5]

In an effort to unite the various campaigns against nuclear weapons and nuclear power into a nationwide movement, activists formed Mobilization for Survival (MFS) in 1977. MFS was an umbrella organization that prioritized four goals: "zero nuclear weapons," "ban nuclear power," "stop the arms race," and "fund human needs." Yet the organizations that affiliated with MFS still struggled to find a single issue around which they could coalesce.[6]

In 1979, some activists began touting the bilateral nuclear freeze proposal as the issue that could unite and expand the anti-nuclear movement.[7] Although the nuclear freeze gained traction among American anti-nuclear activists as the 1970s ended, it was Lyndon Johnson who had first proposed a nuclear freeze in a message to the 18-Nation Disarmament Conference on January 21, 1964. Johnson called for the superpowers and their allies to "explore

a verified freeze of the number and characteristics of strategic nuclear offensive and defensive vehicles." In this message, Johnson presented the freeze as
the first step toward significant nuclear arms reduction, just as anti-nuclear
activists would fifteen years later.[8] But the Johnson administration actually
wanted to use the freeze to codify existing U.S. nuclear superiority. It wrongly
believed that Soviet leaders were so eager to avoid the economic burdens of a
prolonged nuclear arms race that they would accept a freeze agreement that
left them with an inferior nuclear force, albeit one still capable of execut-
ing a devastating retaliatory strike. Soviet officials, however, had no interest
in a freeze agreement. They thought that the 1962 Cuban missile crisis had
shown that nuclear inferiority forced a superpower to back down in a crisis.
Instead of exploring a freeze, the Soviet Union accelerated its missile program
in order to achieve nuclear parity with the United States.[9]

U.S. and Soviet leaders resurrected versions of the nuclear freeze proposal
at various points during the Strategic Arms Limitation Talks (SALT), which
opened in November 1969 and produced the Anti-Ballistic Missile (ABM)
Treaty and SALT I agreement in 1972 and the SALT II Treaty in 1979.[10]
Richard Nixon and Leonid Brezhnev signed the five-year SALT I agreement
on May 26, 1972, during the Moscow summit. SALT I included a freeze on
U.S. and Soviet intercontinental ballistic missiles (ICBMs) at their existing
levels, which were 1,054 for the United States and 1,618 for the Soviet Union.
Yet SALT I did not curb multiple independently targetable reentry vehicles
(MIRVs), which enable a missile to launch multiple warheads at different targets. By developing MIRVs, the superpowers could continue to enhance the
quality of their ICBM forces despite the freeze provision in SALT I. In fact,
SALT I permitted the United States and the Soviet Union to improve and
replace their strategic missiles as long as they did not dramatically increase
the dimensions of ICBM silo launchers or exceed missile limits. SALT I also
allowed the United States to build up to 710 submarine-launched ballistic
missiles (SLBMs), while the Soviets were permitted 950 SLBMs. Bombers
were excluded from the agreement.[11]

The SALT II Treaty included more sweeping limits than SALT I, but its
ceilings were so high that they would not force the United States to make any
substantive modifications to its nuclear weapons programs.[12] The nonpartisan
Arms Control Association estimated that SALT II would have only required
the Soviet Union to cut its forces by about 270 delivery vehicles.[13] Signed by
Carter and Brezhnev at the Vienna summit on June 18, 1979, SALT II limited each superpower to 2,400 strategic nuclear delivery vehicles, which were

ICBMs, SLBMs, heavy bombers, and air-to-surface ballistic missiles. No more than 1,320 of these delivery vehicles could be MIRVed missiles or heavy bombers with air-launched cruise missiles. No more than 1,200 could be MIRVed missiles, of which no more than 820 could be ICBMs. On January 1, 1981, the limit on strategic nuclear delivery vehicles would decrease to 2,250. A host of additional restrictions on U.S. and Soviet strategic nuclear forces made SALT II a long and complex agreement, although it would not require the superpowers to make dramatic changes to their strategic nuclear programs.[14]

The nuclear freeze proposal resurfaced as U.S. senators considered SALT II ratification. Senator Mark Hatfield, a liberal Republican from Oregon, expressed frustration that the SALT II Treaty would not end the nuclear arms race, but rather "legitimate its escalation." Shortly after the Vienna summit, Hatfield proposed a nuclear moratorium amendment to SALT II. Hatfield's amendment called for the United States and the Soviet Union to freeze "further development, testing, and deployment" of their strategic nuclear arsenals. Hatfield believed that this bilateral strategic nuclear moratorium would halt the arms race and allow the superpowers to focus on reducing strategic nuclear weapons.[15]

Hatfield's moratorium amendment inspired Randy Kehler, a thirty-five-year-old community organizer who had founded the Traprock Peace Center in Deerfield, Massachusetts.[16] Kehler had a long history of peace activism and would play a leading role in the U.S. nuclear freeze movement during the 1980s. As an undergraduate at Harvard, Kehler was horrified to learn that the United States was using napalm in Vietnam and decided to spearhead a letter-writing campaign against the war in 1965. After college, Kehler worked for the War Resisters League office in San Francisco, where he mobilized protesters against the Vietnam War and personally engaged in tax and draft resistance.[17] On August 28, 1969, Kehler spoke about his willingness to go to jail to protest the Vietnam War and advocated "nonviolence as a way of life." Daniel Ellsberg was so moved by Kehler's words that he cried uncontrollably for more than an hour after the speech, which Ellsberg credited with setting him on the path to leaking the Pentagon Papers.[18] Kehler spent nearly two years in prison for his refusal to participate in the draft.[19]

After the Vietnam War, Kehler's focus shifted toward protesting nuclear power and nuclear weapons. He was arrested for participating in a nonviolent occupation of the Seabrook nuclear power plant site in New Hampshire.[20] As a protest against U.S. defense spending, Kehler and his wife, Betsy Corner, stopped paying federal income taxes in 1977, donating the money to charity instead. (This would ultimately lead the Internal Revenue Service to seize their home in Colrain, Massachusetts, in 1989.) In 1979, Kehler helped establish the Traprock Peace Center, which prioritized stopping the nuclear arms race.[21]

Kehler was immediately drawn to the clarity and simplicity of Hatfield's nuclear moratorium amendment, which he thought would make it a perfect organizing vehicle for local peace activists. Ordinary Americans could comprehend the nuclear freeze proposal without having to master all of the intricacies of U.S. and Soviet nuclear policy. The bilateral nature of the freeze also made it appealing to Kehler, who thought that local activists would have more success building support for a proposal that called on both superpowers to take action rather than just the United States. Kehler and the other Traprock Peace Center activists viewed the freeze as a meaningful first step toward the reduction and elimination of nuclear weapons. They began collecting signatures to put a nuclear freeze referendum on the November 1980 ballot in three state senate districts in western Massachusetts.[22]

Even before Hatfield proposed the nuclear moratorium as an amendment to SALT II, some peace and anti-nuclear weapons activists had been arguing that the freeze could end the nuclear arms race and serve as the basis for a nationwide grassroots anti-nuclear movement.[23] One such individual was Randall Forsberg, who was asked to give a speech on the freeze at the MFS convention in December 1979.[24] Forsberg was a thirty-six-year-old PhD student in international studies at the Massachusetts Institute of Technology. She had become interested in nuclear disarmament while working as a typist at the Stockholm International Peace Research Institute (SIPRI) in the late 1960s. Living in Stockholm with her Swedish husband, Forsberg thought that it would be "interesting" for an American to work at SIPRI while the United States was waging war in Vietnam. She quickly became stunned by the material that she was typing. Forsberg was dismayed by the size of the U.S. nuclear arsenal and the lack of sincere efforts to reduce nuclear weapons. Deciding to devote her life to disarmament, Forsberg vowed to master nuclear and defense issues and then focus on public education.[25]

Forsberg wanted to provide objective information that anti-nuclear activists could use to advance their campaigns. She rose through the ranks at SIPRI, working as an editor and analyst before moving to Boston for graduate school in 1974. Forsberg became renowned for her detailed knowledge of nuclear policy, even mentoring Helen Caldicott, who became arguably the most prominent anti-nuclear activist in the world during the 1980s. Forsberg would establish her own think tank, the Institute for Defense and Disarmament Studies (IDDS), in Brookline, Massachusetts, in 1980.[26]

During her speech at the MFS convention in December 1979, Forsberg urged the fragmented anti-nuclear movement to unite in support of a bilateral nuclear freeze. In her view, the key to building a powerful nationwide movement against nuclear weapons was to advocate one significant yet moderate demand of both the United States and the Soviet Union. It would take a positive goal to mobilize ordinary Americans, who would become disheartened and indifferent if the anti-nuclear movement concentrated solely on the devastating effects of nuclear war. Americans were unenthusiastic about proposals that merely eliminated a single weapons system, but they were also uninterested in "utopian" calls for immediate nuclear disarmament. They also generally opposed unilateral initiatives that applied only to the United States. Forsberg believed that the bilateral nuclear freeze proposal met all of the criteria to appeal to not only veteran activists, but also mainstream, middle-class individuals from middle America who had no political experience.[27]

Forsberg formally presented the case for a bilateral nuclear freeze in a pamphlet titled *The Call to Halt the Nuclear Arms Race*. In *Call*, Forsberg argued that the freeze was an "essential, verifiable first step" toward averting the danger of nuclear war, drastically reducing or eliminating nuclear weapons, and preventing nuclear proliferation. In the late 1970s, the United States and the Soviet Union had begun developing a new generation of nuclear weapons with counterforce capabilities. Forsberg explained that counterforce weapons, like the U.S. MX ICBM and the Soviet SS-18 ICBM, "will increase the pressure on both sides to use their nuclear weapons in a crisis, rather than risk losing them in a first strike." She insisted that a bilateral nuclear freeze was needed to stop the development of these destabilizing weapons, which heightened the risk of nuclear war.[28]

In Forsberg's view, a freeze on the testing, production, and deployment of new nuclear weapons was also a necessary prerequisite for successful arms reduction negotiations. If negotiations were begun without first halting the production of new nuclear weapons, then any reductions achieved on existing systems would be "token" because an entirely new generation of weapons would be on the way.[29] In order to achieve meaningful arms reduction, the superpowers needed to stop producing new nuclear weapons and then work for deep cuts in existing systems. *Call* also noted that the adoption of the freeze could help the United States and the Soviet Union fulfill their Article VI obligations under the Nuclear Non-Proliferation Treaty to work for "effective measures relating to cessation of the nuclear arms race at an early date and to nuclear disarmament." A U.S.-Soviet nuclear freeze would make it easier for non-nuclear-weapon states to refrain from acquiring nuclear weapons and for other members of the nuclear club to restrain their own nuclear weapons programs.[30]

As Forsberg hoped, the bilateral nuclear freeze proposal won support from both factions of the anti-nuclear movement in 1980. Traditional pacifist and peace organizations embraced the freeze first and most fully. In April 1980, AFSC, CALC, and FOR joined with Forsberg's IDDS to print and distribute the *Call* pamphlet.[31] As freeze supporters began considering a strategy for the nascent freeze movement over the summer, Terry Provance of AFSC and Carol Jensen of CALC submitted draft strategy papers.[32] Representatives of pacifist and peace organizations dominated the interim steering committee that freeze supporters established on September 29, 1980, to spearhead the freeze campaign.[33]

Yet these peace activists often wanted to expand Forsberg's freeze proposal and link it with other issues. For example, AFSC's conception of the freeze included a moratorium on research and development of nuclear weapons, which Forsberg thought would be too difficult to verify.[34] AFSC argued that the nuclear freeze should be coupled with a ban on the construction of new nuclear power plants, which would facilitate a transition away from nuclear power. According to AFSC, activists should also work to win U.S. and Soviet acceptance of an agreement not to use nuclear weapons in a crisis. Conventional weapons production and U.S. military intervention abroad should be critiqued alongside the nuclear arms race. Despite their differences with Forsberg, AFSC activists pledged to continue distributing *Call* and strategizing with other freeze supporters.[35]

Individual leaders of more moderate anti-nuclear organizations also supported a nuclear freeze in 1980, albeit more tentatively than pacifist and peace groups. For example, David Cortright, the executive director of SANE, noted that the nuclear freeze "has great appeal to me personally, but I'm not sure it can become a popular crusade for Middle America." He wondered whether the freeze proposal would generate sufficient excitement among ordinary Americans to build a mass anti-nuclear movement.[36] Cortright had been active in the GI movement against the Vietnam War, participating in mass demonstrations and petition drives while serving in the United States Army Band at Fort Wadsworth, New York, and Fort Bliss, Texas.[37] After the war ended, Cortright earned a PhD in political science from the Union Institute while working at the progressive Institute for Policy Studies think tank in Washington, DC. He assumed SANE's executive director post in 1978.[38]

Cortright believed that a freeze movement should work first to stop two or three single weapons systems, since "a freeze against the arms race would of course be meaningless if such enormous new systems as the MX were allowed to enter production." Successful campaigns against single weapons systems would generate momentum for a freeze in the future.[39] CALC and AFSC leaders actually agreed with Cortright on this point, even though they wanted to link the freeze to other issues.[40] SANE, however, pledged to "actively participate" in the budding freeze movement, because it shared the freeze campaign's goal of ending the nuclear arms race. SANE was also eager to unite and expand the anti-nuclear movement.[41]

Despite pacifists' critique that the freeze proposal was not extensive enough and moderates' charge that it was too extensive, Forsberg maintained her definition of the freeze and her view that it should be the focus of the anti-nuclear movement. She believed that goals that were narrower or broader than her freeze proposal would fail to mobilize widespread popular support. According to Forsberg, the size and composition of the freeze movement would determine its ability to influence policy. Only a large and broad-based movement would be able to overcome "the forces of inertia, of confused ideologists, and of organized groups with a personal stake in the arms race" and persuade Congress and the president to stop the nuclear arms race.[42] Yet different visions of the freeze movement's goals would persist for much of the 1980s, with implications for the movement's effectiveness.

From the outset, the freeze movement adopted a grassroots strategy. *Call* ended with a series of "action suggestions," each of which involved action on the local level, such as sending the *Call* pamphlet to community leaders, purchasing newspaper advertisements advocating the freeze, urging the city council to pass a freeze resolution, or creating a local freeze group to gather signatures for a freeze petition that would be submitted to the group's members of Congress and governor.[43] The freeze movement was a decentralized one that operated primarily on the local and state levels in 1980 and early 1981, as activists began implementing the "action suggestions" in *Call*. For example, activists in Buffalo, New York, handed out excerpts of *Call* at a picnic, march, and vigil held to commemorate the thirty-fifth anniversary of the U.S. atomic bombings of Hiroshima and Nagasaki on August 6 and 9, 1980. In early 1981, freeze supporters from Chicago's North Shore purchased a two-page advertisement urging their members of Congress and Reagan to prioritize a bilateral nuclear freeze agreement. This advertisement ran in ten editions of several area newspapers. Meanwhile, the thirty-five freeze groups that composed the Connecticut Coalition for a Nuclear Arms Freeze conducted a freeze petition drive aimed at gathering five thousand signatures in each of the state's six congressional districts. This petition drive was the centerpiece of the activists' efforts to teach Connecticut residents about the dangers of the nuclear arms race and the need for a freeze.[44]

The most notable local freeze work was Kehler's 1980 campaign to win passage of a nuclear freeze resolution in three state senate districts in western Massachusetts. Local peace activists joined with members of various religious, labor, and community groups to mount a massive public education campaign focused on the necessity of a nuclear freeze. These activists distributed literature; took out radio, television, and billboard advertisements; and delivered speeches to local groups about the freeze. On November 4, 1980, nearly 60 percent of the voters in the three districts approved the nuclear freeze measure. Liberals, moderates, and conservatives backed the freeze referendum in western Massachusetts, showing that the appeal of the freeze concept could transcend the partisan divide.[45] Forsberg and other local peace activists were inspired by the success of the freeze resolutions in Massachusetts and began working to put freeze initiatives on their local and state ballots.[46]

Freeze movement leaders were pleased with the flurry of local freeze activism in 1980 and early 1981. As the inaugural March 1981 edition of the *Freeze Newsletter* explained, "The immediate goal of the national campaign for a Nuclear-Weapon Freeze is to have the largest possible number of organizations and local citizens' groups publicly endorse the idea and gain support for a Freeze in their communities. Local activities lie at the heart of a national movement."[47] Freeze activists believed that strong support for the nuclear freeze in local communities would be essential for convincing elected officials to pursue a freeze.[48]

While the freeze movement was emerging in the United States, the April 1980 "Appeal for European Nuclear Disarmament" (or END Appeal) launched the British organization END and the annual transnational END Conventions. Rather than pursue a nuclear freeze as the first step toward disarmament, END supporters sought a nuclear-free Europe as a precursor to a world without nuclear weapons. E. P. Thompson, a fifty-six-year-old British historian and activist, was the primary drafter of the END Appeal. A former member of the British Communist Party, which he joined as a Cambridge student in 1941, Thompson had left the party after the Soviets violently suppressed the Hungarian Revolution in 1956. After he quit the Communist Party, Thompson quickly emerged as a major figure of the early British New Left. He advocated "socialist humanism" and envisioned a peaceful revolution from below, in which ordinary Britons would organize and act at the grassroots level to build a socialist society. In the late 1950s and early 1960s, Thompson served as a contributor and editor of New Left journals and worked to establish New Left clubs across Britain.[49]

Yet Thompson believed that the Cold War's ideological divide was hindering the achievement of "socialist humanism."[50] He played an active role in the British Campaign for Nuclear Disarmament (CND), which a group of British intellectuals, religious leaders, and anti-nuclear activists established in January 1958. Founded amid growing public concern over British hydrogen bomb tests and the possibility of nuclear war, CND advocated unilateral British nuclear disarmament, which it hoped would ease international tensions and serve as an example for other nations. CND activists sought to mobilize public opposition to nuclear weapons to pressure British members of Parliament (MPs), especially those in the Labour Party, to pursue unilateral nuclear disarmament.[51] Together with his wife, Dorothy, Thompson spearheaded the local CND group in their town of Halifax. Thompson hoped that CND might be able to pressure the British government to withdraw from NATO. This could spark a revolution from below, as ordinary Britons worked to transcend the Cold War and make British society more equitable and just.[52]

In addition to being an activist, Thompson was also a renowned historian. Michael Bess has noted that Thompson explored many of the same questions as a historian that he grappled with as an activist, especially the question of how ordinary individuals can remake their societies. A self-described "historian of radical movements," Thompson received international attention for *The Making of the English Working Class*, which was published in 1963. It became a major work in the field of social history, and Thompson assumed leadership of Warwick University's new Centre for the Study of Social History in 1965. After leaving Warwick University in 1971, Thompson spent much of the 1970s concentrating on historical research and writing.[53]

In late 1979, however, the NATO dual-track decision prompted Thompson to shift his focus to anti-nuclear activism.[54] On December 12, 1979, NATO foreign and defense ministers adopted the dual-track decision in response to the Soviets' modernization and expansion of their long-range theater nuclear forces (LRTNF) aimed at Western Europe, which began in the mid-1970s with the deployment of SS-20 missiles and Tu-22M "Backfire" bombers.[55] The first track of the decision consisted of a proposed modernization of NATO's LRTNF through the deployment of 108 U.S. Pershing II missiles and 464 U.S. ground-launched cruise missiles in Belgium, Britain, the Federal Republic of Germany (FRG), Italy, and the Netherlands. A simultaneous offer of U.S.-Soviet arms control negotiations on both sides' LRTNF constituted the second track of the decision. If these proposed arms control negotiations were successful, they ostensibly would reduce the number of missiles that NATO planned to deploy in Western Europe in 1983.[56]

The dual-track decision galvanized Thompson and other Europeans who feared that an intensifying nuclear arms race might lead to a nuclear war in Europe. Thompson also regarded the planned U.S. missile deployments as a challenge to European sovereignty, calling them "a visible symbol of United States hegemony." In Thompson's view, the British government's support for the dual-track decision was part of a broader militarization effort that included increased policing at home. After learning from the television news that U.S. cruise missiles were headed for Britain, Thompson vowed to prevent their deployment.[57]

A phone call from Ken Coates to Thompson set in motion the formation of END. In this conversation, Coates advocated the creation of a transnational movement seeking the elimination of nuclear weapons located in and targeted on Europe.[58] Coates, a forty-nine-year-old director of the Bertrand Russell Peace Foundation, had been active in British left-wing politics for more than two decades. Like Thompson, Coates had been a member of the British Communist Party but broke with it after Joseph Stalin condemned Yugoslav leader Josip Broz Tito in 1948. Dismayed by the Soviet suppression of the Hungarian Revolution in 1956, Coates helped organize British Trotskyites into what became the International Marxist Group. A veteran peace activist, Coates took part in earlier British campaigns against nuclear weapons and the Vietnam War. In 1968, Coates founded the Institute for Workers' Control in an effort to increase workers' influence in industry. His dedication to organized labor had begun twenty years earlier, when he chose to work as a coal miner rather than perform national service fighting with the British Army in Malaya.[59]

By the beginning of 1980, Coates was focused on the rising international tensions that spelled the end of détente. He feared that a nuclear war was increasingly likely, due to the escalating superpower nuclear arms race and the growing risk of nuclear proliferation. In his view, the denuclearization of Europe would create "a complex of multinational mediators between the two super powers" and slow nuclear proliferation. Coates believed that a nuclear-free Europe was a worthwhile goal for a new anti-nuclear movement.[60]

In advocating a denuclearized Europe, Coates was inspired by earlier proposals for nuclear weapons free zones, including in Central Europe, the Balkans, and the Nordic countries. He was especially moved by former Swedish prime minister Olof Palme's call for a nuclear-free Europe in 1978.[61] In an address to the Socialist International in Helsinki, Palme noted that Europe was "a ready theatre of war" for the superpowers, given the number of nuclear weapons deployed there. In order to reduce the chance that Europe would be obliterated in a military conflict between the United States and the Soviet Union, Palme called for the eventual elimination of nuclear weapons in Europe, particularly Northern and Central Europe.[62] Coates wondered, "If Europe is the most vulnerable region, the prime risk, with a dense concentration of population, the most developed and destructible material heritage to lose, and yet no obvious immediate reasons to go to war, why is there any hesitation at all about making Olof Palme's 'ultimate objective' into an immediate and urgent demand?"[63] With a campaign for European nuclear disarmament, Coates sought to do just that.

Coates enlisted Thompson to write a draft appeal for European nuclear disarmament, which Coates then circulated for comments. One person to whom he sent the draft appeal was Mary Kaldor, a thirty-three-year-old fellow at the Science Policy Research Unit at the University of Sussex who would play a major role in END.[64] Kaldor's interest in nuclear disarmament began at the age of twelve, when she started participating in CND demonstrations. After graduating from Oxford in 1967, Kaldor became a researcher at SIPRI, where her work focused on the global arms trade. At SIPRI, Kaldor developed friendships with many of her colleagues, including Forsberg. Alva Myrdal, the Swedish sociologist and politician who served as SIPRI's first chair, significantly shaped Kaldor's thinking during this period. Kaldor was drawn to Myrdal's argument that the Cold War was a "mutual enterprise" pursued by the United States and the Soviet Union, as well as her belief that ordinary individuals should have access to independent sources of information on disarmament efforts. Kaldor spent two years working in Stockholm before leaving for a research fellow position at Sussex University. While at Sussex, Kaldor researched and wrote on the innovation of military technology, the military industry, economic conversion, and disarmament.[65]

Kaldor brought not only expertise, but also British Labour Party connections to the movement for a nuclear-free Europe. Her father, Nicholas, was a renowned economist who had worked for the United Nations Economic Commission for Europe in the late 1940s and served as an advisor to Harold Wilson's Labour government. Her mother, Clarissa, was elected a Labour Party councillor in the early 1960s. Kaldor had started advising the Labour Party on defense policy in 1975, participating in the party's National Executive Committee Study Group on Defence Expenditure, the Arms Trade and Alternative Employment. This group considered ways to reduce defense spending, as well as the broader impact of such reductions. Coates later noted that Kaldor and Dan Smith, a former CND general secretary who had also participated in the Labour Party study group on defense spending, "were institutionally connected with all the people who could be most helpful in the Labour Party in taking up the issues of European nuclear disarmament."[66]

Yet the END Appeal was not simply a British effort. Coates also convened a meeting of prominent individuals from across the European left to discuss Thompson's draft appeal and the development of a campaign for a denuclearized Europe.[67] Attendees at this March 8, 1980, meeting in London included Thompson; Coates; Kaldor; Stuart Holland, a British Labour MP; Arthur Scargill, a British trade union leader; Bruce Kent, a Roman Catholic priest who was the CND general secretary; Claude Bourdet, a leader of the noncommunist French left; Ulrich Albrecht, a peace studies professor at the Free University of Berlin; and Antonio Bronda, a journalist working for the Italian communist newspaper *L'Unità*.[68] Thompson later reflected that the END Appeal was "greatly revised, to its advantage" by his wife, Dorothy; Coates; Kaldor; Smith; Kent; Albrecht; Bourdet; and Zhores Medvedev, a biologist and dissident who was stripped of his Soviet citizenship in 1973 while working at the National Institute for Medical Research in London.[69]

A press conference in the House of Commons on April 28, 1980, officially launched END, as Thompson, Kaldor, Kent, and Medvedev joined with Labour MPs Tony Benn and Eric Heffer to unveil the END Appeal. Simultaneous press conferences took place in Paris, Berlin, Oslo, and Lisbon.[70] The END Appeal characterized the 1980s as "the most dangerous decade in human history" and lamented that NATO and the Warsaw Pact continued to develop new nuclear weapons despite the fact that each side already possessed sufficient nuclear forces to destroy the other. It expressed particular concern over the nuclear buildup in Europe, which was "the main geographical stage for the East-West confrontation."[71]

The END Appeal called on ordinary Europeans from East and West to work for the elimination of nuclear weapons "from Poland to Portugal." It also urged the United States and the Soviet Union to remove their nuclear weapons from Europe. In addition to the denuclearization of Europe, the END Appeal demanded human rights protections, the dissolution of NATO and the Warsaw Pact, and the reunification of Europe. Recognizing that European officials often used the threat of nuclear war to justify expanding the power of military and domestic security forces and restricting civil rights, the appeal noted that all Europeans must have the right to participate in the movement to rid Europe of nuclear weapons. It instructed the peoples of Europe to start thinking of themselves as Europeans, rather than as members of one of the blocs, which should be eliminated. "We must commence to act as if a united, neutral and pacific Europe already exists," the appeal insisted. "We must learn to be loyal, not to 'East' or 'West', but to each other, and we must disregard the prohibitions and limitations imposed by any national state."[72]

Although the END Appeal urged Europeans to "mount an irresistible pressure for a Europe free of nuclear weapons," it did not provide them with a specific strategy for achieving the denuclearization of Europe. Rather, activists in each country were free to choose the strategy that they thought would be most effective in persuading political leaders to rid Europe of nuclear weapons. The END Appeal, however, did insist that activists take part in a "transcontinental movement in which every kind of exchange takes place."[73] Only a massive pan-European campaign would be able to generate the intense public pressure necessary to force leaders to eliminate nuclear weapons in Europe.[74] It also would be more difficult for political leaders in NATO and the Warsaw Pact to dismiss anti-nuclear activists as pawns of the opposing bloc if the movement spanned both halves of Europe.[75]

As an organization, END initially consisted of a small British steering committee that sought to coordinate the campaign for a nuclear-free Europe. Its members were Thompson, Coates, Kaldor, Smith, Holland, Kent, and Peggy Duff, a founder and former general secretary of CND who was active in the non-aligned International Confederation for Disarmament and Peace. "Lateral" committees were set up to connect anti-nuclear British parliamentarians, trade union members, churchgoers, women, and university teachers and students with their counterparts in other European countries. END's founders believed that the work of these five lateral committees would pave the way for a pan-European conference of individuals, organizations, and political parties committed to the denuclearization of Europe.[76]

END's initial focus was on building a European-wide campaign that could generate the necessary pressure to convince officials to eliminate nuclear weapons in Europe. One of the major ways in which END sought to develop a transnational movement was circulating and collecting signatures for the END Appeal. Coates and the Russell Foundation took the lead in this effort, amassing hundreds of signatures from across Europe even before the appeal was unveiled publicly on April 28.[77] By September 1980, trade unionists; academics; writers; peace activists; actors; church leaders; social democratic, Labour, socialist, and "Eurocommunist" politicians; and other individuals from twenty-five countries had signed the appeal.[78] Patrick Burke has explained that Coates drew on the network of contacts from the European left that he had developed through his Russell Foundation work when he distributed the appeal, which enabled him to collect signatures quickly.[79]

The END Appeal resonated with Europeans who were anxious about the consequences of the breakdown of détente between the United States and the Soviet Union. As superpower détente collapsed in the late 1970s due to Soviet involvement in Angola and Ethiopia, the United States' failure to ratify SALT II, the NATO dual-track decision, and the Soviet invasion of Afghanistan, fears about world war increased among West Europeans. West Europeans also worried that NATO might use nuclear weapons in a war that broke out in Europe.[80] The END Appeal's call to rid Europe of nuclear weapons was understandably appealing in a time of rising international tension.

END also worked to create a European-wide anti-nuclear movement through its publication of the *END Bulletin*. Appearing quarterly between 1980 and 1983, when the *END Journal* replaced it, the *END Bulletin* contained articles about the activities of END and other anti-nuclear organizations across Western Europe, as well as publicity for their upcoming events. Not only did the *END Bulletin* keep activists from different West European organizations informed about each other's campaigns, but it also encouraged participation in events held in other countries.[81] In addition, the *END Bulletin* provided a forum for individuals and organizations concerned about nuclear weapons to present and debate specific nuclear disarmament initiatives.[82] The editors of the *END Bulletin* explained that their aim was to "express the arguments, strategies and debates that are emerging in different parts of Europe" and to serve as "the main channel of communication between the growing numbers of people and movements who wish to build an alternative in Europe to the arms race and the Cold War."[83]

In late 1980 and early 1981, END activists also participated in two international conferences of European anti-nuclear organizations in order to promote their idea of a European-wide movement for the denuclearization of the continent. At a September 1980 conference in London, END activists presented their proposals for a pan-European movement seeking nuclear disarmament on both sides of the Iron Curtain to representatives from Belgian, Danish, French, West German, Finnish, Irish, and Norwegian anti-nuclear organizations, who agreed to "consider an all-European campaign."[84] END activists also attended a follow-up convention in Frankfurt in March 1981 to discuss European anti-nuclear groups' recent activities and plans for upcoming demonstrations and marches, as well as methods of communication among peace activists from different European countries. The delegates from fourteen countries agreed to back a European-wide communications and information campaign to highlight "the location of nuclear and nuclear-related bases, to shatter the illusion of protection from Civil Defence, [and] to inform the military of their rights." END accepted the task of creating a short newsletter that would be distributed periodically in each European country to facilitate communication among disarmament groups. The activists also tentatively scheduled a pan-European "mass march/demonstration" for Easter 1982.[85] A transnational campaign for the denuclearization of Europe was underway.

Yet END was not solely forging links among European anti-nuclear activists from different countries during this period. In late 1980 and early 1981, END also worked with CND to stage anti-nuclear demonstrations in Britain. Independently of END's efforts to build a transnational movement for a nuclear-free Europe, CND was experiencing a surge of growth after more than a decade of decline. In the mid-1960s, CND went into decline as exhausted activists grew exasperated by their inability to ban the bomb. Popular support for CND waned as nuclear war seemed less likely following the peaceful resolution of the Cuban missile crisis and the signing of the 1963 Limited Test Ban Treaty by the United States, the Soviet Union, and Britain. This agreement banned nuclear tests in the atmosphere, outer space, and underwater. Also, the Vietnam War increasingly preoccupied CND activists, who shifted their focus away from nuclear issues.[86]

CND's revitalization began in the late 1970s, after the 1977 revelation that the United States was on the verge of producing an enhanced radiation warhead for short-range Lance missiles deployed in Europe. By releasing a flurry of neutrons with a minimum of heat and blast, this "neutron bomb" was intended to kill people without obliterating the surrounding infrastructure. Britons worried that these characteristics of the neutron bomb made its use more plausible and suggested that a nuclear conflict could be confined to Europe, thereby making nuclear war more likely.[87] Two hundred and fifty thousand people signed CND's petition against the neutron bomb, the production of which Carter decided to defer in 1978.[88] Yet despite this spurt of activism, only six hundred people turned out for CND's major anti-nuclear rally in 1979.[89]

The intensification of the nuclear arms race, coupled with troubling revelations about the British civil defense program, led to an outpouring of British anti-nuclear protest in 1980. Kent and other CND activists recalled that the NATO dual-track decision, which included a planned deployment of U.S. cruise missiles in Britain, was a major contributor to CND's resurgence. British nuclear modernization also spurred anti-nuclear activism. In January 1980, news of Chevaline, a secret, decade-long, £1 billion program to improve Britain's Polaris SLBMs, broke during a House of Commons debate. Only six months later, Margaret Thatcher's government announced that it would spend billions of pounds on U.S. Trident SLBMs to replace the Polaris missiles.[90]

While escalating the nuclear arms race, the British government published the civil defense pamphlet *Protect and Survive*, which provided instructions to follow before, during, and after a nuclear attack. These instructions were chilling at times, particularly the advice for handling deaths that might occur in a fallout room. Yet they could also be ridiculous, such as the recommendation that a family of four live under a dining-room table for forty-eight hours after a fallout warning.[91] CND activist Philip Bolsover later described *Protect and Survive* as "the best gift CND ever had from any government," because it motivated Britons to join the anti-nuclear movement by making tangible the horrors of nuclear war.[92] Nuclear war seemed increasingly likely as new missiles were developed and a faulty electronic circuit produced two false reports of a Soviet nuclear attack at U.S. Strategic Air Command in June 1980.[93]

When CND held a demonstration on October 26, 1980, fifty thousand people answered the call to march from London's Hyde Park to Trafalgar Square in support of nuclear disarmament.[94] END supporters were among those who marched through the London streets. Carrying signs that read "No SS20s; No Cruise Missiles," END activists demanded the withdrawal of nuclear weapons from both halves of Europe. Thompson was among the featured speakers at the rally in Trafalgar Square, where he reminded the British crowd that Dutch, Belgian, and Norwegian activists were waging similar campaigns against nuclear weapons.[95] Local END and CND groups also coordinated to stage the April 1981 Trans-Pennine Anti-War March, from which a contingent of British activists headed to Brussels for a transnational Easter rally against war.[96]

As Thompson noted, anti-nuclear activism was flourishing in the Netherlands. The leading force in the Dutch anti-nuclear movement was the Interchurch Peace Council (IKV), which Dutch Catholic and Protestant churches had created in 1966. These churches instructed IKV "to study on its own responsibility the problems of war and peace and of development in the world, to publish in popularized form, and to recommend fitting actions to interested parties." Almost immediately, IKV expressed concern about nuclear weapons, focusing its first Peace Week on the theme "proliferation of prosperity, no proliferation of nuclear weapons" in 1967. Two years later, IKV endorsed the opening of the SALT talks in a letter to the Dutch churches. IKV warned of the dangers of the nuclear arms race and called for "replac[ing] the present system of nuclear deterrence with a different system better able to promote peace and justice."[97]

Dutch anti-nuclear activism surged in 1977, as the arms race accelerated and arms control negotiations continuously failed to reduce nuclear weapons. In response to these developments, IKV launched a grassroots campaign for the withdrawal of nuclear weapons from the Netherlands, which it envisioned as the first step toward nuclear abolition. "Help rid the world of nuclear weapons, beginning with the Netherlands," IKV declared in 1977.[98] It sought to build support for a nuclear-free Netherlands among churchgoers, activists in local political party organizations, and labor union members, who were expected to pressure their national organizations to join the campaign. IKV also instructed its supporters to vote only for political parties that planned to denuclearize the Netherlands.[99] News of the Carter administration's planned production of neutron bombs also spurred Dutch anti-nuclear activism in the latter half of 1977. The Dutch Communist Party spearheaded a massive Stop the Neutron Bomb campaign, which received support from the GDR.[100]

As NATO began discussing the modernization of its LRTNF, IKV's focus shifted to preventing new missile deployments, and it sponsored a host of anti-Euromissile meetings and demonstrations.[101] Ruud van Dijk has noted that IKV leaders also had access to Christian Democratic members of parliament due to their shared religious background and social activities. Some of these Christian Democratic parliamentarians supported IKV's call for denuclearizing the Netherlands as a first step toward global nuclear disarmament. At the very least, many of these Christian Democrats opposed the installation of new U.S. nuclear weapons in the Netherlands. As NATO moved toward the dual-track decision, IKV intensified its efforts to persuade Christian Democratic parliamentarians to reject modernization of theater nuclear forces

(TNF). Anti-nuclear sentiment was increasing among the Dutch public, which largely opposed hosting new nuclear missiles.[102]

Van Dijk has shown that the Dutch anti-nuclear movement, as well as opposition among the Dutch public and Christian Democrats to Euromissile deployments, influenced the policies of Prime Minister Andries van Agt and his cabinet. This coalition government of the Christian Democratic Appeal and the People's Party for Freedom and Democracy backed the NATO dual-track decision on December 12, 1979, but deferred a decision on whether to accept the Netherlands' allotted share of missiles until 1981. Determined to prevent the arrival of these missiles, the Dutch anti-nuclear movement continued to mobilize and gain strength.[103]

The Belgian government also faced opposition to the TNF deployments from Flemish socialists and a growing anti-nuclear movement.[104] Belgian anti-nuclear organizations like the National Action Committee for Peace and Development and the Flemish Action Committee Against Nuclear Weapons mounted campaigns against Soviet and U.S. TNF. Fifty thousand people participated in an anti-nuclear rally in Brussels three days before NATO ministers adopted the dual-track decision. These demonstrators called for NATO to abandon its plan to deploy U.S. cruise and Pershing II missiles in Western Europe. They also wanted negotiations aimed at eliminating Soviet SS-20 missiles and denuclearizing Europe.[105] Like the Dutch, the Belgian government endorsed the dual-track decision but with conditions. Belgium would only agree to host missiles if the superpowers had not made headway in arms control negotiations in six months' time.[106]

Anti-nuclear activism was also on the rise in the FRG, although mass demonstrations against nuclear weapons did not take place until 1981. In 1975, opponents of nuclear power staged two dramatic occupations of the Wyhl nuclear reactor construction site, captivating the West German public.[107] By the end of the 1970s, the vibrant West German environmental movement was condemning nuclear power and nuclear weapons and allying itself with West German peace activists.[108]

West German Protestants also highlighted the need for nuclear disarmament in the late 1970s. Inspired by the World Council of Churches' critique of militarism in 1975, the Württemberg-based organization Living Without Arms issued an appeal to all West German Christians in 1978. It urged each Christian to sign a pledge "to live without the protection of military armament" and "campaign in our society for peace developed politically without weapons." Over the next five years, more than 24,000 West Germans signed this pledge. The Christian peace groups Action Reconciliation Service for Peace (ASF) and Action Committee Service for Peace (AGDF) also turned their attention to nuclear issues in the 1970s. Beginning in 1974, they staged an annual Pentecost Festival, which took place in Lower Franconia for three years before relocating to Lower Saxony. These festivals offered Christians a forum for discussing disarmament and recruiting others to work for peace.[109]

Transnational contacts inspired West German Protestants to expand their disarmament work. At the urging of Dutch IKV activists, ASF and AGDF mounted a nationwide Peace Week in late November 1980. They hoped to use this Peace Week to develop peace activists' thinking and attract public support, as Dutch IKV did each year. Planning for this first West German Peace Week began at the Seventh Pentecost Festival, where activists decided on the theme "Create Peace Without Weapons." From November 16 through 22, 350 Peace Weeks took place across the FRG. Protestants played a major role in these events, along with activists from labor unions, women's organizations, and peace and disarmament groups, among others.[110]

The NATO dual-track decision also spurred West German anti-nuclear activism. After two days of discussion in Krefeld on November 15 and 16, 1980, peace activists issued an appeal urging the West German government to rescind its support for the planned U.S. intermediate-range nuclear force (INF) deployments in Western Europe. The Krefeld Appeal also called on government officials to resist the acceleration of the nuclear arms race within NATO.[111] The initial signatories of the Krefeld Appeal included Gert Bastian, a former general who had parted ways with the West German Army over the NATO dual-track decision, and Petra Kelly, a co-spokesperson for the newly established Green Party. Both would become leading figures in the West German anti-nuclear movement during the 1980s. The theologian and pastor Martin Niemöller also signed the Krefeld Appeal in November 1980, as did physicist Karl Bechert, among others.[112]

Yet controversy has plagued the Krefeld Appeal, as contemporaries and historians have debated whether it was a communist initiative. As this debate unfolded after the appeal's launch, Bastian publicly declared in July 1981 that he had written the appeal.[113] By contrast, the historian Gerhard Wettig has argued that Josef Weber of the German Peace Union secretly worked with East German and Soviet officials to initiate the appeal. According to Wettig, this was part of a broader Soviet effort to mobilize West European anti-nuclear sentiment to derail the planned U.S. INF deployments and undermine NATO. Weber recognized that the West German public was unlikely to sign an appeal devised by communists. In an effort to mask the communist origins of the appeal, Weber allegedly convinced Bastian and Kelly to help launch the appeal by claiming that it was inspired by Bastian's criticism of the dual-track decision.[114] Over the next three years, more than four million people signed the Krefeld Appeal.[115]

*   *   *

While U.S. and West European anti-nuclear activism was on the rise in 1980, Reagan was campaigning against Carter for the presidency. Although he shared grassroots activists' desire for nuclear arms reduction, Reagan advocated a starkly different disarmament strategy than the activists. Born on February 6, 1911, in Tampico, Illinois, Ronald Wilson Reagan was the oldest person elected president when he won the 1980 election. He had risen from humble beginnings in Illinois to become a movie star in Hollywood, where he developed an abhorrence of nuclear weapons shortly after the Second World War. In 1945, Reagan became an officer in the Hollywood chapter of the liberal American Veterans Committee. Gilbert Harrison, the American Veterans Committee's founder, recalled that Reagan was attracted to the organization because he liked Harrison's "idea of expanding the Committee into an international lobby under the aegis of the United Nations, working to contain the A-bomb."[116] At a December 10, 1945, dinner in honor of Harvard astronomer Harlow Shapley, Reagan performed a dramatic reading of Norman Corwin's "Set Your Clock at U-235," an anti-nuclear poem that advocated the international control of atomic energy and world government. Reagan was slated to read the poem again at a December 12 rally sponsored by the liberal Hollywood Independent Citizens Committee of the Arts, Sciences, and Professions in support of the international control of atomic energy and nuclear abolition. He did not appear at the rally, however, because he was warned by Warner Bros. studio that he would be in violation of his contract if he participated.[117]

Yet Reagan also developed an antipathy to communism during this period. At the war's end, Reagan was "a New Dealer to the core," believing that "government could solve all our postwar problems just as it had ended the Depression and won the war." To his dismay, however, he discovered that communists were playing a growing role in the liberal organizations that he joined after the war, namely the American Veterans Committee and the Hollywood Independent Citizens Committee of the Arts, Sciences, and Professions. When a dispute between rival unions of set erectors threatened to shut down the movie industry in 1946, Reagan blamed the communists. He worked to negotiate an end to this strike as an officer in the Screen Actors Guild (SAG). His first stint as SAG president coincided with the Hollywood blacklist of suspected communists, although Reagan worked with actors who were targeted by the blacklist but were willing to denounce communism and cooperate with the House Un-American Activities Committee. These postwar experiences in Hollywood made Reagan a fervent anti-communist. "Now I knew from firsthand experience how Communists used lies, deceit, violence, or any other tactic that suited them to advance the cause of Soviet expansionism," Reagan later reflected. "I knew from the experience of hand-to-hand combat [in Hollywood] that America faced no more insidious or evil threat than that of Communism."[118]

Many of Reagan's political views shifted during his time working for General Electric (GE) from 1954 through 1962. Although his primary responsibility was hosting the weekly TV show *General Electric Theater*, Reagan also gave speeches at GE plants across the country. During these GE tours, he became convinced that government regulation was stifling businesses and an expanding federal government was infringing on individual liberty. "By 1960, I realized the real enemy wasn't big business, it was big government," Reagan later wrote. Two years later, he reregistered to vote as a Republican.[119]

Reagan's critique of big government reached a national audience when he delivered a televised speech on behalf of Barry Goldwater's 1964 presidential campaign. Drawing on the ideas that he had been expressing since his GE days, Reagan warned about the dangers of a growing federal government encroaching on individual freedom. He contended that Lyndon Johnson's Great Society would lead the country down the path to totalitarianism. In a rousing conclusion, Reagan told his listeners, "You and I have a rendezvous with destiny. We will preserve for our children this, the last best hope of man on earth, or we will sentence them to take the last step into a thousand years of darkness." Reagan's speech was so well received among Republicans that a group of donors urged him to run for governor of California in 1966.[120] After serving as California's governor from 1967 to 1975, Reagan unsuccessfully challenged Gerald Ford for the 1976 Republican nomination for president.

During this period, Reagan's growing fascination with Armageddon reinforced his anti-nuclearism. Found in the New Testament book of Revelation, Armageddon is the story of the last battle between good and evil that marks the end of the world. While governor of California, Reagan met with evangelical ministers who sparked his interest in this biblical story. Reagan came to associate Armageddon with nuclear war, even declaring that the book of Revelation predicted the destruction wrought by the U.S. atomic bombing of Hiroshima. Determined to protect Americans from the devastation of nuclear Armageddon, Reagan wanted to reduce nuclear weapons as president.[121]

In his 1980 presidential campaign, Reagan asked voters to join him in a "great national crusade to make America great again!" He blamed Carter for rising unemployment and inflation and lambasted his foreign policy as one of "weakness, indecision, mediocrity and incompetence."[122] Although Carter had recently embarked on a nuclear modernization program, Reagan charged him with neglecting U.S. defenses.[123] Meanwhile, the Soviets were engaged in what Reagan hyperbolically called "the biggest military build-up in the history of man." Reagan attacked Carter's record on nuclear arms control, which Carter deemed "the most important single issue" in the 1980 campaign. The SALT II Treaty did nothing to restrain the Soviet buildup, Reagan alleged. He opposed the treaty's ratification on the grounds that it disadvantaged the United States and failed to reduce strategic nuclear weapons.[124]

On the campaign trail, Reagan laid out his "peace through strength" strategy, which called for modernizing U.S. nuclear forces and then pursuing nuclear arms reduction negotiations with the Soviet Union. Reagan argued that the United States' failure to obtain an agreement that actually reduced the superpowers' nuclear weapons was due to the fact that the Soviets maintained a decided nuclear advantage over the Americans. He believed that U.S. nuclear modernization would show the Soviet Union that the United States was not going to let it win the arms race. Realizing that they did not have the resources to keep up with the Americans in a renewed arms race, the Soviets would have an incentive to take negotiations seriously and strive for an agreement that reduced nuclear arsenals, rather than merely limiting their increase. As Reagan explained in a televised address, "The way to avoid an arms race is not simply to let the Soviets race ahead. We need to remove their incentive to race ahead by making it clear to them that we can and will compete if need be, at the same time we tell them that we prefer to halt this competition and reduce the nuclear arsenals by patient negotiation."[125]

Carter characterized Reagan's approach to nuclear arms control as "extremely dangerous and belligerent in its tone." He noted that Reagan had opposed SALT I, the ABM Treaty, the Vladivostok Accords, and SALT II. Dismissing Reagan's contention that he opposed these treaties because they provided for mere arms limitation instead of significant arms reduction, Carter argued that Reagan was averse to arms control. Rather than inducing the Soviets to negotiate arms reduction, Reagan's modernization plan would exacerbate the nuclear arms race, upset U.S. allies, and worsen U.S.-Soviet relations.[126]

Although his modernization plan was aimed at redressing an exaggerated gap in the superpowers' nuclear capabilities, Reagan was sincere in his desire to negotiate arms reduction agreements with the Soviets.[127] While governor of California, Reagan had repeatedly criticized the mutual assured destruction (MAD) doctrine to his aides, later comparing it to "two westerners standing in a saloon aiming their guns to each other's head—permanently." Two of Reagan's closest advisors during the 1980 presidential campaign, Martin Anderson and Michael Deaver, have stated that Reagan's desire to eradicate the threat of nuclear war motivated his involvement in politics, even his decision to run for president.[128] During the campaign, Reagan pledged, "My goal is to begin arms reductions. My energies will be directed at reducing destructive nuclear weaponry in the world—and doing it in such a way as to protect fully the critical security requirements of our nation."[129]

Reagan's desire for sweeping nuclear arms reduction made him a unique figure on the right. Maintaining a position that was far from the conservative consensus, Reagan did not make support for nuclear disarmament a litmus test for serving in his administration. As a result, he assembled a team that did not share his goal of dramatically reducing nuclear weapons and often actively thwarted his pursuit of this aim. Reagan's dislike of confrontation made him reluctant to fire advisors, so the first eighteen months of his administration were plagued by divisions between the president and his top aides on arms control issues.[130] For secretary of state, Reagan chose Alexander M. Haig Jr., who had impressed the president-elect during a conversation about world affairs at Reagan's ranch in the summer of 1979.[131] Haig's record of military and government service sharply contrasted with Reagan's inexperience in foreign policy. After serving in Korea and Vietnam, Haig became Henry Kissinger's military assistant in 1969 and was promoted to deputy national security advisor two years later. He served as Nixon's chief of staff during the embattled days of Watergate before becoming the supreme allied commander Europe in 1974.

Reagan also likely believed that Haig's foreign policy views were compatible with his own. Nixon had written to Reagan during the transition and urged the president-elect to name Haig as his secretary of state on the grounds that the retired general shared Reagan's foreign policy positions and had a breadth of experience. Although Reagan had reservations about Nixon's personality and some of his domestic policies, he believed that the former president "knew more about Washington than anyone else on the Republican side" and followed Nixon's recommendation to tap Haig to lead the State Department.[132]

Although Haig was more interested in crafting serious nuclear arms reduction proposals than many of Reagan's other top advisors, he did not share the president's nuclear abolitionism. Haig later characterized nuclear weapons as the "essential element in the overall Western deterrent." An advocate of linkage, Haig argued that progress in nuclear arms reduction negotiations should be linked to Soviet behavior across the globe. "How can responsible American leaders assume, when the survival of the human species is at stake, that the Soviets have one type of behavior (benevolent and peaceable) when dealing with nuclear weapons and another (brutal and warlike) when invading Afghanistan or intimidating Poland or encouraging terrorism?"[133]

Unlike Haig, Caspar Weinberger had a long-standing relationship with the president. Reagan had appointed Weinberger chairman of the Commission on California State Government Organization and Economy and then state director of finance during his governorship. Weinberger also came highly recommended by Nixon, who had been impressed by Weinberger's work as chairman of the Federal Trade Commission, deputy director and then director of the Office of Management and Budget (OMB), and secretary of health, education, and welfare in his administration. Reagan believed that Weinberger's support for U.S. nuclear modernization made him particularly suited to the position of secretary of defense. Weinberger's reputation for being a cost cutter also made him an attractive choice to lead the Pentagon in Reagan's view.[134] During the conversation in which Reagan asked Weinberger to be his secretary of defense, the president-elect noted that he had been pleased with Weinberger's work as California's finance director, when he had proposed numerous budget cuts.[135] While serving as Nixon's OMB director, Weinberger had won the nickname "Cap the Knife" for his opposition to budget increases.[136] That appealed to Reagan, who wanted to balance the budget and lower taxes while also modernizing U.S. defenses.[137]

Yet Weinberger's actions as secretary of defense quickly revealed that he no longer deserved the moniker "Cap the Knife." Weinberger won a $25.8 billion increase in the fiscal year 1982 defense budget, which the Reagan administration had inherited from Carter. The Carter administration's fiscal year 1982 budget had already included a 5 percent increase in defense spending from the previous year, but Weinberger did not think that it was sufficient. He soon earned a new nickname: "Cap the Ladle."[138]

Unlike Reagan, Weinberger had little interest in pursuing dramatic nuclear arms reduction agreements with the Soviets. In the Reagan administration's first National Security Council (NSC) meeting on February 6, 1981, Weinberger rejected Soviet ambassador to the United States Anatoly Dobrynin's proposal to explore the idea of a Soviet withdrawal from Afghanistan in exchange for the initiation of U.S.-Soviet arms control talks. Weinberger argued that the Reagan administration should wait six months before beginning arms control negotiations with the Soviets. "We don't want to appear too eager [for negotiations] since this weakens our position," he warned.[139]

Richard V. Allen, who had advised Reagan on foreign policy issues during the 1980 presidential campaign, became national security advisor. Allen was a founding member of the revived Committee on the Present Danger, which warned in 1976 that the United States "is in a period of danger, and the danger is increasing." The committee contended that "the principal threat to our nation, to world peace, and to the cause of human freedom is the Soviet drive for dominance based upon an unparalleled military build-up." It emphasized the importance of improving U.S. nuclear and conventional forces.[140] In the late 1970s, Allen set up meetings between Reagan and committee members Jeane Kirkpatrick, Eugene Rostow, and Paul Nitze, each of whom later served in the Reagan administration.[141] While Allen, Kirkpatrick, Rostow, and Nitze shared Reagan's concern that the United States was falling behind the Soviet Union in the nuclear arms race, they did not desire dramatic nuclear arms reduction agreements. Neglecting to make support for nuclear disarmament a condition for joining his administration, Reagan was initially surrounded by advisors who did not share his goal of drastically reducing nuclear weapons.

* * *

Anti-nuclear activists who did share Reagan's desire for nuclear disarmament did not view him as their ally. Rather, Reagan's proposals for nuclear modernization left them deeply troubled by his 1980 election victory. Nuclear freeze activists' devastation was palpable at a steering committee meeting that took place the day after the election. "In terms of creating a new vision for the future or of proposing a way to end the nuclear arms race, we have no competition. We are in position of resistance and people will believe that the gov't has no plan for ending arms race. We are the alternative," freeze activists noted.[142] E. P. Thompson, who was teaching in the United States during the 1980 presidential campaign, was disturbed by the calls for "aggressive nuclear armament" by high-profile Reagan supporters like Richard Burt and Richard Perle, both of whom joined the Reagan administration in 1981.[143] Antinuclear activists believed that Reagan's nuclear modernization plans showed that he had no interest in reversing the arms race.

Reagan's criticism of SALT II reinforced this perception that he would be an obstacle to nuclear disarmament as president. The Krefeld Appeal, which appeared shortly after Reagan's election, criticized the president-elect's unwillingness to press for Senate ratification of SALT II. The appeal's initiators feared that the failure of SALT II would delay INF negotiations. Meanwhile, the "suicidal arms race" would continue, threatening to spiral into a nuclear war.[144]

United in their desire for nuclear disarmament, Reagan and grassroots anti-nuclear activists advocated starkly different strategies for achieving their shared aim. They eyed one another warily, refusing to consider themselves allies in the struggle for disarmament. During Reagan's first term, however, both the president and anti-nuclear activists would play crucial roles in reshaping the U.S. nuclear arms control paradigm.

CHAPTER 2

"We, Too, Are Activists"

On June 22, 1981, the Senate Foreign Relations Committee began confirmation hearings on Eugene Rostow, Reagan's nominee to lead the Arms Control and Disarmament Agency (ACDA). These hearings are best remembered for Rostow's chilling assertion that the United States and the Soviet Union could survive an all-out nuclear war. "The human race is very resilient," Rostow told Senator Claiborne Pell (D-RI), who asked for his views on this issue. In a matter-of-fact way, Rostow pointed out that there would be some survivors in a full-scale nuclear war, even if estimates were correct and one superpower lost ten million citizens while the other lost one hundred million.[1] Rostow's callous statements contrasted sharply with Reagan's horror at learning from the Pentagon that one hundred and fifty million Americans would die in a nuclear war that the United States won. "For Americans who survived such a war, I couldn't imagine what life would be like. The planet would be so poisoned the 'survivors' would have no place to live. Even if a nuclear war did not mean the extinction of mankind, it would certainly mean the end of civilization as we knew it. *No one* could 'win' a nuclear war," Reagan reflected.[2]

In Rostow's confirmation hearings, Pell and Senator Charles Mathias (R-MD) also raised the nuclear freeze proposal and West German anti-nuclear activism, which indicated the growing strength of U.S. and West European anti-nuclear movements in 1981. In a brief response to Pell's question about a "nuclear weapons moratorium," Rostow expressed skepticism but claimed that he needed more information on U.S. and Soviet nuclear forces before he could make a final judgment. After Mathias mentioned the "substantial antinuclear movement" in Germany, Rostow noted that ordinary individuals around the world were concerned about war and wanted political leaders to work for peace.[3] As ACDA director, Rostow would spend more and more time thinking about U.S. and West European anti-nuclear activists. Along with Reagan's nuclear abolitionism, these activists reshaped U.S. arms control policy in profound ways.

This chapter contends that both Reagan and grassroots anti-nuclear activists played essential roles in shifting the U.S. nuclear arms control paradigm from arms limitation to arms reduction during Reagan's first term. This was the first step toward reversing the superpower nuclear arms race and ending the Cold War. Shortly after taking office, Reagan's anti-nuclearism led him to declare that his administration would pursue nuclear arms reduction rather than mere arms limitation. Pressure from U.S. and West European anti-nuclear activists, however, accelerated the Reagan administration's timetable for beginning nuclear arms reduction negotiations with the Soviets and emboldened its initial negotiating proposals. U.S. and West European anti-nuclear activism was particularly crucial in prompting Reagan's advisors, who were not nuclear abolitionists, to support the opening of talks aimed at reducing U.S. and Soviet nuclear weapons.

In 1981 and early 1982, grassroots anti-nuclear activists pressured the Reagan administration by gaining extensive support among the American electorate, working with members of Congress on a nuclear freeze resolution, and urging U.S. allies in Western Europe to reject the planned INF deployments that were slated to begin in late 1983. Reagan was dismayed by the growing support for U.S. and West European anti-nuclear movements, which advocated alternative nuclear disarmament strategies that he considered dangerous and ineffectual. The president feared that these grassroots movements would persuade Congress to reject funding for U.S. nuclear modernization or convince the allies to refuse U.S. INF missiles, which he believed would lock the United States into a position of nuclear inferiority and remove the Soviets' incentive to negotiate arms reduction. In response to grassroots pressure, Reagan became anxious to prove the merits of his own "peace through strength" disarmament strategy: he accelerated his timetable for beginning INF and START negotiations and offered bold opening proposals in these talks. While Reagan hoped that these actions would jumpstart nuclear disarmament, his advisors supported them merely in a cynical effort to curtail anti-nuclear activism. Activists were creating a public, congressional, and allied backlash against U.S. nuclear modernization, which Reagan's advisors thought was vital to ensure the stability and security of U.S. nuclear forces.

*   *   *

Nine days after entering the White House, Reagan's anti-nuclearism led him to declare that his administration would pursue nuclear arms reduction rather than mere arms limitation. In his first presidential press conference, Reagan made it clear that he intended to keep his campaign promise to pursue strategic arms reduction negotiations. After criticizing SALT II as an ineffective agreement that permitted the superpowers to expand their nuclear arsenals, he stated, "We should start negotiating on the basis of trying to effect an actual reduction in the numbers of nuclear weapons. That would then be real strategic arms limitation."[4]

Yet Reagan's "peace through strength" strategy called for pursuing arms reduction negotiations only after modernizing U.S. nuclear forces. The 1980 Republican Party Platform, which Reagan vowed to enact after his election victory, asserted that "before arms control negotiations may be undertaken, the security of the United States must be assured by the funding and deployment of strong military forces sufficient to deter conflict at any level or to prevail in battle should aggression occur."[5] Although Reagan and his top aides publicly expressed a willingness to begin strategic arms reduction talks before U.S. modernization was complete, they privately insisted that the nuclear upgrade should precede the opening of negotiations.[6] Secretary of State Alexander Haig, for example, later reflected that Reagan wanted to build the MX missile, the Trident II submarine, the B-1B bomber, and additional cruise missiles before initiating strategic arms reduction talks with the Soviets.[7]

Reagan's support for linkage also undermined the near-term prospects of strategic arms reduction negotiations. In Reagan's view, U.S.-Soviet negotiations should address not only nuclear arms reduction, but all of the problems plaguing the superpower relationship.[8] With the Soviet war in Afghanistan raging and the threat of Soviet intervention in Poland looming large, there would be a host of issues for U.S. and Soviet officials to discuss.

Reagan's characterizations of the Soviet leadership also contributed to the bleak outlook for strategic arms reduction negotiations in early 1981. An ardent anti-communist, Reagan alleged in his first presidential press conference that Soviet leaders took advantage of détente in the 1970s "to pursue their own aims" and infamously stated that they "have openly and publicly declared that the only morality they recognize is what will further their cause, meaning they reserve unto themselves the right to commit any crime, to lie, to cheat."[9]

The Soviet press agency TASS responded by calling Reagan's statements "unseemly" and "deliberate distortions." It also rejected Reagan's concept of linkage.[10] Thus, despite the president's avowed interest in pursuing strategic arms reduction negotiations with the Soviets, it was unclear when such talks might begin and what form U.S. proposals at those negotiations would take.

A month later, Reagan announced on February 26, 1981, that his administration fully supported both the modernization and arms control tracks of the 1979 NATO dual-track decision. Yet Reagan's announcement of his support for INF negotiations was simply folded into a broader statement that the president made after his meetings with British prime minister Margaret Thatcher during her visit to the United States.[11] As he had with strategic arms reduction negotiations, the president gave no indication in this statement of when he hoped INF negotiations would begin. Moreover, at a March 31 meeting of the NATO Special Consultative Group (SCG) on arms control, Assistant Secretary of State Lawrence Eagleburger assured the allies that the Reagan administration intended to negotiate on INF with the Soviets, but he too declined to provide a specific time frame for the initiation of these talks.[12]

The day before Eagleburger met with NATO allies in Brussels, the Reagan administration was thrown into turmoil when the president was shot as he left the Washington Hilton Hotel after delivering a speech at an AFL-CIO conference. Reagan later reflected, "Perhaps having come so close to death made me feel I should do whatever I could in the years God had given me to reduce the threat of nuclear war; perhaps there was a reason I had been spared." He decided to write a letter to Soviet leader Leonid Brezhnev "to let him know that we had a realistic view of what the Soviet Union was all about, but also wanted to send a signal to him that we were interested in reducing the threat of nuclear annihilation." This signal would be the lifting of the grain embargo that the Carter administration had imposed on the Soviet Union after it invaded Afghanistan.[13]

Haig, however, opposed lifting the grain embargo without a reciprocal conciliatory action from the Soviets and argued that Reagan should allow the State Department to write the letter to Brezhnev.[14] Haig recalled that in the early months of his presidency Reagan had drafted a letter to Brezhnev that called for "a world without nuclear weapons" and "reflect[ed] a demeanor that if only those two men could sit down as rational human beings, the problems of the world would be behind us." Reagan's letter had appalled Haig, who was a firm believer in nuclear deterrence and linkage.[15] Although Haig convinced Reagan not to send this letter to Brezhnev, its contents were likely on the secretary of state's mind when the president penned his missive to the Soviet leader after the assassination attempt. The State Department quickly produced a message that condemned the Soviet military buildup and the Brezhnev Doctrine, which posited that the Soviet Union could intervene in other countries to preserve communist governments.[16]

Averse to confrontation with his advisors but eager to improve relations with the Soviet Union, Reagan decided to send the State Department's letter along with a handwritten missive of his own. In his personal letter, Reagan wrote that he wondered whether "we have permitted ideology, political and economic philosophies, and governmental policies to keep us from considering the very real, everyday problems of peoples." Reagan hoped that lifting the grain embargo would "contribute to creating the circumstances which will lead to the meaningful and constructive dialogue which will assist us in fulfilling our joint obligation to find lasting peace."[17]

Yet it was growing grassroots anti-nuclear activism in Europe, not the assassination attempt, that pushed the Reagan administration to shift from offering general promises to pursue INF negotiations with the Soviets to implementing a concrete plan to begin talks before the end of 1981. IKV was mobilizing across the Netherlands to ensure that the proposed deployment of U.S. cruise missiles was a major issue in the upcoming Dutch general election on May 26, 1981. The stakes of this election were high, as the Dutch government would decide in December whether to accept the forty-eight cruise missiles allotted to the Netherlands under the NATO dual-track decision. In early 1981, anti-nuclear activists mounted more than one hundred local campaigns to persuade Dutch political parties to oppose cruise deployment. They hoped that a Dutch refusal to host U.S. cruise missiles would have ripple effects across Western Europe, bolstering anti-nuclear movements in other countries and specifically undercutting the West German government's willingness to accept U.S. INF. When NATO adopted the dual-track decision in 1979, West German chancellor Helmut Schmidt had been anxious for unanimity, which Dutch rejection of U.S. cruise missiles would shatter.[18] The Belgian government's repeated deferral of a decision on accepting U.S. cruise missiles was further evidence of West European anti-nuclearism.[19]

In West Germany, members of Schmidt's own Social Democratic Party (SPD) were echoing the anti-nuclear movement's call for NATO to cancel U.S. INF deployments in Western Europe. In 1979, the SPD had supported the dual-track decision in the hope that INF negotiations would produce "a military balance at a lower level" of nuclear weapons in Europe. The SPD had also conditioned its support for the dual-track decision on U.S. ratification of SALT II, which Carter ultimately withdrew from Senate consideration after the Soviet invasion of Afghanistan. When the superpowers then failed to pursue substantive INF negotiations in 1980, some SPD members felt that alliance leaders cared only about INF deployments. They worried about an intensifying nuclear arms race, which would destroy détente, increase the likelihood of nuclear war, and divert resources from domestic needs.[20] In December 1980, these SPD members issued the Bielefeld Appeal, which was reminiscent of the Krefeld Appeal that the peace movement had issued the previous month. Both appeals called on the West German government to rescind its support for U.S. INF deployments in Western Europe, with the Bielefeld Appeal demanding that NATO abandon the deployments altogether. The Bielefeld Appeal also urged Schmidt and other SPD politicians to work for the immediate start of INF negotiations and a European disarmament conference, among other things.[21]

A few months later, West European anti-nuclear activists actually confronted NATO defense ministers who gathered in Bonn on April 7 and 8, 1981, to discuss the alliance's planned INF deployments. Caspar Weinberger, making his first visit to Europe as secretary of defense, was among those attending this NATO Nuclear Planning Group meeting at the West German Defense Ministry. Outside the ministry building, protesters voiced their opposition to a nuclear buildup and demanded disarmament. This demonstration took a violent turn when activists began throwing eggs and tin cans at government officials, West German soldiers, and journalists. The police also removed three hundred demonstrators who tried to block the ministry's entrance.[22]

Reagan's advisors feared that rising anti-nuclear sentiment among West European publics would undermine West European governments' support for INF deployments, some level of which were viewed as essential in the face of Soviet SS-20 deployments. Several West European officials contended that a concrete time frame for the initiation of INF negotiations could calm West Europeans who were anxious about the NATO dual-track decision. During the March 31 SCG meeting, Norwegian delegate Johan Jørgen Holst noted that the "lack of effective nuclear arms control was leading to despair in many countries," and Dutch representative Van Vloten emphasized the important role that arms control could play in managing public tensions over the INF issue. Holst "saw the SCG meeting as paving the way towards a more concrete position on [the] timing" of INF negotiations, while West German ambassador Friedrich Ruth, Danish delegate Dyvig, Belgian representative Cassiers, and Van Vloten urged Eagleburger to support tangible signs of movement toward INF talks with the Soviets at NATO's upcoming May ministerial in Rome. Cassiers emphasized that this was vital to secure public support for the dual-track decision.[23]

After meeting with West German foreign minister Hans-Dietrich Genscher in April, British foreign secretary Lord Carrington urged Haig to endorse a paragraph in the forthcoming NATO ministerial communiqué that not only reaffirmed support for U.S.-Soviet INF negotiations, but also indicated that "the U.S. will shortly be approaching the Soviet Union on this subject." Carrington was eager to counteract the impression that only the Soviets wanted INF talks and worried that a delay in pursuing arms control negotiations would undermine West European support for the dual-track decision. Provided that the Soviets did not invade Poland, Carrington pressed Haig to announce at the ministerial that the Reagan administration would approach the Soviets before the summer to set a start date for INF negotiations in the fall.[24]

In response to West European leaders' appeals, Reagan's advisors advocated quickly initiating INF negotiations in the hope of curtailing the West European anti-nuclear sentiment that threatened INF modernization. In preparing for an April 30 NSC meeting on the timing of INF talks, NSC staffers acknowledged that "European Allies, particularly the Dutch, Belgians, and to some extent the Germans, need to be able to point to arms control negotiations as a way to placate the left wing of their socialist parties. Therefore, we need to show progress in moving toward resumption of talks."[25] During the NSC meeting, Haig noted that "in his discussions with Lord Carrington, Prime Minister Thatcher, and above all, Chancellor Schmidt, it became apparent that European leaders cannot maintain domestic consensus behind TNF modernization without a specific date for the start of TNF negotiations." Haig argued that it was "vitally important" that the United States announce a 1981 start date for INF negotiations to the allies at the North Atlantic Council and Defense Planning Committee ministerials in a few days. CIA director William Casey agreed with Haig's views, noting that Italian leaders told him that they needed the United States to set a date for the opening of INF negotiations or they were not going to be able to maintain public support for INF deployments. Frank Carlucci, the deputy secretary of defense, believed that NATO needed to complete studies on the Soviet threat, alliance INF requirements, and arms control objectives before setting a date for negotiations. In order to pacify the European left, however, he maintained that the administration should pledge to finish these assessments by the end of the year and then start negotiations.[26]

Recognizing that West European governments were contending with increasingly anti-nuclear publics, Reagan decided that his administration should tell the allies that it looked forward to beginning INF negotiations by the end of 1981.[27] Reflecting on the NSC meeting in his diary that evening, Reagan noted that the initiation of INF talks "is most important politically to our allies."[28] Haig told the North Atlantic Council in early May that the United States would begin INF negotiations before the end of the year. He planned to approach Soviet foreign minister Andrei Gromyko at the United Nations in September to set a specific date for the opening of talks.[29]

Grassroots anti-nuclear activism also prompted the Reagan administration to accelerate its timetable for pursuing strategic arms reduction negotiations with the Soviets. Reagan's calls for nuclear modernization had left freeze activists distressed by his 1980 victory. Yet they sensed an opening in the wake of Reagan's pledge to pursue strategic arms reduction during his first presidential press conference. These activists sought to build a powerful freeze movement that could hold Reagan accountable for this promise. "A US-Soviet freeze on nuclear weapons would be a first step toward the President's promised 'real reductions' in nuclear weapons," the Freeze Strategy Drafting Committee noted in March 1981. "Widespread public support for the freeze would challenge and encourage President Reagan to honor this commitment." Reagan's vows to cut taxes and balance the budget might also prompt his administration "to seek a politically popular means of cutting the military budget." Activists wanted to build support for the freeze so that it would fit this bill.[30]

Although leading freeze activists believed that local support for the freeze was indispensable for persuading policymakers to implement a freeze, they also wanted to launch a national freeze campaign in early 1981. Pam Solo, a member of the Freeze Strategy Drafting Committee, later explained that the freeze movement "needed national coordination to maintain cohesion and exert the power it was developing by its local presence."[31] On March 20 through 22, 1981, 275 anti-nuclear activists from more than 30 states gathered at Georgetown University for the first national nuclear freeze conference.[32] During this three-day meeting, activists approved a strategy and an organizational structure for a national nuclear freeze campaign.[33]

The national strategy called for "developing widespread public support for the freeze in the U.S. and then making the freeze a national policy objective." Although the *Call* pamphlet demanded that both superpowers adopt a nuclear freeze, the activists decided to focus their efforts on convincing the U.S. government to implement a freeze. To achieve this goal, they agreed to pursue a four-stage strategy over the next four or five years. The first stage sought to "demonstrate the potential of the freeze" through keeping records of the increasing support for the freeze proposal; gaining high-profile endorsements of *Call* and publicizing them; garnering media attention through editorials and print and television coverage of freeze events; reaching out to sympathetic groups that might back the freeze; and winning passage of state and local freeze referenda. In the second stage, which aimed to "broaden the base of public support," the campaign would seek the support not only of an increasing number of ordinary Americans, but also of state and local public bodies, U.S. representatives and senators, Europeans, and the non-aligned nations. The third stage intended to "focus public support for the freeze on policymakers so that it becomes a matter of national debate" through discussions with members of Congress about the freeze, support for congressional freeze resolutions, and cooperation with other organizations working to stop the development of the MX missile, the deployment of INF in Western Europe, nuclear testing, and defense budget increases. In the final stage of their strategy, the freeze would be adopted.[34]

Conference attendees also agreed that the nuclear freeze campaign "should be nationally-coordinated, with locally-based determination of what gets done." Since the early stages of the freeze strategy focused on garnering support for the freeze on the local and state levels, the National Nuclear Weapons Freeze Campaign initially would concentrate on coordinating the efforts of local freeze groups and providing a clearinghouse for activists. An annual national conference would set the Freeze Campaign's overall strategy, while a national committee would meet at least twice in between national conferences to "make the major on-going decisions of the campaign, including the hiring, firing, and supervision of the Clearinghouse staff." The national committee was structured to ensure broad participation in decision-making. Several seats on the national committee were reserved for major constituency groups and organizations that promoted the freeze. Each region of the country and Freeze Campaign task force would also have a national committee seat. The national committee could select an executive committee to make decisions in between its meetings.[35] The activists established eight task forces to focus on government contacts, international contacts, fundraising, resources, media, national events, outreach, and nominations.[36]

In the spring and summer of 1981, freeze activists sought to "demonstrate the potential of the freeze," which was the first stage of the Freeze Campaign's strategy. Across the country, activists worked to build and highlight support for the freeze proposal in their local communities and states. For example, the Freeze Campaign embarked on the Congressional District Endorsement Project, which aimed to launch freeze petition drives in at least one-third of all congressional districts by the end of 1981. Within just four months, petition drives were underway in seventy-five congressional districts across seventeen states in the Northeast, Midwest, and West. In freeze activists' view, petition drives were valuable because they yielded signatures that showed members of Congress the pro-freeze sentiment in their districts. Petition drives also offered freeze activists the opportunity to educate their neighbors about nuclear issues and win publicity for the freeze proposal. People who signed a freeze petition might also be recruited to take a more active role in the burgeoning freeze movement.[37]

Amid the escalating nuclear arms race and the failure of SALT II, these petition drives enjoyed early success. In early June, for example, representatives from the Connecticut Coalition for a Nuclear Arms Freeze delivered 22,500 signatures to their state's congressional delegation. State representatives, mayors, and a local judge signed freeze petitions alongside thousands of ordinary Connecticut residents.[38] These signatures provided concrete evidence of the public's desire for a halt to the nuclear arms race.

Activists also used town meetings and referenda to promote and demonstrate public support for the freeze. In March 1981, activists in fifteen towns in Vermont and two in New Hampshire pioneered the use of the town meeting as a vehicle for endorsing the freeze and calling on U.S. government officials to pursue it.[39] Given that New England town meetings had never debated nuclear issues before, Mary Ellen Donovan, a freeze activist in Plainfield, New Hampshire, expected a real battle over the freeze at her town meeting. She was "frankly surprised and relieved" when the freeze measure easily passed by a vote of 67 to 17. In a *New York Times* op-ed, she explained that "there was a consensus that the [arms] race is our business and that if we continue to pretend it isn't, there's a great chance that there will be no more town meetings." Concerns about the cost of the nuclear arms race and the likelihood that it would lead to nuclear war fueled support for the freeze among Plainfielders not accustomed to voting on nuclear matters.[40]

In fact, freeze movement leaders believed that democratizing nuclear policymaking was essential for stopping the nuclear arms race. Due to its sensitive and highly technical nature, nuclear policymaking had long been the domain of a small group of elite experts and government officials. Yet Randall Forsberg thought that everyone could understand the nuclear arms race and should have a voice in formulating nuclear policy. In her view, democracy meant that all Americans had the right to "participate in the decisions that shape their lives." Based on her experience giving talks on nuclear issues, Forsberg also believed that Americans who understood the arms race wanted to halt it. Taking nuclear matters out of the hands of the elite and allowing ordinary Americans to influence nuclear policy would thus set the United States on the path of disarmament. Forsberg later explained that "it will take a lot of people, concerned, informed, active people in order to reverse the arms race." It was vital to have "enormous, informed, organized, grassroots movements who let our political leaders know that it's not in our interest to continue the arms race."[41]

In the summer of 1981, American attitudes toward the nuclear arms race offered the freeze movement a golden opportunity to foster public support. A Gallup poll conducted in June revealed that 80 percent of Americans wanted U.S. and Soviet officials to meet with the aim of concluding a nuclear disarmament agreement in 1981. Seventy-two percent of Americans would support a U.S.-Soviet agreement "not to build any more nuclear weapons in the future," which was a key element of the freeze proposal. Forty-seven percent of Americans, a plurality, would approve a more sweeping agreement to eliminate existing U.S. and Soviet nuclear weapons. This public support for disarmament was even more striking given that it existed alongside doubts that the Soviets would adhere to an arms control agreement. For example, 60 percent of Americans thought that the Soviets were "not at all likely" to comply with a treaty to halt nuclear weapons construction.[42] Yet 65 percent of this group still wanted such an agreement.[43]

With this widespread desire for disarmament, the freeze movement was able to organize across the United States, even in conservative areas that had voted for Reagan in 1980. For example, freeze rallies had taken place in Des Moines and Decorah, Iowa; Albuquerque, New Mexico; Helena, Montana; and Columbus, Ohio, on Mother's Day 1981.[44] In addition, the South Dakota Peace and Justice Center and the Oregon Fellowship of Reconciliation launched freeze speaking tours across their respective states. These tours involved public education and recruitment of freeze supporters into the movement.[45] Growing support for the freeze in conservative cities and states would be hard for the Reagan administration to ignore and would increase pressure on the president to pursue a freeze as a first step toward disarmament.

In addition to the increasing public pressure that the freeze movement was asserting, Reagan was beginning to feel pressure closer to home. The participation of Patti Davis, Reagan's youngest daughter, in anti-nuclear events forced Reagan to reckon personally with the American anti-nuclear movement and its contrasting disarmament strategy. Davis's relationship with her parents was often strained, but she developed a sincere interest in anti-nuclear activism during her father's 1980 presidential campaign. Troubled by Reagan's anti-Soviet rhetoric and nuclear modernization plans, Davis began "discreetly" talking to activists from the Alliance for Survival, an anti-nuclear organization in California. As Reagan's electoral victory appeared increasingly assured, Davis formulated "idealistic plans" to invite her fellow anti-nuclear activists to dinner at the White House, where they could talk with her father and his top advisors. She also hoped to use the media's new-found interest in her to promote an end to the threat of nuclear war.[46]

As part of her efforts to avert a nuclear war, Davis accepted an invitation to speak at "Survival Sunday," an anti-nuclear rally that took place at the Hollywood Bowl on June 14, 1981. This star-studded event featured performances from Jackson Browne, Bonnie Raitt, Bruce Springsteen, and Graham Nash, as well as speeches from civil rights activist James M. Lawson Jr., Carter administration official Midge Costanza, and labor leader Dolores Huerta, among others.[47] Eighteen thousand people filled the Hollywood Bowl to capacity to protest nuclear weapons and nuclear power.[48]

Ronald and Nancy Reagan were deeply upset by their daughter's participation in the "Survival Sunday" rally and repeatedly tried to convince her to withdraw from the event. They told Davis that the Alliance for Survival was simply using her to humiliate her father. Nancy Reagan even used the assassination attempt against the president to try to guilt Davis into pulling out of the rally. "'Well, I just assumed you wouldn't do something like this after your father was shot,'" Nancy Reagan told her daughter. "'You're going to wound him more than the bullet did.'" Shortly after this conversation, Ronald Reagan told Davis that everyone would turn against her for publicly opposing her parents. He wrongly charged that all anti-nuclear activists wanted the United States to disarm unilaterally and maintained communist sympathies.[49] This false claim that anti-nuclear activists were communists would become a familiar refrain in Reagan's statements about the U.S. nuclear freeze movement.

Amid her parents' concerns, Davis redoubled her commitment to the anti-nuclear movement. In her speech at the "Survival Sunday" event, she advocated bilateral nuclear disarmament and a shift away from nuclear power. Davis also decided to implement her plan to bring anti-nuclear activists to the White House. She resolved that Helen Caldicott, an Australian pediatrician who was a leading figure in the international anti-nuclear movement, should be the first activist to meet with her father.[50] Caldicott and Reagan would meet on December 6, 1982, in the White House library.[51]

The surge in anti-nuclear activism accelerated the Reagan administration's timetable for initiating strategic arms reduction talks. Though Rostow continued to emphasize that modernized U.S. nuclear forces would incentivize the Soviets to strive for real progress in negotiations, he also recognized the power of the growing grassroots anti-nuclear movement. In an August 17, 1981, NSC meeting, Rostow declared, "I am not suggesting that we wait to negotiate until we are rearmed. That is a rational position. [French president François] Mitterrand has recently spoken favorably of it. But we can't go so far, and the President has decided otherwise. As we have been forced to realize, the mystic faith in arms control agreements as guaranties of peace is simply too strong among our people and the people of Europe to be ignored." Reagan had decided that the administration would not postpone strategic arms reduction negotiations until it had completed a strategic modernization program. In light of the increasing anti-nuclearism of Americans and West Europeans, there was widespread agreement with the president, even from hardline advisors like Rostow, who had faced questions about the nuclear freeze proposal during his confirmation hearing in June.[52] At the August 17 NSC meeting, Rostow sought only "firm commitments to rearm," which should come in the form of "Presidential decisions, [congressional] votes, appropriations," before negotiations began.[53]

Less than two months later, Reagan unveiled his plans for a strategic modernization program that would enhance all three legs of the U.S. strategic nuclear triad, as well as upgrade communications and control systems and strategic defenses. Reagan believed that this modernization would not only deter Soviet aggression against the United States and its allies, but also give the Soviets an incentive to negotiate strategic arms reduction.[54] Yet Reagan made it clear that he would begin strategic arms reduction talks with the Soviets while U.S. strategic modernization was underway. In discussing his proposed deployment of MX missiles, for example, Reagan asserted, "We really mean that we're going to go forward with them [the Soviets] and try to persuade them into a program of not limitation, but a program of actual reduction of these strategic weapons. . . . So, we're hopeful that maybe some of the systems, the very systems we're talking about, won't ever have to be completed."[55] Reagan's willingness to abandon the strategic modernization program shows that he truly envisioned it as an incentive for the Soviets to engage in meaningful arms reduction negotiations.

Reagan's reassurances notwithstanding, American anti-nuclear activists were not persuaded that the administration's strategic modernization program was part of an effort to achieve arms reduction agreements with the Soviets. SANE argued that the program would endanger, rather than enhance, U.S. national security. By improving the ability of U.S. strategic forces to threaten Soviet ICBM silos, U.S. modernization efforts would encourage the Soviets to resort quickly to a nuclear first strike in a crisis, thereby engaging in a catastrophic example of the "use it or lose it" phenomenon. At the very least, SANE believed, U.S. modernization would "touch off a new, more deadly spiral in the nuclear arms race," as the Soviets tried to match and then surpass U.S. innovations. The group also decried the $180 billion price tag of the plan, which would likely lead to cuts in domestic social programs. SANE dismissed Reagan's claim that his modernization plan would incentivize the Soviets to reduce their nuclear weapons, neglecting to even address it in an official statement on the program.[56]

Popular discontent with nuclear weapons was even more palpable in Western Europe, where anti-nuclear activism surged during the summer and fall of 1981. This protest was largely a reaction against NATO's planned installation of U.S. Pershing II and cruise missiles in Western Europe and the Soviets' ongoing deployment of SS-20 missiles aimed at Western Europe. As 1981 progressed, however, the Reagan administration's nuclear modernization efforts and rhetoric about nuclear war intensified anti-nuclear activism. Two months before Reagan unveiled his strategic modernization program, his administration announced on August 9 that it would produce the neutron bomb. U.S. Defense Department officials justified the move as a sign to the world that the Reagan administration intended to build up its military strength.[57] The administration's insensitivity in making this announcement on the thirty-sixth anniversary of the U.S. atomic bombing of Nagasaki was not lost on European anti-nuclear activists. They were deeply troubled by Weinberger's statements about the effectiveness of the neutron bomb against Soviet tanks. Along with the scheduled Pershing II and cruise deployments, neutron bomb production suggested that the Reagan administration was gearing up for a limited nuclear war in Europe.[58]

Reagan's statements only exacerbated Europeans' fears that his administration was preparing for nuclear war. In reply to a newspaper editor's question on October 16, Reagan observed that it would theoretically be possible for the superpowers to use tactical nuclear weapons in battle without triggering an all-out nuclear war. In this same exchange with editors, however,

Reagan repeatedly expressed support for INF and strategic arms reduction negotiations. He also claimed that the Soviets believed that nuclear war was winnable, a view that he insisted he did not share. In fact, Reagan hoped to "disabuse" the Soviets of this belief. He spoke of his nuclear modernization plans as a deterrent to Soviet aggression and an incentive for Soviet nuclear arms reduction.[59] Yet it was his frank comments about limited nuclear war that stood out, stoking the fears of Europeans who were already on edge about U.S. nuclear modernization. They recognized that Reagan's talk of limited nuclear war meant nuclear war that is "limited to us, the Europeans," in the words of anti-nuclear activists at a London demonstration eight days later.[60]

In the FRG, concerns about U.S. INF deployments sparked the country's first mass anti-nuclear demonstration on June 20, 1981. At the close of the Protestant Church Congress in Hamburg, one hundred thousand rallied against the planned installation of Pershing II and cruise missiles in Western Europe, which they feared would make nuclear war more likely. The theme of the Congress was "do not be afraid," which the angel told the shepherds in Luke 2:10 before announcing the birth of Christ. Turning this theme on its head, the anti-nuclear protesters proclaimed, "Be afraid, atomic death threatens us all!" Desperate to halt the escalating nuclear arms race and avert nuclear war, over 180 groups called for the abandonment of the NATO dual-track decision and an outpouring of anti-nuclear activism. Among the co-organizers of this protest were the Young Socialists, the youth organization of Schmidt's SPD. Much to Schmidt's dismay, anti-nuclear sentiment was making inroads in his own party.[61]

The Protestant Church Congress also launched cooperative mechanisms that allowed West German peace activists to coordinate their efforts and stage record-breaking anti-nuclear rallies in the future. Near the end of the Congress in Hamburg, Christian peace activists from Action Reconciliation Service for Peace and Action Committee Service for Peace held a planning meeting for an anti-nuclear demonstration that was scheduled to take place in Bonn on October 10. Activists from twenty peace, religious, environmental, and communist organizations attended this session, which launched the West German peace movement's "breakfast meetings." These meetings offered West German peace activists the opportunity to coordinate strategy and plan joint events. In early 1982, the "breakfast meetings" gave rise to the first Action Conference, which elected the first Coordinating Committee to plan an anti-nuclear demonstration coinciding with the NATO summit in Bonn on June 10, 1982.[62] For the October 10, 1981, demonstration in Bonn, three hundred thousand turned out, while four hundred thousand took part in the June 10, 1982, protest.[63]

In 1981, END was also accelerating its anti-nuclear work in Britain and throughout Europe. For example, END cofounders E. P. Thompson and Bruce Kent, who was also general secretary of CND, discussed nuclear issues and advocated disarmament at meetings across England. Both Thompson and Kent fondly recalled that these meetings were "packed," with Thompson noting that crowds turned out even in conservative areas. Ordinary Britons were troubled by the state of the nuclear arms race, particularly the planned deployment of U.S. cruise missiles in Britain. Kent described the atmosphere of these meetings as "electric," as attendees vowed to press the British government to stop the slide toward nuclear Armageddon.[64] Local anti-nuclear organizations began sprouting up across Britain, and CND's membership skyrocketed from three thousand in early 1980 to thirty thousand in the fall of 1981.[65]

Along with its campaigning in Britain, END remained determined to build a European-wide movement that could pressure political leaders to rid Europe of nuclear weapons. As part of this effort, END cofounders Mary Kaldor and Dan Smith began organizing transnational peace researcher conferences to discuss concrete disarmament proposals and strategies for advancing them. At their first meeting in Amsterdam in late May 1981, for example, the researchers agreed to advocate the cancellation of U.S. Pershing II and cruise deployments and a freeze on Soviet SS-20 deployments. Reductions should be the goal of any U.S.-Soviet INF talks that opened. The researchers decided that the British and Dutch anti-nuclear movements, which were the two strongest, would present these demands in a joint statement that other organizations could endorse. This presumably would illustrate the wide-ranging popular opposition to U.S. and Soviet INF deployments in Europe. Meanwhile, activists would also push West European Social Democratic parties to reply to a letter from Brezhnev with a call to reduce or freeze Soviet SS-20s.[66]

These researchers recognized that it was essential to create a "massive political movement" in order to achieve their goal of a nuclear-free Europe. The denuclearization of Europe was a mammoth undertaking that would only be achieved by a large anti-nuclear movement pursuing a variety of short-term goals using a range of tactics. Thus, the researchers also discussed ways to spark anti-nuclear activism in southern Europe, where the movement had been relatively inactive. Kaldor and Smith noted that this first research conference "became more of a political consultation than a meeting of researchers."[67]

By the fall of 1981, END was making strides toward the formation of just such a "massive political movement," as it was on the verge of organizing a pan-European convention of individuals, organizations, and political parties advocating a nuclear-free Europe. At a September 1981 conference in Copenhagen organized by IKV and the Danish Nej Til Atomvaben group, European peace activists decided to establish a "European Information Centre (with END help) at IKV" offices. Intended to facilitate the development of an "integrated strategy in European peace movements," it became known as the International Peace Communication and Coordination Center (IPCC).[68] The IPCC began hosting a small meeting of West European anti-nuclear activists every three months in a different West European city.[69] Although the creation of the IPCC was a step in the direction of END's aim of a European convention on nuclear disarmament, it did not include representatives from Eastern Europe or delegates from any European political parties committed to the denuclearization of Europe.

The November 1981 Rome consultation, however, set the END Convention process in motion. END supporters from across Europe gathered in Italy's capital to consider the prospects for a pan-European conference on nuclear disarmament.[70] Recognizing that European anti-nuclear movements had different ideas about how to achieve their shared goal of a nuclear-free Europe, the Rome consultation delegates agreed to hold an END Convention in 1982 to provide the movements with an opportunity to discuss their views. "But if we do not talk these matters through at the international level, we shall reduce our contact to a process of marching and demonstrating, which is not enough to maintain the physical momentum of the movement, still less to develop its thinking," END cofounder Ken Coates warned. An END Convention would enable anti-nuclear activists and politicians to discuss specific disarmament initiatives and strategies for promoting them. It would also strengthen transnational ties among individuals committed to the denuclearization of Europe, which would enrich the discussion of how best to realize this aim.[71]

The Rome consultation established the END Convention Liaison Committee, which was open to anyone who had signed the END Appeal and was interested in planning the upcoming conference. At its opening meeting in December 1981, the Liaison Committee decided that the first END Convention would take place in Brussels from July 2 through 4, 1982, coinciding with the United Nations' Second Special Session on Disarmament.[72]

END supporters also participated in the massive anti-nuclear demonstrations that swept across Western Europe in the fall of 1981.[73] In the largest demonstration in West German history, three hundred thousand protesters marched through the streets of Bonn on October 10 expressing opposition to the Euromissiles. In a similar feat in Belgium, two hundred thousand people demonstrated against nuclear weapons in Brussels on October 25. Two hundred and fifty thousand rallied in London's Hyde Park on October 24 in opposition to nuclear weapons. On the same day, five hundred thousand demonstrated in Rome. On November 21, four hundred thousand people turned out for an anti-nuclear rally in Amsterdam, making it one of the largest demonstrations in Dutch history. Protesters hoped that they could convince West European governments to refuse U.S. Pershing II and cruise missiles.[74] They also hoped to show Reagan, whom an END editorialist called "the arch enemy" surely "watching on television," that Western Europe did not want to host U.S. INF missiles.[75]

END's reference to Reagan as "the arch enemy" shows that West European anti-nuclear activists did not consider him an ally in their fight for nuclear disarmament. They wondered: If Reagan was serious about nuclear arms reduction, why was he building new nuclear weapons that increased the risk of nuclear war and consumed economic resources? Viewing Reagan's "peace through strength" strategy as nonsensical, the activists believed that his nuclear modernization efforts revealed the insincerity of his calls for disarmament.[76] In fact, Reagan's nuclear modernization program and talk of nuclear war spurred individuals to engage in grassroots anti-nuclear activism.[77]

Reagan similarly viewed West European anti-nuclear activists as adversaries rather than allies in his crusade for nuclear arms reduction. In the summer of 1981, he argued that many West European activists were "really carrying the propaganda ball for the Soviet Union," as he falsely claimed that they were not concerned about Soviet SS-20 deployments.[78] After three hundred thousand anti-nuclear protesters took to the streets of Bonn on October 10, Reagan escalated his attacks on the activists. He charged that Soviet propaganda had instigated their demonstrations, although he admitted that some protesters might be "very well meaning."[79]

West European peace movements' platforms and outreach to independent activists in Eastern Europe show that the Soviets did not control these movements. The 1980 END Appeal, for example, blamed both superpowers for the nuclear arms race and called for the removal of U.S. and Soviet nuclear weapons from Europe.[80] As part of the effort to construct a massive pan-European anti-nuclear campaign, END's founders sought to extend the movement into Eastern Europe. Although an initial meeting with Czechoslovaks in the spring of 1980 was unproductive, END's contacts with independent peace and human rights activists in the Soviet bloc increased over the 1980s and ultimately influenced its agenda.[81] In December 1982, END's political positions and relations with Soviet bloc dissidents drew the ire of Soviet Peace Committee president Yuri Zhukov, who charged that END sought to "conceal and justify an aggressive militarist policy of the USA and NATO."[82] E. P. Thompson recalled that the Soviet Peace Committee condemned "the Dutch Interchurch Peace Council, END, myself, Mary Kaldor, [and] some of the Eurocommunists" for refusing to act in accordance with Soviet wishes, insisting that these movements and activists were "CIA agents."[83] The attacks leveled at West European peace movements by both superpowers highlight their independence.

Although Reagan publicly hailed allied governments' willingness to host U.S. INF missiles, his administration privately worried that West European anti-nuclear activism would undermine West European officials' support for the deployments.[84] This concern led Reagan's advisors to support the bold "zero option" proposal for the INF talks, which were scheduled to begin in Geneva on November 30, 1981. The zero option called for the elimination of U.S. and Soviet land-based INF missiles. This proposal naturally appealed to Reagan's anti-nuclear streak. Reagan's advisors, however, primarily backed it in an effort to curb anti-nuclear opposition to U.S. INF deployments. Reagan's aides viewed these deployments as vital, especially in light of the Soviets' predicted disinterest in reaching an INF agreement in the near future.

As the Reagan administration worked to devise its opening INF proposal, several West European officials pushed for a dramatic initiative that could placate anti-nuclear activists and garner public support for NATO's dual-track decision. In a meeting on July 17, 1981, Carrington cautioned Haig that "in Britain, for example, very many middle of the road people were worried about the increasing lethality of nuclear weapons and wished to see a reduction on numbers."[85] Sensitive to public debates about the zero option, West German officials soon raised this proposal to the allies.[86] The zero option called for the cancellation of U.S. INF deployments if the Soviets dismantled all of their existing INF missiles. In 1979, Dutch and West German leaders had advocated this proposal as their publics increasingly turned against nuclear weapons. The Dutch government had made an unsuccessful bid to reference the zero option in the dual-track decision, and Schmidt had raised the zero option as "the ideal case" with the Carter administration in the fall of 1979.[87] Eager to win public support for the Reagan administration's forthcoming INF proposal in 1981, West German officials called an August 27 meeting to discuss public relations for the upcoming INF negotiations. In a paper for this meeting with American, Italian, Belgian, and British officials, the West Germans suggested that "the zero option could be presented as the ultimate consequence of the western proposal to negotiate de jure equal ceilings at the lowest possible level."[88]

Genscher also urged Haig to adopt an INF proposal that the West German government could portray as "fully compatible with the zero option" during a meeting in Bonn in mid-September.[89] Haig and Genscher ultimately agreed that the zero option would be the best outcome of INF negotiations "in ideal circumstances."[90] At an SCG meeting in Brussels on September 16, West German ambassador Friedrich Ruth noted that Haig's "reference to achieving the zero option as the ideal case had struck a chord in the FRG." Ruth thought that it was politically savvy to seek INF ceilings at the lowest level that the Soviets would accept, because this would force the Soviets to take responsibility for any agreement that did not eliminate INF. Dutch representative Van Vloten similarly saw political advantages to the zero option and thought that it should be a possible outcome of negotiations.[91]

Although Belgian delegate Comte de la Barre d'Erquelinnes and British representative David Gillmore supported the zero option as an ideal goal, they warned U.S. officials that Reagan should not solely pursue the zero option in talks with the Soviets. If the Reagan administration proposed the zero option and the Soviets rejected it, then it would be difficult to deploy INF in 1983, because these missiles would contravene the U.S. negotiating position. Gillmore also worried that the zero option would raise public expectations for a dramatic agreement that the Soviets were unlikely to endorse. In addition, Gillmore was wary of allowing public relations concerns to determine the substance of the U.S. INF proposal.[92] The zero option, however, was gaining popularity across Western Europe. Two weeks later, Gillmore expressed concerns to his British colleagues that "the zero option has a considerable head of steam behind it in Western Europe." He admitted that "in the end we may have to concede to strong German, Dutch and other West European views."[93]

While the Reagan administration was consulting the allies on its negotiating position, an internal interagency group was also meeting to discuss the specifics of the U.S. proposal. Prior to an October 13 NSC meeting on the INF talks, the group agreed that U.S. negotiators should "propose a phased, comprehensive approach to TNF arms control negotiations which seeks reductions to the lowest possible levels on land-based TNF missiles in the first phase."[94] Since both the Americans and the Soviets viewed fast-flying land-based INF missiles as the most threatening, they would be the initial focus of negotiations.[95] U.S. negotiators would be prepared to address intermediate-range aircraft at a later stage of the talks. They would seek "equal, global limits" on U.S. and Soviet INF missiles, and they would neither negotiate nor compensate for British and French nuclear weapons. Strict verification measures would be an essential element of any agreement. The group had yet to agree on specific ceilings for U.S. and Soviet INF missiles when Reagan met with his top advisors on October 13 to discuss the upcoming negotiations.[96]

During this NSC meeting, Reagan's advisors expressed pessimism about reaching an agreement with the Soviets due to the Kremlin's superiority in INF missiles. Their main concern was ensuring that the U.S. negotiating position fostered support among West European publics and governments for the administration's INF approach, including the planned missile deployments in 1983. As Haig put it, "The primary purpose of the negotiations is political, i.e., to update the TNF modernization program. An actual arms control agreement is secondary and has little prospect because of the imbalance of forces."[97]

Anxious to win over West European publics and shore up West European governments' support for INF deployments, Weinberger set forth a negotiating proposal even bolder than the one that West German and Dutch officials were advancing. He urged the administration to propose the zero option only and stop touting the "'lowest possible numbers' formula," which merely envisioned the zero option as the ideal goal. In advocating the zero option, Weinberger contended that the United States had no answer for the Soviets' 750 SS-20 warheads aimed at America's allies in Western Europe and Asia. "In this light," he argued, "we might need to consider a bold plan, sweeping in nature, to capture world opinion. If refused by the Soviets, they would take the blame for its rejection." Weinberger saw the zero option as the dramatic proposal that could turn the tide of West European opinion in the administration's favor. If negotiations did not succeed, the United States would not be blamed and deployments would proceed on schedule.[98]

In pitching the zero option to Reagan, Weinberger also argued that it was a sound arms control position. After initially raising the zero concept, Weinberger noted, "If the Soviets agreed, we would achieve the balance [in INF] that we've lost." Adding their support, Casey and Counselor to the President Edwin Meese contended that the zero option would be the most easily verifiable arms control position that the administration could adopt. Yet Weinberger did not hesitate to admit that the Soviets were unlikely to accept the zero option. "But whether they reject it or they accept it, they would be set back on their heels. We would be left in good shape and would be shown as the White Hats."[99]

Like Weinberger, Haig was also concerned with ensuring that West European anti-nuclear sentiment did not compel West European governments to scuttle U.S. INF deployments. He feared, however, that the zero option might facilitate such an outcome. "What would happen in one or two years when it comes time to deploy," Haig asked, "if we have a 'zero option' on the table? With such an option, the Europeans will surely reject any new deployments." Echoing Gillmore's concerns, Haig argued that West European governments would not want to risk public ire by installing new missiles when there was a proposal on the negotiating table that would obviate the need for these controversial deployments. Reagan reserved his final judgment on the zero option, and the NSC planned to reconvene in a month for further discussion.[100]

Pressure on the Reagan administration to incorporate the zero option into its INF proposal increased when the NATO Nuclear Planning Group referred to the "zero-level" in its Gleneagles communiqué. West German, Dutch, Norwegian, and Danish officials pushed for the inclusion of the zero option in the statement issued at the end of the Nuclear Planning Group's meeting in Gleneagles, Scotland, on October 20 and 21. During a discussion of the zero option, Denmark's permanent representative to NATO, Anker Svart, noted that the zero option "had taken on a political life of its own." With anti-nuclear activism surging in the FRG, Hans-Georg Wieck, the West German representative to NATO, argued that "to mention the zero-option was in the end a political requirement and several [defense] Ministers would support such a reference." This included West German defense minister Hans Apel, who also expressed Chancellor Schmidt's desire for a reference to the zero option.[101] In the Gleneagles communiqué, the NATO defense ministers noted that "on the basis of reciprocity, the zero-level remains a possible option under ideal circumstances."[102] This statement showed the world that NATO was prepared to consider the zero option, as Eagleburger noted several days later.[103]

By the November 12 NSC meeting, Haig had come to support the idea of a zero proposal, provided that U.S. negotiators also "indicate from the outset a willingness to consider equal ceilings greater than zero." This "zero plus" proposal would show that the U.S. negotiating position was not so inflexible that it should be dismissed as unserious. If negotiations did not succeed by the time that INF deployments were scheduled to occur, such deployments would still be in line with a U.S. position that preferred zero, but "allowed from the outset the possibility of arms control agreements above zero."[104] Meanwhile, Weinberger and the Joint Chiefs continued to advocate the pure zero option. They argued that it was "a bold initiative that will appeal to the broad public, here and in Europe, on whose support Allied governments depend."[105]

For his part, Reagan was attracted to the zero option's promise of abolishing an entire class of nuclear missiles. He hoped that this would be just the start of significant U.S. and Soviet nuclear arms reduction. In the November 12 NSC meeting, Reagan explained, "It is my belief that we can begin negotiations with the hope that we can eliminate all of these missiles totally, verifiably, and globally. Then in good faith, we can with regard to other nuclear weapons, look to a realistic reduction." He viewed the zero option as a sound negotiating position, and unlike his advisors, thought that the Soviets could find it compelling. Acknowledging that European publics skeptical of his administration's handling of the INF issue "may be expecting slogans" from him on arms control, Reagan argued that "properly worded, our position can be convincing and can persuade."[106]

Although Reagan wanted to eliminate INF missiles, he realized that it might not be possible to get an agreement that accomplished this feat in one fell swoop. In order to set the superpowers on a course of INF reductions, which he hoped would lead to the liquidation of INF missiles, Reagan was willing to accept an agreement that called for equal INF ceilings above zero. In explaining his ideal negotiating approach to the Soviets, Reagan said that U.S. negotiators should "simply go in and say that we are negotiating in good faith for the removal of these systems on both sides. We should ask the Soviet Union to share in this effort. We should not say this is what we would like to have, but we will settle for less. One should ask for the moon, and when the other fellow offers green cheese, one can settle for something in between."[107] He repeatedly stated that his administration should determine the number of Soviet INF systems that it would be willing to accept in an INF agreement so that it would be ready to respond seriously to a Soviet counteroffer.[108] This willingness to compromise demonstrates that Reagan had a sincere interest in reaching an INF agreement with the Soviets.

The administration adopted the zero option as its opening position for the INF talks, which Reagan announced in a speech to the National Press Club on November 18, 1981. In addition to presenting the zero option for INF, Reagan laid out a broader program of arms reduction in this speech. He called for "the mutual reduction of conventional, intermediate-range nuclear and strategic forces," as well as U.S. and Soviet adoption of measures "to reduce the risks of

surprise attack and the chance of war arising out of uncertainty or miscalcula-
tion." His discussion of strategic arms reduction was especially noteworthy, as
he pledged to begin talks with the Soviets on these systems "as soon as possible
next year." To symbolize the break from his predecessors' pursuit of strategic arms limitation, he announced that the new negotiations would be called
START (for Strategic Arms Reduction Talks) rather than SALT.[109]

The various drafts of this speech reveal a divide between Reagan and his
advisors on the extent of arms reduction that the United States should pursue.
A November 14 draft stated, "The United States proposes to reduce conventional, theater nuclear and strategic forces to the lowest level the Soviet Union
is willing to accept."[110] This sentence suggests that the Americans would be
seeking a truly radical reduction of nuclear arms, shrinking their nuclear
arsenal as much as the Soviets would agree to reciprocate. By November 17,
this line had disappeared from the speech but was handwritten back in by
Reagan.[111] Nevertheless, it did not make it into the final speech, which simply
stated, "The United States proposes the mutual reduction of conventional,
intermediate-range nuclear and strategic forces."[112] Reagan's aides clearly
thought that the administration should refrain from making nuclear arms
reduction proposals as dramatic as the president desired. Averse to confrontation, Reagan backed down in the face of his advisors' opposition.

For their part, anti-nuclear activists were wholly unimpressed with
Reagan's zero option proposal. END publicly condemned it as a "mislead-
ing" proposal that "stands little chance of being accepted at the negotiating
table." END activists thought that the Soviets were unlikely to agree to dismantle missiles that they had already deployed in exchange for a U.S. offer
to eliminate missiles that had not even been developed yet. END vowed to
continue pressuring West European governments to refuse U.S. INF missiles
and "call[ed] upon the peoples of Eastern Europe and the Soviet Union to
press for the unconditional elimination of the SS-20 missiles and all 'theatre'
nuclear weapons."[113] Petra Kelly, a leader of West Germany's Green Party and
anti-nuclear movement, characterized the zero option as "a kind of voodoo
arms reduction."[114] She lamented that the U.S. proposal did not call for any
actual reduction of NATO's nuclear weapons, instead "only removing those
[NATO] missiles still on paper and not yet deployed in Europe." Kelly also
argued that all nuclear weapons threatening Europeans should be part of
the INF negotiations in Geneva, including sea- and air-based systems, U.S.
forward-based systems, and British and French nuclear weapons.[115]

In the Netherlands, peace activists and leftist politicians moved forward with plans to hold an anti-nuclear demonstration in Amsterdam on November 21. Five days earlier, Prime Minister Andries van Agt had declared that the Dutch government would further delay its decision on whether to accept U.S. cruise missiles. In the largest anti-nuclear demonstration of the fall, 400,000 rallied under the slogan "no new nuclear weapons in Europe." They called on the Dutch government to rescind its support for the NATO dual-track decision and encourage other allies to rethink their endorsement of the decision.[116]

The record-setting anti-nuclear demonstrations that took place across Western Europe contributed to the growth of the freeze movement in the United States. In October and November 1981, Americans were transfixed by the media coverage of anti-nuclear protests that drew hundreds of thousands of people onto the streets of Bonn, Brussels, London, Rome, and Amsterdam. Kehler later explained that ordinary Americans developed "sympathy for the European people as victims of superpower politics and militarism and ultimately perhaps the victims of nuclear war."[117] A nuclear conflict seemed increasingly likely, given Reagan's nuclear modernization programs and talk of limited nuclear war. Americans flocked to the freeze movement to try to convince leaders to halt the dangerous arms race.[118]

At the end of 1981, the Freeze Campaign Clearinghouse, which provided information and assistance to local and state freeze groups, relocated from Forsberg's Institute for Defense and Disarmament Studies in Brookline to St. Louis. Leading freeze activists believed that St. Louis would highlight the grassroots nature of the freeze movement and its aim of developing widespread popular support for the freeze. Kehler became the Freeze Campaign's national coordinator.[119] He recalled that in late 1981 and early 1982 the clearinghouse "couldn't possibly keep track of the number of groups calling themselves 'freeze groups'" because so many new local and state freeze organizations were emerging. "And it was the same way with raising money," Kehler reflected. "I mean it was the only time in my life when we would have people calling us, both individuals and foundations saying, 'To whom do we write a check?' And I would say, 'Well, don't you want a proposal? . . . Do you need a fund appeal?' 'No, no, no,' they said, 'don't bother with that. We like so much what you're doing; just tell us where to send the money.'"[120]

As 1981 drew to a close, activists were working to get the freeze on the ballot in several states and large cities. Inspired by the successful freeze referenda in western Massachusetts, Los Angeles activists Jo and Nick Seidita launched a campaign in December 1980 to gather the 346,119 signatures required to put the freeze on California's ballot in November 1982. A ballot initiative promised educational opportunities and publicity for the freeze proposal. If ultimately passed by the voters, it would pressure political leaders to end the nuclear arms race and avert a nuclear war. Signature gathering began the first week of December 1981 with home petition parties across California. The Seiditas won the support of California businessman Harold Willens, who tapped his Hollywood and corporate connections to raise money for the campaign. They ultimately collected over seven hundred thousand signatures for the freeze initiative, more than twice the number necessary to secure a spot on the ballot. The Seiditas, who had spoken about their efforts at the Freeze Campaign's First National Conference, also encouraged and advised other activists who were working for freeze referenda across the country.[121] Freeze measures would appear on ballots in ten states and several metropolitan areas in 1982.[122] The disarmament strategies of Reagan and grassroots activists would continue to clash in the year ahead.

*   *   *

Reagan assumed the presidency with a sincere desire for dramatic nuclear arms reduction. By March 1982, he was publicly embracing the more radical idea of completely eliminating nuclear weapons. On March 16, Reagan told reporters that he was willing to talk to Brezhnev about a zero option for INF missiles and strategic nuclear weapons.[123] In an interview with members of the *New York Post* editorial board a week later, Reagan lamented the Soviet nuclear buildup and emphasized the importance of modernizing U.S. nuclear weapons to force the Soviets to negotiate arms reduction. "Militarily they have been an industrial giant," Reagan said of the Soviet Union. "And this is one of the reasons why we can't retreat on what we're doing, because I believe we've come to the point that we must go at the matter of realistically reducing, if not totally eliminating, the nuclear weapon, the threat to the world."[124]

In the years after his involvement in anti-nuclear organizations in Hollywood, Reagan had talked of the threat of nuclear war, most notably at the 1976 Republican National Convention.[125] Yet it was not until March 1982 that he publicly set forth the idea that the abolition of nuclear weapons was the best way to avert nuclear war. In his autobiography, Reagan suggested that it was during the first year of his presidency that his desire to achieve significant nuclear arms reduction became a dream of eliminating nuclear weapons. He wrote, "One of the first statistics I saw as president was one of the most sobering and startling I'd ever heard. I'll never forget it: The Pentagon said at least 150 million American lives would be lost in a nuclear war with the Soviet Union—even if we 'won.' . . . No *one* could 'win' a nuclear war. Yet as long as nuclear weapons were in existence, there would always be risks they would be used, and once the first nuclear weapon was unleashed, who knew where it would end? My dream, then, became a world free of nuclear weapons."[126] In seeking nuclear abolition, Reagan thought that it was vital to negotiate from a position of strength.[127]

As Reagan also acknowledged in his autobiography, however, his advisors did not share his goal of eliminating nuclear weapons.[128] Although they disagreed with one another on specific arms reduction proposals, Reagan's team was united in opposition to nuclear abolition. While the replacement of Richard Allen with William P. Clark as national security advisor in January 1982 meant that Reagan had a longtime friend in the post who had direct access to the president, Clark was not a nuclear abolitionist. When Reagan raised the issue of nuclear abolition, his advisors would band together either to ignore or stymie his advocacy of a nuclear-free world. The president's trusting nature, detachment from the process of policy implementation, and dislike of confrontation enabled his aides to disregard his statements about the desirability of eliminating nuclear weapons. Reagan biographer Lou Cannon has noted that the president's guileless personality made him assume that those working for him were acting in line with his goals. According to Cannon, Reagan also believed that it was his responsibility to set forth a general policy direction, but that the implementation of policy should be left to his aides. Reagan's avoidance of conflict with his advisors likely led them to believe that they could ignore his statements about nuclear abolition without risking a confrontation with him.[129]

When Reagan's advisors were unable to ignore the president's dream of a nuclear-free world, such as when he drafted a speech mentioning this goal, they worked to convince him to moderate his language or approach. Reagan aide Martin Anderson has written that the president's inexperience in foreign affairs prompted him at times to defer to his more knowledgeable advisors on foreign policy issues.[130] An example of this can be seen in the formulation of a March 31, 1982, statement on the administration's nuclear arms reduction efforts. A March 30 draft of the statement, which was based on Reagan's input, declared, "I pledge to them [members of Congress]—and to all people who yearn for the day when the threat of global holocaust is eliminated for once and all—that this Administration is committed, heart and soul, to pursuing this vital goal."[131] Yet this line alluding to nuclear abolition did not make it into the final version of the speech that Reagan delivered from the East Room of the White House.[132] After Reagan spent three days writing drafts of the statement, his top national security aides gathered to write the final draft. Talking points for this meeting note that after having received the input of Weinberger, Haig, and Rostow, Reagan "accepts that we cannot: call for a freeze in any respect or call for the ultimate elimination of nuclear weapons."[133] Stifled by domineering aides who did not want nuclear abolition, Reagan refrained from pledging that he would pursue a nuclear-free world when he gave the speech.

By the spring of 1982, when Reagan delivered his speech, the freeze proposal was gaining support not only at the grassroots level, but also in the U.S. Congress. In December 1981, the Freeze Campaign's U.S. government contacts task force devised a plan to meet with House members to discuss the freeze. The task force thought that it was too early to advocate specific freeze legislation, however.[134] Delegates to the Freeze Campaign's First National Conference had envisioned the introduction of congressional freeze resolutions as part of the third phase of the movement's four- or five-year strategic plan. They wanted to "demonstrate the potential of the freeze" and "broaden the base of public support" before "focus[ing] public support for the freeze on policymakers so that it becomes a matter of national debate."[135]

Prominent senators' desire to introduce freeze legislation accelerated the Freeze Campaign's timetable for pursuing a freeze in Congress. Shortly after the Freeze Campaign's Second National Conference in late February 1982, Senator Edward Kennedy (D-MA) told Forsberg and Kehler that he and Senator Mark Hatfield (R-OR) wanted to introduce bipartisan freeze legislation. Eyeing a presidential run in 1984, Kennedy thought it would be advantageous to support a cause that was winning adherents across the United States. Hatfield had proposed a nuclear moratorium amendment to SALT II in 1979.[136] Forsberg and Kehler knew that Kennedy and Hatfield could win the freeze more media exposure and high-profile endorsements. Yet they also worried about deviating from the Freeze Campaign's strategy. They ultimately decided to support Kennedy and Hatfield's efforts, however, as it seemed too good of an opportunity to pass up.[137] On March 10, 1982, Kennedy and Hatfield introduced a bipartisan freeze resolution in the Senate, and Edward Markey (D-MA), Jonathan Bingham (D-NY), and Silvio Conte (R-MA) introduced the same resolution in the House. As a joint resolution, this freeze measure was simply advisory. It urged the superpowers to negotiate a freeze and then reduction of their nuclear weapons and delivery vehicles.[138] Nevertheless, this freeze resolution quickly became a way for members of Congress to express their displeasure with Reagan's nuclear policy.[139]

A month later, an anti-nuclear organization called Ground Zero sponsored activities across the country to teach Americans about the threat of nuclear war. Founded by Roger Molander, a former NSC official, Ground Zero was strictly an educational organization. Activities during Ground Zero Week, which lasted from April 18 to 25, included lectures, rallies, and small group discussions. Although some events were sparsely attended, particularly in the South, Ground Zero activities took place in more than 600 communities and on 350 college campuses across the United States. The media coverage of Ground Zero Week also raised awareness of nuclear issues among millions of Americans who did not participate in the week's events, but followed the news.[140]

Ground Zero Week activities prompted Clark to urge the Reagan administration to pursue bold arms reduction proposals in an accelerated time frame. In an April 22, 1982, memo to Meese, Chief of Staff James Baker, and Deputy Chief of Staff Michael Deaver, Clark repeatedly acknowledged that Reagan and grassroots anti-nuclear activists had the same goal of averting nuclear war, but different strategies for achieving it. Unsurprisingly, he argued that the administration's strategy was the better one. Clark noted, "Our effort should be directed toward convincing Americans whose anxieties are heightened by this movement that *our* policy solutions best meet their desire that the United States do something to lessen the prospect of a nuclear holocaust." In order to further its strategy for avoiding a nuclear war, Clark argued that the administration should not just wage a public relations campaign, but should actually pursue bold arms reduction initiatives. He wrote, "We must also focus on concrete policy and new initiatives; otherwise, our 'peace offensive' will be met with cynicism, both at home and abroad." Clark recommended that Reagan announce a "new initiative in connection with START" in May. This announcement "should be designed to capture the initiative by its boldness."[141]

Although grassroots anti-nuclear activism was prompting Clark to urge the Reagan administration to pursue dramatic arms control initiatives in an accelerated time frame, the national security advisor did not think that the administration should acknowledge publicly the effects that anti-nuclear activists were having on its policy. "The fact that the activists have our attention should be kept secret," Clark wrote. "We want to demonstrate that we,

too, are activists—seeking resolution to the same concerns."[142] The administration should be seen as proactive, not reactive.

As a nuclear abolitionist, Reagan wanted a bold opening START proposal.
In an April 21, 1982, NSC meeting, he declared, "It's too bad we cannot do
in START what we did in INF, or what Ike (Eisenhower) proposed on all
nuclear weapons. First, we need to restore the balance."[143] Reagan wished that
U.S. negotiators could propose the elimination of strategic nuclear weapons,
as they had called for the eradication of land-based INF missiles in the zero
option. He also admired Dwight Eisenhower's "Atoms for Peace" speech,
which he misinterpreted as a disarmament proposal. The same day that he
met with the NSC to discuss the U.S. START position, Reagan expressed his
desire to abolish nuclear weapons in a reply to a concerned citizen who had
written him a letter about his nuclear policy.[144] Although Reagan believed
that the conventional imbalance between NATO and the Warsaw Pact made
a proposal to eliminate strategic nuclear weapons impractical at present, he
eagerly sought a dramatic START initiative.

Under pressure from freeze activists, Reagan's advisors, who did not share
the president's nuclear abolitionism, also came to favor a striking START
proposal. Prior to the April 21 NSC meeting, State Department officials contended that the administration must devise a negotiating proposal that will
"elicit broad support in the US and with our allies, enhancing the credibility of
U.S. arms control policy. . . . This is clear in view of the political challenges of
the freeze movement in the US and the peace movement in Europe. We must
keep this in mind in choosing a negotiating approach."[145] Haig reiterated this
point during the NSC meeting, telling Reagan, "We need a dramatic proposal
to reverse the momentum over the peace movement and put you on the side
of the Angels."[146]

Reagan's advisors were anxious to placate the anti-nuclear movement
with a bold arms reduction proposal, largely because they thought that it
was endangering congressional support for the U.S. strategic modernization
plan. Haig emphasized the importance of setting forth a START proposal
that garnered public support, "not only to reinforce our START negotiating
position, but also to ensure Congressional approval of our defense budget,
and maintain support for the firm foreign policy line we have taken with the
Soviet Union across the board."[147] Rostow similarly worried that anti-nuclear
activists were putting U.S. nuclear modernization at risk. He lamented the
strength of the "anti-nuclear movement" in the April 21 NSC meeting, arguing that there was another "more serious movement under the surface, i.e.

move to isolation." In Rostow's view, the United States could not give in to this movement and "must restore the credibility of our nuclear guarantee."[148]

Reagan, for his part, wanted to craft a START proposal that was plausible to the Soviets. After all, he eventually wanted to eliminate nuclear weapons. In late March, Reagan had written a note to Clark suggesting that the congressional Jackson-Warner resolution, which called for nuclear arms reduction, might "tie in a conventional weapons reduction which could then open the door to zero nuclear weapons."[149] Although critics later argued that the opening U.S. START position was unserious because it required the Soviets to engage in steeper reductions in ICBM warheads and strategic missile launchers than the Americans, Reagan chose the most credible proposal set forth by his advisors. Alternative Defense Department and ACDA proposals called for seeking immediate reductions of throw-weight (a metric of the number and size of warheads a missile could carry) below the U.S. level. Haig rightly pointed out that the Soviets would never accept these proposals, which would have mandated a 65 percent reduction in Soviet throw-weight without subjecting the Americans to any real cuts.[150] Concerned about the plausibility of the U.S. START position, Reagan ultimately backed an initiative advocated by the State Department, the Joint Chiefs, and Deputy National Security Advisor Robert "Bud" McFarlane to wait until a later phase of negotiations to seek direct reductions in throw-weight.[151]

The Reagan administration's START position called for two phases of negotiations. In the first phase, U.S. negotiators would propose that the superpowers reduce their strategic ballistic missile warheads to 5,000 apiece, with no more than 2,500 of those warheads deployed on ICBMs. Each side would also reduce its deployed strategic ballistic missiles to 850, of which only 210 could be heavy and medium ICBMs. Each superpower could only deploy 110 heavy missiles. In the second phase, U.S. officials would call for direct reductions in ballistic missile throw-weight to an equal level below the current U.S. level. Each superpower would also reduce its bombers to 250.[152] Reagan outlined this proposal in a commencement address at his alma mater, Eureka College, on May 9, 1982.[153]

Anti-nuclear organizations were sorely disappointed in Reagan's START proposal. The Friends Committee on National Legislation issued a statement condemning the initiative as one-sided in favor of the United States. Since large ICBM warheads composed the bulk of Soviet strategic nuclear forces, the Soviets would have to engage in sharper reductions of ICBM warheads, strategic ballistic missiles, and eventually throw-weight than the Americans.

The Friends Committee also criticized the proposal for failing to include a freeze on weapons production and deployment during negotiations. "This proposal is so partial and one-sided that by the time the Soviets respond with their own initial positions, and by the time negotiators, after long sessions, finally hopefully reach agreement years hence, the proposals are likely to be overtaken by events and new weapons production." Both the Friends Committee and the Freeze Campaign argued that the superpowers would only be able to end the arms race if they enacted a freeze on new nuclear weapons while they negotiated significant reductions in existing systems. Anti-nuclear activists urged the United States and the Soviet Union to "start START with the freeze" as June 29, the first day of negotiations, approached.[154]

Reagan, however, was enthusiastic about discussing his arms reduction initiatives. They fit well with his nuclear abolitionism. He viewed the INF and START negotiations as positive steps that "can help free the world from the threat of destruction."[155] In a question-and-answer session with high school students in Chicago, Reagan spoke of his INF zero option as part of a larger effort to accomplish the goal set out by Eisenhower to rid the world of nuclear weapons.[156] In Reagan's mind, an INF proposal to eliminate all land-based INF missiles and a START initiative to reduce ballistic missile warheads by one-third and ballistic missiles by about one-half represented progress toward his goal of a nuclear-free world.[157]

Reagan also characterized his arms reduction proposals as superior alternatives to the freeze for achieving deep cuts in the superpowers' nuclear arsenals and averting a nuclear war. Reagan often stated that he shared anti-nuclear activists' concern about the threat of nuclear destruction and desire to end the arms race. "Today, I know there are a great many people who are pointing to the unimaginable horror of nuclear war. I welcome that concern," Reagan famously declared in an April 17, 1982, radio address. "So, to those who protest against nuclear war, I can only say, 'I'm with you.'"[158] Yet Reagan was eager to criticize the freeze proposal and explain the merits of his disarmament strategy. He argued that a nuclear freeze would codify Soviet advantages in the arms race and "make this country dangerously vulnerable to nuclear blackmail."[159] A freeze also would remove the Soviets' incentive to negotiate arms reduction agreements by halting the administration's modernization program.[160] Misconstruing the nuclear freeze as the ultimate goal of the anti-nuclear movement rather than a first step on the path to sweeping nuclear arms reduction, Reagan also declared that his START proposal would lead to real reductions in the superpowers' nuclear arsenals instead of just a halt in place.[161]

Yet the clear and simple nuclear freeze concept continued to resonate with Americans who feared that the Reagan administration's nuclear modernization program might be a precursor to nuclear war, rather than a prerequisite for meaningful arms reduction negotiations. In one of the largest political demonstrations in U.S. history, 750,000 people marched from the United Nations to Central Park on June 12, 1982, demanding nuclear disarmament. Tens of thousands of children led the march that included Vietnam veterans, Quakers, lawyers, physicians, labor union members, and students of arms control. Activists who had protested to ban the bomb in the 1950s, promote civil rights in the 1960s, and stop the Vietnam War in the late 1960s and early 1970s walked alongside suburbanites who eschewed the label of "anti-Establishment" and declared that they had never been to a political demonstration before. Survivors of the atomic bombings of Hiroshima and Nagasaki marched in the same columns as Americans who had served in the armed forces during the Second World War. Puppeteers wielding doves that loomed above the crowds shared the streets with engineers, musicians, and Hollywood elites. Catholics, Baptists, and Buddhists marched toward the Central Park rally that had been timed to coincide with the United Nations' Second Special Session on Disarmament. Alex Willentz, a demonstrator, told reporters optimistically, "There's no way the leaders can ignore this now. It's not just hippies and crazies anymore. It's everybody."[162] Freeze activists were determined to convince the Reagan administration of the merits of their strategy for reversing the nuclear arms race.

Despite their dueling disarmament strategies, both Reagan and anti-nuclear activists were playing essential roles in shifting the U.S. nuclear arms control paradigm from arms limitation to arms reduction. Reagan's budding nuclear abolitionism led him to set his administration on the course of pursuing nuclear arms reduction, rather than mere arms limitation, upon taking office. Pressure from grassroots anti-nuclear activists in the United States and Western Europe, however, accelerated the Reagan administration's timetable for pursuing arms reduction negotiations with the Soviets and emboldened its negotiating proposals. U.S. and West European anti-nuclear activism was particularly important in prompting Reagan's advisors, who were not nuclear abolitionists, to support the opening of talks aimed at reducing U.S. and Soviet nuclear weapons. This shift in the U.S. nuclear arms control paradigm was the first step toward reversing the nuclear arms race and ending the Cold War.

CHAPTER 3

"Merely the Illusion of Peace"

In the late afternoon of December 6, 1982, Reagan entered the White House library for what promised to be an uncomfortable meeting. As a favor to his daughter, Patti Davis, Reagan had agreed to meet with anti-nuclear activist Helen Caldicott. Davis was convinced that the modernization element of her father's "peace through strength" strategy might precipitate a nuclear war. She hoped that a conversation with Caldicott, an Australian pediatrician who had revived Physicians for Social Responsibility and created Women's Action for Nuclear Disarmament, would change her father's policies.[1] While Reagan consented to meet with Caldicott and his daughter for more than an hour, he suggested that this be a "personal private visit" and that none of the participants should mention it to the press.[2]

The meeting disappointed both sides. Reagan and Caldicott could not even agree on the basic state of the nuclear arms race, with Reagan arguing that the Soviets were ahead, while Caldicott insisted that parity existed between NATO and the Warsaw Pact.[3] Reagan confided in his diary that evening that Caldicott was "all steamed up & knows an awful lot of things that aren't true. I tried but couldn't get through her fixation."[4] Caldicott described the meeting as "the most disconcerting hour and a quarter of my life."[5] Caldicott and Reagan each presented a disarmament strategy that the other viewed as dangerous. Caldicott called for a nuclear freeze followed by reductions of existing nuclear systems. She feared that a nuclear buildup would lead to a nuclear war, as the superpowers would be more likely to use new counterforce weapons in a crisis rather than chance losing them in a first strike. Reagan contended that the United States needed to modernize its nuclear forces in order to incentivize the Soviet Union, which he believed was winning the arms race, to negotiate arms reduction. He warned that a freeze would lock the United States into a position of nuclear inferiority.[6]

This chapter contends that Reagan became even more anxious to prove the merits of his "peace through strength" disarmament strategy as U.S. and West European anti-nuclear movements gained strength in 1982 and 1983. Pressure from grassroots anti-nuclear activists led the Reagan administration to modify U.S. START and INF proposals in an effort to address Soviet concerns. Most importantly, Reagan's anxiety about the growing freeze movement prompted him to expand the U.S. ballistic missile defense program in an attempt to add a new element to his disarmament strategy that would make it more viable and popular at the expense of the freeze. While Reagan hoped that these decisions would jump-start nuclear disarmament, his advisors supported them merely in an effort to curtail anti-nuclear activism. Grassroots movements were undermining public, congressional, and allied support for U.S. nuclear modernization, which Reagan's aides considered vital to strengthen U.S. nuclear forces.

In 1982 and 1983, U.S. anti-nuclear activists continued to pressure the Reagan administration by winning passage of numerous state and local freeze measures. They also lobbied Congress to withhold funding for Reagan's strategic modernization program and approve a freeze resolution. West European activists persisted in pressing West European governments to refuse the U.S. INF missiles that were scheduled to arrive in late 1983. Reagan worried that these grassroots movements would convince Congress to defund his nuclear modernization efforts or persuade the allies to reject U.S. INF deployments. While Reagan valued U.S. nuclear modernization primarily as an incentive for the Soviets to negotiate nuclear arms reduction, many of his advisors still advocated modernization solely because they wanted to enhance U.S. nuclear forces.

*   *   *

As American public opinion coalesced behind the freeze in the spring of 1982, several Reagan administration officials called for a major public affairs campaign to promote the president's disarmament strategy and undercut the freeze movement. An NBC News poll conducted at the end of March 1982 showed that 74 percent of Americans supported a bilateral freeze.[7] Red Cavaney, the deputy director of the Office of Public Liaison, noted that public support for the freeze transcended the political divide. He warned Michael Deaver, the deputy chief of staff who was personally close to the Reagans, that "more than almost any issue in recent times, the subject of nuclear freeze is rapidly gaining a momentum and is likely to capture the public debate at the expense of virtually everything other than jobs." Eugene Rostow was similarly troubled by the breadth of the anti-nuclear movement, which had attracted three powerful new groups: "the churches, the 'loyal opposition' and, perhaps most important, the unpoliticized public." He cautioned William P. Clark that surging anti-nuclear activism could impede administration policies like defense modernization. Both Cavaney and Rostow advocated a public affairs effort to curb the freeze movement and tout Reagan's "peace through strength" approach.[8]

Clark agreed and urged Reagan to endorse a sweeping public affairs effort.[9] Along with the pursuit of bold arms reduction proposals in an accelerated time frame, this public affairs campaign constituted Clark's "grand strategy to deal with what may be the most important national security opportunity and challenge of this Administration," namely the growth of the anti-nuclear movement and the demand for nuclear arms control.[10] In pressing Reagan to approve his grand strategy, Clark echoed Rostow's concerns that a failure to counter freeze activists could have negative effects "on the Defense budget, on arms control, on allied relationships, etc."[11]

Reagan was troubled by the freeze movement's growing strength and anxious to persuade Americans of the superiority of his "peace through strength" disarmament strategy. He authorized a "comprehensive arms control and defense information effort," which Clark launched at an interagency meeting on April 28, 1982.[12] This meeting marked the start of the interagency Arms Control Information Policy Group, which met regularly under the leadership of Deputy National Security Advisor Robert "Bud" McFarlane.[13] A former Marine officer who spent twenty years in the Corps, McFarlane served two combat tours in Vietnam before becoming Kissinger's military assistant in 1973. Working on the Senate Armed Services Committee staff in 1979 and 1980, McFarlane had been "immersed in defense budgets and the SALT II treaty." In the Reagan administration, he supported nuclear arms reduction negotiations with the Soviets.[14]

As the freeze movement pressured the Reagan administration on multiple fronts in the second half of 1982, the work of the Arms Control Information Policy Group seemed all the more urgent to U.S. officials. In the summer, anti-nuclear activists lobbied members of the U.S. House of Representatives to pass a freeze resolution sponsored by Clement J. Zablocki (D-WI). They also worked to put the freeze on the 1982 ballot in states and cities across the country and persuade voters to support the freeze. U.S. Roman Catholic bishops were increasingly endorsing the freeze just as the National Conference of Catholic Bishops' Ad Hoc Committee on War and Peace was drafting a high-profile pastoral letter addressing nuclear issues. The Reagan administration, often through the Arms Control Information Policy Group, sought to counter the freeze in each of these arenas.

On June 23, in what the *New York Times* termed "a rebuff to President Reagan," the House Foreign Affairs Committee approved the Zablocki freeze resolution by a vote of 26 to 4, setting up a full House vote on the measure. The Zablocki resolution included an amendment sponsored by Representative Jonathan Bingham (D-NY) that incorporated language from his March 10 freeze resolution. Bingham's amendment called for a "mutual and verifiable freeze" followed by nuclear arms reduction, as well as a merger of the INF and START talks. Another key amendment to the Zablocki resolution urged the U.S. Senate to "approve" the SALT II treaty.[15]

In the run-up to the House vote on August 5, the Freeze Campaign and other anti-nuclear organizations pressed House members to pass the Zablocki resolution. Although the introduction of bipartisan freeze resolutions in the House and Senate on March 10 had accelerated the Freeze Campaign's timetable for pursuing a congressional freeze, it did not establish a Washington, DC, office with a dedicated congressional liaison until July 1982.[16] Thus, the Freeze Campaign primarily put pressure on House members in their districts rather than in Washington. It sponsored pro-freeze rallies and petitions and encouraged freeze supporters to write, call, or visit the district office of their representative. Meanwhile, the Council for a Livable World, the Coalition for a New Foreign and Military Policy, Physicians for Social Responsibility, and other more established anti-nuclear organizations took the lead on the pro-freeze lobbying efforts in Washington. They targeted the approximately 135 House members who had not yet taken a position on the freeze.[17]

The Reagan administration launched its own effort to derail the Zablocki resolution. The Arms Control Information Policy Group directed State Department, Defense Department, and ACDA officials to prepare a packet for members of Congress touting Reagan's nuclear arms reduction proposals and criticizing the freeze. This packet included fact sheets on the U.S. START proposal and strategic modernization program, as well as a State Department pamphlet on the nuclear freeze.[18] In this pamphlet, State Department officials contended that the freeze would cement Soviet advantages in the nuclear arms race, leaving the United States at risk and eliminating Soviet incentives to negotiate nuclear arms reduction. The freeze would also be difficult to verify and yield less sweeping results than Reagan's arms reduction initiatives. According to State Department officials, the freeze would also amount to "a unilateral decision by the United States to withdraw" from the NATO dual-track decision, which would damage America's reputation with the allies. Meanwhile, Reagan's proposals called for dramatic and verifiable reductions in U.S. and Soviet nuclear weapons to equal levels.[19]

Reagan's participation in the campaign against the Zablocki resolution highlights the seriousness of his administration's efforts to prevent passage of a congressional freeze measure. In meetings and phone calls on August 4 and 5, Reagan personally urged House members to vote against the Zablocki resolution. In addition to offering his usual criticisms of the freeze, Reagan claimed that the Zablocki resolution would hamper the INF and START negotiations by revealing Americans' skepticism of the talks. "Negotiations require full support of American people and Congress. Lack of support encourages Soviet intransigence at bargaining table, diminishes prospects for agreement on reductions." According to Reagan, House members should vote for a substitute amendment to the Zablocki resolution that William Broomfield (R-MI), William Carney (R-NY), and Samuel Stratton (D-NY) were sponsoring.[20] This Broomfield substitute supported Reagan's START initiative and declared that reductions must precede a freeze. If passed, the Broomfield substitute would replace the text of Zablocki's freeze resolution.[21] On the evening of August 5, Reagan noted in his diary, "I had to be a little stern in some of the meetings but it paid off. So did the phone calls on the nuclear freeze. We've just won it 204 to 202."[22] The Broomfield substitute was triumphant.[23]

Although the Zablocki freeze resolution failed in the House, freeze activists and congressional freeze supporters were optimistic. Randy Kehler later characterized the close vote as "our real peak in Congress." He noted that the Zablocki resolution was not encumbered by amendments that diluted the freeze, so "it was the clear, what I think of as the pure freeze, was right there, and it missed by one vote, with virtually no work on our part."[24] Representative Edward Markey, who had introduced a House freeze resolution on March 10, and his aides Peter Franchot and Douglas Waller shared Kehler's hopefulness. House rules state that an amendment must win by a majority vote, so the Broomfield substitute would have been doomed if one of its supporters had altered his vote. "We could already hear the battle cry from freeze activists across the country: 'Change one vote and pass the freeze,'" Waller later wrote. They hoped to use the close House vote to rally support for congressional candidates who backed the freeze in the upcoming midterm election.[25]

Congress, however, was not the only vehicle through which freeze activists could pressure the Reagan administration to pursue their disarmament strategy. The American electorate was another such vehicle. During the summer and fall of 1982, state and local freeze campaigns across the country worked to persuade voters to support freeze referenda. Ballots in ten states and several large cities included a freeze resolution in 1982. The National Freeze Campaign aided state and local freeze referenda campaigns by developing television and radio advertisements for their use and providing financial assistance, among other things. The National Freeze Campaign initially focused on Wisconsin, which was the first to hold a statewide freeze referendum during its primary election on September 14. The Freeze Campaign Clearinghouse pledged to share insight from the Wisconsin effort with other state and local referenda campaigns.[26]

To build support for the freeze referendum, the Wisconsin Nuclear Weapons Freeze Campaign distributed pro-freeze literature, canvassed voters in person and by phone, and sent speakers to address organizations across the state. In advocating the freeze, Wisconsin activists made the familiar claim that an escalating nuclear arms race increased the likelihood of nuclear war. A nuclear freeze therefore was crucial for preventing nuclear conflict. Yet Wisconsin activists also made a powerful economic argument for the freeze. In 1982, the United States was mired in a recession. The unemployment rate was over 10 percent, the highest since the Great Depression. "At a time when millions are out of work, including many here in Wisconsin, the sanity of spending billions of dollars on additional nuclear weaponry at the expense of our domestic economy must be questioned," freeze activists asserted on a referendum flyer.[27] A freeze was important for averting a nuclear war and restoring economic prosperity.

Just as it had worked against the Zablocki freeze resolution in the House, the Reagan administration mobilized to convince voters to oppose freeze referenda. Administration officials actively tracked the progress of campaigns to put freeze resolutions on state and local ballots in 1982.[28] In August, the Arms Control Information Policy Group launched a major effort to counter state freeze referenda campaigns. For example, State Department, ACDA, and Defense Department officials met with newspaper editorial boards and appeared on television and the radio in the key media markets of states with freeze resolutions on the ballot. During these trips, administration officials also worked to educate "religious, ethnic, veterans, women and other interest groups" about Reagan's nuclear arms reduction proposals and the disadvantages of the freeze.

An interagency group crafted a speech insert and fact sheets to enable leading spokespeople to promote Reagan's disarmament strategy in the national
media, as well as answer questions about U.S. nuclear policy and the freeze.[29]
This speech insert included a reminder that the Reagan administration was
already pursuing sweeping and verifiable nuclear arms reduction with the
Soviet Union. In addition to the administration's usual charges against the
freeze, this insert suggested that the passage of nuclear freeze referenda could
undercut U.S. negotiators by indicating a lack of support for their efforts.[30] This
claim was similar to the one Reagan had made against the Zablocki freeze resolution to great effect.

The administration's efforts were in vain, however. On September 14,
Wisconsin voters passed the freeze measure by a 3-to-1 margin.[31] This success
excited referenda campaigns across the country, leading the National Freeze
Campaign to worry about "some over-confidence as a result of the Wisconsin victory."[32] Freeze activists, however, continued to build support for the
referenda in the run-up to the November general election. Even movie stars
became involved in Reagan's home state of California, which had a freeze
measure on the ballot. In the October 30 episode of the ABC News program
The Last Word, Paul Newman advocated the freeze in a heated debate against
Charlton Heston.[33]

The Reagan administration similarly pressed on with its effort to counter
freeze referenda campaigns. Administration officials tried to spin the Wisconsin vote to their advantage, noting that they "share the objective of the
Wisconsin nuclear referendum insofar as it calls for mutual nuclear weapons reductions." They also claimed that the text of the Wisconsin referendum "is unclear as to whether a moratorium should precede or follow actual
arms reductions," even though the referendum plainly called for "a mutual
nuclear weapons moratorium and reduction."[34] As the November election
approached, administration officials continued to tout Reagan's arms reduction proposals and disparage the freeze in states and cities with freeze resolutions on the ballot.[35]

In discussing the drawbacks of the freeze proposal and the merits of his
disarmament strategy, Reagan sometimes veered into ad hominem attacks
on freeze activists. He falsely claimed that the Soviet Union had started the
freeze movement to undermine U.S. national security. Referring to anti-
nuclear protesters gathered outside of the ballroom in which he was speaking to veterans' organizations on October 4, Reagan declared, "They were
demonstrating in behalf of a movement that has swept across our country

that I think is inspired by, not the sincere, honest people who want peace, but by some who want the weakening of America, and so are manipulating many honest and sincere people."[36] At a press conference a month later, Reagan wrongly stated, "There is no question about foreign agents that were sent to help instigate and help create and keep such a movement going."[37] Despite later being confronted by a reporter with the House Intelligence Committee's findings that "proponents of the nuclear freeze are not being manipulated by Soviet agents," Reagan refused to abandon his wildly inaccurate view that the freeze movement was subject to Soviet influence. He answered the reporter by incorrectly claiming that Brezhnev originated the freeze proposal in February 1981.[38] To make his point, Reagan sometimes quoted from John Barron's *Reader's Digest* article "The KGB's Magical War for 'Peace,'" in which Barron argued that the Soviet Union had initiated the freeze movement.[39] It appears that Reagan was relying on *Reader's Digest*, rather than objective intelligence assessments, for his information about the makeup of the freeze movement.

Americans found Reagan's message unpersuasive, however, as they approved freeze resolutions in eight of the nine states with such a measure on the ballot in the November 1982 election. The freeze resolution won in California, Massachusetts, Michigan, Montana, New Jersey, North Dakota, Oregon, and Rhode Island, while it lost in Arizona. In addition to these statewide measures, voters in major cities like Chicago, Denver, Philadelphia, and Washington, DC, adopted freeze resolutions. The *New York Times* reported that "the voting on the resolution, which is purely advisory, constituted the largest referendum on a single issue in the nation's history," as the states and cities that passed a freeze resolution "include about one-fourth of the country's population."[40] Freeze activists also counted fifteen House races in which an incumbent opposed to the freeze lost.[41] Overall, Democrats gained twenty-six House seats in the 1982 midterm election, which suggested that the House likely would pass a freeze resolution in 1983.

The freeze was making inroads not only with the American electorate, but also with U.S. Catholic bishops, which deeply troubled the Reagan administration. Pax Christi, a Catholic peace organization, had endorsed the freeze in 1980.[42] Amid the continuing nuclear arms race, Pax Christi decided in early 1982 to urge U.S. bishops to support the freeze proposal. It advocated the freeze in a mass mailing and asked bishops to return a card endorsing the freeze. By the end of April, nearly half of the active bishops had returned pro-freeze cards. Supporters of Pax Christi's freeze appeal included three of the five bishops on the ad hoc committee writing the pastoral letter on war and peace issues.[43]

Through meetings and correspondence with the ad hoc committee in 1982, senior Reagan administration officials sought to influence the substance of its pastoral letter.[44] The administration wanted to forestall criticism of U.S. nuclear policy, which it feared would undercut public support for nuclear modernization and bolster U.S. and West European anti-nuclear activism.[45] By contrast, the bishops' endorsement of U.S. arms control proposals would underscore the sincerity of these initiatives and pressure the Soviets to accept them.[46] Reagan had won the Catholic vote in the 1980 presidential election, and his aides viewed Catholics as an important constituency. By late 1982, they were concerned about Catholics' interest in the freeze.[47] If the bishops advocated a freeze in their pastoral letter, this likely would increase support for the freeze among a key bloc of voters.

The Reagan administration's contact with the ad hoc committee did not yield a pastoral letter that endorsed U.S. nuclear policy. Instead, the first draft of the pastoral, which the committee released in June 1982, criticized the "deterrence relationship" between the U.S. and Soviet blocs as "a sinful situation because of the threats implied in it and the consequences it has in the world." Deterrence, however, was temporarily tolerable because it helped keep the peace. Yet this moral toleration of deterrence depended on an escalation of disarmament efforts. The committee endorsed the idea of a freeze and urged the Reagan administration to pursue "'unilateral initiatives' toward disarmament." It also condemned the first use or threat of first use of nuclear weapons. Contrary to the Reagan administration's wishes, the committee left the call for a freeze on strategic nuclear weapons and no nuclear first use in the pastoral's second draft, which it released for the National Conference of Catholic Bishops' meeting in November. The committee also denounced first-strike weapons, which could include the MX missile.[48]

When the committee's second draft again criticized U.S. nuclear policy, the Reagan administration intensified its efforts to shape the pastoral. Clark, a devout Catholic, wrote a letter to Archbishop Joseph Bernardin, the committee's head, chiding the bishops for failing to mention Reagan's nuclear arms reduction efforts. Clark reiterated the administration's criticisms of the freeze and his belief that the bishops would back U.S. arms reduction proposals if they studied them. In Clark's view, the U.S. nuclear deterrent met the pastoral's own criteria for being "morally defensible," as it aimed to avert war and existed alongside negotiations to reduce U.S. and Soviet nuclear weapons.

Not only did Clark call on Bernardin to circulate his letter at the National Conference of Catholic Bishops' November meeting in Washington, but he also had it published in the *New York Times* on November 17.[49]

Anxious to improve the pastoral's assessment of U.S. nuclear policy, Reagan offered to meet with some of the bishops attending the November conference in Washington. Secretary of State George Shultz expressed an interest in speaking at this conference. Rostow also requested a meeting with the bishops in late 1982. Yet the bishops passed on each of these invitations to discuss nuclear issues directly with Reagan or his top advisors.[50] A Shultz speech at the November meeting would have violated the National Conference of Catholic Bishops' rule permitting only bishops to address such gatherings. A straw poll at the meeting revealed that over 70 percent of the bishops were in "basic agreement" with the second draft of the pastoral letter. Of the nearly 26 percent who maintained "major reservations," many wanted a more critical pastoral.[51] In light of these attitudes, it was unsurprising that the bishops were not inclined to meet Reagan or Rostow. Desperate for a more positive evaluation of U.S. policy, administration officials floated the idea of asking the Vatican to press U.S. bishops to revise their pastoral letter.[52]

The Reagan administration's problems were compounded on December 7, when the House voted 245 to 176 to delete production funds for the MX missile from the fiscal year 1983 defense appropriations bill. The growing popularity of the nuclear freeze proposal and the persuasiveness of antinuclear activists' arguments against the MX fueled congressional opposition to MX production funding. The House vote on December 7 marked the first time since the Second World War that the House or Senate had rejected production funds for a major weapon system desired by a president.[53]

Anti-nuclear organizations, including SANE, the Council for a Livable World, and Women's Action for Nuclear Disarmament, had teamed up with environmental and religious groups to wage a large-scale campaign against the MX. Lobbyists representing these organizations in Washington urged members of Congress to vote against the MX, while grassroots activists across the country contacted their legislators to express their opposition to the missile.[54] SANE directed an extensive phone-tree operation to intensify grassroots pressure on Congress to reject the MX. As part of this operation, SANE volunteers called activists in swing districts and states who then alerted their own networks to write or call members of Congress about the MX.[55] Between the midterm election on November 2 and the House vote on December 7, SANE volunteers called 1,294 individuals, who in turn encouraged more than 27,000 people to petition House members to elim-inate MX production funding.[56]

In letters to members of Congress, anti-nuclear activists and lobbyists criticized the MX as a destabilizing and expensive missile that would under-mine nuclear arms control efforts. As a first-strike weapon, the MX would increase the chance of nuclear war, particularly in times of international ten-sion. With a price tag of at least $20 billion, the MX force was a wasteful expense during a recession. Anti-nuclear groups also dismissed the Reagan administration's claim that the MX would be a bargaining chip in arms con-trol negotiations with the Soviets, noting that the administration was sending mixed signals about whether it would actually give up the MX in an arms reduction agreement. They reminded members of Congress that "there is not a single instance in the history of modern arms negotiations of a weapon in production being given up in the course of such talks." Rather, the con-struction of a new U.S. missile would make the Soviets less likely to agree to nuclear arms reduction.[57]

Anti-nuclear activists and lobbyists also condemned the proposed "dense pack" basing mode for the MX missile. Under the "dense pack" plan, MX missiles would be placed so close to one another in such a small area that incoming Soviet warheads theoretically would destroy one another without obliterating the majority of the MX missiles. UCS, for example, sent infor-mational packets to senators detailing the flaws of "dense pack." Based on the questionable and untested theory of fratricide, it was unclear if "dense pack" would even work. This basing mode would also violate SALT I and SALT II, which banned construction of additional fixed ICBM silos. Military experts had even acknowledged that the Soviets could develop countermeasures to "dense pack" as early as the late 1980s. In order to address concerns about the survivability of the MX in the "dense pack" basing mode, the Pentagon was considering the deployment of an ABM system to protect the MX missiles in Wyoming, which would be a violation of the ABM Treaty. With all of these problems, "dense pack" was still estimated to cost at least $28 billion.[58]

Anti-nuclear activists' opposition to the MX and "dense pack" influenced some members' positions on MX production funding. During a September 1982 conversation with anti-nuclear activists, Mike Rock, a staffer for Repre-sentative Virginia Smith (R-NE), brought up the strength of the National Cam-paign to Stop the MX and Clergy and Laity Concerned's anti-MX campaign. He noted that Smith would likely continue to vote against the MX. Luanne Bloom told anti-nuclear activists that her boss, Representative Daniel Akaka

(D-HI), had been influenced by the many letters he had received about the MX. He would probably vote against the missile.[59] In November, Peter Sloan, a staffer for Representative William Ratchford (D-CT), urged anti-nuclear activists to send his office "materials so Ratchford can speak to issue in full [House Appropriations] committee." Mike Merek, who worked for Representative David Obey (D-WI), told anti-nuclear activists that "calls like this are key" and encouraged them to show up when the House Appropriations Committee marked up the defense appropriations bill.[60]

In speeches on the House and Senate floor, opponents of the MX often referenced Americans' desire for a nuclear freeze as one of the main reasons that they planned to vote against MX production funding. On November 29, Senator William Proxmire (D-WI) noted that voters passed freeze resolutions in eight of the nine states with such a measure on the ballot in the recent midterm election. "The people of this democracy have gone on record on the nuclear arms race. They want their leadership to negotiate now to find an agreement with the Soviet Union to stop testing, development and production of nuclear weapons," he declared.[61] In the House debate on the amendment eliminating MX production funding, Representative Les AuCoin (D-OR) stated that "the people in this country came the closest to a national referendum in the history of this Republic on November 2, when they endorsed overwhelmingly the nuclear weapons freeze. And one of the weapons they had in mind was the MX."[62] Markey and Representatives Patricia Schroeder (D-CO) and Harold Ford (D-TN) made similar statements during this debate.[63]

House members also set forth many of the same arguments against the MX that anti-nuclear activists had been making throughout the fall. They lambasted the cost of the missile, as well as the impracticality of the "dense pack" basing mode. Rather than serve as a bargaining chip that could induce the Soviets to agree to nuclear arms reduction, the MX would violate the SALT and ABM treaties.[64] The skepticism of members of Congress and anti-nuclear activists about the viability of the "dense pack" basing mode was vindicated the day after the House vote when John W. Vessey, the chairman of the Joint Chiefs of Staff, told the Senate Armed Services Committee that a majority of the Joint Chiefs opposed the "dense pack" plan.[65]

Reagan viewed the House vote to eliminate MX production funding as a serious challenge to his disarmament strategy. He was unable to perceive the contradiction between building MX missiles and pursuing START talks. Rather, Reagan believed that the MX vote had removed a major incentive for the Soviets to negotiate seriously. Calling the December 7 vote "a grave

mistake," Reagan warned that "unless reversed in coming days, it will seriously set back our efforts to protect the nation's security and could handcuff
our negotiators at the arms table."[66] There would be dangerous consequences
if the START negotiations stalled in the wake of the House MX vote. Reagan
cautioned McFarlane, "It's coming, Bud. This inexorable building of nuclear
weapons on our side and the Russians' side can only lead to Armageddon.
We've got to get off that track."[67]

Yet Congress dismissed Reagan's warnings, listening instead to anti-
nuclear activists' concerns about the MX missile and the "dense pack" basing
mode. Following the House vote to eliminate MX production funding, anti-
nuclear organizations focused on persuading the Senate to follow suit. The
leaders of SANE, the Coalition for a New Foreign and Military Policy, and
UCS sent letters to senators highlighting the flaws of the MX and "dense pack"
and urging them to halt MX production funding.[68] Local grassroots groups
from across the country also contacted senators to express their opposition to
the MX.[69] Senator Arlen Specter (R-PA), for example, received roughly 1,800
calls or letters on the MX issue.[70] In a speech on the Senate floor, Alan Cranston (D-CA) listed public support for the freeze as one of the reasons that he
was offering an amendment to delete MX production funds. "The country is
also activated by the proposal of a bilateral, verifiable nuclear weapons freeze.
More than 20 million Americans have voted on this issue this year: 60 percent
in support," he noted.[71]

Anti-nuclear activists scored a major victory when a House-Senate conference committee rejected MX production funding on December 19, 1982.
While the conference committee did provide $2.5 billion for MX research
and development, most of these funds could not be spent until Congress
approved a basing mode for the MX.[72]

Anti-nuclear activists' success in the 1982 election and influence on the
congressional MX debate prompted Reagan and a small circle of aides to
accelerate the U.S. missile defense program by launching SDI on March 23,
1983. Reagan was troubled by the increasing popularity of the freeze proposal, which he viewed as a dangerous initiative that would hinder the pursuit of dramatic nuclear arms reduction. In the wake of anti-nuclear activists'
triumphs in late 1982, Reagan was even more determined to prove the superiority of his disarmament strategy to the American people and Congress.
By publicly embracing a major missile defense research program, he hoped
to increase the viability and popularity of his disarmament strategy at the
expense of the freeze movement. Although advisors like McFarlane were

not nuclear abolitionists, they were frustrated that the freeze movement was undermining congressional and public support for the administration's nuclear policy. McFarlane hoped that SDI would be a creative and popular way to achieve the same goals of that stymied policy: the conclusion of significant arms reduction agreements and the deterrence of a nuclear attack on the United States.

The 1972 ABM Treaty placed significant constraints on U.S. and Soviet ABM systems. Under the agreement, each superpower could maintain only two limited ABM sites: one to safeguard its capital and the other to protect an ICBM field. Nationwide ABM systems were prohibited. In 1974, U.S. and Soviet leaders signed a protocol reducing the number of permitted ABM sites to one apiece. The ABM Treaty was in line with the MAD doctrine, which posited that both superpowers' vulnerability to nuclear attack by the other would ensure that neither launched a nuclear strike. Both superpowers' possession of a "second-strike" capability, the ability to retaliate after enduring a nuclear attack, would deter each side from striking the other. By banning the deployment of nationwide ABM systems, the ABM Treaty helped to maintain the mutual vulnerability that MAD claimed was critical to deterring nuclear war.[73]

Although Reagan's strategic modernization program called for "research and development on ballistic missile defense," he did not prioritize this issue until the freeze movement made significant inroads with the American public and Congress in late 1982.[74] Six weeks after the record-setting anti-nuclear demonstration in New York City on June 12, 1982, Edward Teller, the "father of the hydrogen bomb," wrote a letter to Reagan extolling the recent advances in directed energy weapons, which he argued could be used to destroy incoming nuclear missiles. Contending that the Soviets were likely ahead of the Americans in developing these defenses, Teller urged Reagan for "a mandate to vigorously explore and exploit the technological opportunities in defensive applications of nuclear weaponry." Teller argued that not only would an "accelerated developmental program" of defensive nuclear weapons likely yield technologies that would protect the United States against a Soviet missile attack, but "commencing this effort may also constitute a uniquely effective reply to those advocating the dangerous inferiority implied by a 'nuclear freeze.'"[75] Although Reagan favored using nonnuclear technologies to defend against missile strikes, he wrote Clark that "we should take this [Teller's letter] seriously and have a real look."[76]

The freeze movement's influence on the 1982 election and the House MX vote prompted McFarlane to begin seriously considering a major missile

defense research effort. After Reagan faced questions about the freeze movement during a campaign trip to New York in the fall of 1982, McFarlane told
the president that he was pursuing a project that might finally allow the administration to get the better of the freeze movement.[77] The MX vote in Congress
made McFarlane believe that the United States would never be able to build as
many offensive nuclear weapons as the Soviet Union, whose leaders were not
restrained by congressional action or public sentiment. McFarlane thought that
the administration needed to direct its efforts to harnessing American strengths,
which were in high technology. ABM systems would allow the United States to
make full use of its technological advantages. By intercepting and destroying
incoming ballistic missiles, ABMs would compensate for the Soviet advantage
in ICBMs—an advantage that the freeze movement was making it difficult for
the administration to redress through nuclear modernization.[78] McFarlane also
envisioned SDI as a bargaining chip that could induce the Soviets to conclude a
sweeping nuclear arms reduction agreement. Fearing that a major U.S. missile
defense program would yield advances in offensive weapons, the Soviets would
oppose it. According to McFarlane's plan, U.S. officials would then offer to
abandon their missile defense program in exchange for dramatic cuts in Soviet
strategic nuclear forces, which would make an ABM system unnecessary.[79]

McFarlane did not detail the specifics of his missile defense research proposal to Reagan in late 1982, but simply explained to the president that he
had an idea that could "outflank the freeze movement while also solving the
problem of the nuclear imbalance and improving the negotiating position
of the United States in strategic arms talks." Responding positively, Reagan
instructed McFarlane to provide an update on his progress in January.[80]

Meanwhile, burgeoning anti-nuclear sentiment led the chief of naval
operations James D. Watkins to seek an alternative to offensive nuclear deterrence. As a devout Catholic, Watkins monitored the efforts of the National
Conference of Catholic Bishops' Ad Hoc Committee on War and Peace to
draft a pastoral letter addressing nuclear issues. Although he personally
believed in the morality of nuclear deterrence, Watkins was dismayed to learn
that the pastoral's criticism of U.S. nuclear policy was leading some Americans to abandon military service on moral grounds. Watkins realized that
public opinion was turning against offensive nuclear deterrence. Coupled
with the difficulty of finding an MX basing mode, this realization made Watkins eager to rethink U.S. deterrence.[81]

An accelerated missile defense research program offered the alternative
to offensive nuclear deterrence that Watkins sought. After a review of the

Defense Department's existing ABM program and a meeting with Teller on January 20, 1983, Watkins became convinced that missile defense was technologically feasible. He now believed that missile defense research would facilitate a transition away from deterrence based solely on offensive nuclear weapons to deterrence that relied also on ABM technology. He gained the unanimous support of the Joint Chiefs on February 5 to present this idea to Reagan at a meeting scheduled for February 11.[82]

During this meeting, Reagan responded enthusiastically to Watkins's arguments for an accelerated missile defense research program, believing that it could further his own goal of nuclear abolition. After touting the recent technological advances that he thought warranted a new ABM research effort, Watkins asked Reagan, "Would it not be better if we could develop a system that would protect, rather than avenge, our people?" This appeal to Reagan's abhorrence of nuclear weapons was effective because the president instructed the Joint Chiefs to write a report outlining the contours of a major missile defense research program.[83] That evening, Reagan wrote in his diary that missile defense could make his dream of a nuclear-free world a reality: "An almost 2 hr. lunch with Joint Chiefs of staff. . . . Out of it came a super idea. So far the only policy worldwide on nuclear weapons is to have a deterrent. What if we tell the world we want to protect our people not avenge them, that we're going to embark on a program of research to come up with a defensive weapon that could make nuclear weapons obsolete? I would call upon the scientific community to volunteer in bringing such a thing about."[84] Reagan reasoned that by making it impossible for nuclear missiles to strike their targets, missile defense would make nuclear missiles obsolete. He believed that if nuclear missiles were obsolete, U.S. and Soviet officials would agree to eliminate them. ABM research became a major element in the president's disarmament strategy.

Reagan insisted on quickly developing and announcing a significant missile defense initiative because he was anxious to curb the freeze movement, which continued to show strength in early 1983. In a move that received national media attention in early February, the Freeze Campaign's Third National Conference adopted a strategy for 1983 focused on influencing Congress and the 1984 elections. As part of its congressional strategy, the Freeze Campaign vowed to pressure the House and Senate to pass a bilateral, comprehensive freeze resolution. Yet it also decided to pursue immediate, bilateral, interim restraints on the nuclear arms race. Freeze activists would push Congress to stop funding the testing, production, and deployment of nuclear systems and urge the Soviets to "exercise corresponding restraint."

Special attention would be given to halting nuclear testing and INF deployments. Eager to play a consequential role in the 1984 elections, the Freeze Campaign's Third National Conference established the Project 84 task force. This task force would examine opportunities and make recommendations for freeze participation in the 1984 presidential and congressional campaigns.[85]

As the race for the Democratic presidential nomination kicked off, it appeared that freeze activists could play a pivotal part in the campaign. In announcing their presidential bids in February 1983, Senator Gary Hart and former vice president Walter Mondale called for a nuclear freeze.[86] Senator Alan Cranston also emphasized the importance of ending the nuclear arms race and reducing nuclear weapons in his campaign launch.[87] Nuclear arms control looked to be an important issue in the 1984 presidential race, providing freeze activists with an opening to influence the Democratic presidential nomination process at the very least.

In the weeks leading up to his announcement of SDI, Reagan was distressed by the increasing popularity of the freeze. During a February 25 NSC meeting, for example, he lamented that the freeze movement was constantly condemning his administration's policies, specifically censuring "a film by anti-nuclear advocate Helen Caldicott, noting that it represents the type of criticism to which U.S. security planning is continually subjected to."[88]

Reagan set forth his usual criticisms of the freeze proposal in a March 8, 1983, address to the National Association of Evangelicals in Orlando, which is best remembered for his description of the Soviet Union as an "evil empire." He claimed that his disarmament strategy was superior to the freeze, declaring, "The truth is that a freeze now would be a very dangerous fraud, for that is merely the illusion of peace. The reality is that we must find peace through strength." He exhorted the audience to "resist the attempts of those who would have you withhold your support for our efforts, this administration's efforts, to keep America strong and free, while we negotiate real and verifiable reductions in the world's nuclear arsenals and one day, with God's help, their total elimination."[89] Reagan later wrote that he had hoped that this speech would "reach" freeze supporters and convince them to support his policies instead.[90]

Reagan was eager to unveil a new ABM research program that could undercut the freeze movement. According to McFarlane, Reagan repeatedly urged the Joint Chiefs and the few White House staffers working on the missile defense issue to wrap up their efforts quickly in March. Reagan wanted to "break something new" in a defense speech in late March, specifically an initiative that could diminish support for the freeze. An expanded missile defense research effort seemed to be such a proposal.[91] By explaining the ways in which missile defense could facilitate the elimination of nuclear weapons, Reagan hoped to increase support for his disarmament strategy.

Within his administration, Reagan was alone in his pursuit of nuclear abolition. His vision of SDI as the key to a nuclear-free world was also unique, even among supporters of accelerated missile defense research. To safeguard his conception of SDI as a tool for eliminating nuclear weapons, Reagan displayed a new assertiveness in nuclear policy. He deliberately kept the circle of aides working on SDI's announcement small, purposely excluding those who he believed would oppose and undermine his vision for SDI. McFarlane later wrote that after the Joint Chiefs endorsed an accelerated missile defense research effort and Reagan approved a new ABM program, the president told him, "I want you to keep this tightly under wraps. Do the work in your own staff and write the speech and let's get ready to give it." Reagan feared that members of his administration who opposed an expanded missile defense research effort would go public with their criticism after finding out about SDI, thereby killing the program before it had even been formally announced. McFarlane recalled that "no more than half a dozen people, outside the military, even knew about the initiative."[92] The State Department was kept completely out of the loop on SDI until two days before Reagan announced the program.[93] Although Weinberger had attended Reagan's February 11 meeting with the Joint Chiefs, the Defense Department had no idea that Reagan was planning to unveil a major ABM research effort in his March 23 address until the day before the speech.[94] Even the Joint Chiefs did not realize until March 20 that Reagan was preparing to announce a significant ABM research program.[95] Reagan's speechwriters were told to craft a speech on the proposed defense budget for the upcoming fiscal year, but to expect the addition of "a significant insert" right before the president went on the air.[96]

Reagan's vision of SDI prevailed in his March 23 announcement of the program. Contending that "the human spirit must be capable of rising above dealing with other nations and human beings by threatening their existence," Reagan encouraged Americans to consider "wouldn't it be better to save lives than to avenge them?" In this vein, the Reagan administration would launch a major initiative to research and develop ballistic missile defenses. The president urged "the scientific community in our country, those who gave us nuclear weapons, to turn their great talents now to the cause of mankind and world peace, to give us the means of rendering these nuclear weapons impotent and obsolete." If the "threat posed by strategic nuclear missiles" could be eradicated, then "this could pave the way for arms control measures to eliminate the weapons themselves."[97] In a repudiation of MAD, Reagan expressed his hope that SDI would facilitate the transition to a nuclear-free world.

Six days later, Reagan revealed that he was willing to share SDI with the Soviets to help bring about nuclear abolition. Reagan told a reporter that after a viable missile defense was developed, a U.S. president "could offer to give that same defensive weapon to them [the Soviets] to prove to them that there was no longer any need for keeping these missiles. Or with that defense, he could then say to them, 'I am willing to do away with all my missiles. You do away with all of yours.'"[98]

Prominent technical experts, however, questioned the feasibility of SDI. Jerome Wiesner, a former MIT president who had advised Eisenhower and Kennedy on science and technology issues, told the *New York Times* that "most technical people doubt that antimissile devices in space will work. But even if they do, it's wishful thinking to believe that they would provide impenetrable defenses." He noted that utter devastation would result even if just 5 or 10 percent of Soviet nuclear weapons penetrated U.S. missile defenses.[99] George Rathjens and Jack Ruina, MIT professors who had held leadership positions in the Defense Department's Advanced Research Project Agency, also believed that it would be "virtually impossible" to create a "100 percent effective" defense. In light of this, SDI would be unable to achieve Reagan's goal of making nuclear weapons obsolete.[100] Congressional Democrats also argued that SDI was far-fetched, and they likened it to the fantasy films *Star Wars* and the science fiction character Buck Rogers.[101] The "Star Wars" moniker stuck.

For their part, leading freeze activists did not share Reagan's view that SDI was the key to a nuclear-free world. Rather, they deemed the program risky or simply nonsensical. Marta Daniels, a Connecticut freeze activist and active participant in the national campaign, characterized SDI as "dangerous and destabilizing." In a pamphlet criticizing the initiative, Daniels cited the concerns of prominent scientists and engineers who argued that ballistic missile defense was not technologically feasible. Daniels also maintained that SDI would foster "space warfare development," as the superpowers worked to create weapons that could cripple a ballistic missile defense system. The country without ballistic missile defenses would surely accelerate its offensive missile deployments so that it could penetrate the adversary's defenses. Ballistic missile defenses would also give a superpower a first-strike capability. Protected by its missile defense system, it could launch a nuclear attack against the other superpower without fear of retaliation. SDI also appeared to violate existing agreements like the ABM Treaty, which prohibited the United States and the Soviet Union from "develop[ing], test[ing], or deploy[ing] ABM systems or components which are sea-based, air-based, space-based, or mobile land-based." In Daniels's view, SDI would have grave consequences across the board.[102]

In light of expert opinion that SDI was technologically unsound, Kehler initially "thought it was laughable. I thought it was a joke." He later admitted, however, that he underestimated the popular appeal of a program that pledged to defend the United States against a nuclear attack and facilitate nuclear disarmament. By the summer of 1984, Kehler recognized that the Reagan administration had used SDI to get "the jump on us, in terms of public relations."[103] Forsberg similarly acknowledged that SDI "somewhat pacified" the freeze movement, although she argued that this did not occur until after 1984.[104]

*   *   *

While the growing influence of the U.S. nuclear freeze movement prompted Reagan to unveil SDI, the increasing popularity of the West European peace movement led the administration to make its INF proposal more flexible in 1983. Both Reagan and his advisors hoped that a new INF proposal would curtail West European anti-nuclear sentiment, which threatened to undermine West European governments' support for the planned U.S. INF deployments. The Reagan administration was determined to install the INF missiles, given Soviet intransigence in the INF negotiations. Reagan and some of his advisors also believed that the deployments would prompt the Soviets to negotiate INF reductions in the future.

Anti-nuclear activism was on the rise throughout Western Europe in 1982, as U.S. INF deployments loomed on the horizon. The June 12, 1982, anti-nuclear march and rally in New York City was only one of a series of global demonstrations timed to coincide with the opening week of the United Nations' Second Special Session on Disarmament. On June 5, 300,000 anti-nuclear protesters marched through the streets of Rome, and 10,000 rallied for nuclear disarmament in Dublin. The next day, 15,000 demonstrated in Madrid.[105] Also on June 6, 250,000 activists from across Western Europe gathered for a CND demonstration in London's Hyde Park. They released a joint declaration of European peace movements to the Second Special Session on

Disarmament. In a passage clearly aimed at preventing U.S. INF deployments, the statement urged governments to refuse to produce or deploy nuclear weapons on their territory. In addition to rejecting the concept of nuclear deterrence, the activists declared, "We refuse also every measure which seeks to marshal humankind into two opposed blocs. We refuse the Cold War and we disown allegiance to its ideologies and to its opposed security systems. We affirm our citizenship of a healed human world."[106]

Although these demonstrations were scheduled to take place during the UN's Second Special Session on Disarmament, they also occurred while Reagan was traveling in Europe. The London protest took place on the eve of Reagan's arrival in the United Kingdom. A June 10 anti-nuclear demonstration in Bonn, which drew four hundred thousand participants, coincided with Reagan's visit for a NATO summit. Marchers hoped to show the president that they wanted "active steps to disarmament now, not cosmetic talks," indicating that they viewed U.S. proposals in the INF and START negotiations as unserious.[107]

Yet END activists recognized that the European anti-nuclear movement needed to do more than simply organize demonstrations in order to convince government officials to pursue nuclear disarmament in Europe. The European peace movement also needed to devise "a constructive alternative" to the nuclear arms race and war. One of the major forums for examining these issues was the inaugural END Convention that took place in Brussels from July 2 through 4, 1982.[108]

Drawing about a thousand people from twenty-five countries, the 1982 END Convention brought together anti-nuclear activists and politicians from the European left to discuss concrete disarmament proposals, strategies for advancing disarmament, and ways to strengthen transnational cooperation.[109] "Affinity groups" enabled scientists, trade unionists, church leaders, residents of local nuclear-free zones, peace movement activists, medical professionals, and peace educators, among others, to connect with their counterparts in other European countries. "Thematic workshops" were held to consider topics such as the ongoing U.S.-Soviet arms reduction negotiations; disarmament and the economy; the establishment of nuclear-free zones; nuclear disarmament and the division of Germany; Europe, the Third World, and the peace movement; and chemical and biological weapons.[110]

END Convention delegates agreed that "the great peace marches" alone would not persuade government leaders to rid Europe of nuclear weapons.[111] Another strategy for denuclearizing Europe was expanding efforts to convince local and regional governments to establish nuclear-free zones in their cities and districts. Activists who had already been lobbying for local nuclear-free zones noted that local governments "can open an official channel of discussion with central government." They can also "obstruct central government proposals. For example, they can refuse to build access roads to missile bases; refuse to participate in NATO war games; publicize sites in the area; educate the public to the dangers [of nuclear weapons] and various alternatives."[112] Activism on the local level could have a national or international impact.[113]

More radical forms of direct action were also debated at the END Convention. The most popular conference session was the thematic workshop on "opposition to Euromissile bases," which featured British, Italian, and Belgian anti-nuclear activists who were protesting INF missiles at their proposed deployment sites.[114] In August 1981, a group of women had walked 120 miles from Cardiff, Wales, to Royal Air Force Station Greenham Common in England, which was one of the planned deployment sites for U.S. cruise missiles in Britain. Upon reaching RAF Greenham Common, they had established a "peace camp" outside of the military base that would remain in existence for the next nineteen years. Living at the camp, these women hoped to block the deployment of cruise missiles through acts of civil disobedience. Demonstrations were also taking place in the Sicilian town of Comiso, which was the proposed deployment site for U.S. cruise missiles in Italy. In April 1982, sixty thousand people rallied against the U.S. INF deployments, while two-thirds of those living in the town of Comiso signed a petition to stop the construction of the cruise missile base.[115] Workshop attendees proposed a peaceful invasion of RAF Greenham Common, the establishment of a summer peace camp in Comiso, war tax resistance, and a five-minute general strike across Europe, among other actions.[116] One convention delegate wrote that the call for direct action at proposed INF deployment sites "was greeted with the longest applause of the entire Convention."[117]

In view of its aim to facilitate "the creation of links and the pooling of information among peace organizations from Western Europe," the 1982 END Convention was a success.[118] The transnational END Convention Liaison Committee decided to hold a second END Convention in West Berlin from May 9 through 15, 1983. Preparations for this Berlin convention began shortly after the Brussels convention concluded.[119]

West European anti-nuclear activism prompted Paul Nitze, the lead U.S. INF negotiator, to seek a compromise agreement with Yuli Kvitsinsky, his Soviet counterpart, in July 1982. Nitze and his deputy, Maynard Glitman, were well aware of the massive anti-nuclear demonstrations roiling Western Europe, particularly the FRG. After meeting with Schmidt and Genscher in mid-April 1982, Nitze and Glitman believed that the West German government would uphold its commitment to deploy U.S. missiles if the INF negotiations failed. Yet Glitman later recalled, "Both of us were concerned, however, that the result might resemble a Pyrrhic victory, with considerable damage inflicted upon the Alliance as a result of the disaffection of a large portion of the public in several Alliance member states." With West German anti-nuclear activism surging and the Soviets planning to review their INF position in the summer of 1982, Nitze began quietly considering concessions that each side could make to reach a deal.[120]

By this point, the Soviets had rejected the U.S. zero option proposal. Instead, they sought an agreement restricting the Soviet Union and NATO to "300 'medium-range' missiles and aircraft" in Europe. The Soviets used "NATO" to encompass U.S., British, and French forces. Although NATO would be allowed three hundred medium-range systems, U.S. Pershing II and cruise missile deployments were prohibited under this proposal, which also failed to limit Soviet INF deployments in Asia.[121]

Mindful of West Europeans' desire for an INF treaty, Nitze decided to "explore informally" a compromise deal with Kvitsinsky. Following weeks of clandestine conversations, Nitze and Kvitsinsky finally agreed on an INF package during their "walk in the woods" in the Jura Mountains on July 16, 1982. In reaching this agreement, the two negotiators were speaking only for themselves and still had to present the terms of the deal to their governments for approval. The Nitze-Kvitsinsky package limited the United States and the Soviet Union to 225 "medium-range nuclear delivery systems in Europe," of which only 75 could be missile systems. The Americans would deploy only ground-launched cruise missiles in Europe, forgoing the installation of Pershing II missiles in the FRG. The Soviets would freeze their INF deployments in Asia. After the superpowers signed a START agreement, they would begin talks for additional INF reductions.[122] Although Nitze and Kvitsinsky acted on their own initiative in striking this compromise, their dramatic encounter eventually leaked and captured the public imagination, inspiring Lee Blessing's 1988 Broadway play *A Walk in the Woods*.[123]

U.S. and Soviet leaders, however, did not find the deal inspiring in the late summer of 1982. Reagan, Weinberger, and the Joint Chiefs opposed granting the Soviets a monopoly on fast-flying intermediate-range ballistic missiles in Europe while the Americans were restricted to slow-flying cruise missiles.

They did not want to cancel the deployment of Pershing II missiles, which the Soviets found particularly worrisome given their ability to strike Soviet targets in mere minutes. It seemed unwise for the United States to give up its greatest leverage as part of a flawed deal. Reagan administration officials also believed that the Soviets' silence on the Nitze-Kvitsinsky package after the "walk in the woods" indicated their disapproval of it. If Reagan embraced the package in this situation, he would appear to be offering unilateral concessions to the Soviets.[124]

As the third round of INF negotiations opened in Geneva on September 29, 1982, Kvitsinsky announced the Soviets' rejection of the package. The Soviet leadership refused to endorse any INF agreement that excluded British and French nuclear forces, restricted Soviet INF deployments in Asia, or failed to reduce aircraft dramatically. Kvitsinsky later told Nitze that the Kremlin did not want to consent to any U.S. INF deployments for fear that this would undermine West European peace movements and stem the controversy surrounding the U.S. missiles. Soviet leaders were hoping that the INF issue would divide and weaken NATO.[125]

West European peace movements continued to flourish in the fall of 1982. Even celebrities campaigned against the Euromissiles through vehicles like Artists for Peace, an international group of musicians, actors, and writers who galvanized opposition to the nuclear arms race through art. On September 11, 1982, Artists for Peace staged a festival in Bochum in support of the Krefeld Appeal, which called on the West German government to rescind its support for U.S. INF deployments in Western Europe. Although more than two million people had already signed the Krefeld Appeal, festival performers like Udo Lindenberg, Marius Müller-Westernhagen, Fabrizio de Andre, and Harry Belafonte hoped that the event would expand the movement against U.S. deployments in the FRG. More than two hundred thousand people attended this disarmament festival.[126]

By the time of the Artists for Peace festival in Bochum, however, the West German government was in turmoil. Disagreements over U.S. INF deployments had strained the governing coalition between the Social Democratic Party (SPD) and the Free Democratic Party (FDP). Staunch supporters of both tracks of the NATO dual-track decision, the Free Democrats were troubled by the growing number of Social Democrats who opposed hosting U.S. Pershing II and cruise missiles.[127] Yet it was a clash over economic policy that finally brought down the coalition on September 17. The FDP then formed a coalition with the conservative Christian Democratic Union (CDU). In a constructive no-confidence vote on October 1, the Bundestag removed Helmut Schmidt from power and elected Christian Democratic leader Helmut Kohl as chancellor.[128] The new West German government pledged to hold elections on March 6, 1983.[129] After this dramatic turn of events, a Reagan administration spokesperson expressed "pleasure in seeing a Government that is more in tune with the Reagan philosophy" in the FRG. Yet American officials were also concerned that the SPD would increasingly embrace anti-nuclear policies now that it was in opposition.[130]

Meanwhile, the Dutch and Belgian governments continued to defer their decisions on accepting U.S. cruise missiles in the face of popular anti-nuclear sentiment. The Dutch opposed hosting U.S. cruise missiles by a 2-to-1 margin, while more than 150 Belgian towns were self-proclaimed nuclear-free zones by late 1982.[131]

As 1982 turned into 1983, some of Reagan's advisors worried that the zero option was making U.S. negotiators seem inflexible and fueling West European anti-nuclear sentiment. They feared that surging anti-nuclearism among West European publics would undermine West European governments' support for U.S. INF deployments. To curb West European anti-nuclear sentiment and forestall West European pressure for a flawed INF agreement that cemented Soviet superiority, some of Reagan's aides advocated a more flexible U.S. INF proposal.

Visits to Bonn and London in November 1982 spurred Nitze's call for a new INF proposal. He warned Deputy Secretary of State Kenneth Dam that West European publics, particularly the West Germans, viewed Soviet INF proposals as reasonable. Meanwhile, "public opinion in Europe, and most significantly, in Germany and the UK, no longer supports the zero/zero solution; what they want is a negotiated settlement that makes US deployments unnecessary." Conversations with West German and British officials convinced Nitze that they also "desperately" wanted movement in INF negotiations. With elections looming in both countries in 1983, these governments did not want INF deployments to dominate the upcoming campaigns. Nitze predicted that "if no agreement is reached by March, and we stick to the zero/zero option, it is unlikely that in Germany the CDU will continue to back deployment as scheduled. It is certain, however, that the SPD and the Greens will more and more violently oppose" U.S. missiles. To counter this anti-nuclear sentiment and gain West European support for Reagan's handling of INF, Nitze argued that the administration should pursue an alternative to the zero option when the fourth round of INF negotiations opened in early 1983.[132]

In a National Security Planning Group meeting on January 13, 1983, Shultz also raised the possibility of offering an interim INF proposal to shore up West European support for U.S. deployments. While maintaining the zero option as its ultimate goal, the Reagan administration should indicate its readiness to conclude an INF agreement that limited the Soviet Union and the United States to an equal number of INF missile warheads between zero and 572.[133] State Department officials believed that the Soviets were not going to accept the zero option, making U.S. INF deployments in 1983 essential. Yet they cautioned that "Allied governments cannot maintain the support of the political Center for deployments unless they can show that we are making every effort to reach an agreement. We are engaged in a battle for the heart and mind of Europe, and we cannot let the Soviets appear to be more reasonable than we." If the United States seemed obstinate in INF negotiations, West European publics and governments would be increasingly drawn to Soviet proposals for NATO to abandon its planned deployments in exchange for mere cuts in Soviet INF missiles. The allies would then push the United States to endorse these Soviet initiatives as well. In making the case for an interim INF proposal, State Department officials acknowledged that the Soviets were unlikely to accept it, given their opposition to any U.S. INF deployments in Western Europe. For the same reason, an interim INF proposal would not completely curb the West European peace movement. Yet it would show the majority of West Europeans that the Reagan administration was not "intransigent and unreasonable in insisting on the complete destruction of the Soviets' entire force." It would also compel the Soviets to "attack the principle of equality—and we can win that fight."[134]

Despite the dim prospects for an INF agreement in early 1983, Shultz wanted the administration to engage constructively with the Soviets and shift the superpower relationship "away from confrontation and toward real problem solving."[135] In a January 19, 1983, memo to Reagan, Shultz advocated a superpower dialogue covering arms control, regional issues, human rights, and bilateral relations, which the administration ultimately pursued as its four-part agenda for U.S.-Soviet relations.[136] President of the Bechtel Corporation when Reagan tapped him to replace Haig as secretary of state on June 25, 1982, Shultz had served as secretary of labor, OMB director, and secretary of the treasury in the Nixon administration.[137] Although Shultz did not have Haig's military or national security credentials, he believed that he was the only one of Reagan's top advisors who had experience negotiating successfully with the Soviets. As secretary of the treasury, Shultz had conducted trade negotiations with the Soviets and developed a good relationship with Nikolai Patolichev, the Soviet minister of trade.[138] In early 1983, however, Shultz and other State Department officials thought that U.S. INF deployments were the key to improving arms control prospects, because they would give the Soviets a tangible incentive to negotiate INF reductions.[139]

Although Reagan was deeply concerned about the growth of West European anti-nuclear activism in the winter of 1982–83, he did not approve an interim INF proposal in January. Rather, Weinberger and General Robert Barrow of the Joint Chiefs convinced Reagan that altering the U.S. INF proposal would actually help West European politicians who opposed U.S. deployments and upset West European peace activists. In the January 13 National Security Planning Group meeting, Weinberger told Reagan that the adoption of an interim INF proposal would be in line with the wishes of West German SPD leaders Hans-Jochen Vogel and Egon Bahr and so might help the SPD in the upcoming West German elections at the expense of the CDU/CSU. U.S. officials regarded the election of Kohl's CDU/CSU government as imperative because Kohl supported missile deployments if an INF agreement was not concluded by the end of 1983. Barrow echoed Weinberger's concern that an interim INF proposal might undermine Kohl's election, noting that West German minister of defense Manfred Wörner recently asked the administration not to alter its zero option proposal before the upcoming West German elections on March 6.[140]

Weinberger also argued that an interim INF proposal would intensify West European anti-nuclear activism. "If we abandon 0/0 now," he told Reagan at the National Security Planning Group meeting, "the peace movement would insist that we go back to it."[141] Defense Department officials argued that "European opponents of our deployment now have a stake in the negotiations, because the negotiations might eventually—if we stay the course— lead to the zero outcome. Abandon it and their interest in the negotiations will diminish sharply."[142] Although British officials privately called this claim "spurious," it appeared to carry weight with Reagan.[143] The president decided to maintain the zero option.[144]

Although the Reagan administration did not offer an interim proposal when a new round of INF negotiations began in late January 1983, it did declare its readiness to consider alternatives to the zero option. During a trip to Rome in early February, Vice President George Bush told Italian foreign minister Emilio Colombo that the "zero option remained the goal of the U.S.

government, but they were determined to explore in Geneva every opportunity of reaching agreement. The zero option was not a 'take it or leave it' proposal."[145] This became Bush's refrain as he traveled across Western Europe, and it "caught the public imagination," as Thatcher later noted.[146] At Thatcher's urging, Reagan expressed the same message in a speech to the Annual Washington Conference of the American Legion on February 22.[147]

By the spring of 1983, anti-nuclear sentiment was so widespread in Western Europe that it permeated music and books. In Britain, artists attacked the government's civil defense pamphlet *Protect and Survive*. For example, in the song "Protect and Survive" (1980), the band Jethro Tull sang of the futility of British civil defense measures, which it warned would not save Britons in a nuclear war.[148] This was also the message of Raymond Briggs's graphic novel *When the Wind Blows* (1982), which became so popular that it spawned a 1986 animated film of the same name with music by David Bowie, Genesis, and other famous British rockers.[149] Amid deteriorating superpower relations and an escalating nuclear arms race, the danger of nuclear war pervaded West German music during the early 1980s. The most famous example was Nena's "99 Luftballons" (1983), a song about ninety-nine balloons sparking a nuclear war when political leaders mistook them for nefarious objects. "99 Luftballons" was a global hit, and Nena recorded an English-language version, "99 Red Balloons," the following year.[150] Nuclear war and its aftermath also featured prominently in West German novels of the early 1980s, most notably Gudrun Pausewang's *Die letzten Kinder von Schewenborn* (*The Last Children of Schewenborn*) (1983). In depicting the bleak lives of nuclear war survivors in the fictional West German town of Schewenborn, Pausewang hoped to spur readers to pursue peace.[151]

Other West European artists advocated nuclear disarmament or peace in their work. This included the Dutch band bots, whose 1979 song "Das weiche Wasser" ("The Soft Water") became popular among peace activists in the 1980s. In 1982, the West German singer Nicole won the Eurovision Song Contest with "A Little Peace," which became a hit record across Western Europe. After her Eurovision victory, however, Nicole told the media that her song was about "personal peace," not the Cold War. She also said that she would not join in a peace demonstration, which she did not think could influence government policy. Despite these statements, Martin Klimke and Laura Stapane have argued that the widespread popularity of songs like "A Little Peace" highlighted the extent of West Europeans' concern about nuclear weapons in the early 1980s.[152]

Despite this prevalent nuclear anxiety, the economy was the pivotal issue in the West German elections on March 6, 1983. Heading to the polls while unemployment was at a historic high, voters believed that the Christian Democrats would improve the economy. Winning 48.8 percent of the popular vote, the CDU/CSU secured 244 of the 498 seats in the Bundestag. With the FDP winning 6.9 percent of the vote and 34 seats, the coalition between the Christian Democrats and Free Democrats would remain in power. Yet the Green Party, which maintained close ties with the West German peace movement, also had success in the 1983 election. The Green Party's advocacy of nuclear disarmament enabled it to win 5.6 percent of the popular vote, thereby crossing the 5 percent threshold for sending representatives to the Bundestag. Securing 27 seats in the Bundestag, the Greens claimed to have a popular "mandate" to block U.S. INF deployments. They vowed to work against the installation of U.S. missiles from their new Bundestag posts.[153]

By mid-March, the Reagan administration was facing significant West European pressure to set forth an interim INF proposal. The British, Dutch, Italian, and West German governments, all slated to host INF missiles, were urging the Reagan administration to modify its INF position. Many of the other NATO allies were doing the same.[154] For example, British and Italian officials told Bush in February that the Reagan administration should maintain the zero option as its ultimate goal but also work for an interim INF agreement that established equal ceilings on U.S. and Soviet INF.[155] As Thatcher explained to her advisors during their preparations for Bush's visit to London, "If the United States did not show signs of flexibility soon, Western public opinion could increasingly turn against them. . . . In the light of the discussions with Dr. Kohl, she would tell Mr. Bush that the credibility of the United States negotiating position could be put at risk, with serious effects on the cohesion of the Alliance, if the United States did not take a new initiative in the INF negotiations in the direction she had indicated."[156] An interim INF proposal would show that the Americans were negotiating in good faith. This would hopefully undercut the appeal of the Soviets' flawed INF proposals and shore up West European support for U.S. INF deployments at the end of the year.

On March 30, 1983, Reagan announced an interim INF proposal. Nitze told Kvitsinsky that the United States was "prepared to negotiate an interim agreement in which the United States would substantially reduce its planned deployment of Pershing II and ground-launched cruise missiles, provided the Soviet Union reduce the number of its warheads on longer range INF missiles to an equal level on a global basis." The zero option, however, remained Reagan's ultimate goal.[157]

In scheduling the announcement of this interim proposal, Reagan sought to maximize the initiative's impact on West European public opinion and undercut the West European peace movement. Reagan initially intended to unveil his new INF position on March 31, meaning that it would be reported in Europe on April 1, which was Good Friday. This troubled Thatcher, who recognized that the interim INF proposal would receive little media coverage in the United Kingdom because national newspapers did not print Good Friday editions. In a letter to Reagan asking him to move up his announcement by twenty-four hours so that it would hit the newspapers before Good Friday, Thatcher wrote, "We all have an interest in ensuring that your statement is given the widest possible publicity. This will also help to pre-empt some of the impact of Easter peace movement demonstrations both here and elsewhere."[158] Persuaded by Thatcher's reasoning, Reagan agreed to issue a statement on the interim INF proposal on March 30.[159] By showing that U.S. negotiators were flexible in their efforts to reach an INF agreement, this new proposal hopefully would curtail European anti-nuclear sentiment and maintain European governments' support for INF deployments.

The Conservatives' decisive victory in the UK elections on June 9, 1983, virtually ensured U.S. cruise missile deployment in Britain. Victory in the Falklands War had boosted the popularity of Thatcher and the Conservatives, which they translated into sweeping electoral success in 1983. Meanwhile, the Labour Party ran on a radical platform that one Labour member of Parliament famously deemed "the longest suicide note in History." It vowed to pursue unilateral nuclear disarmament, pull out of the European Community, and nationalize industry. Although there was significant opposition to U.S. cruise missile deployments among Britons, most did not want the government to renounce nuclear weapons unilaterally (or pursue Labour's other proposals, for that matter). In the 1983 election, Labour managed to capture just 27.6 percent of the vote, its worst showing in over 60 years.[160] James Hinton, a historian who was active in END and CND in the 1980s, later admitted that "after June 1983, with Mrs. Thatcher safely back in Downing Street, the deployment of cruise missiles was just a matter of time."[161] The Italian elections of June 26 and 27 also led to the formation of a government that supported the NATO dual-track decision. In his first speech as Italy's prime minister, Bettino Craxi pledged to accept U.S. cruise missiles at the end of the year if the INF negotiations did not produce an agreement.[162]

Despite the election results in the FRG, Britain, and Italy, West European peace activists did not abandon their efforts to stop U.S. INF deployments in 1983. They recognized that the U.S. Congress was another possible vehicle for blocking the Euromissiles. In an *END Journal* editorial, Kaldor reported that the U.S. Freeze Campaign was advocating a congressional resolution to delay U.S. INF deployments. This would give U.S. and Soviet negotiators additional time to reach an agreement before the installation of Pershing II and cruise missiles complicated their efforts. Kaldor called on activists to "publicize the resolution in Western Europe," presumably to win West European endorsements that could convince Congress to pass it.[163]

Yet the Freeze Campaign's efforts to delay U.S. INF deployments were too little, too late. Although the Freeze Campaign and European movements like END were in frequent contact during the early 1980s, they failed to pursue a joint program of action that might have enhanced their policy influence.[164] Instead, the Freeze Campaign and West European movements remained wedded to their specific goals. During a meeting of West European, American, and Canadian anti-nuclear movements in Paris on September 11, 1982, Kehler declared that "the Freeze Campaign could not at this point discuss seriously, much less commit ourselves to, any actions aimed at stopping the Cruise and Pershing missiles." In Kehler's view, a bilateral freeze on all nuclear weapons was a more sweeping step toward disarmament than halting the deployment of two missile systems. Believing that a major strength of the Freeze Campaign was its bilateral approach to ending the arms race, Kehler also did not want to issue a unilateral call for the United States to forego its INF deployments. For their part, the European activists at this meeting expressed support for the Freeze Campaign, but most refused to make the freeze one of their main aims.[165] European activists thought that the freeze proposal was too conservative because it would not eliminate any nuclear weapons that had already been deployed. E. P. Thompson explained, "Here in Europe we have to get *rid* of weapons. To campaign in Europe for a freeze would be a step back from the campaign for a nuclear-free Europe, and also from the unilateralist demand for disarmament by direct initiatives by our own nations."[166]

In early 1983, however, it appeared that the Freeze Campaign would prioritize the Euromissile issue. Freeze activists became concerned that the impending U.S. INF deployments would make a bilateral freeze harder to achieve, as the Soviets would likely respond to U.S. missiles with their own counterdeployments. Freeze activists also feared that U.S. and Soviet INF would move Europe closer to the brink of nuclear war. On February 6, 1983, the Freeze Campaign's Third National Conference called for an agreement canceling U.S. INF deployments and reducing Soviet INF. If this proved impossible before the end of 1983, the Freeze Campaign wanted Soviet INF reductions and a one-year delay in U.S. INF deployments so that negotiators could continue working for an INF treaty.[167]

In practice, however, the Freeze Campaign did not devote much attention to the INF issue until the fall of 1983, just before U.S. deployments were slated to begin. Rather, the Freeze Campaign's leaders and congressional allies prioritized a nonbinding, comprehensive freeze resolution, which the U.S. House of Representatives passed on May 4, 1983. Even after the House endorsed the freeze resolution, Freeze Campaign leaders worried about the unilateralism of working for a one-year delay in U.S. INF deployments. Pam Solo, the chair of the Freeze Strategy Committee, later reflected that this "obsession with bilateralism" prevented the Freeze Campaign from really taking aim at U.S. INF deployments in the summer of 1983, just when it was most critical to do so.[168] Although several Democratic House members introduced amendments and resolutions to delay U.S. INF deployments in the summer and fall, they were unsuccessful.[169]

Parliaments in Britain, Italy, and West Germany, however, were scheduled to vote on accepting U.S. INF missiles in late October and November. This provided activists with another chance to stop the U.S. deployments, although it was a long shot that they would succeed. Just before these votes, massive anti-nuclear demonstrations took place across Western Europe. On October 22, four hundred thousand protested in London, while a demonstration in Rome drew between half a million and one million participants. More than a million turned out for protests across the FRG, with four hundred thousand gathering in Bonn. West Germans also formed a human chain that stretched the seventy miles between U.S. military installations in Stuttgart and Neu Ulm. In the largest demonstration in Belgian history, three hundred thousand rallied in Brussels on October 23. In a similar feat in Norway, twenty thousand marched through the streets of Oslo the next day. On October 29, half a million Dutch took part in anti-nuclear demonstrations.[170]

With pro-missile governments in Britain, Italy, and the FRG, these demonstrations were not enough to convince parliamentarians to reject U.S. missiles. In a Halloween vote that drew CND protesters dressed like witches, the UK House of Commons decided 362 to 218 to endorse cruise missile deployment.[171] On November 16, Italy's Chamber of Deputies voted 351 to 219 in support of hosting cruise missiles in Sicily.[172] Six days later, the West

German Bundestag agreed to deploy Pershing II and cruise missiles. The 286-to-226 vote broke down largely along party lines, with Christian Democrats and Free Democrats supporting the Euromissile installation and Social Democrats and Greens opposing it.[173] Although Reagan's interim proposal did not eliminate West European activism against the Euromissiles, it helped maintain West European governments' support for deployments.

*   *   *

While a surge in West European peace activism led to a more flexible U.S. INF proposal, the nuclear freeze movement's growing influence in Congress prompted the Reagan administration to alter its START proposal throughout 1983 to try to accommodate Soviet concerns. Reagan hoped that these changes would yield a quick START agreement that would vindicate his disarmament strategy and quash support for the freeze. Reagan's advisors, however, backed the modifications in order to secure congressional support for the MX.

After the House voted to eliminate MX production funds on December 7, 1982, the Reagan administration established a commission of outside experts to study the MX basing mode, the overall strategic modernization program, and U.S. strategic arms control policy. Brent Scowcroft, who had been Ford's national security advisor, chaired this bipartisan panel. In its April 1983 report, the Scowcroft Commission recommended a long-term shift from producing large ICBMs with multiple warheads to small, single-warhead ICBMs, which it deemed more survivable and stable. In the meantime, however, the commission advised deploying 100 MX missiles in current Minuteman ICBM silos to improve deterrence and incentivize the Soviets to conclude an arms control agreement.[174]

The Scowcroft Commission also urged Reagan to use arms control to facilitate the transition to an ICBM force of small, single-warhead missiles. Arms reduction proposals should be framed "not in terms of launchers, but in terms of equal levels of warheads of roughly equivalent yield." If launchers or missiles were the unit of account in arms reduction proposals, there was "an incentive to build launchers and missiles as large as possible and to put as many warheads as possible into each missile."[175]

As the anti-nuclear movement lobbied Congress to defund the MX permanently, several influential House and Senate members declared that their support for the MX depended on the Reagan administration modifying its START proposal. These members of Congress wanted Reagan to align his START position with the Scowcroft Commission's recommendations and pursue new arms reduction initiatives.[176] Senators Charles Percy (R-IL), Sam Nunn (D-GA), and William Cohen (R-ME) urged the president to establish a bipartisan arms control advisory commission and pitch the idea of a "build-down" to the Soviets. Under the "build-down" proposal, the superpowers would eliminate two nuclear warheads for every new nuclear warhead deployed.[177]

While the congressional debate over the MX raged, the Freeze Campaign worked for House passage of a nuclear freeze resolution. Activists recognized in January 1983 that a House vote on the freeze "will be the next major political test" for the freeze movement, and the Freeze Campaign's Third National Conference prioritized congressional approval of a freeze resolution in 1983.[178] Freeze movement leaders encouraged freeze supporters to press their House members to cosponsor the freeze resolution, oppose any amendments or substitutes designed to dilute the freeze, and urge their colleagues on the House Foreign Affairs Committee to back the freeze.[179] The Freeze Campaign also staged a Citizens Freeze Lobby in Washington, DC, on March 7 and 8 to meet with House members and personally encourage them to support the freeze resolution. Letters, petitions, and lobby proxies from freeze supporters who could not travel to Washington were delivered to House members by freeze activists who did attend the Citizens Freeze Lobby.[180] Five thousand freeze supporters from forty-three states met with members of Congress and rallied during this event.[181] Reuben McCornack, the Freeze Campaign's congressional liaison, spearheaded the lobbying efforts in Washington, DC, and sent information to local and state freeze organizations on promoting congressional support for the freeze.[182]

Anti-nuclear organizations that had lobbied House members to pass the freeze resolution in the summer of 1982 joined the Freeze Campaign's efforts in early 1983. The Council for a Livable World, Physicians for Social Responsibility, SANE, and UCS lobbied representatives to back the freeze, as did members of the newly formed Citizens Against Nuclear War. Established by the National Education Association in October 1982, Citizens Against Nuclear War was a coalition of national labor unions, professional organizations, religious groups, and women's organizations that sought an end to the nuclear arms race and the prevention of nuclear war. Protestant denominations like the American Baptist Churches–USA, the Episcopal Church, and the Presbyterian Church in the United States also organized letter-writing campaigns to members of Congress in early 1983 to urge them to support the freeze resolution.[183]

Anti-nuclear activists' lobbying efforts were rewarded when the House passed a nuclear freeze resolution by a vote of 278 to 149 on May 4.[184] Yet the resolution was diluted by 33 amendments that ranged from exempting submarines from the freeze to implying that the freeze could be abandoned if nuclear arms reduction did not follow "within a reasonable, specified period of time."[185] Nevertheless, Kehler viewed the passage of the House freeze resolution as a victory for the freeze movement. "I think you can look at those amendments today and see that the freeze was basically intact," Kehler later reflected.[186] McCornack agreed, declaring after the House vote that "the nut of the freeze was preserved." Even with the amendments, the resolution maintained the basic principle that the superpowers should freeze before negotiating nuclear arms reduction agreements.[187] By setting forth an alternative approach to arms control, the freeze resolution expressed dissatisfaction with the Reagan administration's arms control policies. Some House members supported it for this very reason.[188]

As the freeze movement stoked congressional discontent with Reagan's pursuit of arms control, the administration reassessed its START position. In early May, Reagan sent letters to members of Congress vowing to shift U.S. arms reduction policy into line with the recommendations made by the Scowcroft Commission and Congress. In response to these presidential promises, the House Appropriations Subcommittee on defense and the Senate Appropriations Committee voted to release research and development funds for the MX.[189]

So began the horse-trading between the Reagan administration and Congress that resulted in a host of modifications to the U.S. START proposal in exchange for a series of congressional votes in support of the MX, culminating in congressional appropriation of MX production funds in November 1983.[190] As the fourth START negotiating round began on June 8, Reagan announced that the new U.S. position included a "relax[ation] [of] our current proposal for an 850 deployed ballistic missile limit." This was a response to the Scowcroft Commission's recommendation that Reagan avoid making launchers the unit of account in arms reduction proposals in order to foster the transition to small, single-warhead ICBMs. Reagan also noted that "high priority work is continuing on how the mutual and guaranteed build-down concept proposed by several United States Senators can be applied in our quest for significant and stabilizing strategic arms reduction."[191] During the fourth round of negotiations, the United States collapsed the two negotiating phases so that the strategic nuclear weapons of concern to both sides were on the table; agreed to air-launched cruise missile restrictions below SALT II levels; and showed flexibility on throw-weight reductions. On October 4, the day before the start of the fifth negotiating round, Reagan announced that U.S. negotiators would propose a build-down on ballistic missile warheads and bombers and would be willing to limit air-launched cruise missiles further if the Soviets showed flexibility on U.S. concerns. Reagan emphasized that the two sides needed to engage in "tradeoffs" and indicated that the United States would agree to reductions in its areas of advantage if the Soviet Union did the same.[192]

Although many of Reagan's advisors hoped that a modified START proposal would secure congressional support for the MX, Reagan and Clark thought that it might actually result in some type of strategic arms reduction agreement. Reagan sincerely wanted to reach a START agreement in 1983. In fact, in the initial draft of his July 11 letter to Soviet general secretary Yuri Andropov, Reagan asked, "If we can agree on mutual, verifiable reductions in the number of nuclear weapons we both hold, could this not be a first step toward elimination of all such weapons?"[193] Clark believed that the changes to the U.S. START position might make possible "either a Vladivostok type agreement on the way to a full START Treaty and/or the implementation of some build-down provisions in the context of such an agreement."[194] After announcing modifications to the U.S. START proposal on October 4, Reagan declared, "The door to an agreement is open. All the world is waiting for the Soviet Union to walk through."[195]

It is unsurprising that Reagan hoped for a START agreement in the fall of 1983, as the freeze movement continued to mobilize and events reinforced his desire to avoid nuclear war. In a September 1983 public diplomacy plan, his advisors contended that "the freeze movement does not appear to be gaining momentum, and is attracting far less media attention than a year ago." Yet they also noted that freeze activists would keep lobbying Congress to eliminate funding for strategic modernization and INF deployments, which were vital incentives for the Soviets to negotiate nuclear arms reduction. "Public opinion polls continue to show that a substantial majority of Americans (70–30) favor a nuclear freeze, but much of the support for a freeze is 'soft,' and represents, in part, a desire for continuing arms control efforts on the part of the Administration."[196] Surely some type of START agreement would curb support for the freeze, which Reagan viewed as a dangerous threat to his own disarmament strategy.

By the fall of 1983, anti-nuclear films were hitting the American market, and activists sought to capitalize on this phenomenon to increase support for the freeze. *The Day After*, the most famous nuclear film of the decade, aired on ABC on November 20, 1983. A few months before ABC broadcast *The Day After*, the feature films *WarGames* and *Octopussy* raised the specter of a nuclear war triggered by a computer hacker or a rogue general, respectively. In both of these films, however, nuclear conflict was ultimately averted. By contrast, *The Day After* depicted a Soviet nuclear attack on Lawrence, Kansas, and its ghastly aftermath. By showing that nuclear war would bring mass death and environmental destruction, director Nicholas Meyer hoped to spur initiatives to prevent nuclear war.[197]

Freeze activists sought to use *The Day After*, which nearly 100 million Americans watched, to strengthen their movement.[198] Recognizing that the film would raise awareness of the danger of nuclear war and its disastrous effects, the Freeze Campaign and SANE devised a strategy for channeling nuclear anxiety into support for the freeze, a concrete proposal that could help avert nuclear war. They encouraged members of local freeze and SANE organizations to host viewing parties of *The Day After* and set up informational tables at shopping centers during the three days after the film aired.[199] The Freeze Campaign and SANE also urged activists to appear on local media to promote the freeze after the film and provided a guide for engaging the media. As activists noted, *The Day After* afforded the freeze movement with a "unique opportunity to reach out to millions of people who otherwise would not be open to the concept of a nuclear weapons freeze," typically because they did not like contemplating nuclear issues.[200]

Like the freeze movement, the Reagan administration was determined to translate concerns raised by *The Day After* into support for its strategy of preventing a nuclear war through deterrence, nuclear arms reduction, and strategic defense. Reagan noted in his diary two days before *The Day After* aired, "We know it's 'anti-nuke' propaganda but we're going to take it over & say it shows why we must keep on doing what we're doing."[201] In editorials for the *New York Times*, the *Washington Post*, and *USA Today*, Bush, Weinberger, and Kenneth Adelman, who had succeeded Rostow as ACDA director in April 1983, touted the administration's strategy for averting a nuclear war. Weinberger and Adelman also highlighted Reagan's belief that "a nuclear war can never be won and must never be fought," which the president had reaffirmed in a speech to the Japanese Diet on November 11, 1983.[202] In the days preceding ABC's broadcast of *The Day After*, administration officials also appeared on national television news programs and radio stations in twenty-seven major media markets across the country. Most notably, Shultz participated in a panel discussion on nuclear issues that ABC aired immediately after *The Day After*. Hosted by Ted Koppel, this ABC *Viewpoint* special also featured former government officials Robert McNamara, Henry Kissinger, and Brent Scowcroft, as well as William F. Buckley Jr., a conservative commentator; Elie Wiesel, a writer who had survived the Holocaust; and Carl Sagan, a scientist who warned about "nuclear winter."[203] Shultz was eager to ensure that *The Day After* did not boost the efforts of those seeking to derail U.S. INF deployments in Western Europe, which were slated to begin three days after the film aired. On *Viewpoint*, he emphasized Reagan's commitment to dramatic nuclear arms reduction and his abhorrence of nuclear war.[204]

Events in the fall of 1983 also prompted Reagan to think deeply about the consequences of nuclear war and reinforced his determination to pursue nuclear arms reduction and strategic defenses to prevent nuclear disaster. On September 1, a Soviet air commander shot down Korean Airlines Flight (KAL) 007, believing it to be an American reconnaissance plane after it strayed into restricted Soviet airspace. The downing of this commercial airliner killed all 269 people aboard, including U.S. congressman Larry McDonald. Reagan condemned the KAL 007 incident as a "terrorist act" and criticized the Soviets' unwillingness to provide a forthright account of what happened.[205] Yet he also believed that "the KAL incident demonstrated how close the world had come to the precipice and how much we needed nuclear arms control: If, as some people speculated, the Soviet pilots simply mistook the airliner for a military plane, what kind of imagination did it take to think of a Soviet military man with his finger close to a nuclear push button making an even more tragic mistake?" In Reagan's view, the prospect of "a Soviet military man" mistakenly initiating a nuclear attack also highlighted the importance of SDI, which could defend against nuclear missile strikes.[206]

Reagan's own viewing of *The Day After*, which he screened at Camp David on October 10, also bolstered his determination to avert a nuclear war. Reagan was deeply affected by the film, which he described in his diary as "powerfully done—all $7 mil. worth. It's very effective & left me greatly depressed." He noted, "My own reaction was one of our having to do all we can to have a deterrent & to see there is never a nuclear war."[207] Lou Cannon has demonstrated that the former actor Reagan relished watching films, which often influenced him more than memoranda or briefing books.[208] In fact, Reagan's thoughts returned to *The Day After* during a November 18 briefing from Weinberger and Vessey on U.S. plans for responding to a nuclear attack. Describing the briefing as "a most sobering experience," Reagan later wrote, "In several ways, the sequence of events described in the briefings paralleled those in the ABC movie. Yet there were still some people at the Pentagon who claimed a nuclear war was 'winnable.' I thought they were crazy." Reagan felt more strongly than ever that arms reduction agreements and strategic defenses were essential for averting the horror of nuclear war, which *The Day After* so vividly illustrates.[209]

NATO's Able Archer 83 exercise heightened Reagan's desire to prevent a nuclear conflict. Recent scholarship has persuasively challenged the conventional view that Able Archer 83 sparked a Soviet war scare in November 1983.[210] The concluding exercise of Autumn Forge 83, Able Archer 83 took place from November 7 to 11, and it focused on the shift from conventional to nuclear warfare. While the Soviets did not view Able Archer 83 as a cover for a U.S. nuclear strike, they did engage in "counter-mobilizing and -signaling." As Simon Miles has argued, this was standard behavior during the rival alliance's military exercises. When Reagan learned of these Soviet actions, however, he became concerned and even more determined to avert nuclear war.[211] In his November 18 diary entry, Reagan noted, "I feel the Soviets are so defense minded, so paranoid about being attacked that without being in any way soft on them we ought to tell them no one here has any intention of doing anything like that."[212]

Yet Reagan's hope that a modified U.S. START proposal would facilitate a strategic arms reduction agreement was not realized in 1983. By the end of the year, Reagan's disarmament strategy was failing. In response to the beginning of U.S. INF deployments, the Soviets walked out of the INF talks on November 23. A couple of weeks later, as the fifth START round concluded, the Soviets refused to set a date for resuming negotiations. As the INF and START talks collapsed, Reagan vowed to push for the reopening of negotiations leading to meaningful nuclear arms reduction agreements.[213]

At the end of 1983, grassroots anti-nuclear activists and Reagan were facing serious challenges in their pursuit of disarmament. The installation of U.S. Pershing II and cruise missiles in Britain, Italy, and the FRG was a major defeat for West European peace movements, which had devoted significant effort to blocking these deployments. American nuclear freeze activists were similarly powerless to stop the Euromissiles. Meanwhile, the U.S. Senate rejected the freeze resolution in October, and Congress appropriated funding for the MX in November. Rather than incentivize the Soviets to negotiate nuclear arms reduction, Reagan's INF deployments led to the breakdown of the INF and START talks. Reagan and U.S. and West European activists would respond differently in the wake of these setbacks, and their visions for ending the Cold War would diverge in 1984 and 1985.

CHAPTER 4

"We Have to Take Our Campaign into a New Phase"

On February 27, 1984, U.S. Secretary of Defense Caspar Weinberger and END cofounder E. P. Thompson squared off in a debate at the Oxford Union. At issue was the motion "There is no moral difference between the foreign policies of the U.S. and the U.S.S.R." Thompson spoke in favor of the motion, and Weinberger opposed it. The debate attracted significant media attention, with the BBC airing it live in Britain and PBS showing it several months later in the United States. Originally scheduled to take place in May 1983, the debate had been postponed after British defense secretary Michael Heseltine convinced Weinberger not to take part in such a high-profile event before the UK elections. Heseltine's move was controversial, likely heightening interest in the debate when it finally occurred in February 1984.[1]

In making their cases before the Oxford Union, Thompson and Weinberger provided glimpses of the policies that END and the Reagan administration would adopt after the setbacks of late 1983. Thompson pointed out that both the Americans and the Soviets built up their offensive arsenals and maintained a military presence far from their borders. He advocated European autonomy from the superpowers, arguing that Europeans "need to play the part of making a space between the two superpowers, a more tranquil space."[2] In 1984, END would broaden its focus to include European autonomy alongside nuclear disarmament.

In defending the morality of U.S. foreign policy at Oxford, Weinberger stressed that it could be changed by Congress or the American electorate. By contrast, just a handful of powerful men devised Soviet policies. Any Soviet citizen who questioned government policies faced serious punishment. Weinberger also noted that the Reagan administration sought to transition away from offensive nuclear deterrence. Reagan hoped to develop strategic defenses that could "remove the shadow of these terrible [nuclear] weapons from the earth." Weinberger's statements won over a majority of the audience members, who voted for his position 271 to 232.[3] His words also highlighted Reagan's continued commitment to SDI and negotiating arms reduction from a position of strength, which only intensified after Reagan's landslide victory in the 1984 presidential election.

This chapter contends that West European peace activists, U.S. nuclear freeze supporters, and Reagan responded to the challenges of 1983 in different ways, and their visions of how to end the Cold War diverged in 1984 and 1985. Concerns about the viability of their movement after their failure to halt U.S. INF deployments, coupled with increased contact with East European activists, led many West Europeans to broaden their focus beyond European nuclear disarmament in 1984. East European dissidents helped West European activists become more aware of the interconnections among nuclear disarmament, the dissolution of the blocs in Europe, European autonomy, and human rights. West European activists increasingly sought to end the Cold War through the denuclearization and reunification of an autonomous and free Europe.

By contrast, U.S. nuclear freeze activists narrowed their focus. They urged Congress to defund elements of the U.S. nuclear program, thereby enacting the freeze in stages. After Gorbachev announced a unilateral moratorium on nuclear tests in July 1985, U.S. activists worked for a permanent ban on U.S. and Soviet nuclear testing. Although Reagan administration officials continued to monitor the freeze movement's activities in 1985, freeze activists did not influence U.S. nuclear policy during Reagan's second term.

Reagan continued to believe that negotiating from a position of strength and pursuing SDI would yield sweeping nuclear disarmament.[4] After the collapse of the INF and START talks, Reagan's nuclear abolitionism led him to pursue the resumption of U.S.-Soviet arms reduction negotiations in 1984. Once the Soviets agreed to reopen talks, Reagan worked with Shultz to enshrine nuclear abolition as the official long-term U.S. goal in National Security Decision Directive (NSDD) 153 in January 1985. When Gorbachev came to power on March 11, 1985, Reagan finally had a partner in the Kremlin with whom he could work for a nuclear-free world.

Gorbachev and Reagan sought to end the Cold War by achieving sweeping nuclear arms reduction agreements that would spur the elimination of nuclear weapons. They believed that their personal diplomacy with one another could pave the way for global nuclear abolition and thus placed a high value on their correspondence and summit meetings. Yet their disagreements over SDI frustrated their first attempt to reach a dramatic arms reduction agreement at the November 1985 Geneva summit.

∗   ∗   ∗

West European peace activists mourned the arrival of U.S. INF missiles in Britain, the FRG, and Italy in November 1983. After U.S. cruise missiles landed at Greenham Common on November 14 and 15, there was crying and wailing among the women who had been living in a peace camp at the site since 1981. Some of the women chained themselves to a gate and fence at one of the entrances to the base, while others obstructed access to a road leading to Greenham Common. Nearly two hundred miles away, fifty demonstrators took part in a "die-in" on a Manchester street during Heseltine's visit on November 15. Other British anti-nuclear activists reacted to the missiles' arrival with anger. Demonstrators sprayed Heseltine with red paint at Manchester University, while onlookers shouted "better red than dead, Michael." In their view, communism would be preferable to a fiery demise in a nuclear war. After Heseltine cleaned the paint from his face, protesters physically blocked him from entering the room where he was scheduled to address Conservative students. Once Heseltine finally took the stage with the help of police, demonstrators launched two eggs at him while audience members yelled "jobs not bombs!"[5]

Funereal protests marked the arrival of U.S. missiles in the FRG. On November 26, West German demonstrators descended on the picturesque town of Schwäbisch Gmünd, advancing toward the headquarters of the U.S. 56th Artillery Brigade, which would control a share of the Pershing IIs slated for deployment in the FRG. The activists then marched five miles to the U.S. military base at Mutlangen, where Pershing II components had arrived in the early hours of the morning. At Mutlangen, nearly six hundred protesters blockaded the entrance to the base, where they had ceremoniously placed a coffin.[6] While British and West German protesters were mourning their governments' decision to risk the survival of humanity by escalating the nuclear arms race, they just as easily could have been lamenting the challenges that the missile deployments posed to the survival of their own movements.

In the wake of its defeat on the INF issue, END debated its future direction. This debate revolved around two central questions. The first was whether

END should focus only on nuclear disarmament or address broader issues. The second was whether END should concentrate on promoting European autonomy or adopt a more global program that would also benefit Third World countries and the superpowers.[7] The two main camps in this debate were represented by two of END's founders, Mary Kaldor and E. P. Thompson, who faced off during an intense meeting on March 17, 1984.

In an editorial in the December 1983–January 1984 issue of the *END Journal*, Kaldor promoted the "freeze and withdraw" proposal, which reflected her view that END should continue to prioritize nuclear disarmament and pursue a program that benefited not only Europe, but also Third World countries and the superpowers. This proposal "combine[d] the demand for a freeze on the development and production of nuclear weapons with the demand for the withdrawal of all nuclear weapons on foreign territory." The plan had a global scope, meaning that all nuclear-weapon states would be required to abide by the freeze provisions and no country in the world would be allowed to host foreign nuclear weapons. Kaldor hoped that this integration of U.S. and West European goals would alleviate the concerns that freeze activists and END supporters had about each other's aims and facilitate future cooperation. "By taking on the freeze explicitly in our European campaign, we can further demonstrate our desire to avoid anti-Americanism. By including the demand for withdrawal, we retain the integrity of our demand for nuclear-free Europe and we get over the absurdity of demanding a freeze on deployment *after* cruise has been deployed," Kaldor explained. Contending that "we have to take our campaign into a new phase," Kaldor believed that END should focus on advocating the "freeze and withdraw" proposal moving forward.[8]

At the March 17 meeting, Kaldor defended her view that nuclear disarmament should remain END's primary focus. She contended that over the last four years, END had formed a massive coalition of supporters who all wanted nuclear disarmament but were not all seeking European autonomy from the superpowers. If END began concentrating on European autonomy, some supporters would be alienated and the movement would wane. Kaldor also argued that END should work for general demilitarization and disarmament in Europe rather than European autonomy in order to forestall the possibility that individual European countries or Europe as a whole tried to become a third superpower. "It's not clear to me whether it would be better to have British and Dutch and other forces in Germany, say, than American forces. If it were at the same level it could be worse."[9]

Although Kaldor argued that END should pursue nuclear disarmament as its main goal, she acknowledged that nuclear arms reduction would give countries across the globe, including the superpowers, more autonomy. Freed from the threat of nuclear blackmail and unencumbered by the ties of alliance nuclear strategy, states would be able to pursue "more independent and more diverse policies." In other words, a consequence of nuclear disarmament was greater autonomy—not just for Europe, but also for the United States, the Soviet Union, and the Third World. Yet Kaldor thought that END's stated aim should remain nuclear disarmament. In her view, framing END's message around European autonomy would obscure the organization's actual goal of ending the Cold War. "We [should] make the point that we emphasize the European situation because it's Europe that provided the base for cold war ideology, but it's not because we want Europe as such to be independent, it's because we want to get rid of the Cold War."[10] In Kaldor's view, a post–Cold War world was one in which nuclear weapons were being eliminated and no country was subject to another's influence. Since nuclear disarmament was a prerequisite for greater autonomy for all nations, however, it should be END's priority.

Thompson, by contrast, was fed up with END's "exclusive obsession with nukes." While he still strongly supported the denuclearization of Europe, Thompson thought that END needed to embrace explicitly the larger political rationale for removing nuclear weapons from Europe, namely that it would help eliminate the division of Europe and give Europe greater autonomy from the superpowers. Unlike Kaldor, he believed that individuals protesting the Euromissiles were demanding not only the rejection of cruise and Pershing II deployments, but also greater independence for European countries and an end to the bloc system. Activists resented the deployment of American missiles on European soil and believed that the United States had bullied its NATO allies into accepting the deployments through the 1979 dual-track decision. Thompson noted that other West European anti-nuclear organizations were grappling with these larger aims of overturning the bloc system in Europe and promoting European autonomy from the superpowers, as were East European movements like Charter 77. Even individuals on the left and right of the American political spectrum were questioning the U.S. military presence in Western Europe. Thompson viewed END's explicit advocacy of these larger political goals as "an idea whose time has come."[11]

In Thompson's view, Kaldor's "freeze and withdraw" proposal was "concealing a *political* case beneath the forms of an arms control (or nuclear disarmament) proposal." Rather than promote the "freeze and withdraw" concept, END should respond to the INF deployments with a new appeal on the scale of the one that launched the organization in 1980. Thompson wrote that it should begin by acknowledging, "Well, we lost that one. The missiles are here. On both sides. Now we must stop tinkering with armaments proposals and go directly at the underlying political conditions." The new appeal should demand "the withdrawal not only of nukes but of all US and USSR troops and bases from Europe East and West." Nuclear-free zones should be established and conventional forces should be reduced across the continent. European governments should permit increased communication between citizens in the two blocs, and the superpowers should allow European governments to loosen their connections to the blocs. Ordinary Europeans should be encouraged to "strain every effort to break through the blocs, begin to act as if they do not exist, and re-assert the autonomy of the continent against the superpower domination."[12] According to Thompson, an appeal for an autonomous and reunified Europe would be an appeal for "breaking down the cold war."[13]

Recognizing the challenges that INF deployments posed to the viability of the anti-nuclear movement, END's leadership accepted Thompson's offer to draft a new appeal calling for the dissolution of the blocs in Europe and European autonomy from the superpowers.[14] Thompson began writing a draft appeal that could be debated at the April 1984 meeting of the IPCC.[15]

Thompson's correspondence with East European activists, particularly the Czech dissident Jaroslav Šabata, significantly shaped the substance of his appeal. A psychology professor and reform-minded Communist Party official, Šabata was expelled from the Party and fired from his university post for condemning the 1968 Soviet-led invasion of Czechoslovakia. He spent much of the 1970s in prison, serving five years for distributing leaflets encouraging Czechoslovaks not to vote in corrupt elections in 1971 and two years after trying to meet Polish Workers' Defense Committee activists in 1978. Šabata was one of the first individuals to sign the "Declaration of Charter 77," which launched the Charter 77 movement in Prague.[16]

On New Year's Day in 1977, 240 writers, intellectuals, and oppositionists began the Charter 77 movement to advance respect for human rights in Czechoslovakia and across the globe. Although the Czechoslovak government had signed the International Covenant on Civil and Political Rights, the International Covenant on Economic, Social and Cultural Rights, and the Helsinki Final Act, the Charter 77 founders lamented "the extent to which basic human rights in our country exist, regrettably, on paper alone." They hoped to foster Czechoslovak compliance with these agreements by talking with government officials about human rights, highlighting human rights violations, and proposing measures to protect human rights in Czechoslovakia. A rotating group of spokespersons represented Charter 77 in public and signed documents issued by the movement. In April 1978, Šabata was named a Charter 77 spokesperson.[17]

In an April 1983 letter to Thompson, Šabata called on West European anti-nuclear organizations to join with East European civil rights activists to devise "a joint strategy for transforming Europe into a single entity" and "a strategy for the democratic transformation of Europe." He forcefully criticized the West European peace movement's tendency to prioritize nuclear disarmament over civil rights issues, which West Europeans justified on the grounds that "the right to life," which nuclear war would extinguish, trumped all other rights. Šabata, however, passionately argued that "the right to life implies a life of dignity" and that the struggle for civil rights could not be discounted. He also contended that the key to reunifying Europe, a goal that he knew that Thompson shared, was the extension of civil rights and democracy in Eastern Europe, not nuclear disarmament. Only if East Europeans were free and democratic would they be able to engage in a genuine dialogue with West Europeans that could possibly eliminate the blocs in Europe.[18]

In advocating a new appeal for a reunified, autonomous Europe, Thompson highlighted Šabata's April 1983 letter. Both he and Jerry Turner, an active member of END's Czech Task Group, called it "one of the most important documents that we've had before us in the past year" and urged a serious consideration of Šabata's ideas within END.[19] Thompson's appeal, "European Declaration of Peace," showed that he had embraced many of Šabata's views. In this appeal, Thompson condemned the division of Europe fueled by the "artificial state of superpower domination" and called on East and West Europeans to join together to "search for ways of bringing to an end the abnormal state of the 'Cold War' itself."[20] While Thompson's 1980 END Appeal briefly mentioned the dissolution of the blocs in Europe as a long-term aim, its focus was squarely on the denuclearization of Europe.[21] In the 1984 "European Declaration of Peace," however, Thompson's emphasis had shifted to European reunification and autonomy. In a paragraph that could just as easily have been written by Šabata, Thompson expressed support for all disarmament initiatives, but he warned, "These are not ends in themselves. They must serve as steps towards bringing the division of Europe and the confrontation of the blocs to an end."[22] Thompson also touted the benefits that the reunification of Europe would have for the rest of the world, as Šabata had in his April 1983 letter. The dissolution of the blocs would free up resources for economic development in the Third World, as well as in Europe, the Soviet Union, and the United States.[23]

Šabata's letter to Thompson was just one example of the growing contacts between END supporters and the small independent peace and human rights groups in the Eastern bloc. END established working groups on Hungary, the Soviet Union, Poland, the German Democratic Republic (GDR), and Czechoslovakia in late 1982 and 1983.[24] In addition to monitoring, analyzing, and publicizing developments in these countries, the working groups also cultivated relationships with independent activists living in these states.[25] These interactions had an important influence on END's agenda. Through correspondence and meetings, East European activists helped West Europeans become more aware of the interconnections among nuclear disarmament, the reunification of Europe, European autonomy, and human rights.

Czechoslovaks were initially unreceptive to END's efforts to establish ties. In June 1980, Thompson told END's steering committee that his wife, the historian Dorothy Thompson, had a "rather unencouraging meeting with Czech historians, who were very isolated and in no strong way drawn to our [END] appeal."[26] Two Czech exiles living in Britain, Jan Kavan and Zdena Tomin, explained Czechoslovaks' initial reluctance to partner with West European anti-nuclear activists. They noted that ordinary East Europeans generally had less access to information on the nuclear arms race than West Europeans and often believed that Western nuclear weapons acted as a check on Soviet aggression. For many East Europeans, the daily violations of their human rights by the government eclipsed the danger posed by nuclear weapons.[27]

When Charter 77 expressed support for the West European peace movement on November 15, 1981, however, new possibilities emerged for END to develop contacts in Czechoslovakia. Charter 77's "Statement on West European Peace Movements," a copy of which was sent to END, marked the beginning of a dialogue with Czechoslovak human rights activists that eventually helped END supporters appreciate the interconnections among nuclear disarmament, human rights, the elimination of the blocs, and European autonomy.[28] In this statement, Charter 77 spokespersons Bedřich Placák, Václav Malý, and Jiří Hájek contended that the Helsinki Final Act recognized respect for human rights as essential for extending détente in Europe. Governments that refused to respect their citizens' human rights were therefore unserious about pursuing East-West détente. "One can hardly believe in the sincerity of peace efforts where people are persecuted for demanding that the undertakings of détente policy in the area of human rights and basic freedoms should be carried out," they wrote. In addition, political leaders who escalated the nuclear arms race threatened human rights by endangering individuals' right to life. "On the other hand, one cannot regard as defenders of these rights and freedoms those who are stepping up the arms race and bringing closer the danger of war, particularly in Europe ... the civilisation from which sprang the concept of human rights in which the right to life is given pride of place."[29]

In their ensuing correspondence with West European peace activists, Charter 77 repeatedly stressed the indivisibility of peace and human rights.[30] "For indeed the greatest threat to peace is the failure to respect other people's dignity and freedom, the treatment of others not as fellow human beings (albeit mistaken or misguided) but as enemies who must be treated with brutality and violence," wrote Charter 77 spokespersons Radim Palouš, Anna Marvanová, and Ladislav Lis in an open letter to Dutch IKV dated August 27, 1982. Since respect for human rights was a necessary condition of peace, any effort to advance human rights was a contribution to peace.[31]

A year and a half after Charter 77 began corresponding with END, the Polish Committee for Social Resistance (KOS) also initiated contact with END through an open letter to West European anti-nuclear movements.[32] Founded a few days after the introduction of martial law in December 1981, KOS sought to support Polish political prisoners and promote their ideals. It consisted of five-person underground cells operating across Poland, and it published a bulletin every two weeks.[33] While KOS activists shared END's aim of a nuclear-free Europe, they also emphasized the importance of European autonomy and the indivisibility of peace and human rights. In an October 20, 1983, statement, KOS called for "an all-European peace movement" pursuing a "Europe, from the Urals to the Atlantic, free from nuclear weapons." Yet KOS believed that only Europeans could construct a peaceful Europe and thus urged European anti-nuclear activists to seek autonomy from the superpowers. "Our continent has been, for almost 40 years, deprived of political autonomy," KOS lamented. "The Yalta agreement submitted half of Europe to Soviet domination, and made the security of the other half dependent on American military protection." Superpower actions, particularly Soviet aggression, had endangered Europe. Only a Europe free from external interference could establish true peace.[34]

Like Charter 77 in Czechoslovakia, KOS also advocated the indivisibility of peace and human rights. Maintaining that "peace is indivisible," KOS

activists called on Eastern bloc peace movements to highlight "the totalitarian system's threat to peace" and "defend human and civic rights" in their
societies. Meanwhile, West European anti-nuclear activists should press their
governments to work for "self-determination" for East Europeans.[35]

While END supporters largely developed relations with Charter 77 and
KOS by exchanging letters, they were able to visit East German peace activists in East Berlin. The autonomous East German peace movement began
attracting Western attention following the launch of the Berlin Appeal on
January 25, 1982. "The Berlin Appeal—Make Peace Without Weapons" was
the work of Robert Havemann, a chemist and former East German official
who criticized the East German government's brutal actions, and Rainer
Eppelmann, a pastor who organized "Blues Masses" that provided thousands
of young East Germans with an opportunity to discuss peace.[36] Asserting that
any war in Europe would inevitably turn nuclear, the Berlin Appeal called for
the elimination of nuclear weapons in Europe. It argued that the division
of Germany was heightening the risk of nuclear war, as "divided Germany
has become the deployment area for the two nuclear superpowers." In order
to reduce the chance of nuclear war, the victors of the Second World War
should conclude peace agreements with the GDR and the FRG, withdraw
their troops from these countries, and pledge not to interfere in "the internal affairs of the two German States." The Berlin Appeal also called on the
East German government to respect citizens' freedom of speech so that they
could discuss and advocate peace.[37] Although the GDR banned petitions that
had not received official government approval, more than two thousand East
Germans signed the Berlin Appeal.[38]

Women quickly assumed a prominent role in the autonomous East
German peace movement and became key contacts for END supporters.
In October 1982, hundreds of women sent a letter to East German leader
Erich Honecker condemning a new law that conscripted women into military service during emergencies.[39] The next month, female END supporters
began visiting East Berlin to meet with the women who signed the letter to
Honecker. These East German activists staunchly opposed conscription and
the militarization of education in the GDR. Recognizing that civil defense
measures were unlikely to save lives, they also disliked civil defense drills for
a nuclear attack. These activists believed that the East German government
should work to prevent war instead of preparing citizens for war through civil
defense. They thought that any conventional war would inevitably escalate
into a nuclear conflict.[40]

These female East German peace activists did not emphasize the indivisibility of peace and human rights during their conversations with END supporters. Yet the December 1983 arrests of END supporter Barbara Einhorn and East German activists Bärbel Bohley, Ulrike Poppe, Jutta Seidel, and Irene Kuckuz in East Berlin highlighted the urgent need to advocate individuals' right to work for disarmament and peace. The women were arrested in connection with the END Women's Committee's plans to publish a book on women and peace activism in the GDR. During Einhorn's visit to East Berlin at the beginning of December 1983, Bohley, Poppe, Seidel, and Kuckuz gathered contributions for the proposed volume. Einhorn also took notes on a conversation with these women for inclusion in the book. East German authorities charged the women with "a crime against the state," specifically "gathering (unclassified) information which could be passed to a person or organization in another country where it could potentially be used to the detriment of the image of the GDR." Einhorn was detained and interrogated for four days after she unsuccessfully tried to leave East Berlin on December 10.[41] Arrested on December 12, Bohley and Poppe spent six weeks in prison.[42] Although Einhorn received milder treatment than Bohley and Poppe, she now had personal experience of the repression facing peace activists in the Eastern bloc.

The arrests of these women also showed that the escalation of the nuclear arms race created an atmosphere of tension and fear that governments used to stifle civil liberties. Einhorn's visit to East Berlin began only nine days after the West German Bundestag voted to accept U.S. Pershing II and cruise missiles and a little more than a month after the Soviet Union vowed to respond to U.S. INF deployments by stationing new missiles in the GDR and Czechoslovakia.[43] After being released from jail, Einhorn wrote, "My interrogator made it very clear that my arrest was a fairly direct by-product of the sharply deteriorated political situation. By extension, this also applies to the GDR women. There is a great deal of evidence to suggest that until very recently, the state was prepared to tolerate their activities to a certain degree."[44] New U.S. and Soviet missile deployments heightened East-West tensions, which the East German government used to justify restricting individual rights.

Thompson's 1984 "European Declaration of Peace" made it clear that East Europeans were influencing West European activists' thinking about the reunification of Europe and European autonomy. The IPCC, however, rejected Thompson's new appeal on the grounds that "the existing [1980] END Appeal still provided an adequate framework" for the European peace movement and it would be too difficult to devise a statement that every

IPCC-affiliated organization could endorse.[45] Nevertheless, END did not abandon the "European Declaration of Peace," but rather reproduced it as a discussion document in the *END Journal*.[46]

Yet East Europeans felt that West European peace activists were still too focused on nuclear disarmament at the expense of human rights concerns. In a letter to the July 1984 END Convention in Perugia, Charter 77 spokespersons wrote that "it is becoming increasingly obvious that your hopes are our hopes and *vice versa*," noting that both Charter 77 and West European peace groups shared a desire to overturn the division of Europe and help Europe achieve autonomy from the superpowers. Both also opposed militarism. Yet Charter 77 condemned Western activists' actions at the 1983 Prague World Peace Assembly, during which a West Berliner received resounding applause for his declaration that democracy and human rights issues had no place in the peace movement. Had not the 1938 Munich agreement and the 1968 Soviet-led invasion of Czechoslovakia shown that it was unwise to pursue "peace at any price"? Charter 77 encouraged West European activists to recognize that there could be no true peace without democracy, human rights protections, and respect for the dignity of all individuals.[47]

Although East European dissidents were critical of the West European peace movement, West European activists were learning from their East European counterparts and altering their movement to reflect the East Europeans' ideas. At the July 1984 END Convention in Perugia, to which Charter 77's critical letter of the Western peace movement was addressed, the division of Europe into blocs was a major subject of discussion, alongside traditional disarmament issues.[48] In July, the French anti-nuclear group Comité pour le Désarmement Nucléaire en Europe (CODENE), the Italian environmental organization Legambiente, and KOS also issued a joint declaration vowing to work together for their common aim of "building a free and peaceful Europe, beyond the order of Yalta." Much of the declaration was devoted to explaining the indivisibility of peace and human rights and included a pledge to ensure that "all European peoples are guaranteed their democratic rights: freedom of opinion, of the press, of worship, of organization." The aim of securing human rights protections across Europe was given equal weight to the goals of promoting East-West dialogue, the denuclearization of Europe, conventional arms reductions, and military budget cuts. In fact, CODENE, Legambiente, and KOS declared that their first joint actions would focus on "freedom of action for all citizens and independent organizations everywhere, and for the release of all those who are illegally imprisoned for their ideas."[49]

In a November 1984 letter to Charter 77, END activists wrote of the Czechoslovak dissidents' influence on their views on human rights issues, noting, "From our point of view, the dialogue which we have had during the past two years has greatly enriched our understanding of the principle of the indivisibility of peace and the struggle for civil rights." END and CND activists put this concept of the indivisibility of peace and human rights into practice when they held a demonstration on December 8 against both the Soviet Union's deployment of SS-21 missiles in Czechoslovakia and the GDR and the imprisonment of Jan Pukalik, a young Czech who was arrested for gathering signatures for a petition against the Soviet deployments in Czechoslovakia. END activists asserted, "It is the right and duty of all European citizens who oppose nuclear weapons to make their views known to governments. We also believe that the freedoms of public speech, assembly and petitioning are basic civil rights and play a vital role in this process."[50]

In January 1985, END officially endorsed East German and Czechoslovak dissidents' joint declaration condemning the Soviet SS-21 deployments and calling for governments to recognize the dignity and rights of all individuals, which they deemed a necessary condition for peace. Peter Crampton, the chair of END, vowed to publicize this joint declaration in the West.[51] In demands presented at the beginning of the Nuclear and Space Talks, CND, the West German Green Party, IKV, the Swiss Peace Council, the Freeze Campaign, and SANE called on all governments to respect the right of individuals to work for disarmament. Governments should not abridge activists' freedom of speech or right to organize for an end to the arms race.[52]

In the aftermath of their failure to stop U.S. INF deployments in late 1983, many West European activists realized that they needed to broaden their aims beyond nuclear disarmament if they were going to maintain their movements' viability. Influenced by their contacts with East European dissidents, END activists in particular began to emphasize the dissolution of the blocs in Europe and greater autonomy for Europe from the superpowers. They also began advocating the indivisibility of peace and human rights. West European activists' failure to give human rights and democracy the same attention as disarmament, however, would be an ongoing source of contention with East European dissidents.

Unlike many West European peace movements, the Freeze Campaign began narrowing its efforts following the setbacks of late 1983. In early December 1983, the Freeze Campaign's Fourth National Conference reaffirmed that a bilateral, comprehensive nuclear freeze was its overall goal. In 1984, however, the Freeze Campaign would concentrate on securing an immediate freeze on nuclear warhead testing and ballistic missile testing and deployment. Freeze activists would urge Reagan to pursue these initial moves toward a comprehensive freeze, as long as the Soviets did the same. In light of Reagan's opposition to the freeze, however, the Freeze Campaign would also lobby Congress to defund nuclear warhead testing and ballistic missile testing and deployment. This funding cutoff would depend on Soviet reciprocation. In addition, freeze activists would contest funding for individual weapons systems like the MX, Trident II, and Pershing II and cruise missiles. They also planned to seek the withdrawal of U.S. INF missiles from Britain, the FRG, and Italy, as well as a reduction in Soviet INF missiles aimed at Western Europe.[53] Recognizing that Congress was unlikely to endorse a comprehensive nuclear freeze in 1984, the Freeze Campaign hoped that "break[ing] the freeze down into little bite-sized pieces" might make it more palatable to Congress.[54]

After the Fourth National Conference, the Freeze Campaign worked with Markey and Kennedy to craft legislation that would facilitate a bilateral freeze on the testing of nuclear warheads and the testing and deployment of new ballistic missiles and anti-satellite weapons. Formally titled the "Arms Race Moratorium Act," this legislation was colloquially known as the "quick freeze." Markey introduced it in the House on May 2, and Kennedy followed suit in the Senate a day later. In the spring and summer of 1984, the Freeze Campaign sought to foster grassroots support for "quick freeze" legislation and pressed members of Congress to pass it. These efforts were undermined, however, by Massachusetts freeze activists who disagreed with the national conference decision to narrow the freeze movement's legislative aim. These Massachusetts activists urged members of Congress to support a rival comprehensive freeze bill that Representative Nicholas Mavroules (D-MA) introduced in the House. With a breakaway faction of the freeze movement challenging the idea of a "quick freeze," Congress failed to rally around even this more modest goal in 1984.[55]

Although the Freeze Campaign narrowed its legislative aim for 1984, it also sought to influence the 1984 elections, particularly the presidential race. Freeze activists believed that the election of a president who supported the freeze could be a breakthrough for their efforts to halt the nuclear arms race. They embraced the slogan "If You Can't Change the Politicians' Minds, Then Change the Politicians!"[56]

Following the recommendation of its Project 84 task force, the Freeze Campaign established a separate political action committee (PAC) called

Freeze Voter '84 in June 1983. This PAC sought "to create such a potent grass-roots force that current incumbents and potential challengers at the national level dare not ignore the Freeze issue."[57] Freeze Voter's strategy was to "identify, recruit and mobilize freeze voters," particularly in states in which Reagan was considered vulnerable or districts in which a congressional race clearly pitted a freeze supporter against a freeze opponent. Freeze Voter '84 ultimately targeted seven states in the presidential race, as well as forty House contests and eight Senate races.[58]

Other anti-nuclear organizations, like SANE, also worked to influence the presidential and congressional elections. Like freeze supporters across the country, SANE's executive director, David Cortright, was dismayed by Senate rejection of the freeze resolution and congressional appropriation of MX production funds and refusal to vote on INF deployments. In light of these congressional actions and Reagan's continued opposition to the freeze, Cortright argued in December 1983 that "the best way to campaign for a nuclear freeze in 1984, in our view, is to work for the defeat of Ronald Reagan and the election of a more peace-oriented Congress." To maximize the freeze movement's influence on the 1984 elections, Cortright called for workshops to train local activists in electoral work, voter registration and get-out-the-vote campaigns targeting freeze supporters, and voter education initiatives to familiarize Americans with nuclear issues. SANE decided to join with Freeze Voter '84 and the Council for a Livable World to target close congressional races that clearly matched a freeze supporter against a freeze opponent. Cortright also encouraged activists to mobilize against Reagan in predicted swing states. In addition, activists should focus on "keeping the Democrats honest," pressuring Democratic candidates to endorse the freeze as a first step toward dramatic nuclear arms reduction.[59]

In contrast to West European and U.S. anti-nuclear activists, Reagan stood by his disarmament strategy of negotiating from a position of strength and pursuing SDI. After the collapse of INF and START talks, Reagan's abhorrence of nuclear weapons led him to insist that his advisors work for the resumption of U.S.-Soviet negotiations in 1984. Despite opposition from some of his top aides, Reagan urged his administration to devise arms reduction proposals that could form the basis of a future superpower agreement.

Weinberger was the key opponent of Reagan's efforts to restart arms reduction negotiations in 1984. In a March 23 memo to Reagan, Weinberger wrote, "Our strategy since January has been predicated on the assumption that there is at least a fair chance for an improvement in the US-Soviet relationship, including an arms control agreement on terms that the Reagan Administration could defend. Private diplomatic activity, public pronouncements and our approach to the compliance issue have all been aimed at coaxing the Soviets along a path of accommodation." Weinberger noted that the administration had "deliberately downplayed the Soviet walk-out from Geneva and the Soviet record on compliance" in the hope that this restraint would convince the Soviets to resume arms reduction negotiations. Administration officials also had been working on devising new negotiating frameworks that might entice the Soviets back to the bargaining table. Weinberger wanted to abandon these policies because they were not prompting a Soviet return to negotiations. He also feared that the administration's efforts to restart negotiations were diverting it from defending its arms control record, which was likely to be attacked in the upcoming 1984 presidential election.[60]

During the first two years of Reagan's presidency, when he alone sought dramatic nuclear arms reduction, Reagan often retreated in the face of hardline advisors' criticism of his disarmament efforts. By early 1984, however, he could count on McFarlane and Shultz to support his arms reduction initiatives, which led him to be more assertive in nuclear policymaking. In advance of a March 27 National Security Planning Group meeting, for example, McFarlane wrote Reagan, "While Cap's position (which is not supported by the Joint Chiefs) is subtle, it masks a proposal to 'hardline it' by not exploring even internally in our government more flexible positions on START or INF. . . . If we do that and nothing else, we risk having you cast in the image of being inflexible and responsible for the breakdown." McFarlane encouraged Reagan to instruct his advisors to devise "solid flexible positions on both START and INF" that "take part of their [the Soviets'] approach and melds it with ours so that they have a figleaf for coming off their position."[61]

Reagan agreed with McFarlane and told his advisors at the March 27 meeting that "the Senior Arms Control Policy Group should accelerate their work and present me with options for new START/INF positions within a few weeks. This is for us, not for the public."[62] Reagan's directive that new arms reduction proposals were not for public consumption shows that he was not acting merely out of concern for public opinion. Rather, Reagan was serious about crafting positions that could convince the Soviets to return to negotiations.

With arms reduction talks still dormant in the fall of 1984, Reagan met with Soviet foreign minister Andrei Gromyko at the White House on September 28 to try to reinstate negotiations. Reagan had high confidence in both his interpersonal skills and negotiating abilities and believed that he would achieve positive results in a face-to-face meeting with a top Soviet official. He often likened U.S.-Soviet arms reduction negotiations to those he had conducted in Hollywood while president of the Screen Actors Guild.[63] In his meeting with Gromyko, Reagan sought to convince the Soviet foreign minister that his administration had no aggressive intentions toward the Soviet Union, but rather felt threatened by the Soviets' military buildup and interventions in the Third World. If he and Gromyko could dispel their mutual suspicions, Reagan thought that they could catalyze the resumption of arms reduction negotiations, which he hoped would ultimately lead to nuclear abolition.[64]

In order to emphasize his support for the elimination of nuclear weapons, Reagan arranged to speak with Gromyko alone for a few minutes. Reagan later informed Shultz that Gromyko privately said that the Soviets wanted to reduce the superpowers' growing nuclear arsenals. Reagan replied, "My dream is for a world where there are no nuclear weapons."[65] Dobrynin similarly recalled, "The president emphatically told him [Gromyko], as if this was a big secret, that his personal dream was a 'world without nuclear arms.' Gromyko answered that nuclear disarmament was 'the question of all questions.' Both agreed that the ultimate goal should be the complete elimination of nuclear weapons."[66] Reagan and Gromyko, however, failed to restart arms reduction negotiations. After the meeting, Gromyko asserted that the Reagan administration needed to prove its desire for peace through "practical deeds," not just words.[67]

While Reagan wanted to use his meeting with Gromyko to resurrect nuclear arms reduction talks, some White House aides hoped that it would improve voters' perceptions of Reagan's foreign policy as the November 6 election approached.[68] Freeze activists, however, were not having a major impact on the presidential race. As Forsberg later admitted, both the freeze movement and the Democratic Party failed to bring the nuclear arms race to the forefront of the presidential contest.[69] In a March 1984 letter to the Democratic presidential candidates, Forsberg warned that a Democrat would not beat Reagan by paying "lip service to the freeze while supporting traditional arms control." In order to distinguish themselves from Reagan and "tap the wellsprings of popular American support for the freeze," Democrats needed to make clear that they would pursue a bilateral freeze as president.[70] Yet the front-runners for the Democratic presidential nomination, Walter Mondale and Gary Hart, backed a nuclear freeze, strategic modernization, and increased military spending. Divided over whether to support the candidate with the strongest freeze credentials (such as George McGovern, Jesse Jackson, or Alan Cranston) or the one most likely to beat Reagan in November

(Mondale or Hart), Freeze Voter '84 did not make an endorsement in the Democratic primary. It thus wielded little influence in the process of selecting the Democratic presidential nominee.[71]

After Mondale won the Democratic nomination, many freeze activists were unenthusiastic about joining his campaign because he shared Reagan's desire to modernize U.S. nuclear forces. Karen Mulhauser, a Citizens Against Nuclear War activist who worked for Mondale, recalled, "When I tried to get local activists to attend Mondale rallies with freeze signs, I inevitably had to spend several hours trying to convince them that there was a real difference between Mondale and Reagan. They often said they'd vote for Mondale but they couldn't 'stomach' working for him."[72] Freeze activists would not have a decisive impact on the 1984 presidential election.

Neither Freeze Voter '84 nor SANE PAC wielded significant influence on the congressional races either. Political scientist David Meyer has shown that Freeze Voter '84 and SANE PAC spent most of the money that they raised on overhead costs, rather than distributing it to congressional candidates. Of the nearly $1.5 million raised by Freeze Voter '84, only $17,147 reached candidates. SANE PAC donated to candidates nearly $149,000 of the more than $251,000 that it raised.[73] Although Freeze Voter '84 declared that it won "four of eight Senate races" and "25 of 35 marginal House races," Meyer has pointed out that only one of those Senate races was close. While freeze supporter Paul Simon did prevail narrowly in the Illinois Senate race, he campaigned as a centrist and distanced himself from the freeze movement. Out of the twenty-five House victories for which Freeze Voter took credit, twenty were incumbents, and nearly 97 percent of House incumbents were reelected in 1984. In the six races for open House seats in which Freeze Voter made an endorsement, only two of its candidates won.[74] In its own comparison of the incoming Ninety-Ninth Congress and the sitting Ninety-Eighth Congress, Freeze Voter '84 acknowledged that the freeze movement suffered a seven-vote net loss in the House, while winning only a three- or four-vote net gain in the Senate.[75]

Meanwhile, Reagan was reelected in a landslide on November 6. After winning 49 states, 525 electoral votes, and 59 percent of the popular vote, Reagan felt that he had a mandate to continue his domestic and foreign policies.[76] Eleven days later, Konstantin Chernenko, who had become Soviet general secretary on February 13, 1984, after Andropov's death, agreed to begin negotiations on nuclear arms reduction and space issues. In his November 17 letter to Reagan, Chernenko wrote, "We are prepared to seek most radical solutions which would allow movement towards a complete ban and eventually liquidation of nuclear arms."[77] Thrilled by Chernenko's support for eliminating nuclear weapons, Reagan worked with Shultz to enshrine nuclear abolition as the official long-term goal of the U.S. government in NSDD 153.

Chernenko was genuinely interested in arms reduction agreements, which would enable him to cut defense spending and boost the Soviet economy. Yet he was also plagued by health problems throughout his time in power. In late August 1984, Chernenko was so ill that U.S. intelligence officers engaged in a "Death Watch." When Chernenko's health suffered, Gromyko assumed control of Soviet foreign policy. Long known in the West as "Mr. Nyet" (Mr. No), Gromyko was reluctant to engage the Reagan administration in 1984.[78]

Reagan, however, used Chernenko's call for nuclear disarmament to bolster his argument that U.S. negotiators should seek nuclear abolition in talks with the Soviets. Shultz supported Reagan on this point. On November 28, Reagan noted in his diary, "Met with Geo. S. re the upcoming arms reduction talks. We agree that since Chernenko has talked as I have of total elimination of nuclear weapons that should be our goal in the negotiations."[79]

Reagan could talk of little besides nuclear abolition in the four National Security Planning Group meetings held to prepare for Shultz and Gromyko's January 1985 talks on resuming negotiations. Reagan emphasized the importance of arms reduction negotiations and SDI in creating a nuclear-free world. During the December 5 meeting, Reagan declared, "We need to look at reducing and ultimately eliminating nuclear weapons." He derided proposals that called for only minimal arms reduction, stating that "relative to the goal of eliminating nuclear weapons, an initial reduction of 1,000 is meaningless." Shultz "applauded the President's notion of setting our goal of zero nuclear weapons," emphasizing that "it is important that the President said that, and we must move towards the basis for the elimination of nuclear weapons."[80]

Reagan's other advisors, however, tried to ignore or dismiss Reagan's idea of working for nuclear abolition in the upcoming negotiations. Even McFarlane repeatedly tried to focus the discussion on the stability that he thought would result from deploying SDI to redress the gap in U.S. and Soviet strategic nuclear forces. Kenneth Adelman, the ACDA director, argued that "the elimination of nuclear weapons should not be considered a near-term goal; rather, we should focus on the goal of reducing the number of nuclear weapons."[81] By the December 10 National Security Planning Group meeting, however, McFarlane announced that the U.S. objective would be the elimination of nuclear weapons, although he characterized it as a long-term goal. Following

McFarlane's statement, Reagan eagerly interjected, "Yes, that's right."[82] He was happy that his newfound decisive demeanor, along with Shultz's support, was moving U.S. policy in the direction he desired.

The NSDD that emerged from these National Security Planning Group meetings established nuclear abolition as the official long-term goal of the United States. NSDD 153, "Instructions for the Shultz-Gromyko Meeting in Geneva," set forth specific aims for the foreign ministers' meetings on January 7 and 8. It also laid out the Reagan administration's approach to arms reduction negotiations and its view of the relationship between offensive nuclear weapons and strategic defenses. The paragraph characterizing the U.S. approach to future negotiations with the Soviets clearly embodied Reagan's vision for achieving a nuclear-free world:

> During the next ten years, the U.S. objective is a radical reduction in the power of existing and planned offensive nuclear arms, as well as the stabilization of the relationship between offensive and defensive nuclear arms, whether on earth or in space. We are even now looking forward to a period of transition to a more stable world, with greatly reduced levels of nuclear arms and an enhanced ability to deter war based upon the increasing contribution of non-nuclear defenses against offensive nuclear arms. This period of transition could lead to the eventual elimination of all nuclear arms, both offensive and defensive. A world free of nuclear arms is an ultimate objective to which we, the Soviet Union, and all other nations can agree.[83]

By assuming an assertive role in nuclear policymaking and enlisting the help of Shultz, who viewed arms control negotiations as a promising vehicle for improving superpower relations, Reagan was finally able to move U.S. policy into line with his goal of nuclear abolition.

In Geneva, Shultz and Gromyko forged an agreement to resume U.S.-Soviet negotiations. As the name suggests, the Nuclear and Space Talks would address INF, START, and space issues.[84] It was later agreed that the negotiations would begin on March 12 in Geneva.[85]

Reagan's reelection and the resumption of U.S.-Soviet nuclear arms reduction negotiations without a freeze were major defeats for the freeze movement. In December 1984, the Freeze Campaign recognized that it had reached an inflection point. According to the Freeze Strategy Committee, the campaign was at the end of "stage one," which witnessed an escalation of both the nuclear arms race and grassroots anti-nuclear activism across the globe. In "stage two," the Freeze Campaign "must build on this essential foundation [laid in the first stage] and create a larger, longer-term, more committed, and better organized Freeze movement."[86]

Despite this realization that the Freeze Campaign was at a crossroads, the Fifth National Conference did not alter the campaign's strategy for 1985. Like the year before, activists would pressure Congress to begin enacting a freeze by defunding elements of the U.S. nuclear program. While the Freeze Campaign still sought a comprehensive freeze, it would also pursue the elimination of funding for nuclear warhead testing and the flight-testing of missiles and anti-satellite weapons as first steps toward a bilateral freeze on nuclear testing. The Freeze Campaign would also lobby Congress to withhold funds for MX production. At the end of 1984, the Freeze Strategy Committee embraced the idea that "a comprehensive freeze can be, and is likely to be, implemented in stages."[87]

The Freeze Campaign's failure to overhaul its strategy in December 1984 shows that it had lost touch with political realities and was unable to adapt in the wake of setbacks. Downplaying the significance of Reagan's reelection, the Freeze Strategy Committee argued that the freeze movement "did *not* 'lose' the White House, because we never had it." It contended that the freeze movement had actually benefited in several ways from the 1984 election, which heightened public awareness of nuclear issues, brought new volunteers and donors into the movement, and showed movement leaders the remaining impediments to securing a freeze.[88] In analyzing the 1984 election results, the Strategy Committee never acknowledged that the president, not Congress, sets the negotiating agenda with the Soviet Union, making the failure to defeat Reagan a major problem for the movement.

In addition, the Freeze Campaign initially ignored the November 1984 announcement that Shultz and Gromyko would meet in Geneva in early January to discuss the resumption of arms reduction negotiations.[89] Instead, the Freeze Strategy Committee advocated public education efforts focused on the consequences of a "bilateral freeze versus a continuously escalating arms race."[90] This was a false choice, however, as the Reagan administration was actively seeking to restart arms reduction negotiations with the Soviets.

The national Freeze Campaign's failure to address the resumption of U.S.-Soviet arms reduction negotiations troubled state freeze organizations. In a January 28, 1985, memo to the national leadership on behalf of the Illinois Freeze Campaign, Bob Stein warned that if the freeze movement did not adapt its strategy to take into account the new Nuclear and Space Talks, Reagan would use the reopening of negotiations to marginalize the freeze movement. Members of Congress would support new nuclear systems so that U.S. negotiators could operate from a position of strength in Geneva. The American people would believe that the freeze movement was "attempting to undermine what they see as very positive developments in arms control," the Nuclear and Space Talks with the Soviets.[91]

Based on suggestions from the Illinois Freeze Campaign, as well as input from Kehler, the national Freeze Campaign unveiled a new "Stop While We Talk" initiative in March 1985.[92] In a March 8 letter to Shultz and Gromyko, the Freeze Campaign called for the United States and the Soviet Union to adopt a "negotiators' pause" as arms reduction talks reopened. The superpowers should immediately halt the testing and deployment of nuclear weapons and their delivery vehicles pending the conclusion of a comprehensive nuclear freeze. By preventing the testing and deployment of new nuclear weapons, this "negotiators' pause" would enable U.S. and Soviet negotiators to concentrate on reducing existing nuclear weapons. Without a freeze, the superpowers would continue to escalate the nuclear arms race, which would undermine prospects for a significant arms reduction agreement.[93] Freeze activists also traveled to Geneva to present this proposal at the opening of the Nuclear and Space Talks on March 12. Along with representatives from SANE, CND, the West German Greens, IKV, and the Swiss Peace Council, the Freeze Campaign urged U.S. and Soviet officials to "stop the arms race while you talk." The activists specifically sought an immediate bilateral freeze on INF deployments and the testing and deployment of strategic nuclear weapons.[94]

This "Stop While We Talk" initiative epitomized the Freeze Campaign's failure to adapt following the challenges of late 1983 through early 1985. The draft proposal for the "Stop While We Talk" campaign noted that in the wake of Reagan's reelection and the reopening of U.S.-Soviet talks without a freeze, "the political winds in Washington have shifted against us and we are losing ground." Changed circumstances seemed to warrant a changed aim and strategy for the freeze movement. Yet this same draft proposal laid out a repackaged freeze proposal that the Freeze Campaign proudly noted "is not a different objective or strategy than what we already have underway."[95] Unable to adjust in the wake of setbacks, the Freeze Campaign would not wield significant policy influence during Reagan's second term.[96]

Rather than focus on the Freeze Campaign, Reagan turned his attention to Mikhail Gorbachev, who took power in the Kremlin on March 11 after Chernenko's death. Reagan immediately penned a letter to Gorbachev expressing his desire to improve U.S.-Soviet relations. He particularly emphasized the need for progress on arms control, noting that the Nuclear and Space Talks "provide us with a genuine chance to make progress toward our common ultimate goal of eliminating nuclear weapons." As the leaders of the superpowers, Reagan and Gorbachev had a unique responsibility to foster peace. Reagan concluded the letter by inviting Gorbachev to a summit in Washington, DC.[97] After three Soviet leaders passed away during his first four years in office, none of whom he had met at a summit, Reagan yearned to make progress with Gorbachev. "How am I supposed to get anyplace with the Russians if they keep dying on me?" he asked his wife, Nancy.[98]

Fifty-four years old when he assumed the post of Soviet general secretary, Mikhail Sergeyevich Gorbachev had neither the health problems nor the outlook of his three elderly predecessors. Born on March 2, 1931, in the small village of Privolnoye in southern Russia, Gorbachev's formative years were defined by the Second World War. Following his father's conscription into the Red Army in 1941, Gorbachev assumed many of his household duties, including tending the vegetable patch that was a key source of food for his family. When German troops occupied Gorbachev's hometown for nearly five months during 1942, they searched his home and arrested and questioned his grandmother, Vasilisa Gopkalo. With rumors swirling of mass executions in nearby villages and fears abounding that the Nazis were planning to target communist families in an upcoming massacre in Privolnoye, Gorbachev's mother and grandmother sent an eleven-year-old Mikhail into hiding outside of town. Red Army troops liberated Privolnoye five days before the villagers thought that the Germans would carry out their mass execution of communists, and Gorbachev's family welcomed them as saviors. Gorbachev would have to endure famine and a false report that his father had been killed in battle before the war's end. "I was fourteen when the war ended," Gorbachev wrote in his memoir. "Our generation is the generation of wartime children. It has burned us, leaving its mark both on our characters and on our view of the world."[99] Gorbachev had an intimate knowledge of the horrors of war.

After the war, Gorbachev became an ardent communist, joining the Komsomol, the communist youth organization. He later recounted, "The war was not only a great victory over fascism but proof that our country's cause was the right one. And by the same token, so was the cause of Communism."[100] Gorbachev earned a law degree from Moscow State University, where he met his wife, Raisa, who studied philosophy. Returning to his native

Stavropol region, Gorbachev quickly rose through the ranks of the Communist Party.

Yet as first secretary of the Stavropol city committee (1966–70) and then first secretary of the Stavropol territorial committee (1970–78), Gorbachev began to have misgivings about the efficacy of the Soviet system. Stavropol's infrastructure was crumbling and it had little industry. Gorbachev embarked on a massive urban development project that would grant more autonomy to individual enterprises and reform the existing system of work planning and incentives. But the central leadership in Moscow slowed Gorbachev's efforts. He soon learned that officials in other parts of the Soviet Union were facing the same challenges. Gorbachev's trips to Italy, France, Belgium, and the FRG in the 1970s only heightened his concern about the Soviet system's functioning. He was struck by the higher standard of living in Western Europe.[101]

During Gorbachev's tenure in Stavropol, he met many of the Politburo members who vacationed at the region's spas, including KGB chairman Yuri Andropov and Chairman of the Council of Ministers Alexei Kosygin. The friendships he developed with these high-ranking Soviet officials helped propel his rise in the party. In 1978, Gorbachev moved to Moscow to serve as the Central Committee secretary overseeing agriculture. He became a full member of the Politburo in 1980. When Chernenko was too sick to attend Politburo meetings in 1984, Gorbachev ran them, making him a likely successor to Chernenko. Gorbachev was eager to lead the Soviet Union, believing that he could carry out meaningful reforms. "We can't go on living like this," he told Raisa on the night before he became general secretary.[102]

Gorbachev assumed leadership in the Kremlin with the aim of dramatically improving East-West relations. This goal was motivated partly by his moral aversion to nuclear weapons and his desire to avert a nuclear war between the blocs. He feared that rising tensions between NATO and the Warsaw Pact, each of which possessed sufficient nuclear capabilities to destroy the other many times over, might lead to a nuclear conflict. The two sides needed to reduce hostility before their disagreements precipitated a nuclear war. During a visit to the United Kingdom three months before he became general secretary, Gorbachev noted that "the nuclear age inevitably dictates *new political thinking*, that 'now more than ever' there was a need for constructive dialogue, for a search for solutions to key international problems, an attempt to find areas of agreement that could lead to greater trust among different countries, the creation of an atmosphere in international relations that would be free of nuclear threats, suspicion, fear, and animosity."

Two days after Gorbachev became general secretary, he asked Mitterrand, "Is it not time to make decisions corresponding to the interests of all nations and all peoples, decisions that would not allow the world to slide into the abyss of nuclear catastrophe, the consequences of which it is difficult even to predict?"[103] Cold War tensions must be reduced so that the world did not succumb to nuclear war.

Gorbachev found nuclear weapons morally abhorrent. He worried about the horrific consequences that would result from their use, and he called for serious negotiations to reduce and eventually eliminate these weapons. In a discussion with Thatcher on December 16, 1984, Gorbachev dramatically presented the British leader with a diagram representing the superpowers' nuclear arsenals, remarking that "only a fraction of this would be needed to bring about nuclear winter." He warned, "If both sides continued to pile up weapons in ever increasing quantities it could lead to accidents or unforeseen circumstances. With the present generation of weapons, decision-making time could be counted in minutes. There was a Russian proverb that said: 'Once in a year even an unloaded gun can go off.' If one had to have nuclear weapons it must be at the lowest possible level." Gorbachev vowed to Thatcher that the Soviets would approach the upcoming discussions on restarting nuclear arms reduction negotiations "with serious new proposals."[104] In a speech before the House of Commons Select Committee on Foreign Affairs two days later, he characterized Soviet proposals as "envisag[ing] the most radical reduction in nuclear armaments—with a view to eventually dismantling them completely." He urged his listeners to recognize that "for all that separates us, we have one planet, and Europe is our common home, not a theater of operations."[105]

After Gorbachev became Soviet general secretary, his moral opposition to nuclear weapons persisted. He later told Soviet nuclear physicist Yuri Smirnov that he was morally repulsed by the fact that his new position made him liable for the nuclear arms race and any nuclear war that might break out. During an exercise meant to train the Soviet leadership in the response protocols to a Western nuclear attack, Gorbachev refused to press a button launching nuclear weapons.[106] In a Central Committee plenum on his first day as general secretary, Gorbachev exhorted his colleagues to recognize that "never before has such a terrible danger hung over the heads of humanity as in our times. The only rational way out of the current situation is for the opposing forces to agree to immediately stop the arms race—above all, the nuclear arms race—on the earth's surface and not allow it into outer space."[107]

Gorbachev's desire to improve superpower relations was also motivated by his aim of economically and politically revitalizing the Soviet Union. Soviet economic growth rates had been declining for twenty-five years when Gorbachev became general secretary in March 1985. The Soviet economy was also inordinately militarized, with defense consuming "roughly 40 percent of the budget and 15–20 percent of GDP in the early 1980s, or at least four times the U.S. level."[108] The Soviet economy was therefore a distorted one, as its bloated defense sector was maintained at the expense of consumer industries. This militarized economy also enabled the reactionary Soviet military-industrial complex to wield enormous influence in political and social affairs.[109] Gorbachev quickly realized that if he were going to introduce much-needed economic and political reforms in the Soviet Union, he would have to remove the justification for the Soviets' militarized economy: the Cold War with the West. Gorbachev later recounted, "We had to develop our own initiative aimed at ending the Cold War because without that it would have been impossible to take the decisive steps of perestroika."[110] Even before he became the top Soviet leader, he admitted to the House of Commons Select Committee on Foreign Affairs, "The Soviet Union needs peace to implement its huge development programs."[111]

Gorbachev's nuclear abolitionism led him to seek to end the Cold War by halting the superpower nuclear arms race and concluding sweeping nuclear disarmament agreements. He later wrote that Soviet nuclear arms reduction initiatives in 1985 were motivated by "the desire to give material content to the idea of a renewal of international relations, based on the principle of equal security for both sides and freeing them both from a confrontational approach."[112] Anatoly Chernyaev, who was the deputy chief of the International Department of the Central Committee when Gorbachev took power, recalled that the new Soviet leader initially believed "that he could end the Cold War solely by proposing to cut weapons."[113]

Gorbachev affirmed his desire to reduce nuclear weapons and improve U.S.-Soviet relations in a March 24 letter to Reagan. In this missive, Gorbachev noted that the superpowers had a "common interest" in averting nuclear war. He argued that the two leaders should devote significant personal attention to the Geneva arms reduction negotiations. Gorbachev also accepted Reagan's invitation to hold a summit, although he deferred the questions of where and when the leaders should meet. In consenting to a summit with Reagan, Gorbachev abandoned the condition imposed by Brezhnev in 1977 that U.S. and Soviet leaders would only meet to sign an agreement.[114]

Although Reagan and Gorbachev wanted to spur arms reduction negotiations and improve superpower relations, SDI was a major source of contention between them. Gorbachev believed that SDI was an effort to give the United States a first-strike capability, and he worried that SDI components might be used in a first strike from space to hit targets on Earth.[115] In the Nuclear and Space Talks, Soviet officials linked reductions of offensive nuclear weapons to a ban on "space-strike weapons," which they defined as space-to-earth weapons, anti-satellite weapons, and space-based ABM defenses.[116] Reagan, by contrast, insisted that SDI would enable both superpowers to eliminate their nuclear weapons. By rendering nuclear weapons ineffective, SDI would protect the world if a country clandestinely kept some nuclear systems or a "madman" redeveloped nuclear weapons after they had been abolished. Desperate to protect the initiative that he thought would make nuclear abolition possible, Reagan refused to accept any ban on strategic defense research.[117] Disagreements over SDI's purpose would complicate Reagan and Gorbachev's arms reduction efforts over the next two years.

Nevertheless, Gorbachev was anxious to reverse the nuclear arms race and improve relations with the United States. On April 7, 1985, he announced a seven-month unilateral moratorium on deployments of SS-20 missiles aimed at Western Europe. Calling the move a gesture of "good will," Gorbachev indicated that the Soviets would be willing to extend the moratorium beyond November if the United States agreed to stop deploying Pershing IIs and cruise missiles in Western Europe.[118] On July 29, Gorbachev declared that the Soviets would begin observing a unilateral moratorium on nuclear tests on August 6, the fortieth anniversary of the U.S. nuclear bombing of Hiroshima. Announcing that the unilateral moratorium would remain in effect through the end of the year, Gorbachev stated that the Soviets would extend it if the United States joined the moratorium.[119] Although the Reagan administration dismissed both initiatives as propaganda, Andrei Grachev, an advisor to Gorbachev, has argued that "for Gorbachev they represented genuine attempts to announce to the West his intention to do 'real business' in foreign policy."[120]

After Gorbachev's July 29 announcement, SANE and other U.S. antinuclear organizations accelerated their efforts to secure a nuclear test ban. SANE viewed a nuclear test ban as "the first concrete step" toward a nuclear freeze. Its regional canvassing directors had already found strong public support for a nuclear test ban, and the fortieth anniversary of the Hiroshima bombing provided a symbolic opportunity to mobilize opposition to nuclear testing.[121] U.S. anti-nuclear activists believed that Gorbachev's unilateral moratorium on nuclear tests had removed a major obstacle to achieving a permanent nuclear test ban. Now the activists only needed to convince the Reagan administration to accept Gorbachev's invitation to join the testing moratorium.[122]

With Reagan and Gorbachev set to meet in Geneva on November 19 and 20, SANE and the Freeze Campaign embarked on a crusade to convince both leaders to agree to a permanent, mutual halt to nuclear testing at the summit. The centerpiece of this campaign was a signature drive for "An Appeal to World Leaders," which urged Reagan and Gorbachev to use the Geneva summit to "announce an immediate halt to nuclear testing, leading to negotiations for a Comprehensive Test Ban Treaty" and to "begin negotiations toward reduction and eventual elimination of nuclear weapons."[123] By demonstrating a high level of public support for a nuclear test ban, U.S. activists hoped to pressure Reagan to join Gorbachev's moratorium.

While U.S. anti-nuclear groups pursued elements of a nuclear freeze in 1985, activists across Europe continued to advocate the dissolution of the blocs in Europe, greater European autonomy, and the indivisibility of peace and human rights. East European activists took the lead in promoting these goals and offering suggestions for how they could be implemented, while West Europeans primarily endorsed and publicized East European appeals and proposals. This led East European dissidents to become increasingly frustrated with West European peace activists, who they felt still devoted too much attention to nuclear issues at the expense of human rights concerns in particular. East European dissidents urged West European activists to work for disarmament, the reunification of Europe, and human rights.

Across Eastern Europe, independent activists called for a reunified, autonomous, and free Europe and set forth proposals for achieving this goal. The most notable example was the Prague Appeal, which Charter 77 issued on March 11, 1985. Addressed to the upcoming END Convention in Amsterdam, the Prague Appeal identified the division of Europe as the primary threat to peace on the continent. Recognizing that any war in Europe would turn into a world war, the Prague Appeal's signatories argued that the division of Europe also endangered the peace of the entire globe. They believed that it was imperative for government officials and ordinary citizens to overcome the Iron Curtain's divide. The appeal's signatories argued that the creation of nuclear-free and neutral zones in Europe, the establishment of relations spanning the Iron Curtain, the adoption of nonaggression treaties, and the conclusion of agreements between the European Economic Community and the Council for Mutual Economic Assistance could help bridge Europe's divide. In order to break down the blocs in Europe, they also called for self-determination for the Germans "to decide if or how they wish to unite their two states within their present frontiers," as well as negotiations between NATO and the Warsaw Pact on the elimination of their military organizations, the denuclearization of Europe, and the withdrawal of U.S. and Soviet troops from Europe.[124]

Yet the appeal's signatories emphasized the Conference on Security and Cooperation in Europe (CSCE) process, also known as the Helsinki process, as the key to reunifying Europe. They noted that "throughout this process, the negotiations have not been conducted between the blocs but between equal partners, a fact which has underlined the independence of all participating states and established in principle the sort of relations which, if implemented, would open the way to the unification of Europe." The Helsinki Final Act, the product of the CSCE, also provided protections for human rights, which would enable citizens to criticize government policies and offer proposals for eradicating the bloc system. The appeal's signatories lamented that "the requirement that governments should fulfill all their undertakings and obligations [under the Helsinki Final Act] has not been made full use of by the peace movement." They also advocated the indivisibility of peace and human rights, arguing that individuals have the right to "take part in decisions affecting . . . their very survival." Only governments that respected the rights of their citizens would be able to transform Europe into a unified, peaceful continent.[125]

Similarly, German peace activists called for negotiations to break down the blocs in Europe. In April 1985 letters to the U.S. Congress and the Supreme Soviet of the Soviet Union, Berlin activists called on both superpowers to join with European states in negotiations for the complete withdrawal of U.S. and Soviet troops, conventional weapons, and nuclear forces from both German states; the reduction and eventual withdrawal of the superpowers' troops, conventional weapons, and nuclear forces from the rest of Europe; and the establishment of nuclear-free zones in Scandinavia, the Balkans, and Central Europe as a first step toward removing all weapons of mass destruction from Europe. European countries would also undertake a second set of negotiations for a "system of agreements which will secure the conditions for durable peace as well as ensuring the re-establishment of ecological balance, economic relations and cultural cooperation."[126] While twenty-one prominent East German peace activists endorsed the Prague Appeal, which called for similar negotiations, they also expressed reservations about using the CSCE process as a vehicle for reunifying Europe. In a letter to the Prague Appeal's signatories, they argued that "Helsinki did not question the political and military *status quo* in Europe in the years of détente," but rather accepted the Soviet domination of Eastern Europe. While peace activists could try to make better use of the Helsinki Final Act, might it not be wiser to start new sets of negotiations to end the division of Europe?[127]

Members of the newly formed Freedom and Peace (WiP) movement in Poland also offered suggestions for overcoming Europe's divide and demanded human rights protections. Following the October 1984 sentencing of Solidarity Student Committee member Marek Adamkiewicz to two and a half years in prison for refusing to take the military oath, Adamkiewicz's fellow students organized a hunger strike in support of him. Inspired by Pope John Paul II's sermons on peace, those participating in the hunger strike decided to establish a peace movement in Krakow in April 1985. Recognizing that the concept of "peace" had been distorted by Polish and Soviet leaders, who talked of peace while engaging in violence against their own people and other nations, WiP activists sought to "give peace activities back their moral and political value" and encourage their fellow Poles to engage in peace activism. Affirming the indivisibility of peace and human rights, WiP members campaigned for freedom within Poland and also cooperated with international and domestic organizations to promote nonviolence around the world. WiP groups quickly spread to Warsaw, Wroclaw, Gdansk, Szczecin, and other Polish cities in the spring and summer of 1985.[128] In a letter to the 1985 END Convention in Amsterdam, WiP activists called for the disarmament and demilitarization of Central Europe as a first step toward the dissolution of Europe's blocs. They cautioned against unilateral and unverifiable disarmament initiatives, so as to ensure that the Soviet Union did not take advantage of a Western force reduction. WiP also urged that "the question of struggle against totalitarian systems be treated on an equal level with endeavors for disarmament" by European peace movements.[129]

West European peace activists publicly supported East European appeals for the reunification of Europe and the extension of human rights protections in the East. In a statement on the Prague Appeal, END "welcome[d]" it and endorsed all of its aims. END activists admitted that "the Western peace movement has neglected to discuss the Helsinki process," attributing this to their lack of knowledge of the specifics of the Helsinki Final Act and their skepticism that West European leaders were eager to work for disarmament. Yet they wrote that they "are intrigued by the way you use your government's signature on the Final Act as a real campaigning tool" and believed that "it is high time we remedied our past neglect of the Helsinki process." END activists asked Charter 77 "to share with us in detail the way you think it [the Helsinki process] can be used as a framework for our work too."[130] At the July 1985 END Convention in Amsterdam, which was attended largely by West European peace activists, East European proposals for the reunification of Europe and the extension of human rights protections throughout the continent were publicized and debated.[131] END activists also made trips to the GDR, Hungary, and Poland during 1985 to meet with independent peace activists, discuss their views on peace and human rights issues, and consider ways that East European and West European activists could collaborate to promote their common goals.[132]

The Western peace movement's continued focus on nuclear issues, however, irritated East European activists, who urged West Europeans to spend more time advancing human rights and overcoming the division of Europe. During END activist Paul Anderson's visit to Budapest in February, prominent Hungarian oppositionists Miklós Haraszti and Ferenc Rusza repeatedly criticized the direction of the Western peace movement. Highlighting the human rights abuses taking place in the Soviet bloc, Haraszti argued that "a movement arguing for peace *and* human rights should be a priority in Western Europe." Rusza was more concerned that Western activists were not devoting sufficient attention to breaking down the blocs in Europe, which he viewed as the underlying cause of the nuclear arms race. He reproached the Western movement for "its focus on missiles to the exclusion of serious consideration of the strategies and political structures of which the missiles were the most visible symbol."[133] In its letter to the END Convention in Amsterdam, WiP activists encouraged their Western counterparts to recognize that in Eastern Europe "it is just as possible to be killed by a death-dealing rocket as by a truncheon in a militia station, though death from a weapon of mass destruction is a question of tomorrow, whereas we face truncheons every day." Human rights violations were an immediate concern throughout the Soviet bloc and should be so across Europe. "As long as there are nations which are oppressed, exploited, terrorized and murdered—there is no peace in the world, irrespective of whether the aggressors are foreign armies or their own governments." WiP insisted that Western peace activists prioritize human rights alongside traditional disarmament issues.[134] These words had an impact, as West European activists would devote more attention to human rights in the latter half of the 1980s.

In November 1985, the attention of Reagan, Gorbachev, and U.S. freeze activists was on the upcoming Geneva summit, where the new Soviet general secretary would be joined by a new foreign minister. In July, Gorbachev had "promoted" the hardline Gromyko to the largely ceremonial post of Soviet president and named Eduard Shevardnadze his successor in the Ministry of Foreign Affairs.[135] Gromyko's inflexibility made him ill-suited to carry out the foreign policy reforms that Gorbachev sought.[136] Shevardnadze, the top communist official in Georgia, was a daring choice to replace Gromyko, as he had no foreign policy experience, spoke only Georgian and Russian, and had spent little time outside of the Soviet Union.[137] Gorbachev and Shevardnadze had known each other for decades, however, having risen through the Communist Party ranks together. They shared a strong desire to reform the Soviet Union's economy and foreign policy and had developed a deep sense of trust with one another.[138]

The stakes of Reagan and Gorbachev's first meeting in Geneva were high. Both leaders believed that they would only be able to realize their dream of a nuclear-free world if they forged a strong partnership to move the Nuclear and Space Talks toward nuclear abolition. In their first private meeting, which had been scheduled for fifteen minutes but lasted an hour, Reagan and Gorbachev each emphasized the importance of working together to find a way out of the nuclear arms race.[139] Reagan opened the session by urging Gorbachev to recognize that their "primary aim" should be "to eliminate the suspicions which each side had of the other." If the two leaders could dispel their mutual mistrust and form a personal relationship, they could make progress on a range of issues, including nuclear arms reduction. "Countries do not mistrust each other because of arms," Reagan told Gorbachev, "but rather countries build up their arms because of the mistrust between them." Gorbachev was similarly convinced that "he and the President could not ignore each other," but needed to engage each other. Identifying the avoidance of nuclear war and the termination of the nuclear arms race as the most important tasks facing the two leaders, Gorbachev argued, "We needed to say something to the world about this. . . . We need to find a formula at this meeting which would give impetus toward moving towards resolution" of these issues.[140]

Between the first and second plenary sessions in Geneva, Gorbachev met with a delegation of anti-nuclear activists that included Jesse Jackson, Freeze Campaign director Jane Gruenebaum, and Cortright. Armed with nearly 1.2 million signatures in support of "An Appeal to World Leaders," U.S. activists had traveled to Geneva on November 17 to present their petitions to Reagan and Gorbachev. Although Reagan declined to see them, Gorbachev spent nearly an hour with them on the first day of the summit.[141] In this meeting,

Jackson emphasized the need for the Soviet Union to adopt a permanent, verifiable ban on nuclear testing, improve its treatment of Soviet Jews, and take a stand on apartheid in South Africa. Although Gorbachev expressed a desire "to discuss real disarmament," he denied that the Soviet government was violating the rights of Jews. He completely ignored the apartheid issue.[142] Nevertheless, Cortright recalled, "It had been a remarkable event. The meeting that was supposed to last just a few minutes had gone on for almost an hour. In the midst of his first encounter with the president of the United States, Gorbachev had taken time for a dialogue and meeting with the peace movement." Dismissing the idea that Gorbachev may have met with the peace delegation to embarrass Reagan, Cortright believed that the meeting vindicated the U.S. anti-nuclear movement.[143]

Yet Cortright failed to acknowledge that the nuclear freeze movement no longer exerted the influence on U.S. nuclear policy that it had during Reagan's first term. George Keyworth, the president's science advisor, received reports on the anti-nuclear movement's activities in 1985, but he does not appear to have forwarded these reports to more senior administration officials.[144] Neither Reagan nor his principal advisors referenced the nuclear freeze movement when formulating arms control policy in NSC meetings in 1985. The U.S. anti-nuclear movement would never again exercise the policy influence that it had during the early 1980s.

At the Geneva summit, Reagan and Gorbachev's discussions of specific arms reduction proposals were marred by their disagreements over SDI, which often became heated. Gorbachev vigorously attacked SDI in four of his six meetings with Reagan, arguing that it was an American attempt to gain a first-strike capability and would "lead to an arms race in space, and not just a defensive arms race but an offensive arms race with space weapons." Gorbachev warned Reagan that "if the U.S. embarks on SDI, the following will happen: 1) no reduction of offensive weapons; and 2) Soviet Union will respond" with its own defensive system.[145] Reagan repeatedly insisted that SDI was designed to facilitate nuclear abolition, making an analogy between SDI and a gas mask that he would repeat many times in the coming years. He reminded Gorbachev, "In 1925 in this city of Geneva all of the countries that had participated in World War I had met and had reached agreement not to use poison gas warfare. Nevertheless, all had kept their gas masks." Reagan believed that the two leaders should similarly "go forward to rid the world of the threat of nuclear weapons, but at the same time retain something like that gas mask, i.e., a shield that would protect our countries should there be an unforeseeable return to nuclear missiles." Reagan vowed that the United States would share SDI with not only the Soviet Union, but also all nuclear states, so that nuclear weapons could be eliminated.[146] In an emotional exchange during the third plenary session, Gorbachev asked Reagan how he could trust the president's pledge to share SDI with the Soviet Union when the United States did not even share all of its advanced technology with NATO allies.[147] SDI would remain an obstacle to progress on arms reduction.

Nevertheless, the Geneva summit was significant in that it produced an agreement for two additional summits and a joint statement affirming the need to avoid nuclear war and engage in 50 percent reductions of nuclear arsenals. Following their famous private meeting next to a roaring fire in a boathouse on the banks of Lake Geneva, Reagan and Gorbachev agreed to two additional summits during their walk back to the Villa Fleur d'Eau. Gorbachev accepted Reagan's invitation to visit the United States in 1986, and Reagan agreed to travel to the Soviet Union.[148] As Reagan and Gorbachev noted in their toasts during dinner on the last night of the summit, the two leaders had not abandoned dialogue even though they disagreed on many issues. They would continue to try to work together to reverse the nuclear arms race.[149]

The joint U.S.-Soviet statement on the Geneva summit declared that "a nuclear war cannot be won and must never be fought" and reaffirmed Reagan and Gorbachev's commitment "to prevent an arms race in space and to terminate it on earth, to limit and reduce nuclear arms and enhance strategic stability." The two leaders called on their negotiators in the Nuclear and Space Talks to make "early progress, in particular in areas where there is common ground, including the principle of 50% reductions in the nuclear arms of the U.S. and the U.S.S.R. appropriately applied, as well as the idea of an interim INF agreement."[150] Although Reagan and Gorbachev had not reached an agreement in Geneva that would force their negotiators to draft a treaty eliminating nuclear weapons, they made it clear that they expected their delegations to work for significant arms reduction.

By late 1985, it was clear that grassroots and government nuclear abolitionists' visions for ending the Cold War had diverged. Reagan and Gorbachev hoped to reach an agreement to eliminate U.S. and Soviet nuclear weapons. East European dissidents and West European activists pressed world leaders for a denuclearized, reunified, autonomous, and free Europe. U.S. anti-nuclear activists lobbied for a nuclear test ban as the first step toward a nuclear freeze, which they deemed necessary to ensure that U.S.-Soviet arms reduction negotiations yielded meaningful results.

By the end of the Geneva summit, each group believed that its strategy was succeeding. Reagan and Gorbachev had agreed that nuclear war must never be waged and instructed their delegations to draft a treaty for a 50 percent reduction in nuclear weapons. They also had scheduled two additional summits, where they could try again to reach an agreement to abolish their nuclear arsenals. East European and West European activists' goals were converging, and there were some joint efforts to promote their common aims taking place. U.S. anti-nuclear activists had mobilized public support for a nuclear test ban and met with Gorbachev in Geneva to discuss nuclear testing. As a new year began, however, these divergent visions would begin to intersect in unexpected ways.

CHAPTER 5

"The Time Is Right for Something Dramatic"

On a bitterly cold October afternoon in the Icelandic capital of Reykjavik, Reagan and Gorbachev sat in the reputedly haunted Hofdi House and discussed a plan for abolishing their nuclear weapons in ten years.[1] Initially proposed by Gorbachev as "a quick one-on-one meeting" that would lay the groundwork for a summit in the United States, the Reykjavik meeting of October 11 and 12, 1986, rapidly evolved into a full-blown summit once underway.[2] By the summit's final, unplanned session, Reagan and Gorbachev had dispensed with their talking points and were negotiating the terms of a ten-year framework for the elimination of strategic nuclear missiles. Reagan looked forward to the day when "he and Gorbachev would come to Iceland and each of them would bring the last nuclear missile from each country with them. . . . He would be very old by then and Gorbachev would not recognize him. The President would say, 'Hello Mikhail.' And Gorbachev would say, 'Ron, is it you?' And then they would destroy the last missiles" and "give a tremendous party for the whole world."[3] When the two leaders and their foreign ministers began an argument over whether "strategic offensive arms" or "offensive ballistic missiles" should be liquidated in the second five-year period of the framework, Reagan noted, "It would be fine with him if we eliminated all nuclear weapons."[4] Gorbachev immediately replied, "We can do that. We can eliminate them." Shultz excitedly stated, "Let's do it."[5]

Yet the Reykjavik summit would produce no disarmament agreement. The leaders' discussion of a ten-year plan for eliminating all nuclear weapons quickly became mired in a dispute over the type of strategic defense research that would be permitted while nuclear weapons were being liquidated. Reagan had agreed to Gorbachev's demand that neither superpower would withdraw from the ABM Treaty and deploy strategic defenses during the ten years in which they were eliminating nuclear weapons. The president balked, however, at Gorbachev's insistence that both sides limit strategic defense research to the laboratory during these ten years. Reagan thought that such a restriction would kill SDI, which he believed would facilitate nuclear abolition by ensuring against any rogue attempts to revive nuclear weapons in the future. Gorbachev, however, believed that SDI would allow the United States to deploy offensive weapons in space or an ABM system that would give it a first-strike capability. He refused to drop his demand that SDI research remain confined to the laboratory while nuclear weapons were liquidated.[6] Realizing that the two leaders were at an impasse, Reagan abruptly broke off the session and walked out of the room.[7] The Reykjavik summit was over. Forgoing the ceremonial send-off that usually concludes meetings between heads of state, Reagan and Gorbachev simply left Hofdi House with the grim looks on their faces that would become famous all over the world.

This chapter contends that the period from the November 1985 Geneva summit through the October 1986 Reykjavik summit was the peak of Gorbachev and Reagan's efforts to end the Cold War by negotiating agreements that would jump-start global nuclear abolition. Keenly aware that the Soviet economy could not sustain another round of the nuclear arms race, Gorbachev also had a moral aversion to nuclear weapons that was strengthened by the accident at the Chernobyl nuclear power plant on April 26, 1986. Anxious to begin the process of nuclear disarmament, Gorbachev set forth a series of sweeping nuclear arms reduction proposals in 1986 that contained significant Soviet concessions. European peace activists influenced many of these proposals, particularly those dealing with nuclear weapons in Europe. Gorbachev linked the reduction and elimination of offensive nuclear weapons with restrictions on strategic defenses and hoped that Reagan might agree to limit SDI in exchange for the abolition of nuclear weapons. The leaders' disagreement over the nature and purpose of SDI, however, stymied their efforts to eliminate nuclear weapons.

While Gorbachev and Reagan sought an agreement in late 1985 and 1986 that would begin ridding the world of nuclear weapons, West European peace activists continued to follow the lead of their East European counterparts in advocating an end to the Cold War through the denuclearization and reunification of an autonomous and free Europe. These European activists' arguments influenced Gorbachev's nascent views of a "common European home," although the Soviet leader diverged from the activists in envisioning a place for the Soviet Union in a unified Europe. Gorbachev also advocated greater autonomy for East European states from the Soviet Union, which European peace activists favored. Yet Gorbachev did not prioritize the construction of an integrated Europe or greater autonomy for Eastern Europe until 1987, when Soviet economic interests reinforced the attractiveness of peace activists' arguments for a reunified, autonomous, and free Europe. By 1987, it was also clear that Reagan was unlikely to compromise on SDI, which made Gorbachev more amenable to European activists' vision for ending the Cold War.

*   *   *

Eleven months before the dramatic Reykjavik summit, Reagan and Gorbachev had met for the first time in Geneva on November 19 and 20, 1985. Anti-nuclear activists were largely unimpressed by the summit, ridiculing it as an empty meeting full of "nice smiles."[8] END noted that both Reagan and Gorbachev supported a 50 percent reduction of nuclear weapons, but they disagreed on critical elements of a START agreement. Most notably, the two leaders had different definitions of "strategic" weapons. The Soviets argued that "all weapons capable of reaching the territory of the other superpower" were strategic, while the Americans classified "long-range weapons" as strategic. Under the Soviet definition, a START treaty would include U.S. INF missiles in Western Europe, which could reach the Soviet Union, but exclude Soviet SS-20 missiles, which could reach only U.S. allies in Western Europe. Similarly, both Reagan and Gorbachev supported an interim INF treaty in principle, but they clashed over whether to include British and French nuclear weapons in the agreement. In addition, Gorbachev wanted major restrictions on SDI, which Reagan staunchly opposed.[9]

END activists blamed both superpowers for the lack of substantive progress in Geneva, charging that divisions within the Reagan administration on nuclear policy hindered U.S. preparations for the summit. Recent Soviet proposals "seemed as keen to score public relations points as to stake out the ground in preparation for serious negotiations." For example, Gorbachev offered merely token reductions in Soviet SS-20s aimed at Western Europe in October. Arms reduction agreements would require both superpowers to compromise, which neither seemed willing to do.[10]

In the wake of the Geneva summit, activists across Europe continued to advocate an end to the Cold War through the denuclearization and reunification of an autonomous and free Europe. One of the most dramatic examples was a spontaneous protest for "freedom and peace" in Prague on December 8, 1985. With his appeals to "give peace a chance" and "imagine all the people living life in peace," rock musician John Lennon had become a hero to young Czechoslovaks who wanted peace in their own country and across Europe. Following his assassination in New York City on December 8, 1980, young Czechoslovaks turned a wall on Prague's Kampa Island into a symbolic tomb for Lennon, drawing images of the late Beatle and writing bits of poetry about peace and freedom. Crowds of young Czechoslovaks gathered at what became known as the Lennon Wall each year on the anniversary of the musician's death.[11]

On the fifth anniversary of Lennon's assassination, several hundred young demonstrators decided to march from the Lennon Wall to Prague Castle. After playing rock and folk music, which represented a repudiation of state-sanctioned cultural activities, the young activists chanted as they marched to the castle: "We want freedom!" "Give peace a chance!" "No missiles are peaceful!" "Red bourgeoisie out!" "SS-20s Out!" Three hundred young students and workers signed "an improvised anti-missile petition," which "reject[ed] the siting of any nuclear weapons on either side of Europe!" The petition was sent to Czechoslovakia's president and prime minister, as well as to the U.S. and Soviet embassies. Although several demonstrators were arrested and questioned by the police, they were ultimately released. Charter 77 representatives lauded the spontaneous demonstration as "the first event of its kind in our capital for fifteen years." Impressed by the passion of the young demonstrators, Charter 77 characterized the event as "a challenge to us all" to do more for peace and human rights.[12]

Asserting that the way to end the Cold War was to overturn the bloc system in Europe and achieve European autonomy from the superpowers, a group of peace activists from Britain, Denmark, the FRG, Italy, Spain, and the United States promoted a process called "dealignment" to achieve these ends. Dealignment, or "bloc erosion," called for increased contacts between ordinary citizens and government leaders in Eastern and Western Europe; respect for differences among European states; and a gradual loosening of military ties between states. Recognizing that peace activists working for bloc erosion in different parts of Europe naturally would focus on different discrete goals, the group also sought to devise a common set of criteria that could unify their efforts. "A British campaign against Trident [missiles] or a Turkish campaign to secure the release of imprisoned peace activists may seem very different. But if they share a common philosophy, they can be mutually supportive." Regardless of their immediate goal, activists should promote political rather than military solutions to conflicts in Europe; the democratization of security policy; and increased internationalism. By devising a common framework for peace activities, the group hoped to increase the European peace movement's unity and effectiveness in 1986.[13]

Convinced by East European activists of the indivisibility of peace and human rights, West Europeans also campaigned for human rights protections throughout Europe. In the fall of 1985, West European activists publicized instances of government repression of Eastern bloc dissidents. Contending that all individuals have the right to work for disarmament, END highlighted the KGB's growing persecution of Moscow Trust Group activists, who were frequently arrested or sent to psychiatric hospitals for their membership in an organization that sought nuclear disarmament and the reunification of Europe.[14] Founded by a small group of intellectuals in Moscow on June 4, 1982, the Group to Establish Trust Between the USSR and the USA, better known as the Moscow Trust Group, argued that the development of mutual trust between the superpowers was the key to preventing a nuclear war that would destroy humanity. It wanted to democratize nuclear disarmament negotiations, and it called on ordinary Soviets and Americans to devise concrete proposals for trust-building and nuclear arms reduction.[15] In addition to publicizing Soviet mistreatment of Moscow Trust Group activists, END also drew attention to the arrests and trials of two WiP members, Mariusz Ganic and Tomasz Kulczewski. Both men were pacifists who were arrested for refusing to be drafted into the Polish army.[16]

END activists believed that publicizing the arrests and detention of East European peace activists would help mobilize international pressure that could secure their release. They pointed to the cases of Natasha Akulyenok and Olga Kabanova as examples of their strategy's success. These two Moscow Trust Group members were sent to psychiatric hospitals on May 15, 1985, in order to prevent them from meeting with peace activists from other countries at the Moscow Youth Festival. Both were released, however, after an international outcry over their detention.[17]

Like European peace activists, Gorbachev was disappointed in the Geneva summit. Although he toasted the joint communiqué issued at the end of the summit and wrote glowingly about the meeting in letters to Reagan, he privately lamented the leaders' failure to reach substantive arms reduction agreements.[18] Speaking about the summit at a conference of the Central Committee on November 28, Gorbachev declared, "Reagan is maneuvering. Of course, the essence of his policy—the policy of the military-industrial complex—has not changed, there was no increased love toward us." Yet Gorbachev also believed that the Soviets could induce the president to make compromises that would lead to arms reduction agreements. He told the Central Committee, "Our pressure, the pressure of the public opinion are producing results, forcing him [Reagan] to make steps toward us."[19]

Gorbachev specifically hoped to convince Reagan to restrict or abandon SDI in connection with an agreement to abolish the superpowers' nuclear weapons. U.S. ambassador to the Soviet Union Arthur Hartman recalled that "Gorbachev decided that Reagan meant what he said at Geneva. He did want to rid the world of nuclear weapons, and he was deadly serious about S.D.I. Gorbachev's idea was to persuade Reagan to take the one [abolition] without the other [Star Wars]. He seems to have decided at Geneva that he could bring it off."[20] Reagan had been unwilling to restrict SDI in exchange for an agreement to *reduce* nuclear weapons. Gorbachev hoped, however, that an offer to *eliminate* Soviet nuclear weapons would be too enticing for Reagan, a fellow nuclear abolitionist, to pass up. Surely restrictions on SDI would be a small price to pay for an agreement that would go a long way toward achieving their shared goal of a nuclear-free world.

Shortly after the Geneva summit, Gorbachev instructed the sections of the Ministries of Foreign Affairs and Defense responsible for arms reduction negotiations to devise a bold new initiative that he could present to Reagan.[21] Gorbachev and Shevardnadze had already agreed on the need for a plan to rid the world of nuclear weapons shortly after Shevardnadze became foreign minister in July 1985. "By the autumn we had made a start—a scientific analysis of the international situation, contacts and meetings we had had in the past months," Gorbachev wrote in his memoir. "It was then that we decided to formulate our ideas and intentions in a long-term agenda which would serve as a basis for our 'peace offensive.'"[22] Oleg Grinevsky, head of the Soviet delegation to the CSCE, recalled that the Politburo agreed around December 30 "to come out with a specific realistic program of disarmament and of policies to decrease tension in the international arena." The program would include a 50 percent reduction of strategic nuclear weapons, the elimination of INF missiles in Europe, and measures to guarantee European security, among other things. The Politburo directed the Big Five, its arms control planning commission, and the Little Five, experts who reported to the Big Five, to formulate the details of the disarmament program.[23] The Big Five, which consisted of representatives from the Central Committee of the Communist Party (CPSU), the Ministry of Foreign Affairs, the Ministry of Defense, the KGB, and the Military-Industrial Commission, quickly set to work.[24]

Unbeknownst to nearly everyone, including Gorbachev, Georgy Korn-ienko, first deputy foreign minister, and Marshal Sergei Akhromeyev, chief of the general staff of the Soviet armed forces, had spent the past few months secretly devising "the broadest possible program of nuclear disarmament on their own initiative."[25] The Kornienko-Akhromeyev initiative called for the global elimination of nuclear weapons in fifteen years. Lieutenant General Nikolai N. Detinov, a member of the Little Five; General Nikolai Chervov, dep-uty to the chief of the general staff; and General Viktor Starodubov, an arms reduction negotiator, have asserted that the Soviet military did not think that the Reagan administration would accept this proposal. Rather, they saw it as a useful propaganda tool. The Soviet leadership could use the proposal to show its willingness to eliminate nuclear weapons and tar the Americans as obsta-cles to peace when they rejected it.[26] While many in the Soviet military may have discounted the initiative as propaganda, Akhromeyev appears to have viewed it as a serious arms reduction proposal. The chief of the general staff was keenly aware of the dangerous potential of the superpowers' nuclear arse-nals, which contained tens of thousands of nuclear weapons. "This unimag-inable nuclear power, if used, could incinerate all life on Earth in the course of ten minutes," he reflected.[27] He therefore was anxious to avert nuclear war by reducing and eventually eliminating nuclear weapons.

After the Politburo instructed the Big Five and the Little Five to work out the details of a sweeping new arms reduction initiative, Kornienko and Akhromeyev decided to unveil their secret proposal. Grinevsky recalled that Akhromeyev sent his deputy, Chervov, to present the initiative to Gorbachev in Crimea, where the general secretary was ringing in the new year.[28] After Gorbachev expressed support for the Kornienko-Akhromeyev initiative, it was taken up by the Big Five, which produced the final draft of the plan to abolish nuclear weapons by 2000 that the Politburo endorsed.[29] Gorbachev described the plan in a letter to Reagan on January 14, 1986, and he publicly presented it the following day.[30]

In the letter unveiling his disarmament plan to Reagan, Gorbachev appealed to Reagan's nuclear abolitionism and contended that this initiative would provide a realistic path for achieving the president's goal of a nuclear-free world. While the Soviet plan would require the United States to curtail SDI, Gorbachev argued that the enactment of his proposals would make SDI unnecessary. Reagan justified SDI on the grounds that it would make nuclear abolition possible, but the implementation of Gorbachev's plan would elimi-nate nuclear weapons long before SDI was ready for deployment. Gorbachev urged Reagan to forget SDI and instead focus on destroying offensive nuclear weapons. "Instead of spending the next 10–15 years developing new sophisticated weapons in space, which are allegedly intended to make nuclear weapons 'obsolete' and 'impotent,' wouldn't it be better to address those weapons themselves and take that time to reduce them to zero?" Gorbachev asked Reagan.[31]

Gorbachev's proposal laid out a comprehensive three-stage plan for the global liquidation of nuclear weapons by the end of 1999. By establishing a specific timeline for the elimination of nuclear weapons, the January 15 initiative differed from the vague Soviet disarmament proposals made by Gorbachev's predecessors, which called for nuclear abolition but offered no details for achieving this goal. During the first phase of Gorbachev's plan, the Soviet Union and the United States would reduce by 50 percent their nuclear delivery vehicles that could reach the other superpower's territory. They would also reduce the nuclear "charges" on this type of delivery vehicle to six thousand. These cuts were contingent on the superpowers' rejection of the development, testing, and deployment of "strike space arms." The Soviet Union and the United States would also eliminate their INF missiles in Europe and adopt a nuclear test ban during this phase. The United States would vow not to provide strategic or INF missiles to other countries, and Britain and France would agree not to engage in a nuclear buildup. Gorbachev anticipated that this phase would last from five to eight years.[32]

During the second phase, which would begin by 1990, the other members of the nuclear club would begin reducing their nuclear arsenals. They would implement a nuclear freeze and withdraw any weapons stationed in other countries. The Soviet Union and the United States would continue their phase one reductions and also eliminate INF missiles deployed outside of Europe. All tactical nuclear weapons would be abolished. The bans on "strike space arms" and nuclear testing would become multilateral. This phase would last from five to seven years. In the final phase, which was slated to begin by 1995, the nuclear powers would abolish the rest of their nuclear weapons by the end of 1999.[33]

European anti-nuclear activists influenced the substance of several proposals contained within this January 15 initiative. In the first phase of his disarmament plan, Gorbachev proposed the complete elimination of INF missiles in Europe "as a first stage on the path of freeing the European continent of nuclear weapons."[34] This proposal marked the first time that the Soviets had offered to abolish INF in Europe, and its inclusion in the earliest phase of the disarmament plan suggested that the Soviet leadership prioritized the elimination of nuclear weapons in Europe. From its inception in 1980, END's primary goal had been the denuclearization of Europe. The April 1980 END Appeal called upon the people of Europe "to free the entire territory of Europe, from Poland to Portugal, from nuclear weapons." It also urged "the two super-powers to withdraw all nuclear weapons from European territory. In particu-lar, we ask the Soviet Union to halt production of the SS-20 medium range missile and we ask the United States not to implement the decision to develop cruise missiles and Pershing II missiles for deployment in Europe." END had asserted that the removal of Soviet and U.S. INF missiles from Europe would go a long way toward advancing its goal of a nuclear-free Europe.[35]

In addition, the second phase of Gorbachev's disarmament plan called for the nuclear powers to adopt a nuclear freeze and withdraw any nuclear weap-ons deployed on foreign territory. Kaldor had set forth a "freeze and with-draw" proposal in an editorial in the December 1983–January 1984 edition of the END Journal.[36] In the spring of 1984, the IPCC had taken up the "freeze and withdraw" concept as part of its effort to devise a joint U.S.-European disarmament platform.[37] The END Journal had published the IPCC's "freeze and withdraw" proposal in its December 1984–January 1985 issue.[38]

The Soviet leadership closely monitored the proposals of Western peace organizations and expressed a particular interest in those set forth by END. Tair Tairov, the Soviet representative of the communist World Peace Council from 1979 until early 1986, recalled the Central Committee's keen interest in END's initiatives: "Moscow was always asking me to inform the Soviet lead-ership about the trends in the Western peace movements—what were the priority issues, and so on. Although the Soviet media—and especially articles by the Soviet peace committee leaders—described the END conventions as an anti-Soviet happening, the Soviet Party leaders took the END movement very seriously and the Central Committee was anxious to know as much as possible about it." According to Tairov, Central Committee members were drawn to END's arms reduction proposals, although they "wanted to exploit its disarmament platform for Moscow's foreign policy without paying a price for it." They did not want to implement the human rights protections that END demanded.[39]

Tairov also recalled European peace activists' influence on Gorbachev in particular. "During the last twenty to thirty years, peace research institutes, disarmament campaigns, civil rights activists, and outstanding individuals in Europe have elaborated a long list of peace proposals," he wrote in 1990. "What Gorbachev did was to face the challenge of common sense presented in those peace proposals. Thus he himself has been shaped, as far as foreign policy is concerned, by peace and new social movements in Europe and inside the USSR as well; part of Gorbachev is the work of millions in the streets of Europe and the result of the tireless efforts of human rights activists."[40]

END's proposals reached Party leaders not only through Tairov's reports, but also through the Soviet Peace Committee's accounts of its correspondence and meetings with END activists. Directed by the CPSU, the Soviet Peace Committee was the official state-sponsored peace organization in the Soviet Union and the Soviet affiliate of the World Peace Council. Although END was a non-aligned peace movement, meaning that it was not affiliated with the communist World Peace Council, it maintained contacts with the Soviet Peace Committee so that it could present proposals directly to Soviet officials. Yet relations between END and the Soviet Peace Committee were often strained. In an infamous December 2, 1982, letter to Western peace activists, the Soviet Peace Committee's president, Yuri Zhukov, lambasted END for its relations with East European dissidents and its claim that both superpowers bore responsibility for the nuclear arms race. Zhukov concluded that END's positions showed that the organization "aimed at the disorientation, demobilization, and undermining of the anti-war movement and is called upon to conceal and justify an aggressive militarist policy of the USA and NATO."[41] In its response, END contended that Zhukov sought to "slander" END simply because it refused to support Soviet policies blindly and noted that his letter "could weaken and divide the peace movement."[42]

Despite the Soviet Peace Committee's inflammatory statements, END activists valued their meetings with committee representatives because they provided "occasions for argument and debate" and served as "a way of learning and understanding different positions, seeing each other as human beings, and developing our own thinking." Discussions with the Soviet Peace Committee allowed END to present and explain its proposals, as well as advocate respect for the human rights of Soviet activists like those in the Moscow Trust Group. Days before the END Journal ran Kaldor's editorial promoting the "freeze and withdraw" concept that later appeared in Gorbachev's disarmament plan, a group of END activists met with the Soviet Peace Committee on November 30, 1983, and presented the idea.[43] Representatives from the Soviet Peace Committee also attended the July 1984 END Convention as observers and would have been exposed to END proposals during the convention's sessions.[44]

Although Zhukov and other Soviet Peace Committee officials viewed END as "a pro-NATO, anti-socialist movement," they provided reports of their meetings with END activists to Party leaders.[45] In fact, some independent peace activists in the Eastern bloc encouraged END's leadership to meet with the Soviet Peace Committee for this reason. In a March 1986 letter, Yuri Medvedkov, an active member of the Moscow Trust Group, encouraged END activists to continue expressing their views to Zhukov because "with reluctance, perhaps, he must report it higher up."[46]

Alexei Pankin also highlighted END's influence on Gorbachev's nuclear arms reduction proposals. While working at the Institute of USA and Canada, Pankin grew close to Director Georgy Arbatov, who advised Gorbachev. In 1988, Pankin became the deputy editor of the Moscow journal *International Affairs* and started assisting Shevardnadze's speechwriters. Discussing the influences on Gorbachev's foreign policy, Pankin recalled, "Since all ideas relating to nuclear disarmament and security, etc. were coming from the West, a large part of the 'new thinking' basically was simply a copying of books and articles by Mary Kaldor, E. P. Thompson, and George Kennan, etc."[47]

In a statement on Gorbachev's January 15 initiative, the Soviet Peace Committee acknowledged the influence of European activists' proposals on Gorbachev's disarmament plan. "The new Soviet proposals are proof of the highest responsibility, the manifestation of a new thinking and a new policy determined by the realities of the nuclear age, and the reflection of many initiatives and proposals put forth by peace movements in different countries," the Soviet Peace Committee declared.[48] In a letter written on January 20, Zhukov solicited Western peace activists' reactions to Gorbachev's disarmament plan and encouraged these activists to submit ideas for joint action to promote the January 15 initiative.[49]

While END activists were pleased that Gorbachev's plan incorporated some of their proposals, they nevertheless characterized the January 15 initiative as "a masterly move in the peace propaganda game." In an article in the *END Journal*, Kaldor expressed her fear that Gorbachev might be "making utopian-sounding proposals in the confident expectation that the United States will never agree" to them. She noted that the Soviets already had made many of the stage one proposals in October 1985. One striking exception was Gorbachev's call to eliminate INF missiles in Europe as a first step toward ridding Europe of nuclear weapons. While it was apparent that Gorbachev would not agree to reductions in strategic nuclear weapons without significant restrictions on SDI, it was unclear if Gorbachev would be willing to conclude a separate INF agreement without a U.S. pledge to curb SDI. If Gorbachev would not negotiate a separate INF treaty, then "the medium range offer is nothing more than a way of increasing European political pressure on the US to halt Star Wars. . . . The proposal means that Gorbachev may be serious about stopping Star Wars but is less serious about disarmament in Europe." Kaldor noted, however, that a separate INF agreement would show that Gorbachev genuinely wanted disarmament. "It would make the Gorbachev package much more convincing, indicating in practice that real benefits could be obtained if the US was willing to give up Star Wars. More important, perhaps, it could mark the beginning of a real disarmament process in Europe, with profound consequences for the very structures of the Cold War."[50]

Ironically, the Reagan administration was largely in agreement with END's assessment of Gorbachev's January 15 initiative. Many U.S. officials similarly believed that Gorbachev's disarmament plan contained many elements of propaganda and recycled several old Soviet arms reduction proposals. John Poindexter, who succeeded McFarlane as national security advisor in December 1985, contended that Gorbachev's initiative had "a large measure of propaganda."[51] An NSC paper concluded that the January 15 initiative did not set forth any new START proposals or any constructive proposals on defense and space, but did acknowledge that it contained a new offer to eliminate INF in Europe.[52] Even Reagan initially feared that Gorbachev's disarmament plan might be propaganda, writing in his diary on January 15, "Then a long meeting with Geo Shultz & John Poindexter on . . . our response to a letter from Gorbachev who surprisingly is calling for an arms reduction plan which will rid the world of nuclear weapons by yr. 2000. Of course he has a couple of zingers in there which we'll have to work around. But at the very least it is a h—l of a propaganda move."[53]

Reagan's advisors were at odds over the proper response to Gorbachev's January 15 initiative. Weinberger and the Joint Chiefs did not think that the United States should alter any of its current arms reduction positions, because they believed that Gorbachev's disarmament plan did not contain any substantially new START, INF, or defense and space proposals. Weinberger and the Joint Chiefs also opposed expressions of support for the principle of nuclear abolition, arguing that it "will cause the [upcoming Washington] summit to become, in effect, a deadline for reaching some agreement with the Soviets, and, therefore, it will be much more difficult to deal with the Soviet proposal, protect our interests, and pursue our agenda." On the opposite end of the spectrum, Shultz and Nitze thought that U.S. negotiators should respond to Gorbachev's plan by offering new START, INF, and defense and space proposals. They also wanted to keep open "the possibility of some limited general agreement about the elimination of nuclear weapons which could be reached at the next summit." Adelman, Edward Rowny, the Geneva negotiators, and the NSC staff shared Shultz and Nitze's willingness to support the goal of nuclear abolition on U.S. terms, but thought that the new INF initiative in Gorbachev's plan was the only one that warranted a new U.S. proposal.[54]

After hearing these three options, Reagan endorsed the position of Adelman, Rowny, the Geneva negotiators, and the NSC staff at a National Security Planning Group meeting on February 3. He did not believe that the January 15 initiative, which repackaged many existing Soviet proposals, merited new U.S. proposals across the board. On the other hand, the president rejected Weinberger and the Joint Chiefs' idea of essentially characterizing Gorbachev's plan as propaganda. Reagan asserted, "The US should go to the negotiations, point out that the Soviets have made a general, overall offer, and agree on the overall aims of the process. We should emphasize that what the US seeks now is a *practical* way forward: a way to achieve verification in a concrete agreement, even if such involves a proposal we have already made." Reagan did want to revise the current U.S. INF proposal, which called for an interim agreement limiting each superpower to 140 INF missile launchers in Europe and requiring the Soviets to reduce their SS-20 launchers in Asia comparably. This interim INF agreement would establish an equal global limit on U.S. and Soviet INF missile warheads. In instructing his aides to develop a new INF proposal, Reagan declared that "it was clear that we needed to work in INF for total elimination of those systems."[55]

In its official response to the January 15 initiative, the Reagan administration affirmed its support for the principle of nuclear abolition. The elimination of nuclear weapons, however, should be preceded by "correcting conventional and other force imbalances and problems, full compliance with existing and future treaty obligations, peaceful resolution of regional conflicts in ways that allow free choice without outside interference, and a demonstrated commitment by the Soviet leadership to peaceful competition." The administration also rejected Gorbachev's assertion that nuclear abolition would "obviate the need for defenses against such weapons, particularly to protect against cheating or breakout by any country."[56] Contending that the superpowers should concentrate on "the first steps of this process" of eliminating nuclear weapons, U.S. officials urged the Soviets to focus on achieving a 50 percent reduction of nuclear weapons and an interim INF agreement in the near term.[57]

In response to Gorbachev's new proposal to eliminate INF missiles in Europe, the Reagan administration set forth an INF counterproposal after consultation with its allies in Europe and Asia. Troubled by Gorbachev's failure to address Soviet SS-20 missiles in Asia, which could easily be moved to target Western Europe, the Reagan administration made a proposal that would eliminate INF globally.[58] Under the U.S. proposal, the superpowers would reduce their INF missile launchers in Europe to 140 by the end of 1987. The Soviet Union would make "concurrent proportionate reductions in Asia." During the next year, the United States and the Soviet Union would reduce their remaining INF missile launchers by 50 percent. By the end of 1989, both sides would have eliminated their INF completely. While the reductions were being implemented, there would be "a parallel series of global LRINF missile warhead ceilings under which the U.S. retains the right to global equality."[59] In a February 24, 1986, statement, Reagan asserted that this new INF proposal could lay the foundation for "immediate progress" in the INF talks. He also reminded Gorbachev that "the place to make real progress in reducing nuclear and other forces is at the confidential negotiating table" rather than in the public arena.[60]

*   *   *

As 1986, the UN-designated "International Year of Peace," got underway, European peace activists continued to promote not only a nuclear-free Europe, but also an end to the division of Europe, greater European autonomy from the superpowers, and respect for human rights.[61] Like in the year before, East European dissidents often took the initiative in promoting the goal of a reunified, autonomous, and free Europe, while West Europeans primarily endorsed and publicized East European appeals and proposals. West European and East European activists in the Network for East-West Dialogue, however, did join forces in 1986 to craft a memorandum explaining how the Helsinki process could facilitate the denuclearization, reunification, and democratization of Europe.

Affirming the indivisibility of peace and human rights, Initiative for Peace and Human Rights activists Rainer Eppelmann, Peter Grimm, Ralf Hirsch, and Wolfgang Templin sent a letter to the East German government on January 24, 1986, calling for "internal peace" within their country. "In our view only a state which is peaceful in its domestic affairs can really convincingly work for peace in its foreign policy," these four prominent East German activists wrote. Defining "internal peace" as respect for the rights set forth in the UN's Universal Declaration of Human Rights, the East German activists urged their government to adopt a series of measures to safeguard citizens' freedom of movement, freedom of assembly, right to protest, freedom of association, and right to conscientious objection. They also proposed measures to allow anyone to be nominated to run in local and national elections and to facilitate dialogue between the East German government and independent peace activists. The East German activists characterized these proposals as their contribution to the International Year of Peace.[62] END activists translated and published this letter as part of a collection of documents from the autonomous East German peace movement in July 1987. END hoped that this collection would draw attention to the ideas set forth by East German activists in documents "which are inaccessible to the majority of people living in the GDR" and "for the main part little known in the West."[63]

In a petition sent on April 2, 1986, to the Eleventh Party Congress of the Socialist Unity Party, twenty-one East German peace activists called for not only the recognition of the indivisibility of peace and human rights, but also the reunification of Europe, an end to the nuclear arms race, and greater autonomy for the GDR from the Soviet Union. The signatories contended that the existence of the military blocs provided the underlying rationale for the continuation of the nuclear arms race, lambasting Soviet bloc officials who were obsessed with the concept of nuclear parity between the blocs. They also asserted that the Soviet Union used the existence of a hostile military bloc to legitimize its interventions in East European affairs and that the East German government used NATO's existence as an excuse to militarize East German society. In order to facilitate the dissolution of the military blocs, disarmament, and the achievement of greater autonomy, these activists advocated the GDR's withdrawal from the Warsaw Pact, which would force the Soviet Union to remove its troops and weapons of mass destruction from the country. The activists contended that the victors of the Second World War must sign peace treaties with both German states "if complete sovereignty of the GDR is to be established."[64]

Asserting that "peace is a human right and thus each member of society must be able to discuss and help determine everything which affects this right," the signatories called for the creation of a forum in which ordinary citizens and government officials could discuss peace-related issues. They noted that the East German government had refused to accept or even consider numerous proposals made by East German peace activists, including those calling for the demilitarization of society and protections for conscientious objectors.[65] In an effort to publicize this East German petition to the Socialist

Unity Party Congress, END activists devoted an article to it in the Summer 1986 issue of the *END Journal* and translated and published it in the *Voices from the GDR* document collection.[66]

Inspired by young Czechoslovaks' anti-nuclear demonstration in Prague on December 8, 1985, and their creation of "informal groups" dedicated to "religious or ecological concerns or new music appreciation," Charter 77 spokespeople Martin Palouš, Anna Šabatová, and Jan Stern wrote a letter on March 6, 1986, to the Federal Assembly of Czechoslovakia demanding respect for the rights of young activists. Recognizing that young Czechoslovaks often found rock and folk music "capable of expressing the feelings of a generation growing up in the shadow of nuclear missiles," Charter 77 insisted that the state stop persecuting musicians. Since 1983, numerous young singer-songwriters and bands had been banned from performing and some had been tried on false criminal charges. On October 22, 1984, the Ministry of the Interior had even disbanded the official Czechoslovak Musicians' Union, which included the Jazz Section.[67]

The Jazz Section of the Czechoslovak Musicians' Union identified with the European peace movement and declared at the 1983 World Peace Council assembly in Prague that it viewed "music as a universal language, as a way to mutual understanding between people and nations. We believe people searching spontaneously for a common language are as important for peace as professional diplomats negotiating at disarmament conferences."[68] The Jazz Section organized music festivals and concerts in Czechoslovakia, arranged trips to jazz festivals in other Eastern bloc countries, and disseminated information on jazz, rock music, art, and poetry. It even published works that were blacklisted in Czechoslovakia.[69] Charter 77 demanded respect for young Czechoslovaks' right to express themselves freely through music, urging the government to "end the petty despotism over new music. Let the bands play and the singers sing! Lift the ban on the Jazz Section and the Young Music Section."[70]

Appealing to the idea of Europe as a single entity, Charter 77 also advocated the right of young Czechoslovaks to travel throughout the continent. "Even in the most official quarters they talk of Europe as our common home," the Charter 77 representatives wrote. "But what is the good of that, when you cannot walk around this home and its residents cannot visit each other? How can a sense of confidence and belonging be created when nations are artificially divided from each other?" Charter 77 appealed to West European peace activists to help organize and finance "holiday camps where young people from both parts of the European home could meet."[71]

In addition, Charter 77 emphasized the aversion of young Czechoslovaks to the military and nuclear missiles, which "fill them with an even greater sense of insecurity and danger—because they know that every place where missiles are sited becomes a target for enemy missiles." Accordingly, they called on the government to shorten the mandatory military service requirement for Czech youth from two years to eighteen months and create "alternative service" options for conscientious objectors. Palouš, Šabatová, and Stern concluded their letter by demanding an end to discrimination in education and employment on the basis of personal convictions. Young peace activists should have the same opportunities to better their lives as those who did not participate in the peace movement.[72]

END's Czech Working Group, which focused on establishing ties between END and Czechoslovak peace activists, sought to publicize Charter 77's letter to the Federal Assembly, which became known as "Space for the Younger Generation." The Czech Working Group was particularly taken with the idea of transcending the bloc system in Europe by establishing holiday camps at which young West Europeans and East Europeans could meet. During a June 4, 1986, meeting, the group endorsed the holiday camp initiative and decided to seek funding for the program.[73]

In addition to endorsing and publishing East European dissidents' appeals for the reunification of Europe, greater European autonomy from the superpowers, and human rights protections, West European peace activists continued to publicize the government repression of Eastern bloc peace activists in 1986. END drew attention to the growing harassment of Moscow Trust Group members, many of whom were questioned by the Soviet authorities, beaten, sent to psychiatric hospitals, arrested, or dismissed from their jobs.[74] An article in the April–May 1986 issue of the END Journal also spotlighted the February arrests of two WiP activists, Jacek Czaputowicz and Piotr Niemczyk, on charges of membership in an illegal organization. END highlighted the fact that the European peace movement was circulating a petition calling for the release of Czaputowicz and Niemczyk and "condemn[ing] the Polish authorities' repression of peace activists at the precise moment of growing international hope for a new détente."[75]

Hopeful that publicizing the detention of East European peace activists would create international pressure that could secure their release, END proudly reported in the summer of 1986 that the International Physicians for the Prevention of Nuclear War had successfully lobbied the Soviet authorities for the release of Aleksandr Shatravka. Shatravka was a member of the

Moscow Trust Group who was arrested in 1982 for distributing the group's founding appeal.[76] END also encouraged Western peace activists to participate in Moscow Trust Group meetings if they were traveling in the Soviet Union. Trust Group members had reported that the KGB had refrained from interfering with their meetings when Westerners were in attendance. Not only would the presence of Western peace activists lend legitimacy to Trust Group meetings, but Trust Group members also believed that any interactions between Western activists and Soviet citizens would help "break down prejudices and enemy images on both sides."[77]

Peace activists from both halves of Europe also met and corresponded throughout 1986 in an effort to devise a joint strategy for using the Helsinki Final Act to facilitate the reunification of a denuclearized and democratic Europe. Inspired by the March 1985 Prague Appeal's contention that the peace movement had neglected the Helsinki process, the Network for East-West Dialogue, which had been established at the 1984 END Convention, took action. Based on input from West European peace activists and East European dissidents, Network drafted a memorandum setting forth ways in which the CSCE process could create a reunified, denuclearized, and free Europe. Network circulated a first draft of what would come to be known as the "Helsinki Memorandum" in late 1985, and activists from across Europe met in Milan from May 16 through 18, 1986, to discuss drafts of the document. Dutch IKV, which played a leading role in Network, advocated a November 1986 release of the final memorandum to coincide with the opening of the Third CSCE Follow-Up Meeting in Vienna.[78]

The first draft of the Helsinki Memorandum called for the withdrawal of U.S. and Soviet troops and weapons from Europe, the disbanding of NATO and the Warsaw Pact, the creation of a neutral zone extending from Scandinavia to the Balkans, and the denuclearization of Europe. It envisioned Europe as a single entity and advocated increased East-West cooperation on economic, environmental, scientific, and cultural issues. Recognizing the indivisibility of peace and human rights, the memorandum also set forth a plan for instituting human rights protections throughout the continent. In its first draft of the memorandum, Network also envisioned a Europe that would be autonomous from both superpowers. Adopting Thompson's phrase from the 1980 END Appeal, the memorandum encouraged all Europeans "to behave as if a united, neutral and peaceful Europe already existed."[79]

During late 1985 and 1986, European peace activists' calls for a denuclearized and reunified Europe began to influence Gorbachev's nascent concept of a "common European home." Gorbachev came to share the European activists' vision of a united Europe, although he imagined a place for the Soviet Union in the "common European home." During this period, Gorbachev also advocated greater autonomy for East European states, which European peace activists favored.

Gorbachev first invoked the idea of a "common European home" in a speech before the British House of Commons Select Committee on Foreign Affairs on December 18, 1984. Claiming that Soviet proposals for the upcoming Nuclear and Space Talks called for dramatic nuclear arms reduction, he urged the British members of Parliament to recognize that "for all that separates us, we have one planet, and Europe is our common home, not a theater of operations."[80] As historian Marie-Pierre Rey has pointed out, however, the concept of a "common European home" was not new to Soviet foreign policy. Gromyko had used the phrase in 1972 to persuade French president Georges Pompidou to endorse the idea of the CSCE. Brezhnev had also included the phrase in a November 1981 speech in Bonn. When Gorbachev employed the phrase before the British House of Commons in December 1984, its significance was not immediately evident. Was Gorbachev using the phrase in an attempt to drive a wedge between Western Europe and the United States, which did not fit into the "common European home"? Or did the phrase indicate that Gorbachev was contemplating a new vision for Europe?[81]

Gorbachev's next references to a "common European home" showed that he was formulating a new vision for a united Europe that was strikingly similar to the one set forth by the European peace movement. On the eve of his October 1985 visit to France, which was his first trip abroad as general secretary, Gorbachev gave an interview on September 30 to French journalists from TF-1. Answering a question about his desire to improve Soviet relations with Western Europe, Gorbachev stated, "We [Europeans] live in the same house, though some use one entrance and others, another. We need to cooperate and develop communications within that house. I think it natural that the Soviet Union attaches much importance to this cooperation."[82] In an October 3, 1985, address to French parliamentarians, Gorbachev laid out the dimensions of this "common European home," although he did not use this specific phrase in his speech. Foreshadowing his famous July 6, 1989, address on the "common European home" to the Council of Europe in Strasbourg, Gorbachev called for all European countries to cooperate on security, economic, environmental, and humanitarian issues. He also advocated increased contacts between the Warsaw Pact and NATO in the short term and the eventual dissolution of the blocs in Europe. In his view, cooperation among European states and the gradual de-blocking of Europe was necessary to safeguard European security, facilitate economic growth and scientific progress, protect the environment, and enrich European culture.[83]

Gorbachev's proposals for how to reunify Europe were the same as those set forth by European peace activists. He expressed support for the idea of establishing nuclear-free zones in Scandinavia, the Balkans, and in Central Europe "along both sides of the line dividing the two military-political groupings."[84] Contending that the Helsinki process could help Europe overcome its division, Gorbachev urged the continuation of the CSCE process.[85] He advocated ties between the Council for Mutual Economic Assistance (CMEA) and the European Economic Community (EEC), as well as greater contacts between West Europeans and East Europeans at all levels, ranging from government leaders to scientists and artists.[86]

Yet Gorbachev's vision of a united Europe diverged from the one presented by the European peace movement in that it included a place for the Soviet Union. While many European peace activists called for greater European autonomy from the superpowers, Gorbachev contended that the Soviet Union belonged in the "common European home." The 1980 END Appeal defined Europe as extending "from Poland to Portugal."[87] Kaldor explained in March 1984 that END deliberately delineated Europe as "Poland to Portugal" rather than "the Atlantic to the Urals" in order to convey that "nuclear weapons are a way of maintaining a gain in [superpower] domination in Europe and if one had Atlantic to the Urals, and included part of the Soviet Union, one would lose that political significance."[88] Gorbachev, however, contended that the Soviet Union shared a common history and set of traditions with the countries of Europe and therefore fit into a "common European home."[89]

Although Gorbachev promoted the Soviet Union's place in a reunified Europe, he also suggested that people across Europe should have the freedom to choose their own form of government and social system. European peace activists strongly supported the right to self-determination, the exercise of which could bring the autonomy from the superpowers that the activists so desired. In his September 30 interview with French television journalists, Gorbachev declared, "History will have enough time for a peaceful competition of ways of life to ensure for people an opportunity to make a voluntary choice, on their own, to determine which social system is more to their liking."[90] A few days later, Gorbachev told French parliamentarians, "We hold that it is not by force of arms, but only and exclusively by force of example that one must prove the correctness of one's ideology, the advantages of the system that each people has chosen of its own free will."[91] These statements about self-determination were both remarkable and ironic coming from the leader of a country that had repressed an anti-communist uprising in East Germany in 1953 and invaded Hungary in 1956 and Czechoslovakia in 1968 to stop liberalization processes. Would Gorbachev actually allow East European countries to choose their own form of government? Would he permit Eastern Europe to loosen its bonds to the Soviet Union?

European activists influenced Gorbachev's concept of a "common European home" and his budding support for the right to self-determination across Europe. Their proposals for a denuclearized, reunified, autonomous, and free Europe reached the Soviet leadership through the same channels as West Europeans' nuclear disarmament initiatives. Tair Tairov, the Soviet representative of the World Peace Council, provided reports on Western peace movements to the Central Committee, which was especially interested in END's activities. Tairov credited Western peace groups with "play[ing] an instrumental role both in creating an international climate for the changes in Europe and in putting forward an arsenal of peace proposals which contributed to new thinking."[92] In fact, West European peace activists were often supporting and publishing East Europeans' proposals for the reunification of Europe, European autonomy, and human rights protections. West European activists thus lent a powerful voice to the arguments of East European dissidents, who were persecuted in their home countries.

The Soviet Peace Committee also sent accounts of its meetings and correspondence with European peace activists to Party leaders, so it would have conveyed activists' European proposals to the Soviet leadership.[93] Soviet Peace Committee representatives had attended the 1984 END Convention in Perugia, during which the division of Europe was a major subject of discussion, alongside traditional disarmament issues.[94] The work of Mary Kaldor, who was the editor of the END Journal, and E. P. Thompson also provided inspiration for Gorbachev's security policy.[95] It is therefore unsurprising that Gorbachev's calls for a "common European home" and freedom of choice in the fall of 1985 strongly resembled END's demands for a denuclearized, reunified, autonomous, and free Europe.

Gorbachev sincerely wanted a "common European home" and anxiously sought to dispel any notions that his initiative for a reunified Europe was propaganda. Aware that West European leaders might perceive his advocacy of a "common European home" as an effort to split Western Europe from its

American ally, Gorbachev insisted that he was not trying to divide NATO. "We are realists," Gorbachev told the French parliamentarians, "and we understand how strong are the ties—historical, political, and economic—linking Western Europe and the United States."[96] Nevertheless, many West European leaders viewed Gorbachev's "common European home" as propaganda, believing that the Soviet leader was simply trying to pressure U.S. officials into an arms reduction agreement by showing his eagerness to engage with other Western countries. Rey notes that "Margaret Thatcher denounced its 'Utopian dimension,' François Mitterrand found the project premature, and Chancellor Kohl interpreted it as a new attempt to destabilize NATO."[97] Gorbachev was not effective in persuading West European leaders that he sincerely wanted to overcome the division of Europe to promote European security and economic growth, protect the environment, and enliven European culture.

Gorbachev's "common European home" concept was not propaganda, however, as evidenced by the fact that his private statements about the initiative's purpose matched his public pronouncements. In his political report to the Twenty-Seventh Congress of the CPSU on February 25, 1986, Gorbachev set forth the principles of his "new thinking" in foreign policy, one of which was the reunification of Europe. He called for not only "peaceful cooperation among the nations of that [European] continent," but also the "disbandment of military alliances." Gorbachev contended that these aims could be accomplished through "the Helsinki process and a radical reduction of nuclear and conventional weapons" in Europe. He also recognized the importance of "cooperation in the dissemination of the ideas of peace, disarmament, and international security" and "broader contact between peoples for the purpose of learning about one another."[98] In formulating the principles of "new thinking" in early 1986, Gorbachev later recalled that he "found it increasingly difficult to see the multicolored patchwork of Europe's political map as I used to see it before. I was thinking about the common roots of this multiform and yet fundamentally indivisible European civilization, and perceived with growing awareness the artificiality of the political blocs and the archaic nature of the 'iron curtain.'"[99] Thus, the reunification of Europe became part of the "new thinking," which also posited that neither a nuclear arms race nor a nuclear war could ever be won and emphasized the interdependence of countries in the communist and capitalist blocs.[100]

Gorbachev also privately expressed support for greater East European autonomy from the Soviet Union, suggesting that his October 1985 public statements in France about freedom of choice were sincere. In a speech to

Soviet foreign ministry officials on May 28, 1986, Gorbachev insisted, "We have to understand that relations with the socialist countries have entered a new historical era. The time when we helped them to form their economy, their parties, and their political institutions is past. . . . These are full-fledged states, and we cannot lead them by the hand to kindergarten as we would little children. We need a different type of relationship now."[101] On July 3, Gorbachev told the Politburo that the Soviet Union would no longer intervene militarily in East European countries to quell reform movements. "What went on before could not continue. The methods that were used in Czechoslovakia and Hungary now are no good; they will not work!" Gorbachev contended that the Soviet Union could not hope to persuade East European countries to follow the Soviet example through the use of force. "The CPSU's influence can only be ideological, only through example," he asserted.[102] East Europeans must be permitted to run their own affairs.

Although European peace activists influenced Gorbachev's concept of a "common European home" and his support for greater autonomy for Eastern Europe, the Soviet leader did not prioritize these issues until 1987. By that point, Soviet economic interests reinforced the attractiveness of peace activists' arguments for a reunified, autonomous, and free Europe. In 1986, however, Gorbachev did not believe that support for East European countries was a major burden on the Soviet economy that necessitated East European autonomy. He was hopeful about CMEA reform and therefore focused on CMEA, rather than European-wide, integration.[103] Gorbachev was well aware that East European economies were heavily dependent on the Soviet Union, telling Soviet foreign ministry officials on May 28, 1986, that "our friends' situations largely depend on the state of our affairs."[104] The Soviet Union supplied Eastern Europe with oil and gas at well below world market prices. In exchange, Eastern Europe provided the Soviet Union with typically substandard manufactured products. In addition to accepting this disadvantageous system of trade, the Soviet Union provided other subsidies to Eastern Europe.[105] Yet Gorbachev did not view Eastern Europe as a burden to be jettisoned in 1986. In fact, when he learned of the "dangerous position" of the Hungarian economy at the Warsaw Pact's Political Consultative Committee meeting in June 1986, he told Hungarian leader János Kádár to "lean on our shoulder."[106]

Gorbachev believed that the CMEA could be reformed, and he sought CMEA integration in 1986. He recognized that "we have reached the point where we need to build connections [with East European countries] on mutually beneficial grounds, and where we need to press our friends on the quality of the goods they are supplying us." Yet he believed that CMEA integration would accomplish these ends and proudly told the Politburo that the Warsaw Pact had agreed at its June Political Consultative Committee meeting to "liven up our work within the framework of CMEA."[107] Although Gorbachev also understood that the Eastern bloc was lagging behind Western Europe in the process of economic integration, he believed that this could be rectified by "a radical *perestroika* of the economic cooperation mechanism" among CMEA members.[108] Confident that the CMEA could be reformed, Gorbachev did not believe that pan-European integration was the key to spurring Eastern bloc economies.

Rather, Gorbachev's foreign policy priority in 1986 was a Soviet-American agreement that would drastically reduce or eliminate the superpowers' nuclear arsenals. Chernyaev, who became Gorbachev's principal foreign affairs aide on February 1, recalled that the Soviet leader believed in 1986 that he could end the Cold War through nuclear disarmament.[109] The Chernobyl disaster heightened Gorbachev's desire for an agreement that would eliminate nuclear weapons. On April 26, reactor number four at the Chernobyl nuclear power plant in Ukraine exploded, releasing fifty million curies of radiation that spread across the Soviet Union and Europe. As historian Serhii Plokhy has explained, the radioactive fallout from the Chernobyl accident was "the equivalent of 500 Hiroshima bombs." Although the Soviet government did not publicly acknowledge the Chernobyl accident for nearly three days and then understated its severity, it evacuated almost 120,000 people from a thirty-kilometer "exclusion zone" around Chernobyl in the weeks after the explosion.[110] According to historian Kate Brown, the Chernobyl disaster killed at least 35,000 to 150,000 people just in Ukraine. These figures do not include deaths in Russia and Belarus, where much of Chernobyl's fallout struck.[111]

Andrei Grachev, an advisor to Gorbachev, has characterized the Chernobyl disaster as Gorbachev's "personal Cuban missile crisis." The Chernobyl accident showed the Soviet leader the chaos and suffering that would result from a nuclear war. More than ever, he believed that the superpowers must eliminate their nuclear arsenals in order to avert a nuclear war. Speaking to the Politburo on May 8, Gorbachev contended, "We need negotiations. Even with this [American] 'gang' we need to negotiate. If not, what remains? Look at the Chernobyl catastrophe. Just a puff and we can all feel what nuclear war would be like."[112]

Frustrated by the lack of progress on arms control issues since the Geneva summit, Gorbachev decided that the two leaders should "intervene personally" to give the Nuclear and Space Talks "a major impetus; otherwise they would continue to mark time while creating only the appearance of preparations for our meeting on American soil." Gorbachev believed that the two leaders could devise solutions to the issues that stumped their respective negotiators in Geneva. In a September 15 letter to Reagan, he therefore proposed "a quick one-on-one meeting, let us say in Iceland or London, may be just for one day, to engage in a strictly confidential, private and frank discussion (possibly with only our foreign ministers present)." He hoped that this meeting would produce instructions for their negotiators to "draft agreements on two or three very specific questions, which you and I could sign during my visit to the United States."[113]

Within a day of receiving Gorbachev's letter, Reagan assented to the Soviet leader's proposal for a meeting, provided that the Soviets quickly and fairly resolved the Daniloff affair. On August 30, 1986, the Soviets had arrested *U.S. News and World Report* journalist Nicholas Daniloff on trumped-up spying charges in retaliation for the Americans' arrest of Soviet spy Gennady Zakharov.[114] Reagan also indicated his preference for Reykjavik as the site of their meeting. The president liked the symbolism of meeting in a location that was roughly halfway between Moscow and Washington.[115] Reykjavik's remoteness appealed to Shultz, who recognized that the Icelandic government would not insist on being involved in the negotiations or holding distracting social events.[116] Hours after Daniloff's release, Reagan announced on September 30 that he would meet with Gorbachev in Reykjavik on the weekend of October 11 and 12.[117]

During internal Soviet preparations for the Reykjavik meeting, Gorbachev repeatedly emphasized that he sought an agreement eliminating nuclear weapons. On October 4, he told the team preparing for Reykjavik, "We must emphasize that we are proposing the liquidation of nuclear weapons, which we already discussed with the President in Geneva. The talks must be devoted precisely to this goal. We should link this position with my January 15th statement."[118] The official memorandum setting forth the Soviets' "main positions" for the Reykjavik meeting noted, "The Soviet Union proceeds from the assumption that the final result of all the steps in this area should be total liquidation of the nuclear arsenal." It encouraged Soviet negotiators to "underline the importance of the statement of the General Secretary of the Central Committee of the CPSU of January 15, 1986."[119]

Still haunted by the devastation wrought by Chernobyl, Gorbachev also recognized that the Soviet economy could not sustain a renewed nuclear arms race. Understanding that a Soviet-American arms reduction treaty was the only way to stop the costly arms race, Gorbachev insisted that the Soviets should make compromises in order to achieve an agreement. "And if we do not compromise on some questions, even very important ones, we will lose the main point: we will be pulled into an arms race beyond our power, and we will lose this race, for we are presently at the limit of our capabilities," Gorbachev told the group preparing for Reykjavik. "If the new round begins, the pressure on our economy will be inconceivable. That is why to avoid the new round of arms race is the task of tasks for us."[120]

Soviet concessions would also "move" Reagan, which was vital for making the Reykjavik meeting a success. Recognizing that Reagan was surrounded by conservatives who were averse to nuclear abolition, Gorbachev wanted to "pull Reagan into the conversation, so he would agree on directives to the negotiators."[121] The Soviets prepared a host of concessions on INF, START, the ABM Treaty, and nuclear testing for the Reykjavik meeting.[122]

Reagan administration officials had far more modest goals for Reykjavik than their Soviet counterparts. Not expecting the meeting to yield any substantive agreements, Reagan's advisors encouraged the president just to try to make enough progress on arms control issues to set up a productive summit in Washington, DC.[123] The guidance for the U.S. team preparing for Reykjavik stated that the "desired outcome" was "to get [a] specific date for [the] next milestone," presumably referring to the Washington summit.[124]

Since the Reagan administration had set forth a new defense and space proposal on July 25 and new START and INF positions on September 18, it did not prepare any new proposals to present at the Reykjavik meeting.[125] In June 1986, Reagan had told his advisors that he wanted a dramatic arms reduction proposal that could jump-start the Nuclear and Space Talks. At a National Security Planning Group meeting on June 6, Reagan raised the idea of tying the deployment of SDI to the elimination of strategic nuclear missiles, advocating "an agreement now that, if SDI research proves out, and recognizing that both sides are now free to conduct research under the ABM treaty, we would when we got to the point of needing to test, invite the Soviets to observe our tests, but that actual deployment by either side would depend on movement towards total elimination of strategic nuclear missiles—in this way, both sides would see SDI not as a threat, but as a defense against a madman."[126]

Six days later, Weinberger surprised the National Security Planning Group by proposing that "there should be no restraints on SDI research and that we should go for reduction to zero ballistic missiles to be phased in with SDI deployments." Weinberger likely did not want to eliminate ballistic missiles but simply sought to craft a proposal that would give the Reagan administration the appearance of negotiating while still being unacceptable to the Soviets. Just before the meeting ended, Weinberger warned, "We need to be careful with any discussion of ABM or we risk being dragged into an agreement," suggesting that he was not eager for an accord with the Soviets. Reagan, however, jumped at Weinberger's proposal, believing that it would advance his goal of a nuclear-free world. "The time is right for something dramatic," he told his advisors. "We should go for zero ballistic missiles, agree to go forward with research permitted by the ABM treaty, invite the other side to witness testing when we come to that. No deployment of SDI until we eliminate ballistic missiles. Agree to share SDI with the world."[127]

Hoping to address Gorbachev's concern that the United States would use SDI to gain a first-strike capability, Reagan set forth a proposal linking SDI deployment with the elimination of ballistic missiles in a July 25 letter to the Soviet leader. Reagan suggested that both superpowers agree to confine themselves to the research, development, and testing permitted by the ABM Treaty for five years. If either country wanted to deploy strategic defenses after this five-year period, then it would need to offer plans for sharing its defensive systems and abolishing both sides' offensive ballistic missiles. Negotiations on sharing strategic defenses and eliminating ballistic missiles would take place for up to two years. If the United States and the Soviet Union were unable to reach an agreement on these matters after two years, then either country could deploy strategic defenses after giving six months' notice.[128] Reagan believed that this was a sound proposal that could facilitate a breakthrough in arms reduction negotiations with the Soviets. In his diary, he characterized his position as "a good one & [it] should open the door to some real arms negotiations if he [Gorbachev] is really interested."[129] Reagan would personally "lay out the rationale" for U.S. proposals on the first day of the Reykjavik meeting.[130]

Reagan and Gorbachev's summit in Reykjavik would be the peak of their efforts to abolish nuclear weapons. Reflecting on the meeting in his memoir, Reagan wrote, "At Reykjavik, my hopes for a nuclear-free world soared briefly, then fell during one of the longest, most disappointing—and ultimately angriest—days of my presidency."[131] Gorbachev characterized the meeting in 1996 as one in which "truly Shakespearean passions ran under the thin veneer of polite and diplomatically restrained negotiations behind the windows of a cozy little house standing on the coast of a dark and somberly impetuous ocean."[132] Meeting alone or only with their foreign ministers present, Reagan and Gorbachev devised a framework for abolishing their nuclear arsenals in ten years. Their disagreements over the nature and purpose of SDI, however, ultimately prevented the conclusion of any concrete agreements in Iceland.

At Reykjavik, Gorbachev presented a sweeping set of proposals that represented a significant shift toward American positions. In the first session alone, he proposed a 50 percent reduction in strategic nuclear weapons, including significant cuts in Soviet heavy ICBMs, and he accepted the American definition of "strategic" weapons, meaning that U.S. INF missiles and forward-based systems in Europe were excluded. He also proposed the complete elimination of INF missiles in Europe without taking into account British or French nuclear systems. Gorbachev expressed support for the American position that "there must be parity and equality at each stage" of reductions, and he agreed with Reagan on "the importance of effective verification." In terms of defense and space issues, Gorbachev adopted Reagan's framework of a nonwithdrawal period from the ABM Treaty followed by a period of negotiations on strategic defenses. The Soviet leader proposed a ten-year nonwithdrawal period from the ABM Treaty, which was a compromise between the five-year period that Reagan had suggested in his July 25 letter and the fifteen-year period that Gorbachev had advocated in his September 15 letter.[133] Shultz's immediate reaction to these proposals was that Gorbachev "was laying gifts at our feet—or, more accurately, on the table—concession after concession." Nitze remarked after the first session, "This is the best Soviet proposal we have received in twenty-five years."[134] During the third session, Gorbachev also agreed to the U.S. demand to reduce Soviet INF in Asia to one hundred warheads.[135]

After Reagan accepted Gorbachev's proposal for a ten-year nonwithdrawal period from the ABM Treaty, during which massive strategic nuclear arms reduction would take place, the stage was set for a discussion of nuclear abolition during the summit's final session. In an effort to break the impasse over whether "strategic offensive arms" or "offensive ballistic missiles" should be liquidated in the second five-year phase of the nonwithdrawal period, Reagan suggested that the two sides simply agree to eliminate all nuclear weapons in ten years. Gorbachev quickly agreed.[136] Disagreements over SDI, however, blocked the conclusion of any formal agreement to abolish nuclear weapons.

While both leaders agreed to a ten-year nonwithdrawal period from the ABM Treaty, they had vastly different interpretations of the activities permitted by the treaty during these ten years. Gorbachev insisted that the ABM

Treaty allowed strategic defense research and testing in laboratories only, while Reagan maintained that the treaty also authorized research, development, and testing outside of laboratories. Gorbachev contended that it was essential to confine SDI research to the laboratory while the superpowers were eliminating nuclear weapons in order to prevent the deployment of offensive weapons in space or an ABM shield that could give the United States a first-strike capability. Reagan, however, believed that restricting SDI to the laboratory for ten years would kill the very project that could ensure against any attempts to revive nuclear weapons in the future. Desperately pleading with Gorbachev to drop his demand that SDI be confined to the laboratory for ten years, Reagan told the Soviet leader that he "had people who were the most outspoken critics of the Soviet Union over the years, the so-called right wing, and esteemed journalists, who were the first to criticize him. They were kicking his brains out." The president begged Gorbachev for a "favor," noting that "if he did what Gorbachev asked, he would be badly hurt in his own country." Gorbachev refused to change his position, telling Reagan that it was a "question of principle."[137]

Frustrated by Gorbachev's insistence on restricting SDI to the laboratory, Reagan ended the meeting. After accusing Gorbachev of not wanting to reach an agreement, Reagan remarked, "I don't know when we'll ever have another chance like this and whether we will meet soon." Gorbachev retorted, "I don't either."[138] The distraught looks on the leaders' faces as they emerged from Hofdi House showed the world that the meeting had been a failure. Shultz was uncharacteristically emotional in his bleak post-summit press conference, lamenting, "We ended, of course, having worked so hard and come so far, in deep disappointment." Not only had the two leaders failed to reach any formal agreements, but they had not even set a date for the Washington summit. Shultz's eyes welled up with tears as he recalled Reagan's unwillingness to compromise on SDI, but he stated, "I have never been so proud of my President as I have been in these sessions and particularly this afternoon." As Shultz spoke to the press of "the agreement that might have been," U.S. arms control negotiator Max Kampelman openly wept in the front row of the audience.[139]

Gorbachev, however, struck an optimistic tone in his post-summit press conference. In his memoir, Gorbachev admitted that his first inclination had been to denounce Reagan and to blame the summit's breakdown on the president's refusal to compromise on SDI. Yet he also recognized that the two leaders had reached sweeping informal agreements on INF and START during their four sessions. Still unsure how to characterize the meeting when he entered the pressroom, Gorbachev did not make up his mind until he took the podium. He later wrote, "I sensed the anxiety in the air. I suddenly felt emotional, even shaken. These people standing in front of me seemed to represent mankind waiting for its fate to be decided."[140] He realized that he should present Reykjavik as a breakthrough.

After explaining the leaders' inability to reach concrete agreements due to their dispute over SDI, Gorbachev stated, "I think, nevertheless, that the entire meeting here was of major significance. We did, after all, come close to reaching agreements; only they have yet to be endorsed. . . . The very path that we have traversed in reaching these agreements here in Iceland on major cuts in nuclear weapons has given us substantial experience and we have made considerable gains." He firmly believed that "accords are possible" in the future.[141] Gorbachev's speech was met with resounding applause, and members of the press cheered the Soviet leader. Gorbachev's wife, Raisa, burst into tears of joy as her husband deemed Reykjavik "a breakthrough, which allowed us for the first time to look over the horizon."[142] Nuclear abolition had moved from the realm of the imaginary to the negotiating table.

The Reykjavik summit, however, would be the peak of Gorbachev and Reagan's efforts to end the Cold War through global nuclear disarmament. Gorbachev's recognition that Reagan would never compromise on SDI subsequently made him more amenable to European activists' vision for ending the Cold War. Soviet economic interests also reinforced the appeal of European activists' calls for a denuclearized, reunified, autonomous, and free Europe. In 1987, Gorbachev began to focus on eliminating nuclear weapons in Europe, implementing his "common European home" initiative, and supporting the principle of freedom of choice.

CHAPTER 6

"One Cannot Do Business Like This"

Bitterly disappointed after the breakdown of the Reykjavik summit, Reagan slumped in the back seat of the limousine that took him from Hofdi House to the U.S. embassy. "You would have thought that he'd just lost a combination of the Rose Bowl and the Stanley Cup and the Olympics," White House chief of staff Donald Regan said of the president after the summit collapsed. "He was so down. I've never seen a guy so beat in all my life." In the hours after his failure to close a deal with Gorbachev that would have abolished U.S. and Soviet nuclear weapons in ten years, the typically cheerful Reagan was forlorn. Regan recalled the president telling him in the limousine, "'We were that close' and he held up his left hand. Just finger and thumb. That much. He said, 'We were that close to getting rid of all missiles.'"[1] James Kuhn, Reagan's personal assistant, described the president as "distraught" in the summit's immediate aftermath. "I'd just never seen Ronald Reagan that way before, had never seen him with such a look."[2]

After a few hours of reflection on the flight back to Washington, however, Reagan decided that the hope of reaching an agreement to eliminate nuclear weapons had not been lost. Kuhn recalled, "Halfway back across the Atlantic he [Reagan] came back and there was the old Ronald Reagan, smiling, bouncing, and everything. He said, 'I'm okay now. I gave it a lot of thought. I know I made the right decision back there. We couldn't give up SDI, not for America's future.'"[3] Reagan still believed that SDI would facilitate nuclear abolition by ensuring against any rogue attempts to revive nuclear weapons in the future. "Well, the ball is now in his [Gorbachev's] court and I'm convinced he'll come around when he sees how the world is reacting," Reagan wrote in his diary that evening.[4]

After presenting Reykjavik as a breakthrough in his post-summit press conference, Gorbachev privately characterized the meeting as a turning point to Chernyaev. On the flight from Reykjavik to Moscow, Gorbachev told Chernyaev, "Before that [Reykjavik], the conversation was only about limiting nuclear arms. Now it is about reduction and liquidation [of those]." He noted that the two leaders had reached dramatic informal agreements on INF and START reductions, and he hoped that Reagan would reconsider his unwillingness to restrict SDI to the laboratory for ten years. "Everybody saw that agreement is possible," Gorbachev told Chernyaev. "From Reykjavik, we drew the conclusion that the necessity for dialogue has increased even more. That is why I am even more of an optimist after Reykjavik."[5]

Yet an agreement eliminating nuclear weapons would elude Reagan and Gorbachev. This chapter contends that European peace activists' vision for ending the Cold War through the denuclearization and reunification of an autonomous and free Europe became the prevailing one in 1987 and 1988. Although Reagan maintained his dream of a nuclear-free world for the remainder of his presidency, he was unable to translate his vision for over-coming Cold War tensions into an agreement that abolished U.S. and Soviet nuclear weapons. Preoccupied by political crises like the Iran-Contra scandal and Robert Bork's failed Supreme Court nomination, as well as concerns about the health of his wife, Nancy, Reagan shifted into a passive role in his administration's discussions of nuclear arms reduction during 1987 and 1988. Reagan's passivity enabled his advisors, who were not nuclear abolitionists, to assume the dominant role in devising U.S. arms control policy. These aides stymied progress on strategic and tactical nuclear arms reduction, although Reagan and Gorbachev did sign a landmark treaty eliminating land-based INF in December 1987. As the first agreement to abolish an entire class of nuclear weapons, the INF Treaty marked the beginning of the reversal of the superpower nuclear arms race.

Gorbachev's recognition that the Reagan administration was unlikely to compromise on SDI or strategic and tactical nuclear arms reduction made him more amenable to European peace activists' vision for ending the Cold War.[6] Soviet economic interests also reinforced the appeal of European activists' calls for a denuclearized, reunified, autonomous, and free Europe. European peace activists influenced Gorbachev's decision to "untie" the Reykjavik package in February 1987 and pursue an INF treaty separately from agreements on strategic nuclear weapons and strategic defenses. European activists' vision of a united, nuclear-free Europe continued to shape Gorbachev's "common European home" initiative, which he made a priority in a high-profile speech in Prague on April 10, 1987. Gorbachev also advocated freedom of choice for East European states, most notably in his December 7, 1988, address to the United Nations, which fit in with European peace activists' appeals for an autonomous and free Europe.

*   *   *

Since they did not share the president's dream of a nuclear-free world, many of Reagan's advisors were deeply troubled by the revelation that he and Gorbachev had discussed abolishing nuclear weapons during the Reykjavik summit's final session. Hoping to quash any momentum toward nuclear abolition in the days after the summit, these administration officials did not reveal the full extent of Reagan and Gorbachev's conversation during the last summit session. In their statements to the press, for example, Poindexter, Perle, and Nitze spoke only of the last written offer made by Reagan at Reykjavik. This consisted of a 50 percent reduction in strategic nuclear weapons during the first five years of a ten-year nonwithdrawal period from the ABM Treaty. During the last five years, offensive ballistic missiles would be eliminated. These officials did not admit that Reagan and Gorbachev seriously discussed nuclear abolition during the summit's final minutes.[7]

Reagan's advisors also moderated his public remarks on the final summit session, striking a reference to Reagan and Gorbachev's conversation about eliminating nuclear weapons from the president's October 13 address to the nation. In his handwritten first draft of the speech, Reagan wrote that the two leaders considered "a 10 year period in which we began with the reduction of all nuclear explosive devices, bombs, cruise missiles, intermediate range, short range, and strategic missiles. They would be reduced 50% in the 1st 5 years and totally eliminated in the next 5."[8] When Reagan spoke from the Oval Office at 8:00 p.m. on October 13, however, he presented the U.S. offer to halve strategic nuclear weapons in five years and then eliminate offensive ballistic missiles in the next five years as the final proposal discussed at Reykjavik.[9]

After a group of congressional leaders announced on October 14 that Reagan had privately revealed that he and Gorbachev had considered abolishing nuclear weapons in ten years, White House officials launched a concerted effort to conceal the leaders' conversation about a nuclear-free world.[10] Administration officials were instructed to respond to questions about whether Reagan had discussed nuclear abolition at Reykjavik by saying that "both leaders have expressed a common goal of *ultimately* eliminating nuclear weapons. This was discussed in Iceland. The President's proposal in Iceland, however, as he reported in his speech [on October 13], was to eliminate all offensive ballistic missiles during the next ten years."[11]

Poindexter even wrote Reagan a memo urging him to "make no further public comment endorsing the idea of the total elimination of all nuclear weapons in 10 years as something discussed and agreed with the General Secretary." He argued that nuclear abolition would leave NATO vulnerable to Soviet conventional superiority and pose verification challenges. "All this being so," Poindexter wrote, "neither our military experts or our allies would support the idea of moving to the total elimination of all nuclear weapons within 10 years." He implored the president to "step back" from his pursuit of a nuclear-free world and instead focus on the proposal to eliminate offensive ballistic missiles in ten years.[12] On October 27, Reagan authorized U.S. negotiators at the Nuclear and Space Talks to present the proposal to eliminate offensive ballistic missiles during a ten-year nonwithdrawal period from the ABM Treaty.[13]

Infuriated by the Reagan administration's retreat from the Reykjavik discussions of nuclear abolition, Gorbachev began to doubt whether he would be able to reach a comprehensive nuclear arms reduction agreement with the Americans. Particularly enraged by U.S. officials' deceptive descriptions of the summit sessions, Gorbachev gave a televised address on October 22 to set the record straight. After noting that White House spokesperson Larry Speakes had claimed that Reagan did not agree to nuclear abolition at Reykjavik, Gorbachev told the Soviet people, "Things got to the point of outright misrepresentation." He emphasized that Reagan had agreed to abolish strategic nuclear weapons and INF missiles in Europe during the summit.[14] The Reagan administration's continued refusal to admit that Reagan had consented to a time frame for eliminating nuclear weapons prompted Soviet deputy foreign minister Aleksandr Bessmertnykh to take the extraordinary step of publicly quoting from Soviet summit records.[15] During an October 30 Politburo session, Gorbachev wondered, "What does America want after all? They are perverting and revising Reykjavik, retreating from it. They are engaging in provocations again, they are spoiling the atmosphere. I am having more and more doubts whether we can achieve anything at all with this administration."[16]

Although Poindexter had encouraged Reagan to pursue the less radical goal of eliminating offensive ballistic missiles in ten years, a Joint Chiefs of Staff study of this proposal revealed staunch opposition within the Reagan administration even to this more moderate aim. On November 3, 1986, Reagan issued NSDD 250, which instructed the Joint Chiefs to develop a plan that would enable the United States to transition to a world without offensive ballistic missiles by 1996.[17] During a December 19 meeting with Reagan to discuss the Joint Chiefs' initial progress report, both the Chiefs and Weinberger voiced serious concerns about the prospect of abolishing ballistic missiles in ten years. While the chairman of the Joint Chiefs Admiral William Crowe expressed support for the elimination of INF in Europe, he told Reagan that "moving to zero ballistic missiles within ten years is a completely different challenge, 'requiring us to adjust our thinking in every area': nuclear weapons policy; fiscal projections; Soviet force structure and strategy; new technology; and the role of NATO in 1996." He also noted that verifying an agreement to abolish ballistic missiles would be difficult. General Larry D. Welch and General John A. Wickham emphasized the costs associated with building up U.S. conventional forces to compensate for the elimination of ballistic missiles. Welch estimated that the U.S. government would have to spend "tens of billions" of dollars on conventional defenses, while Wickham contended that the modernization of ground forces in ten years would cost $180 billion. Weinberger cautioned that Congress was unlikely to support such expensive conventional modernization programs.[18]

Having already shifted his focus from nuclear abolition to the elimination of ballistic missiles in ten years, Reagan was loath to retreat from the less radical goal of a ballistic missile-free world. He assured the Joint Chiefs that he was "not 'living in a dream world'" and reiterated his support for the abolition of ballistic missiles by 1996. Reagan believed that the U.S. economy could sustain increased spending on conventional forces, but preferred to redress the conventional imbalance with the Soviets through negotiations on conventional reductions. Noting that he had discussed eliminating nuclear weapons with Gorbachev at Reykjavik, the president appeared to be reminding Weinberger and the Chiefs that he had already compromised once on the issue of nuclear arms reduction and did not want to compromise again.[19] In a follow-up memo to Weinberger and the Joint Chiefs, Reagan instructed them to think of the contribution to U.S. national security that would result from the elimination of the Soviet ballistic missile threat. He also reiterated his preference for resolving any NATO–Warsaw Pact force imbalance through arms reduction rather than modernization.[20]

Despite Reagan's clear support for the abolition of ballistic missiles in ten years, opposition to the proposal mounted within the administration, which eventually dropped the idea. In a January 15, 1987, memo to the national security advisor, acting director of central intelligence Robert Gates wrote, "Although I think it is highly unlikely that the Soviets would go along with a move to eliminate ballistic missiles while retaining bombers and cruise missiles, they, in fact, would be in a much better position to take advantage of such a new regime than most people realize."[21] In their February 1987 final report, the Joint Chiefs concluded that the United States could not abolish ballistic missiles by 1996 without either facing heightened risk or increasing projected defense budgets by $390 billion to compensate for the destruction of U.S. ballistic missiles. "Because the fiscal guidance of NSDD-250 cannot be met," the Joint Chiefs wrote, "this baseline report recommends that the goal of transitioning to a world without offensive ballistic missiles within 10 years should be deferred." Rather, "an intermediate goal of deep reductions (as in the 50 percent [reduction of strategic nuclear weapons] proposal) achieved in a reasonable period of time should be pursued as a more immediate alternative."[22] Although Reagan's nuclear abolitionism did not waver in the face of this report, the U.S. proposal to eliminate offensive ballistic missiles by 1996 faded away.

By the time the Joint Chiefs issued their final response to NSDD 250 in late February 1987, the Reagan administration was embroiled in a scandal that consumed its attention and threatened to derail the Reagan presidency. On November 3, 1986, a Lebanese news story claimed that a former Reagan administration official had secretly visited Tehran and declared that the United States would sell arms to Iran in exchange for its help in securing the release of American hostages in Beirut. Throughout his presidency, Reagan had vowed that the United States would never negotiate with terrorists, and this arms-for-hostages scheme clearly violated that pledge. It also contravened the Arms Export Control Act, which prohibited arms exports to Iran because it supported terrorism. On November 13, Reagan acknowledged sending arms to Iran, although he denied that they were "ransom payment for the release of American hostages in Lebanon." Twelve days later, however, Reagan announced that he "was not fully informed" on an aspect of the Iran arms sales and that Poindexter and NSC staffer Oliver North were leaving his administration. Attorney General Edwin Meese then revealed that the profits from U.S. arms sales to Iran, which amounted to $10–30 million, had been diverted to help the Contras fighting the Marxist Sandinista government in Nicaragua. This diversion of funds appeared to contravene the Boland Amendment's restrictions on U.S. aid to the Contras.[23]

Multiple investigations followed these revelations. On November 26, Reagan announced that former senator John Tower, former secretary of state Edmund Muskie, and former national security advisor Brent Scowcroft would form a "special review board" to consider the proper "role and procedures" for the NSC staff in devising and implementing foreign policy.[24] Congress conducted an investigation of Iran-Contra in 1987, and independent counsel Lawrence Walsh spearheaded an investigation of the affair that continued for over six years.[25]

Reagan and his advisors were preoccupied by the Iran-Contra investigations in late 1986 and early 1987. In the very months when the administration should have been capitalizing on the progress made at the Reykjavik summit, it was consumed with minimizing the fallout from the revelations of its illegal activities. Rather than working to formalize the understandings reached at Reykjavik on sweeping INF and START reductions, U.S. officials were focused on the multiple investigations into the Iran-Contra affair. Just a few days after the Joint Chiefs submitted their report on transitioning to a ballistic missile-free world, the Tower Commission released its findings on February 26, 1987. Although appointed by Reagan and led by a Republican, the Tower Commission criticized both the president and his advisors in its report. In the case of U.S. arms sales to Iran, it noted that Reagan "did not force his policy to undergo the most critical review of which the N.S.C. participants and the process were capable. At no time did he insist upon accountability and performance review. Had the President chosen to drive the N.S.C. system, the outcome could well have been different." In light of Reagan's penchant for delegating responsibility, his top advisors "should have been particularly mindful of the need for special attention to the manner in which this arms-sale initiative developed and proceeded."[26]

The Iran-Contra scandal not only diverted the Reagan administration's attention from nuclear arms reduction negotiations with the Soviets, but also led to the ouster of officials who often sided with Reagan on arms control issues. Poindexter, who resigned over his role in the scandal, had been a staunch supporter of the zero ballistic missile proposal and a driving force behind the directive tasking the Joint Chiefs to develop a plan for transitioning to a world without ballistic missiles by 1996. It is no wonder that the proposal was dropped shortly after he left the White House. Another major figure in the Iran-Contra scandal was Bud McFarlane, who continued to play a key role in the arms-for-hostages scheme after he resigned as national security advisor in December 1985.[27] Revelations of McFarlane's involvement in Iran-Contra precluded any possibility that he might advance Reagan's nuclear arms reduction agenda as a former government official. McFarlane had played a major role in the development of SDI and had supported U.S.-Soviet nuclear arms reduction negotiations. Reagan was more assertive in formulating nuclear policy when he could enlist the help of advisors who shared his desire to achieve arms reduction agreements with the Soviets. The loss of two of Reagan's key allies on nuclear issues hampered the president's efforts to keep his administration's policy in line with his goal of eliminating nuclear weapons.

Gorbachev recognized that the Iran-Contra affair hindered his chances of reaching a comprehensive nuclear arms reduction agreement with the Reagan administration. Rather than negotiating a nuclear arms reduction treaty with the Soviets, Gorbachev feared that the Reagan administration would undertake bold, antagonistic actions in an effort to appear strong after Iran-Contra. At a conference with Politburo members and Central Committee secretaries on December 1, 1986, Gorbachev attributed the Reagan administration's recent decision to exceed the missile limits of the unratified SALT II Treaty to the need to seem strong during the "Irangate" crisis. He also warned, "We should not exclude a possibility that as a result of the reaction to Reykjavik and to the 'Irangate,' the administration could undertake a risky venture in either Nicaragua or Seoul, in order to stop our peaceful advance." Gorbachev reminded his colleagues, "We are dealing with political scum. One can expect anything from them. We hate it, but we need a cold head."[28]

*   *   *

While Gorbachev lamented the difficulties of reaching a wide-ranging arms reduction agreement with the Americans, European peace activists continued to advocate a denuclearized, reunified, autonomous, and free Europe. During late 1986 and early 1987, European activists devoted significant effort to convincing Soviet officials to abandon the Reykjavik package, which linked agreements on INF and START reductions with restrictions on strategic defenses. They urged Soviet officials to pursue a separate treaty that would eliminate INF in Europe. Peace activists' arguments in favor of a separate INF agreement influenced Gorbachev's decision to untie the Reykjavik package on February 28, 1987.

During a visit to Moscow from December 2 through 9, 1986, a three-member delegation from British CND lobbied extensively for the de-linking of INF from the Reykjavik package. Joan Ruddock, Stephen Brown, and Paul Rogers met with officials from the Soviet Peace Committee, Ministry of Foreign Affairs, and Ministry of Defense, as well as Vadim Zagladin, who was the deputy head of the International Department of the Central Committee of the CPSU. In addition to these party and government officials, the CND activists also had discussions with researchers from the Institute of USA and Canada and the Institute of World Economy and International Relations. The CND delegation noted that its meetings with the Soviet Peace Committee were "marked by a relative openness and dialogue that has in the past been missing." Even Yuri Zhukov, the notoriously hardline Soviet Peace Committee president, admitted that "we have all made mistakes" and told the antinuclear activists that "criticism is very much *a la mode* these days." The CND delegation also found its discussions with representatives from the Ministries of Foreign Affairs and Defense to be "frank, open, and useful."[29]

In each of their meetings, the CND activists called for the Soviet leadership to untie the Reykjavik package and conclude a treaty eliminating INF in Europe. Ruddock recalled telling Soviet officials that "we were afraid that if the package was immutable, American insistence on SDI would create a stalemate between the two superpowers and prevent any initiative by any other country."[30] The CND team also raised the issue of the Soviet missiles installed in Czechoslovakia and the GDR in response to U.S. INF deployments in 1983. The activists encouraged the Soviets to withdraw these missiles as part of an INF agreement.[31] According to Ruddock, the Soviet response to CND's proposals was "much better than we had expected."[32] Although the Soviet Peace Committee and Ministry of Defense officials opposed the pursuit of a separate INF treaty for the reasons that Gorbachev had cited at Reykjavik, the researchers and Ministry of Foreign Affairs representatives were open to the idea for the sake of making progress on arms control.[33]

In an editorial in the December 1986–January 1987 edition of the *END Journal*, Kaldor criticized Gorbachev's insistence on pursuing an INF treaty in conjunction with agreements on START and strategic defenses. While she condemned Reagan's unwillingness to compromise on SDI at the Reykjavik summit, she also blamed the summit's breakdown on Gorbachev's refusal to de-link INF from the discussions on START and SDI. "Before the summit, it was confidently expected that an agreement to reduce medium-range missiles in Europe would be reached (leaving 100 on each side, said the pundits). Earlier, the Russians had said publicly that such an agreement could go ahead without agreement on strategic weapons," Kaldor wrote. Although the Soviets did agree to eliminate INF missiles at Reykjavik, they reversed policy and made "abandoning SDI" a condition for an INF agreement. Kaldor lambasted the idea of "an all-embracing agreement to be reached at the negotiating table" as a "fairy godmother fantasy," contending that nuclear disarmament could be achieved only through a combination of initiatives.[34] Kaldor's writings were a key source of inspiration for Gorbachev's nuclear arms reduction initiatives, so Soviet officials likely would have read this editorial with interest.[35]

Prominent Soviet dissident Andrei Sakharov also spoke out against the Reykjavik package. Known as the father of the Soviet hydrogen bomb, Sakharov was a nuclear physicist who began working for disarmament and human rights in the late 1960s. His efforts drew the ire of Soviet officials, who stripped him of his position within the Soviet nuclear program, but his work also earned him the 1975 Nobel Peace Prize. Following his criticism of the Soviet invasion of Afghanistan, Sakharov was forced into internal exile in Gorky in 1980. On December 19, 1986, Gorbachev ended Sakharov's exile and permitted him to return to Moscow. During a December 23 press conference at Moscow's Yaroslavl Station, Sakharov urged Soviet officials to abandon the linkage between nuclear arms reduction and restrictions on strategic defenses.[36]

In the weeks following his return to Moscow, Sakharov continued to press for the untying of the Reykjavik package. Yevgeny Velikhov, vice president of the Soviet Academy of Sciences, invited Sakharov to participate in a forum on nuclear disarmament that Gorbachev was hosting in Moscow from February 14 through 16, 1987. Although Sakharov believed that the Forum for a Nuclear-Free World and the Survival of Humanity was "staged primarily for propaganda purposes," he accepted the invitation and told Velikhov of his opposition to the Reykjavik package. During the preparations for the forum, Sakharov presented his case for de-linking INF and START from SDI to the director of the Space Research Institute, Roald Sagdeyev; the president of the Soviet Academy of Sciences, Gury Marchuk; and other academicians.[37]

Over a thousand writers, actors, businessmen, scientists, current and former government officials, and peace activists from across the globe descended on Moscow for the Forum for a Nuclear-Free World and the Survival of Humanity. West German Green politicians and anti-nuclear activists Petra Kelly and Gert Bastian mingled with former Austrian chancellor Bruno Kreisky and former Canadian prime minister Pierre Elliott Trudeau. The Federation of American Scientists sent a delegation, which was led by arms control proponents Jeremy Stone and Frank von Hippel. Singer and antiwar activist Yoko Ono was on hand for the forum, as was actor Gregory Peck, businessman Armand Hammer, and writers Gore Vidal and Norman Mailer. Reporters Dusko Doder and Louise Branson later wrote, "Moscow had never seen anything like it. Never before had any Soviet leader orchestrated an attempt to identify the Kremlin with such an array of prominent intellectuals."[38] On February 16, Gorbachev gave a speech laying out his "new thinking" in foreign policy and hosted a banquet for the forum's participants.[39]

Several activists advocated the abandonment of the Reykjavik package at the Moscow forum. At a February 15 session on anti-missile defenses, Sakharov contended that "a significant cut in ICBMs and medium-range and battlefield missiles, and other agreements on disarmament, should be negotiated as soon as possible, independently of SDI, in accordance with the lines of understanding laid out in Reykjavik. I believe that a compromise on SDI can be reached later. In this way the dangerous deadlock in the negotiations can be overcome." Sakharov had doubts about SDI's technological feasibility and believed that the Soviets could easily develop an offensive countermeasure. In Sakharov's view, Gorbachev's willingness to pursue separate INF and START agreements would undercut political support for SDI in the United States. Stone similarly condemned the linkage of arms reduction agreements with SDI restrictions in his speech later that day.[40] He and von Hippel personally urged Gorbachev to untie the Reykjavik package during the final banquet of the Moscow forum, when they all sat at the same table.[41]

Gorbachev later reflected that his contacts with peace activists at the Moscow forum had convinced him to abandon the Reykjavik package and pursue a separate INF agreement. In his book *Perestroika*, which was published in November 1987, Gorbachev wrote:

> The Moscow forum "For the Nuclear-Free World and the Survival of Humanity" made a very deep impression on myself and other Soviet leaders. We became acutely aware of the sentiments of the world public, its anxiety and concern about the fate of Reykjavik, about the fact that shortly after Reykjavik the Soviet Union had to suspend its unilateral moratorium on nuclear testing, that the United States undermined the SALT-II Treaty and that the ABM Treaty was in jeopardy. We in the Soviet Union gave it much thought and decided to take another step to invigorate the Geneva talks and achieve a positive shift in disarmament. What I have in mind is the singling out of the medium-range missile issue from the package.[42]

Ten days after the Moscow forum concluded, Gorbachev told the Politburo, "Geneva is coming to a dead end." He spoke of "American insolence" in the Nuclear and Space Talks and lamented that Reagan's current priority appeared to be preserving SDI rather than negotiating a comprehensive nuclear arms reduction agreement. If the Soviets de-linked INF from the Reykjavik package, however, it "would make an impression on the outside world, on public opinion." Gorbachev contended that "in the arena of public opinion, we will put pressure on the United States by showing that we are in favor of mutual trust."[43] The Soviet leader hoped that untying the Reykjavik package would jump-start the Nuclear and Space Talks and enable the superpowers to conclude an INF treaty in the near future. On February 28, he announced that the Soviets would seek a separate INF agreement.[44] Gorbachev also invited Shultz to Moscow to reinvigorate U.S.-Soviet arms reduction discussions.[45]

European peace activists called not only for an agreement eliminating INF from Europe, but also for the reunification of a denuclearized and democratic Europe. On November 3, 1986, the European Network for East-West Dialogue presented its Helsinki Memorandum to members of the public and government officials gathered in Vienna for the Third CSCE Follow-Up Meeting. Titled "Giving Real Life to the Helsinki Accords," this memorandum set forth a vision of a denuclearized and bloc-free Europe, in which human rights and self-determination were respected and cooperation on economic, ecological, and cultural issues was widespread. It offered concrete proposals for ways in which the CSCE process could facilitate the creation of this new Europe. Contending that "lasting peace cannot be based on the threat of mutual annihilation," Network activists called for governments and citizens in CSCE countries to work for the elimination of "all medium range missiles and of all nuclear weapon systems with short warning time stationed in or directed at targets in Europe," a comprehensive test ban treaty, and the establishment of nuclear-free zones in which conventional weapons would not be increased, among other things. The activists urged nuclear powers Britain and France to join U.S. and Soviet disarmament efforts and expressed opposition to "any proposal to establish Western Europe as a third military or even nuclear superpower."[46]

Recognizing that "the Helsinki Accords are often presented as confirming the status quo in Europe," Network activists charged that the Accords "do not in letter or spirit cement the bipolar structure of power blocs," but rather "leave the door open for peaceful and gradual change towards a pluralistic Europe which can overcome the bloc structure." They set forth proposals for a range of CSCE initiatives to facilitate political, economic, ecological, and cultural cooperation between Eastern and Western Europe. These included economic agreements between the EEC, the CMEA, the European Free Trade Association, and the United States; joint East-West initiatives to reduce air and water pollution; the creation of a CSCE-backed commission to monitor ecological damage and recommend environmental protection measures; the founding of a pan-European foundation to organize and fund transnational cultural projects; initiatives to promote the study of European languages and literatures; and CSCE scientific and educational exchange programs. Arguing that "mutual trust cannot be created solely by governments," Network activists called on ordinary citizens to engage in "détente from below" through communication with citizens from the other side of the Iron Curtain. West European and East European peace activists envisioned a Europe in which NATO and the Warsaw Pact ultimately ceased to exist.[47]

Throughout the Helsinki Memorandum, Network activists emphasized the indivisibility of peace and human rights. "A lasting peace can only be achieved by overcoming the various political, economic, and social causes of aggression and violence in international relations as well as in the internal conditions of states," the activists wrote. They also believed that individuals should have the right to work for peace and disarmament without fear of persecution. All CSCE governments should respect the human rights laid out in the Helsinki Final Act and the International Covenants on Civil and Political Rights and Economic, Social, and Cultural Rights. Network activists proposed the creation of an "all-European commission on human rights" to which citizens and residents of CSCE countries could appeal if they believed that their rights had been violated.[48]

If the Helsinki process were going to facilitate the denuclearization and reunification of a free Europe, Network activists thought that Europe needed to achieve greater autonomy from the superpowers. Yet they did not believe that it was realistic to keep the United States or the Soviet Union completely out of Europe. This represented a shift in the activists' thinking. In the Helsinki Memorandum, they wrote, "We are aware of the fact that the Europe for which we strive cannot be built in confrontation with or by exclusion of either the USA or the Soviet Union, but only in a common effort of all CSCE countries." Nevertheless, "if we are to radicalize the Helsinki process so as to make it part of a comprehensive democratic program, then we must oppose those superpower policies which contravene the right of countries to self-determination." They urged East and West European movements to pressure the Soviet Union and the United States to recognize and respect European autonomy.[49]

European peace activists' arguments for a united, nuclear-free Europe continued to shape Gorbachev's "common European home" initiative, which he made a priority in early 1987. During the February 26 Politburo session in which he expressed frustration with American behavior in the Nuclear and Space Talks and announced his decision to pursue a separate INF treaty to jump-start negotiations, Gorbachev also called for renewed attention to Europe. "But we should not work only in the direction of America. We need to carefully select other main directions besides the American one," Gorbachev told the Politburo. "We should respond to all the hints from all those who want to work with us. Such hints are coming, directly or implicitly, from Thatcher, Kohl, and Mitterrand."[50] The "common European home" initiative was a vehicle through which the Soviets could reinvigorate their policy toward Europe.

Network activists presented the Helsinki Memorandum to government representatives to the Third CSCE Follow-Up Meeting in Vienna, which Gorbachev touted as an influence on his "common European home" initiative. In his memoir, Gorbachev wrote that in the late fall of 1986, "step by step and brick by brick, I was developing my idea of a 'common European home.' The Vienna CSCE meeting was a significant step forward in this direction." Although Gorbachev had spoken about his "common European home" idea in December 1984 and October 1985, his initiative was often criticized for being "too abstract." Gorbachev recalled that in the spring of 1987, "I decided to state my views on the question in full and was offered a suitable occasion in April 1987 during my visit to Czechoslovakia, the geographical center of Europe."[51]

The idea of a "common European home" that Gorbachev spotlighted in his April 10, 1987, speech in Prague bore a striking resemblance to European peace activists' vision of a denuclearized and reunified Europe. Although Gorbachev noted his "desire to look for mutually acceptable solutions to the entire range of nuclear disarmament issues," he focused primarily on the elimination of nuclear weapons in Europe in his speech. He reminded his listeners that the Soviets sought to conclude a treaty that would abolish INF in Europe. He also proposed the reduction and eventual elimination of shorter-range missiles and tactical nuclear weapons in Europe and called for "drastic" troop and conventional arms reductions.[52]

Lamenting that "our continent is divided into opposing military blocs, with stockpiles of weaponry," Gorbachev called for greater European integration. "The concept of such a 'common European home' assumes a degree of integrity, even if its states belong to different social systems and opposing military-political blocs," Gorbachev said. Although the Soviet leader did not envision the dissolution of the blocs in the near future, he urged East-West cooperation on security, environmental, economic, and cultural issues.[53]

In his speech in Prague, Gorbachev even expressed support for greater East European autonomy from the Soviet Union. He asserted, "No one has the right to claim special status in the socialist world. We consider the independence of every party, its responsibility to the people of its own country, and its right to decide the questions of the country's development to be unconditional principles." Although Gorbachev clearly expected East European governments to remain socialist, he recognized that "no one Party can have a monopoly on truth."[54]

Gorbachev's proposals for how to denuclearize and reunify Europe were the same as those set forth by European peace activists. Like Network activists, Gorbachev believed that the CSCE process could play an important role in creating a united, nuclear-free Europe. He called on the foreign ministers from CSCE states to begin negotiations on reductions of tactical nuclear weapons and conventional forces. The Soviet leader also supported the establishment of nuclear-free zones in Central Europe, the Balkans, and Scandinavia as interim measures that could facilitate the elimination of nuclear weapons in Europe. Contending that the Helsinki process had strengthened ties among European countries, Gorbachev viewed the CSCE process as a vehicle through which to work for greater European integration.[55]

By the spring of 1987, Soviet economic interests reinforced the attractiveness of European peace activists' arguments for an autonomous and integrated Europe. The price of oil started to plummet at the end of 1985, and Gorbachev estimated in July 1986 that the Soviets had already lost nine billion rubles of oil revenue. Furthermore, the first year of Gorbachev's anti-alcohol campaign, which aimed to improve worker productivity by curtailing alcohol abuse, led to an estimated loss of twenty-two billion rubles in revenue from alcohol sales.[56] During a Politburo meeting on October 30, 1986, Gorbachev lamented that Soviet "finances are in the most difficult situation," and he called for a "strict financial plan." He warned that Soviet officials should "be very careful in the question of assistance to other countries. No promises, to nobody, no matter how they ask."[57]

During this period, Gorbachev increasingly viewed support for East European countries as a drain on the Soviet economy that warranted greater autonomy for Eastern Europe. After attending a meeting of the CMEA in

Warsaw, Gorbachev talked to the Politburo on January 29, 1987, about Eastern Europe's inability to pay the Soviet Union in hard currency for the gas and oil that it supplied. Gorbachev also noted, however, that East European states had become indebted to the West because the Soviets were unable to give them advanced technology. Gorbachev called for a "shift to mutually beneficial trade" with Eastern Europe, as well as greater autonomy for East European countries. "And we should hold more firmly to the principle of each communist party being responsible for what happens in its country," Gorbachev declared. "We need this. It is in our interest not to be loaded down with responsibility for what is happening, or could happen, there."[58]

By March 1988, Gorbachev lamented the virtual breakdown of trade within the CMEA and the economic burden of providing foreign assistance to Eastern Europe. In a Politburo session on March 10, Gorbachev spoke again of the Soviet Union's inability to offer Eastern Europe goods that rivaled the quality of Western products, and he acknowledged Soviet disappointment in the substandard manufactured products provided by Eastern Europe. "In CMEA we almost have no trade, only primitive exchange. Oil is the main item. And our representatives feel no need to trade with them. And they do not feel it either. In the European Union there is a market, but not in CMEA." He suggested that either the CMEA needed to be dramatically reformed or the Soviet Union should loosen its ties with Eastern Europe. "We should raise the question in the CMEA candidly: should we become integrated or not? And they must make up their mind, because we cannot remain a provider of cheap resources for them forever. If they tell us 'no,' then our hands are free."[59]

During this session, Gorbachev also characterized foreign assistance, including to Eastern Europe, as an economic burden. "Our [foreign] assistance alone takes 41 billion rubles annually from our budget," Gorbachev announced to the Politburo. "In [our] relations with CMEA, we must take care of our own people first of all. It has become unbearably hard for us to conduct business as we have been doing in previous decades. The comprehensive program is dead. This is a very important issue."[60] Soviet economic interests had converged with the appeal of European peace activists' calls for an autonomous and integrated Europe.

*   *   *

Gorbachev's announcement on February 28, 1987, that he would untie the Reykjavik package paved the way for the landmark INF Treaty, which was the first agreement to eliminate an entire class of nuclear weapons. During his April 14 meeting with Gorbachev in Moscow, Shultz made it clear that the Reagan administration wanted an agreement that abolished INF globally, but would also be willing to conclude a treaty that permitted each side to retain one hundred INF missiles outside of Europe.[61] The secretary of state also raised the issue of shorter-range missiles. Shultz explained that U.S. officials believed that any agreement on shorter-range missiles must include a global ceiling and the right to equality. The United States did not possess any shorter-range missiles in 1987, but it wanted the option to match the number of Soviet shorter-range forces while negotiations on these missiles took place. To Shultz's surprise, Gorbachev declared his desire to eliminate both shorter-range and INF missiles on a global basis and his willingness to address shorter-range missiles in an INF treaty.[62]

Fumbling for a response in the face of Gorbachev's unexpected support for a "global double zero," Shultz merely reiterated the U.S. position that the superpowers should conduct separate negotiations on shorter-range missiles, during which they would seek agreement on a global ceiling and the United States would have the right to equality.[63] Shultz later explained, "I could not accept his offer right there: this was a matter for the alliance to discuss."[64] Nevertheless, Gorbachev was irritated by Shultz's unwillingness to engage his proposal to abolish INF and shorter-range missiles. "You obviously are defending the position you came here with and which you formulated before we proposed elimination of all shorter-range missiles," Gorbachev snapped at Shultz. Becoming emotional, Gorbachev asked Shultz why the United States would need the right to build up shorter-range forces if the Soviet Union was eliminating these missiles. "There is no logic in that at all, with the exception maybe of a purely legalistic interpretation of the right to equality. But this, it seems to me, is just casuistry."[65]

Although Gorbachev prioritized the conclusion of an INF agreement, he had not completely abandoned hope that the superpowers would be able to reach a more comprehensive nuclear arms reduction agreement. During his April 14 meeting with Shultz, Gorbachev offered a concession on SDI that he hoped would jump-start negotiations. Although the Soviet leader continued to insist on restricting SDI to the laboratory while strategic nuclear arms reduction took place, he did present an expanded definition of "laboratory." He proposed that "laboratory research" meant research conducted "in laboratories on the ground, in research institutes, at production plants, [and] at testing grounds and fields." Gorbachev hoped that the two sides could reach a compromise on this issue, particularly since the Soviet Union had already made numerous concessions. "Frankly speaking, we are making our 'final efforts' because the position of the US administration is one of very real extortion from its partner, it is a position of treating its partner disrespectfully," Gorbachev told Shultz. "One cannot do business like this."[66] In the face of Gorbachev's accusations, Shultz sarcastically replied, "I'm weeping for you."[67]

Shultz's behavior reinforced Gorbachev's doubts about whether he could achieve a comprehensive nuclear arms reduction agreement with the Reagan administration. During a Politburo session on April 16, Gorbachev characterized Shultz's trip to Moscow as a "visit to find out what could be 'extracted' from the USSR." Although he pledged to "maintain relations with the present administration to the very end," Gorbachev was pessimistic about the chances of reaching a meaningful, wide-ranging agreement while Reagan was in office. He told the Politburo, "But the question is: can we decide anything with you [the Reagan administration], can we achieve anything? Not a single administration in the past had such chances to achieve something in relations with the USSR. And what's happening? Nothing." Shevardnadze shared Gorbachev's frustration with the Americans, but he also believed that an INF treaty was within reach. "On the medium-range missiles we have [good] prospects and we should look for solutions," Shevardnadze declared.[68]

Gorbachev's outrage at the hardening of U.S. arms control positions was justified. As the year progressed, the Reagan administration appeared to be in full retreat from the informal agreements reached at Reykjavik. When the eighth round of negotiations on START and defense and space began in Geneva in early May 1987, the United States tabled proposals that were a far cry from the plan to eliminate offensive ballistic missiles (or even nuclear weapons) during a ten-year nonwithdrawal period from the ABM Treaty. Although the administration instructed the START negotiating group "to intensify the schedule of negotiations in order to protect options to conclude a START Treaty within the next year," the U.S. draft START Treaty called only for a 50 percent reduction in strategic nuclear weapons in seven years.[69] The defense and space negotiating group presented a proposal calling for a seven-year nonwithdrawal period from the ABM Treaty contingent on the 50 percent START reduction. After 1994, both superpowers would have the right to deploy strategic defenses. The administration instructed the defense and space delegation to explain that "because the Soviet Union rejected the U.S. proposal to eliminate offensive ballistic missiles by the end of 1996 [at Reykjavik], the United States has formulated a new Defense and Space proposal."[70]

U.S. officials were trying to shift blame onto the Soviet Union for their abandonment of the zero ballistic missile proposal.

NATO's endorsement of the elimination of INF and shorter-range missiles on June 12 and Gorbachev's announcement that he supported the "global double zero" on July 22, however, meant that the superpowers were on track to sign an INF treaty in 1987.[71] In September, Shevardnadze traveled to Washington to resolve the remaining INF issues and discuss options for a summit in the United States. Although he was generally pessimistic about reaching a comprehensive nuclear arms reduction agreement with the Americans, Gorbachev held out some hope that an INF treaty might spur progress on START and defense and space. Shevardnadze therefore was ready to engage Shultz in discussions on START and strategic defenses during his time in Washington.[72] The Reagan administration's preparations for Shevardnadze's visit, however, reveal that Reagan's advisors were anxious to stymie any movement toward a sweeping START agreement.

During a National Security Planning Group meeting on September 8, Weinberger went on the offensive against any compromises on U.S. arms control positions. One of the major topics of debate at this meeting was whether the administration should shift its position on mobile ICBMs, abandoning its insistence on a complete ban in favor of permitting a limited number of these missiles. Weinberger opposed such a move, vehemently arguing that the United States would not be able to extract anything from the Soviets in exchange for relaxing its position on mobile ICBMs. When National Security Advisor Frank Carlucci contended that a shift in the U.S. position on mobile ICBMs actually could be "the necessary step to get a START agreement," Weinberger dismissed an agreement permitting mobile ICBMs as "unverifiable." The secretary of defense scoffed at Shultz's argument that mobile ICBMs were more survivable and therefore more stable than fixed ICBMs. He urged Reagan to "hang tough" on START. "I feel they want a START Agreement and I believe we will get a good one if we'll just hold. As far as giving flexibility to a negotiator, I think that is simply another way of telling him he can give up on the issues," he told the president. Adelman agreed. Skeptical of Gorbachev's claims that he wanted a START agreement, Adelman also opposed offering any compromises on START.[73]

Never a master of details, Reagan was frustrated that the issue of mobile ICBMs was stalling progress toward a comprehensive nuclear arms reduction agreement. He urged his advisors to remember that nuclear abolition was his ultimate goal:

You've got to remember that the whole thing was borne of the idea that the world needs to get rid of nuclear weapons. We've got to remember that we can't win a nuclear war and we can't fight one. The Soviets don't want to win by war but by threat of war. They want to issue ultimatums to which we have to give in. If we could just talk about the basic steps we need to take to break the log jam and avoid the possibility of war. I mean, think about it. Where would the survivors of the war live? Major areas of the world would be uninhabitable. We need to keep it in mind that that's what we're about. We are about bringing together steps to bring us closer to the recognition that we need to do away with nuclear weapons.[74]

But rather than craft proposals that would facilitate the elimination of nuclear weapons, Weinberger sought to use Reagan's nuclear abolitionism to convince the president to avoid making any compromises on U.S. positions. Emphasizing that SDI's purpose was to make nuclear weapons obsolete, Weinberger urged Reagan to reject any proposals to lengthen the nonwithdrawal period from the ABM Treaty or place restrictions on America's right to deploy strategic defenses.[75] These compromises, however, were the kind that would facilitate an agreement with the Soviets on strategic defenses, which was a prerequisite for a START treaty.

Weinberger, Adelman, and General Robert Herres, first vice chairman of the Joint Chiefs of Staff, also challenged Reagan's idea of sharing SDI with the Soviets to facilitate nuclear abolition. They argued that the Soviets would use any shared technical data to develop offensive weapons. Unconvinced by this argument, Reagan stressed the need to eliminate nuclear weapons. At the end of the meeting, he told his advisors, "There has to be an answer to all these questions because some day people are going to ask why we didn't do something now about getting rid of nuclear weapons. You know, I've been reading my Bible and the description of Armageddon talks about destruction, I believe of many cities and we absolutely need to avoid that. We have to do something now."[76]

Despite Reagan's instructions to formulate proposals that would precipitate nuclear abolition, no major changes were made to the U.S. START or defense and space positions following the September 8 National Security Planning Group meeting. On September 18, Shultz and Shevardnadze announced that they had agreed in principle to conclude an INF treaty and that Reagan and Gorbachev would sign the treaty at a summit before the end of the year.[77] Nevertheless, Shultz admitted that he could only report progress on some of the minor START issues and that "the big questions remain." He also noted that he "cannot report any narrowing of differences" on defense and space.[78] When the National Security Planning Group met on October 14 to review U.S. arms control positions in advance of Shultz's follow-up trip to Moscow, there was no talk of radically revising U.S. proposals to facilitate an agreement that would eliminate nuclear weapons. In fact, Reagan seemed oddly detached during the meeting. When Carlucci raised some unresolved INF issues, Reagan interrupted to talk about a film on SDI that he had seen recently at Camp David. When the conversation turned to START, Reagan had trouble grasping basic concepts like warhead sublimits and the destabilizing nature of land-based ICBMs.[79] Reagan offered no substantive guidance on the issues debated at the meeting: INF verification, START sublimits, and modifications to the U.S. defense and space proposal.

When Shultz met with Gorbachev in Moscow on October 23, the Soviet leader was exasperated that the United States would not make compromises to facilitate a START or defense and space agreement. On SDI, Gorbachev declared that "while we introduced positive elements, elements of flexibility, into our position, the American side continued to stand on its position of reinforced concrete." Shevardnadze accused the Americans of hardening their START proposal, which now demanded that the Soviets unilaterally eliminate all of their heavy missiles, banned mobile ICBMs, counted medium-range bombers as strategic weapons, and made no effort to resolve disputes over sea-launched cruise missiles. Much to Shultz's surprise, Gorbachev stated that he did not want to travel to Washington simply to sign an INF treaty. Rather, he insisted that the two leaders also sign "key provisions" of a START agreement in Washington, which would pave the way for the signing of a full START treaty during a Moscow summit in 1988.[80] Gorbachev told Shultz, "People will not understand if the two leaders keep meeting and have nothing to show for it, especially since both agreed and said publicly that strategic arms were the key." Gorbachev refused to set dates for a Washington summit, and U.S.-Soviet arms control discussions appeared to be in disarray.[81]

Reagan was facing significant personal and political challenges in October 1987, which likely explain his disengagement from his administration's discussions of nuclear policy. On October 8, Reagan learned from the White House medical staff that they had discovered a possible tumor in Nancy's breast. A biopsy was scheduled for October 17 and doctors warned the first couple that Nancy would need surgery if the tumor was malignant. Reagan later reflected, "The next ten days may have been the longest ten days of our lives." Although Congress was considering Bork's nomination to the Supreme Court, the stock market was turning volatile, and Shultz was trying to finalize the details of the upcoming summit with Gorbachev, Reagan understandably was consumed with concern for Nancy. Reagan later admitted, "I confess this was a period of time in which I was more concerned about the possibility of an even greater tragedy in my own life than I was about the stock market." Nancy's biopsy revealed that her tumor was cancerous and she underwent a mastectomy on October 17.[82]

An examination of Reagan's diary entries from September and October 1987 show that he was also preoccupied by Bork's confirmation battle. On July 1, 1987, Reagan named Bork, a conservative United States Court of Appeals judge, as his nominee to fill the Supreme Court vacancy created by Associate Justice Lewis Powell's retirement. Just hours after Reagan's announcement, however, senators began assailing Bork for his role in the 1973 "Saturday Night Massacre," during which Bork fired Watergate special prosecutor Archibald Cox under Nixon's direction. Senators also condemned Bork's "extremist" views on women's rights and civil rights, among other issues.[83]

Calling and meeting with senators, Reagan took an active part in the White House's efforts to facilitate Bork's confirmation in the fall of 1987.[84] On October 6, however, the Senate Judiciary Committee rejected Bork's nomination by a 9–5 vote. Despite this vote, Bork's nomination was not withdrawn, and the full Senate rejected his nomination by a 58–42 vote on October 23, which was the same day that Shultz met with Gorbachev in Moscow. This was the largest margin of defeat for a Supreme Court nominee in history.[85]

Reagan faced another personal crisis when he learned on October 26 that Nancy's mother, Edith Luckett Davis, had died. "It was extremely difficult for her [Nancy] because I have never known any family with such a close bond between mother and child as there was in Nancy's family," Reagan later reflected. During his trip to Phoenix for his mother-in-law's funeral, Reagan received word that Shevardnadze planned to visit Washington on October 30 with a message from Gorbachev. Leaving a grieving Nancy in Phoenix, Reagan returned to the White House.[86] After meeting with Shevardnadze, who brought a letter from Gorbachev expressing his desire to hold a summit during the first ten days of December, Reagan announced that Gorbachev would arrive in Washington on December 7 to sign the INF Treaty.[87]

During preparations for the Washington summit, many of Reagan's advisors worked to slow progress on strategic and tactical nuclear arms reduction.

Although Weinberger resigned his post as secretary of defense on November 23 due to his wife's poor health, a number of Reagan's advisors feared that sweeping nuclear arms reduction would leave the United States and its NATO allies vulnerable to Soviet conventional superiority. In an October 6 memo to Reagan's principal advisors, Edward Rowny warned against eliminating tactical nuclear weapons. "The issues of the conventional imbalance and the possible denuclearization of Europe are significant fallout from the INF Treaty. We must counter European inclination to move toward a triple zero and not agree to the Soviet proposal that nuclear weapons are negotiated in the conventional forum," he wrote. In the face of Soviet conventional superiority, Rowny believed that the United States should press NATO to carry out the 1983 Montebello decision, which called for the modernization of the alliance's tactical nuclear weapons.[88] Carlucci cautioned Reagan that Gorbachev wanted to denuclearize NATO Europe, which would threaten the security and unity of the alliance.[89]

Several NSC staffers, as well as Carlucci, feared that Reagan and Gorbachev would focus on nuclear abolition in Washington, much as they had during the Reykjavik summit. In a memo to Reagan, Carlucci contended, "We should avoid a lot of discussion of very long-range or possibly impractical goals, e.g., eliminating nuclear weapons, whose impact on our strategic interests is uncertain, particularly as seen by allies."[90] During a November 4 meeting, the interagency Policy Review Group emphasized the importance of avoiding discussion of "a nuclear-free world *and* sharing SDI" during the summit.[91] In a somewhat sinister memo to fellow NSC staffer Robert Linhard, Fritz Ermarth wrote, "We need to come up with a whole list of possible tricks for deflecting the momentum of conversation and buying time." He thought that the administration should delay setting a date for the 1988 Moscow summit, lest it be forced prematurely into concluding wide-ranging arms reduction agreements. "We have to think carefully and talk with our betters about the 1988 summit date. Coming out of this meeting with vaguely new instructions to delegations and a fixed date or even time frame would be a disaster."[92]

Although these machinations by Reagan's advisors impeded progress on strategic and tactical nuclear arms reduction, the INF Treaty heralded the reversal of the superpower nuclear arms race. Six years after U.S. negotiators proposed the zero option, Reagan and Gorbachev signed an agreement to eliminate the entire class of land-based INF missiles at the Washington summit. Both leaders recognized the enormous significance of the treaty. Speaking in the East Room of the White House moments before signing the INF agreement on December 8, Reagan noted, "For the first time in history, the language of 'arms control' was replaced by 'arms reduction'—in this case, the complete elimination of an entire class of U.S. and Soviet nuclear missiles." By signing the INF Treaty, he noted that the two leaders were making "an impossible vision a reality." The president also pointed out that the agreement contained "the most stringent verification regime in history," including unprecedented on-site inspections. "May December 8, 1987, become a date that will be inscribed in the history books," Gorbachev declared, "a date that will mark the watershed separating the era of a mounting risk of nuclear war from the era of a demilitarization of human life."[93]

Although both leaders hoped that the INF Treaty would be merely the first step on the path to a nuclear-free world, their familiar disagreements over SDI derailed their Washington summit discussions. Gorbachev insisted on linking a START treaty with restrictions on SDI, arguing that it was dangerous to build a defensive system that could give one side a first-strike capability while strategic nuclear arms reduction was underway. He also feared that SDI would spark an arms race in space. Reagan was incensed that Gorbachev persisted in linking agreements on START and SDI. He wanted to focus on concluding an agreement to reduce strategic nuclear weapons by 50 percent. Frustrated that Gorbachev did not share his belief that SDI would facilitate nuclear abolition, Reagan reiterated his view that strategic defenses would ensure against any rogue attempt to revive nuclear weapons after the nuclear powers had eliminated them.[94] The two leaders were clearly at an impasse.

By the time of the Washington summit, Gorbachev had conceded that a START treaty would be hard to achieve with the Reagan administration. During a private conversation with the president on the morning of December 9, Gorbachev raised the possibility of a Moscow summit taking place in late May or early June of 1988. Although Gorbachev thought that these dates "would allow for time for a lot of work to be done on a new document on strategic arms and other issues," he did not link Reagan's visit to Moscow with the signing of a START treaty.[95]

The Moscow summit, which took place from May 29 through June 2, 1988, was largely a ceremonial affair. Reagan and Gorbachev exchanged the instruments of ratification of the INF Treaty, and the two sides concluded some minor bilateral agreements on joint verification experiments at nuclear test sites, ballistic missile test launch notifications, and exchange programs, among other things.[96] Nevertheless, U.S. and Soviet negotiators had been unable to ready a START treaty for the leaders to sign during the summit.

The most memorable event of the summit turned out to be Reagan and Gorbachev's stroll through Red Square on May 31. Images of the ardent anticommunist Reagan mingling with ordinary Russians in front of the iconic St. Basil's Cathedral were emblematic of the improvement in superpower relations that had occurred over the previous three years. Gorbachev encouraged the Soviets in Red Square to greet the president. "Shake hands with Grandfather Reagan," the Soviet leader told a young boy. During the leaders' walk, ABC's Sam Donaldson raised Reagan's March 8, 1983, speech to the National Association of Evangelicals, in which the president had called the Soviet Union an "evil empire." "Do you still think you're in an evil empire, Mr. President?" Donaldson asked. "No," Reagan replied. "I was talking about another time and another era."[97]

In an interview with the *Washington Post* a week before the Moscow summit, Gorbachev had been asked about his "new thinking" in foreign policy. Discussing the influences on his foreign policy, the Soviet leader noted, "The new thinking took into account and absorbed the conclusions and demands of the Nonaligned Movement, of the public and the scientific community, of the movements of physicians, scientists, and ecologists, and of various antiwar organizations."[98] As it became clear to Gorbachev that he and Reagan were not going to conclude a comprehensive nuclear arms reduction agreement, he sought to realize the European peace movement's vision of ending the Cold War through the reunification and denuclearization of an autonomous and free Europe.

*   *   *

Throughout 1988, Gorbachev continued to pursue his "common European home" initiative and express support for greater autonomy for Eastern Europe from the Soviet Union. During a toast for Polish leader Wojciech Jaruzelski at a state dinner in Warsaw on July 11, Gorbachev detailed his concept of a "common European home." Building on the Helsinki process, the "common European home" initiative envisioned cooperation between Eastern and Western Europe on security issues. Gorbachev urged European countries to "follow a course toward a continuous process of disarmament— nuclear, chemical, and conventional." The initiative also called for "economic collaboration between the two sides of the continent," with the ultimate goal of "all-European economic integration." Gorbachev hoped that East European and West European countries would be able to develop sufficient trust to permit the elimination of the military blocs in Europe. In endorsing the idea of "socialist pluralism," Gorbachev also indicated his support for greater East European autonomy. He argued that "a respectful attitude to each other's interests, and numerous, often diverging views and experiences—this is not only the basis of mutual understanding and healthy, genuinely friendly ties, it is also a source of acceleration for our movement forward."[99]

Aiming to formulate concrete policies that would advance his "common European home" initiative, Gorbachev created the Institute of Europe within the Soviet Academy of Sciences in early 1988.[100] He had the idea for the institute shortly after Thatcher's visit to the Soviet Union in March 1987. Touting the economic benefits that closer cooperation with Western Europe would yield, Gorbachev told his aides, "We have to plan our European policy seriously. Maybe we should set up a European Research Center."[101] The Institute of Europe was established to research, analyze, and consult on pan-European cooperation and integration.[102] It supplied the Central Committee with reports on the "prospect of European integration and German unification."[103]

Gorbachev took a step toward the realization of the "common European home" in June 1988 when the EEC and the CMEA signed a joint declaration establishing official relations. He hoped that this declaration would pave the way for the eventual creation of a European-wide single market.[104] In an effort to spur additional progress toward the "common European home," the CMEA set forth a plan for economic and technological cooperation with the EEC less than a month after signing the joint declaration.[105] Rather than simply outline his vision of an integrated, nuclear-free "common European home," Gorbachev wanted to pursue concrete initiatives that would facilitate its creation.

When Anatoly Dobrynin, head of the International Department of the Central Committee, suggested that Gorbachev deliver an address to the UN General Assembly in early December, Gorbachev embraced the opportunity to present his vision for ending the Cold War on the world stage.[106] In an October 31 meeting with his top foreign policy advisors on the UN address, Gorbachev declared that "this speech should be anti-Fulton—a Fulton in reverse." If Winston Churchill's famous "Iron Curtain" speech in Fulton, Missouri, on March 5, 1946, marked the beginning of the Cold War, Gorbachev wanted his address to the UN to set forth a vision for ending the Cold War. He emphasized the need to "present the basic principles of our new military-political doctrine, as concretely as possible, and what it means for the international situation." Gorbachev's aim was not merely to call for the establishment of a post–Cold War order, but also to lay out "our contribution to the creation of the new world." In a dramatic departure from the defense policies of his predecessors, Gorbachev wanted to announce unilateral reductions in Soviet forces in the speech.[107]

Taking the podium in the UN General Assembly Hall at 11:05 a.m. on December 7, Gorbachev called for the establishment of a "new world order." Recognizing "the emergence of a mutually interrelated and integral world," the Soviet leader argued that "survival and progress" were contingent on "find[ing] a balance of interests within an international framework." Rejecting the bloc system, Gorbachev declared, "Efforts to solve problems require a new scope and quality of interaction of states and socio-political currents, regardless of ideological or other differences." He believed that the new world order required "de-ideologizing relations among states." Asserting that "the principle of freedom of choice is mandatory," he warned that the failure to recognize a country's right to determine its own sociopolitical system would endanger world peace. Gorbachev also rejected the "use or threat of force" in foreign policy and characterized disarmament as "the main issue without which none of the problems of the coming century can be solved." In order to demonstrate his commitment to creating a post–Cold War order, Gorbachev announced that the Soviet Union would unilaterally reduce its armed forces by 500,000 troops, 10,000 tanks, 8,500 artillery systems, and 800 combat aircraft. These unilateral reductions would include the withdrawal of 50,000 soldiers and 5,000 tanks from the GDR, Czechoslovakia, and Hungary.[108]

"Perhaps not since Woodrow Wilson presented his Fourteen Points in 1918 or since Franklin Roosevelt and Winston Churchill promulgated the Atlantic Charter in 1941 has a world figure demonstrated the vision Mikhail Gorbachev displayed yesterday at the United Nations," declared the New York Times editorial board on December 8.[109] Gorbachev had called for ending the Cold War through cooperation between capitalist and socialist countries, respect for freedom of choice, and disarmament. During 1989, which Gorbachev described in his speech as "a year from which we all expect so much," the Soviet leader would devote his attention to Europe.[110] If the Cold War's end were to come, it would be through the realization of a denuclearized, reunified, autonomous, and free Europe, rather than through global nuclear abolition.

CHAPTER 7

"A Year from Which We All Expect So Much"

After his dramatic address before the UN General Assembly, Gorbachev took a short ferry ride down the East River to Governors Island, where he bid farewell to Reagan and greeted President-elect George H. W. Bush. Although the meeting was intended to be ceremonial, Bush recalled that "there was a feeling of tense expectation" as Gorbachev's ferry approached the dock.[1] Reagan and Bush had been briefed on the substance of Gorbachev's speech, which announced unilateral reductions in Soviet forces and called for an end to the Cold War through international cooperation, respect for freedom of choice, and disarmament.[2] Bush viewed the speech as "encouraging" but considered the Soviets' reduction of their armed forces by five hundred thousand in two years merely a "small but a good start."[3]

In Admiral's House on the island, Reagan, Gorbachev, and Bush reflected on the progress that had been made over the last four years. Reagan presented Gorbachev with a framed photograph of the two leaders in conversation during the Geneva summit. Taken during their walk from the boathouse on the banks of Lake Geneva to the Villa Fleur d'Eau, the image captured the moments when Reagan and Gorbachev had agreed to hold two additional summits in Washington and Moscow. On the photograph, Reagan had written, "We walked a long way together to clear a path to peace, Geneva 1985– New York 1988." Gorbachev appreciated the gift and told the president that he "highly valued their personal rapport, and the fact that in a rather difficult time they had been able to begin movement toward a better world." He "would treasure the memory of all they had been able to do together in these last years."[4] Gazing out at the Statue of Liberty and the Manhattan skyline just before parting, Reagan and Gorbachev agreed that their personal relationship, as well as relations between their countries, had "come a long way" since the Geneva summit.[5]

Although the leaders devoted much of the conversation at Governors Island to fond recollections of the previous four years, Gorbachev was also anxious to "gauge the prospects for our American policy in view of the impending change in the American leadership."[6] Bush, however, remained fairly quiet during the Governors Island meeting, as he was in "the awkward position of having to weigh my present role [of vice president] against my future one."[7] Yet Bush did tell Gorbachev that he "would like to build on what President Reagan had done.... He would need a little time to review the issues, but what had been accomplished could not be reversed."[8] Gorbachev later recounted, "All in all, I had a good impression of this meeting on Governor's Island. The conversation had been frank and friendly, and we could hope to make further headway with the next President of the United States."[9] Gorbachev's optimism would dim as Bush rejected the goal of nuclear abolition in 1989.

This chapter contends that the Bush administration bears responsibility for the superpowers' failure to achieve sweeping nuclear arms reduction agreements as the Cold War drew to a close in 1989. Believing that nuclear weapons were an essential means of compensating for Soviet conventional superiority, Bush and his top advisors exacted a revenge of the establishment by crafting an arms control policy that reinforced a defense strategy based on nuclear deterrence. Upon taking office, they engaged in a protracted review of national security policy that ground U.S.-Soviet relations to a halt. Even after the review ended and START talks resumed, American officials did not prioritize nuclear arms control negotiations with the Soviets. Rather, the Bush administration rebuffed Gorbachev's nuclear arms reduction proposals throughout the final year of the Cold War.

Realizing that U.S. officials were unlikely to seek an agreement eliminating nuclear weapons in 1989, Gorbachev pursued European peace activists' vision for ending the Cold War, just as he had during the last two years of Reagan's second term. In line with European activists' calls for a nuclear-free Europe, Gorbachev announced unilateral reductions in Soviet tactical nuclear weapons in Eastern Europe and proposed negotiations to eliminate these weapons from the continent. He also continued to advocate the creation of a "common European home," which was based on European activists' vision of a denuclearized, reunified, and free Europe. Throughout 1989, Gorbachev supported the principle of freedom of choice, which fit in with European peace activists' appeals for an autonomous and free Europe. As revolutions swept across Eastern Europe in 1989, Gorbachev did not intervene militarily to stop the disintegration of the Soviet empire. He recognized that the use of force would undermine his "common European home" initiative, which he hoped would provide a framework for a stable and peaceful post–Cold War order.

While European anti-nuclear activists continued to promote the idea of a denuclearized, reunified, and free Europe built on a revitalized Helsinki process, new East European peace and human rights groups multiplied in late 1988 and 1989. As ordinary Poles, Hungarians, East Germans, and Czechoslovaks joined the activists' struggle for democracy, human rights, and peace, they remade the very character of their governments and societies. At the dawn of the post–Cold War era, prominent activists with ties to END occupied some of the highest political offices in Poland, the GDR, and Czechoslovakia.

*   *   *

The first sitting vice president to be elected to the presidency since Martin Van Buren, George Herbert Walker Bush was one of the most well-prepared men ever to assume the office of president. He had served as a U.S. congressman from Texas, U.S. ambassador to the United Nations, U.S. envoy to China, CIA director, and vice president. Having graduated Phi Beta Kappa from Yale in just two and a half years, Bush mastered policy details in a way that his predecessor had not.[10] Yet Bush lacked Reagan's ability to articulate a clear vision for the future, or, in Bush's words, "the vision thing."[11]

Neither Bush nor his top advisors shared Reagan's dream of a nuclear-free world. Although interested in pursuing nuclear arms reduction, Bush later recalled, "I wanted to reduce nuclear weapons in a way that would not diminish our deterrent capability." National Security Advisor Brent Scowcroft, who had held the same position in the Ford administration, was horrified by Reagan and Gorbachev's discussion of abolishing nuclear weapons in ten years at the 1986 Reykjavik summit.[12] He even later criticized the 1987 INF Treaty, calling it "a defeat for us in that we got rid of a useful weapon system while the Soviets got rid of one they wouldn't need in any event."[13] In his view, nuclear weapons were an essential means of compensating for Soviet conventional superiority. "It appeared that the Reagan Administration had disregarded the strategic aspects of arms control, placing emphasis on reductions as a goal in itself. It had, I believed, rushed to judgment about the direction the Soviet Union was heading."[14] Bush shared Scowcroft's view that Reagan and his advisors had underestimated the continuing Soviet threat. Even though Gorbachev was pursuing "new thinking" in foreign policy and engaging in domestic reforms, Bush reminded Americans that "the Soviets retain a very powerful military machine in the service of objectives which are still too often in conflict with ours."[15]

Within a month of taking office, the Bush administration embarked on comprehensive reviews of U.S. policy toward the Soviet Union, Eastern Europe, and Western Europe. Reviews of the national defense strategy and U.S. arms control positions began in March and April, respectively.[16] Although Bush had been thinking deeply about U.S. foreign policy as Reagan's vice president for the last eight years, he wrote Gorbachev that he and his advisors "need[ed] some time to think through the entire range of issues, especially those concerning arms control, which occupy a central place in our bilateral relations, and to formulate our position in the interests of further developing these relations."[17] Deputy National Security Advisor Robert Gates later recalled that the reviews were motivated by Bush's desire to "move out of Reagan's shadow" and a widespread concern that the Reagan administration's aim of reaching a START agreement before leaving office ignored the reality of Soviet conventional superiority and the difficulty of verifying strategic nuclear arms reduction. Gates also noted that he, Bush, and Scowcroft wanted to take stock of the changes underway in the Soviet Union and Eastern Europe.[18]

Bush affirmed the importance of nuclear deterrence, which he deemed a "central" part of U.S. containment policy, in the directive for the defense strategy review. Although the Soviets were reforming their economy, political system, and foreign policy, he believed that "it would be reckless to dismantle our military strength and the policies that have helped make the world less dangerous, and foolish to assume that all dangers have disappeared or that any apparent diminution is irreversible." Bush instructed administration officials to study the role of nuclear weapons in the U.S. defense strategy, the requirements for maintaining strategic nuclear deterrence, and the extent to which arms control enhances U.S. security and strategic stability, among other issues.[19] In the directive for the U.S. arms control policy review, Bush tasked the Arms Control Policy Coordinating Committee with evaluating all U.S. negotiating positions in light of the defense strategy review. The president wanted to be sure that his administration's approach to arms control was consistent with its commitment to nuclear deterrence. Setting a June 1 deadline for the submission of defense and space negotiating instructions and a June 7 target for the completion of START negotiating instructions, this directive demonstrated that the Bush administration was in no hurry to begin arms reduction talks with the Soviet Union.[20]

Bush and his top advisors also hoped that these reviews would generate policies that could exploit the changes taking place in the Soviet Union and Eastern Europe to advance U.S. interests. By February 1989, when the Bush administration's comprehensive reviews began, the Soviet Union was in economic disarray. Oil prices began to plummet at the end of 1985, and disintegrating infrastructure was also curbing Soviet oil production. In a Politburo session on February 16, 1989, Prime Minister Nikolai Ryzhkov estimated that falling oil prices had cost the Soviets forty billion rubles of revenue. Meanwhile, Gorbachev's anti-alcohol campaign had led to a loss of thirty-four billion rubles. Ryzhkov informed the Politburo that "in three years of perestroika, government spending exceeded budget revenue by 133 billion rubles." Faced with a rising budget deficit, the Soviet government had printed twenty-one billion rubles over the previous three years. As William Taubman and Svetlana Savranskaya have explained, this led to "a huge monetary overhang—some 40 billion rubles chasing nonexistent consumer goods—thus producing an acute feeling of deficits and shortages among the population." Gorbachev's *glasnost* reforms, which permitted greater freedom of expression, enabled Soviet workers to protest shortages of goods openly.[21]

Yet Gorbachev vowed to continue pursuing *perestroika*, and he made a push for agricultural reform in early 1989. The Soviet leadership also proceeded with plans to hold elections to a new Congress of People's Deputies on March 26, 1989. Gorbachev had spearheaded the resolution for a Congress of People's Deputies at the Nineteenth Party Conference in June 1988. He wanted a reform-minded legislature that would be his ally against conservatives in the CPSU.[22]

The first few months of 1989 were also a period of military retrenchment for the Soviet Union, as it began implementing the reductions that Gorbachev had outlined in his December 7, 1988, speech to the United Nations. By the end of December 1988, Defense Minister Dmitry Yazov told the Politburo that the Ministry of Defense had already devised plans for carrying out the Soviet troop withdrawal from Eastern Europe that Gorbachev had announced in New York.[23] The Soviet Union also completed its withdrawal from Afghanistan on February 15, 1989, bringing an end to more than nine years of military involvement in the country.

Bush believed that the Soviet Union's domestic difficulties and failed foreign adventures had prompted its leaders to "experiment with new political and economic approaches domestically, to make important concessions and withdrawals abroad, and to present a more benign, but in some ways more challenging, face to the world." The president hoped to capitalize on the challenges facing the Soviet Union to promote peace and democracy, including within the Soviet Union.[24]

Bush similarly believed that Eastern Europe was "alive with possibilities" in February 1989, contending that "the potential for real and sustained change in Eastern Europe is greater now than at any time in the post-war period." He noted that "economic problems have become so severe that some of the leaders now seek to revise the outmoded socialist principles on which they have relied for forty years." In addition, "the peoples of Eastern Europe are sending a message to their rulers; political freedom is a precondition for economic improvement."[25] By February 1989, major changes were afoot in Poland and Hungary. After price increases sparked a wave of strikes and protests in 1988, the Polish government agreed to hold roundtable talks on reform with the banned independent trade union Solidarity and the Catholic Church. These talks began on February 6, 1989.[26] That same month, the ruling Hungarian Socialist Workers' Party endorsed the idea of a "multiparty system" in Hungary.[27]

With economic and political reforms underway in the Soviet Union, the Bush administration thought that Gorbachev would encounter political difficulties if he tried to prevent East European leaders from enacting reforms of their own. In the directive for the review of U.S.-East European relations, Bush urged his administration to consider how the United States could help East Europeans exercise self-determination "without bringing a strong and counterproductive reaction from the USSR or the [East European] governments involved." Bush thought that East Europeans should be able to "test" Gorbachev's promise to respect freedom of choice in Europe.[28]

Although Bush had promised Gorbachev that the U.S. review process would not inhibit their efforts to build on the progress made during the Reagan years, his administration's engagement with the Soviets ground to a halt during its first few months in office.[29] Secretary of State James Baker's first visit to Moscow was delayed until the review of U.S.-Soviet relations was completed.[30] In early March, Scowcroft warned the president to avoid "mak[ing] policy precipitously or in a piecemeal fashion" while the comprehensive reviews were taking place. Although Scowcroft recognized that East

Europeans were beginning to "take advantage of Gorbachev's invitation to exercise greater control over their own affairs," he argued that the United States should not embark on any new initiatives in Eastern Europe while the review process was underway.[31]

During Baker's first meeting with Shevardnadze in Vienna on March 7, he refused to discuss a date or even a general timeframe for the resumption of the Nuclear and Space Talks due to the ongoing U.S. reviews. Although Baker pledged that the Bush administration wanted a START treaty, he avoided talking about the substance of U.S. START proposals. He noted that "the U.S. was reviewing its strategic modernization programs and this would of course affect the U.S. negotiating position." Revealing that the U.S. defense strategy review would be completed by the end of April, Baker suggested that a ministerial be held in May, during which the two foreign ministers might be able to set a start date for the Nuclear and Space Talks.[32] Under Baker's plan, the United States and the Soviet Union would be unlikely to begin arms reduction talks until the summer, meaning that they would have lost half a year due to the U.S. comprehensive reviews.

The products of these reviews ultimately were not worth the wait. Baker characterized them as "mush," while Scowcroft and Gates recalled being "disappointed" that the reviews had not yielded new initiatives that took advantage of the changes occurring in the Soviet Union and Eastern Europe.[33] These reviews were largely conducted by members of the bureaucracy, many of whom had been appointed during the Reagan administration. Baker recalled that the Bush team had "changed personnel in a rather genteel way" since it was succeeding another Republican administration.[34] These Reagan holdovers were not enthusiastic about reevaluating the foreign policies that they had helped to craft and implement over the last several years. Two weeks into the reviews of U.S. policy toward the Soviet Union and Eastern and Western Europe, NSC staffers Philip Zelikow and Condoleezza Rice reported, "The review process is not proceeding well. . . . The State people working on it have explained that, as appointees in the previous administration, they were quite satisfied with the Reagan/Shultz approach." The few newly appointed officials in the State Department were often preoccupied by other issues and so were frequently disengaged from the review process.[35] Rather than generating any creative policy proposals, the comprehensive reviews simply put nuclear arms reduction negotiations and U.S. relations with the Soviet Union and Eastern Europe on hold.

*   *   *

After his December 7 UN address calling for an end to the Cold War through cooperation between capitalist and socialist countries, respect for freedom of choice, and disarmament, Gorbachev was eager to begin establishing a "new world order." In an effort to realize his vision of a nuclear-free Europe, which had been shaped by European peace activists, Gorbachev began pursuing the elimination of tactical nuclear weapons in Europe. Speaking at the concluding session of the Third CSCE Follow-Up Meeting in Vienna on January 19, Shevardnadze announced the removal of some of the Soviet Union's tactical nuclear missiles and nuclear-capable artillery pieces from Eastern Europe. The six armored divisions that Gorbachev had told the United Nations would be withdrawn unilaterally from the GDR, Czechoslovakia, and Hungary would take their tactical nuclear systems with them when they left Eastern Europe. Although Western experts estimated that Shevardnadze's announcement amounted to a withdrawal of only twenty-four of the Soviets' roughly 1,400 tactical nuclear missile launchers, the Soviet foreign minister expressed his desire for additional reductions in the future. Shevardnadze also revived the Soviet proposal for negotiations with the United States on tactical nuclear weapons.[36] He reiterated the need for tactical nuclear arms reduction talks to Baker during their March 7 meeting in Vienna.[37]

By early May, Gorbachev was proposing dramatic unilateral reductions of Soviet tactical nuclear weapons and negotiations to eliminate all tactical nuclear weapons in Europe. During his first meeting with Baker in Moscow, Gorbachev repeatedly suggested that the superpowers begin talks on tactical nuclear arms reduction. In what Baker termed a "surprise" move, Gorbachev also revealed that the Soviet Union planned to withdraw five hundred tactical nuclear weapons from Eastern Europe before the end of the year.[38] The Soviet leader told Baker, "If you were willing, we could also examine more radical steps. We are ready to withdraw all of our nuclear ammunition from the territory of our Warsaw Pact allies over the course of 1989-1991, of course, on condition of an analogous step in response by the US."[39]

Recognizing that U.S. officials used Soviet conventional superiority as a reason for maintaining tactical nuclear weapons in Europe, Gorbachev also assured Baker that "a reduction of tactical nuclear weapons in Europe would take place no earlier than the asymmetries in the area of conventional weaponry will be eliminated. Perhaps in parallel with the second stage of reducing conventional weapons." In other words, the elimination of the conventional force imbalance would precede the superpowers' reduction of tactical nuclear weapons to address U.S. concerns. While Gorbachev acknowledged that tactical nuclear arms reduction was a "politically attractive" issue, he believed that its primary value would be in reducing the threat of a nuclear war in Europe.[40]

Gorbachev's focus on tactical nuclear arms reduction mirrored European peace activists' concern about these weapons in 1988 and 1989. In the wake of the 1987 INF Treaty, which eliminated U.S. and Soviet land-based missiles with a range of 500 to 5,500 kilometers, European peace activists feared that the superpowers would modernize their short-range nuclear forces in an effort to compensate for the weapons destroyed under the INF agreement. NATO's debate over the development of a successor to the Lance missile confirmed the activists' worst fears. Since the INF Treaty left tactical nuclear forces in Europe as "the most credible element in extended deterrence," many NATO members were anxious to ensure that these weapons were up to date.[41] In March 1988, NATO reaffirmed its commitment to maintaining the viability of its remaining nuclear forces in Europe, while also continuing the efforts begun at the June 1987 Reykjavik ministerial to develop a "comprehensive concept" of arms control and disarmament.[42]

During 1988 and early 1989, U.S. officials warned NATO governments that the aging short-range Lance missile would soon be in need of modernization. They called on their NATO allies to agree to develop and deploy a follow-on to Lance.[43] The Western European Union similarly argued in 1989 that NATO "cannot avoid the replacement of the Lance. Otherwise the missiles would become obsolete and finally lose their credibility as a deterrent." Noting that the Warsaw Pact had a significant advantage over NATO in short-range nuclear forces, the Western European Union contended that "the countries of WEU should do all the necessary research and make all the preparations for the production of the successor to Lance, but take the final decision on production in, say, two or three years' time," so as not to complicate negotiations on conventional force reductions.[44]

European peace activists eagerly inserted themselves into NATO's debate over tactical nuclear modernization, passionately urging West European governments to refuse a follow-on to Lance. At its October 1987 meeting, the IPCC issued a statement calling on European governments to capitalize on the momentum of an imminent INF treaty to pursue the elimination of tactical nuclear weapons in Europe.[45]

Recognizing West German officials' wariness of modernizing short-range missiles that most likely would be used against other Germans, END activists sought to buoy West German opposition to Lance modernization. They also hoped to convince other West European governments to challenge the development of a follow-on to Lance. In a series of *END Journal* editorials in 1988 and early 1989, Jonathan Steele and Mary Kaldor urged West European peace activists to mobilize against NATO tactical nuclear modernization and put pressure on NATO governments to pursue negotiations with the Soviet Union to reduce and ultimately eliminate these weapons.[46] Contending that public pressure had been one of the major reasons that the superpowers had concluded the INF Treaty, Steele urged West Europeans to make their voices heard in the current debate over short-range nuclear modernization.[47] Kaldor noted that the removal of U.S. and Soviet tactical nuclear weapons from Europe not only would reduce the likelihood of war on the continent, but also would foster greater European autonomy from the superpowers.[48]

Carole Tongue, a member of the European Parliament for London East, argued in an *END Journal* article in early 1989 that "the immediate task for the peace movement is to create a climate of opinion against NATO modernization of short-range nuclear weapons." She encouraged European peace activists to raise the profile of the upcoming June 15, 1989, European Parliament elections and to campaign for anti-nuclear candidates. In her view, an anti-nuclear European Parliament could be an effective counterbalance to voices within the European Community who wanted to create a strong European pillar in NATO based on modernized nuclear weapons.[49]

On the eve of Gorbachev's visit to Britain in April 1989, END released a statement calling on Gorbachev to resist calls to modernize Soviet nuclear weapons in response to NATO's debate over the development of a follow-on to Lance. "In an unfortunate parallel with NATO, there is now talk of 'modernization' and 'compensatory' developments in Soviet weaponry," END activists lamented. "It has proved very difficult to get information on these [conversations], and without such detail it is hard for us to assess to what extent such developments will undo the good done by the INF agreement." They urged Gorbachev to provide more information on the Soviet nuclear program, as well as pursue conventional force reductions, improve the human rights situation in the Soviet Union, and encourage East European leaders to pursue democratic reforms.[50]

Kaldor's writings were a major source of inspiration for Gorbachev's nuclear arms reduction initiatives, so Soviet officials would have been aware of the European peace movement's growing concern over short-range nuclear weapons in 1988 and early 1989.[51] Gorbachev had already proposed the elimination of tactical nuclear weapons, most notably in his January 15, 1986, initiative for abolishing nuclear weapons by 2000 and his April 10, 1987, speech in Prague on the "common European home."[52] With European peace activists' growing opposition to NATO short-range nuclear modernization, however, the environment was ripe for Gorbachev to revive Soviet proposals for the removal of tactical nuclear weapons from Europe. Tair Tairov, who became a department head at the Institute of World Economy and International Relations after leaving his post as Soviet representative of the World Peace Council, recalled that Western peace activists' proposals often influenced Gorbachev's initiatives, which also capitalized on "the fertile soil of European public opinion created by the peace movements."[53]

The Bush administration, however, rejected Soviet proposals to begin negotiations on tactical nuclear weapons in Europe. Despite West German pressure to commence such talks with the Soviets, U.S. officials opposed these negotiations on the grounds that they would facilitate the denuclearization of Europe. The Americans believed that tactical nuclear weapons played a crucial role in NATO's strategy of flexible response, which called on the alliance to maintain a range of possible conventional and nuclear responses to aggression. The elimination of these weapons was therefore out of the question. Since NATO's tactical nuclear weapons were a counter to Soviet conventional superiority, the Bush administration prioritized redressing the conventional force imbalance. U.S. officials would consider reductions in short-range nuclear forces after progress was made in conventional force negotiations.[54]

Baker made these points directly to Gorbachev when they met in Moscow on May 11, 1989. But in presenting the U.S. position, Baker ignored the fact that the proposal Gorbachev made at this meeting actually addressed U.S. concerns. Gorbachev told Baker that the Soviets planned a unilateral reduction of five hundred tactical nuclear weapons from Eastern Europe by the end of 1989. In proposing negotiations on short-range nuclear weapons, Gorbachev also promised that the imbalance in conventional forces would be redressed before the superpowers reduced their tactical nuclear weapons. Nevertheless, Baker lamented near the end of the meeting, "So here we are already in an unfavorable position; you have superiority in tactical nuclear weapons, and in conventional arms. And here, recognizing the political attractiveness of a third zero, you are insisting on [short-range nuclear force] negotiations and thus are trying to put us in an even more unfavorable position."[55] Baker later reflected that Gorbachev had made "a patently one-sided offer," condemning it as "a clear attempt to wrap a strategically insignificant proposal in a broader political context, and score public relations points with European publics."[56] Yet how could this be a one-sided offer when Gorbachev proposed that mutual reductions of short-range nuclear weapons would follow unilateral Soviet cuts in tactical nuclear weapons and the elimination of the conventional force imbalance?

Bush administration officials continued to dismiss Soviet nuclear arms reduction proposals as insignificant and unserious in the days after Baker's meeting with Gorbachev in Moscow. Speaking to the press on May 16, White House spokesman Marlin Fitzwater characterized the Soviet leader's recent arms reduction initiatives as "public relation gambits." He infamously called Gorbachev a "drugstore cowboy," who offered "one arms control proposal after another" that merely repackaged old initiatives or failed to provide for meaningful reductions.[57] While Gorbachev had proposed the elimination of tactical nuclear weapons in 1986 and 1987, his willingness to pursue unilateral reductions in Soviet tactical nuclear and conventional forces before the superpowers began cutting their short-range nuclear forces was new.[58] Also, it is difficult to imagine the arms reduction proposal that Fitzwater would have deemed "meaningful" if he did not consider the abolition of tactical nuclear weapons to be significant.

Bush's unwillingness to engage the Soviets on nuclear arms control frustrated Reagan, whose dream of a nuclear-free world had been spurned by the new administration. Even before Baker rejected Gorbachev's proposals in Moscow, Reagan complained to his friends about Bush's reluctance to pursue nuclear arms reduction with the Soviets. According to *Washington Post* reporter Lou Cannon, "Reagan's friends say he is increasingly concerned at what he considers an excessively cautious approach to nuclear arms reductions negotiations with the Soviets." Reagan had expected Bush to continue his arms control policies and blamed Bush's disparagement of short-range nuclear force negotiations for the discord within NATO on this issue.[59]

Gorbachev was disappointed not only by the Bush administration's refusal to begin negotiations on short-range nuclear forces, but also by its general willingness to put efforts to improve U.S.-Soviet relations on hold while its comprehensive reviews dragged on for months. Chernyaev recalled that the Soviet leader complained in February 1989 that "Bush wasn't drawing the proper conclusions from his U.N. speech." Gorbachev feared that the pause in U.S.-Soviet relations indicated that Bush "even 'has in mind a Western effort to undermine the Soviet Union's international initiatives.'"[60] After his meeting with Baker in Moscow, Gorbachev recalled that the secretary of state seemed to be a "serious person" with a "constructive" attitude. Nevertheless, Gorbachev noted, "We still had no clear answer to the question whether the American administration was prepared to make fast progress."[61]

By the end of July, the head of the International Commission, Aleksandr Yakovlev, was imploring the U.S. ambassador to the Soviet Union, Jack Matlock, to work more seriously for the reduction and elimination of nuclear weapons. Yakovlev and Matlock's July 20 meeting was the first one in months, which was further evidence of the pause in U.S.-Soviet relations. "There is only one danger—nuclear weapons," Yakovlev told Matlock. "As long as they exist, there exists a threat to peace. If we liquidate them, there will be no threat." Yakovlev also noted that the public favored nuclear disarmament.[62]

Matlock's remarks reflected the Bush administration's halfhearted approach to nuclear arms control in 1989. He reminded Yakovlev that Bush supported nuclear arms reduction but did not share Reagan's nuclear abolitionism. Rather, Bush was a firm believer in nuclear deterrence, particularly in light of Soviet conventional superiority. Matlock argued that the Soviets should focus first on cutting conventional forces, which might facilitate nuclear arms reduction at a later date. Worried that the likelihood of nuclear proliferation was increasing, Yakovlev argued that a growing nuclear club would increase the risk of nuclear war and complicate disarmament efforts. He insisted that the superpowers take action now to eliminate nuclear weapons.[63]

Unfortunately, Yakovlev's entreaties fell on deaf ears. The Bush administration did not accelerate its efforts to pursue strategic nuclear arms reduction and maintained its opposition to entering negotiations on tactical nuclear weapons throughout 1989. Although progress toward a START agreement was made at Baker and Shevardnadze's Wyoming Ministerial in September, it was largely the result of Soviet concessions. Even before he arrived in Jackson Hole, Baker was making excuses for the Bush administration's START position. During a press conference a few days before the ministerial, Baker argued that it was hard to craft a START proposal when Congress was delaying votes on elements of the Bush administration's strategic modernization program. In response to a reporter's question about Senate majority leader George Mitchell's criticism of the "timidity" of Bush's foreign policy, Baker contended that the administration was taking care "not to become frantic and rush out here to negotiate a treaty on strategic arms, or anything else for that matter, that would be non-ratifiable." Although he rejected a reporter's assertion that he was implicitly criticizing the Reagan administration's approach to START, Baker nevertheless demonstrated that Bush did not share Reagan's desire to reach a dramatic START agreement as soon as possible.[64]

Eager for a START treaty, the Soviets brought concessions to Jackson Hole. At the Wyoming Ministerial, Soviet negotiators finally abandoned their linkage between strategic nuclear arms reduction and restrictions on strategic defenses. This meant that the two sides could conclude a START agreement without completing a defense and space treaty. The Soviets also announced that they would dismantle the Krasnoyarsk radar station, which U.S. officials had long argued was a violation of the ABM Treaty.[65] At the 1988 Moscow summit, the Reagan administration had made the destruction of the Krasnoyarsk radar a prerequisite for U.S. agreement to a START or defense and space treaty.[66] Baker had reaffirmed that the Krasnoyarsk radar was an obstacle to a START agreement in his March meeting with Shevardnadze in Vienna.[67] While American officials did agree to drop their ban on mobile ICBMs, which pleased Soviet negotiators, their unwillingness to engage on sea-launched cruise missiles and other naval arms thwarted further progress on START in 1989.[68]

*   *   *

Despite the Bush administration's reluctance to pursue nuclear disarmament in 1989, Gorbachev continued to support freedom of choice and advocate his "common European home" initiative, which were the other two aspects of his strategy for ending the Cold War. The principle of freedom of choice fit in with European peace activists' calls for an autonomous and free Europe. Since 1985, European activists' promotion of a denuclearized, reunified, and free Europe had influenced Gorbachev's "common European home" initiative, which he spotlighted in a July 6, 1989, address to the Council of Europe in Strasbourg.

As Hungarian and Polish communist officials embarked on political liberalization during the first half of 1989, Gorbachev's actions lived up to his rhetoric about respecting Europeans' right to choose their own form of government. A few weeks after the Hungarian Socialist Workers' Party endorsed multiparty democracy, Hungarian prime minister Miklós Németh met with Gorbachev, who believed that Hungarian reforms were renewing socialism. No doubt thinking of the upcoming Soviet elections to the new Congress of People's Deputies, Gorbachev boasted to Németh, "Now we are opening the way towards socialist pluralism. The multiplicity of opinions is not a tragedy for the society; on the contrary, it is a real advantage." Gorbachev was glad that "the process of renewal is gradually spreading over the entire socialist bloc, and adds to the political culture and historical experiences of all these countries according to the local conditions."[69]

On March 3, Gorbachev also tacitly endorsed the Hungarian government's plan to begin removing the fences along Hungary's border with Austria. Németh told Gorbachev that these fences "have outlived their usefulness and now serve only to catch citizens from Romania and the GDR who are trying to escape illegally to the West through Hungary. Hungarians no longer violate the border, they have an opportunity to leave the country legally." In response to this declaration that the Hungarians would soon be ripping the fabric of the Iron Curtain, Gorbachev said little. "We have a strict regime on our borders, but we are also becoming more open," he replied.[70] When Hungary began dismantling the barbed-wire fence that ran along its border with Austria in early May, Gorbachev did not intervene.[71]

In Poland, the roundtable talks produced an agreement on April 5 to legalize Solidarity and hold elections to two houses of parliament in June. Solidarity would be able to contest 35 percent of the 460 seats in the lower house of parliament, the Sejm, and all of the 100 seats in the upper house, the Senate.[72] Polish leader Wojciech Jaruzelski hoped that the election results would strengthen the position of reformers within the Communist Party and revitalize communism in Poland.[73] Solidarity, however, emerged as the major victor of the June 4 election, winning all of the 161 Sejm seats that it could contest and 99 of 100 Senate seats.[74] Although the Sejm and Senate elected Jaruzelski president in July, Solidarity activist Tadeusz Mazowiecki became prime minister in August. For the first time since the late 1940s, a non-communist was leading a government in Eastern Europe.[75] Jacek Kuroń, a Solidarity activist who had attended the 1988 END Convention in Lund, became labor minister.[76]

Gorbachev did not try to stop these dramatic events in Poland from unfolding. In a conversation with Jaruzelski on May 9, Gorbachev spoke of the Polish roundtable agreements as an effort to renew socialism, just like his *perestroika* reform program.[77] In the wake of Solidarity's stunning victories in the June elections, Gorbachev still did not threaten the use of force to prevent the formation of a non-communist government in Poland. In fact, Gorbachev actually told Mieczysław Rakowski, the head of Poland's Communist Party, that communists should participate in a Mazowiecki-led government on August 22.[78]

It is important to recognize that Gorbachev initially did not believe that his support for the principle of freedom of choice would lead to the rejection of communism across Eastern Europe. Rather, as Chernyaev later recalled, Gorbachev thought that East Europeans would choose "a good kind of socialism."[79] Speaking to the Politburo on January 21, 1989, about his meeting with the Trilateral Commission, Gorbachev recounted his reply to a question that Kissinger had asked about how the Soviet Union would react if East European countries wanted to join the European Community. "I think that every country should have, and has, its own face," Gorbachev said. "And we will continue to be friends, because the socialist foundation will be preserved in all of them. The paths of our development will be very diverse while we will preserve our commonality."[80] As Gorbachev's support for freedom of choice emboldened non-communists in Eastern Europe, however, he rejected the approach of his predecessors and refused to intervene militarily in East European affairs.

Gorbachev maintained his support for freedom of choice throughout 1989 because he believed that it was the key to the creation of his "common European home," which was another central part of his strategy for ending the Cold War. In an address to the Council of Europe in Strasbourg on July 6, Gorbachev gave the most detailed description of his "common European home" initiative to date. He presented the "common European home" concept as a vehicle for the reunification of Europe that would "put the European common values in the forefront and make it possible to replace the traditional balance of forces with a balance of interests." In his view, the main obstacle to European reunification was a lack of respect for European self-determination. He explained, "The fact that the states of Europe belong to different social systems is a reality. The recognition of this historical fact and respect for the sovereign right of each people to choose their social system at their own discretion are the most important prerequisite for a normal European process. . . . Any interference in internal affairs, any attempts to limit the sovereignty of states—whether of friends and allies or anybody else—are inadmissible." Although Gorbachev's comments were aimed at convincing Western leaders to respect East Europeans who chose socialist systems, he framed freedom of choice as a universal principle, meaning that he was also obliged to recognize it.[81]

Additionally, in describing the security precepts that formed the foundation of the "common European home," Gorbachev declared that "the philosophy of the concept of a common European home rules out the probability of an armed clash and the very possibility of the use or threat of force, above all military force, by an alliance against another alliance, inside alliances, or wherever it may be. It suggests a doctrine of restraint to replace the doctrine of deterrence."[82] If Gorbachev used force to prevent East Europeans from choosing a non-communist system, he would be undermining his own "common European home" initiative.

For their part, West European peace activists and East European dissidents continued to advocate a peaceful, reunified, and democratic Europe in 1988 and 1989. Inspired by independent peace seminars that had been held in Warsaw, Budapest, and Moscow in 1987, Charter 77 and the new Independent Peace Association-Initiative for the Demilitarization of Society (NMS) decided to host their own meeting in Prague from June 17 to 19, 1988. Calling the meeting "Prague 88," its organizers hoped that it would facilitate discussion on "the role of independent groups in fostering peaceful relations between nations." About forty activists from seventeen countries traveled to Prague for the seminar, although many prominent activists from West and East were prevented from attending. Those activists who did make it to Prague found two of the first day's seminar sessions dispersed by Czechoslovak police, who detained the Czechoslovak participants. On the second day of the seminar, all of the nearly fifty activists present at an informal meeting were arrested. Jan Kavan recalled that "ten Czechs spent up to 26 hours in prison and were put under police surveillance after their release. Thirty-four Western participants and Tomas Mastnak from Yugoslavia were expelled from the country after spending six hours in a police station where they continued their discussions."[83]

Despite the Czechoslovak police interference, the Prague 88 attendees were able to finalize a proposal for a European Citizens' Assembly that would take part in the Helsinki process and "would consistently strive for the peaceful and democratic reunification of Europe." Envisioned as a partner for the governments taking part in the CSCE process, the citizens' assembly would set forth proposals for the reunification of a denuclearized, free, and environmentally conscious Europe; offer an independent evaluation of governments' efforts in the Helsinki process; and put pressure on CSCE governments to take action on its proposals. Specifically, the Prague 88 attendees believed that the citizens' assembly should take up the "abolition of military and political blocs; gradual nuclear and conventional disarmament; withdrawal of troops from other countries; implementation of consistently defensive military strategies; protection of the environment; and a transition towards an ecologically conscious economy," as well as proposals to safeguard the free-dom of movement.[84]

The reunified Europe imagined by Prague 88 activists would be demili-tarized. It "would do away with the current practice of disregarding the indi-vidual human being and his/her dignity, and it would pay special attention to environmental issues." These activists' proposal for a citizens' assembly also recognized the links that Europe had with the United States and the Soviet Union, making the proposal a departure from the peace movement's early statements emphasizing the goal of European autonomy from the superpow-ers. The Prague 88 attendees wanted the citizens' assembly to work for a "free, economically strong, ecologically oriented, and socially just society in Europe, North America, and the Soviet Union." They considered "Europe, North America, and the USSR" to be "an area which has a decisive potential for the further development of our civilization as a whole."[85]

END staunchly advocated the proposal to create a European citizens' assembly, and it became one of the movement's top priorities in early 1989. Kaldor had participated in the Prague 88 seminar and signed its final pro-posal.[86] She used articles and editorials in the END Journal to publicize the citizens' assembly initiative and urged other peace activists to campaign for the establishment of the assembly.[87] END also sponsored public meetings to promote the assembly and the vision of a reunified, demilitarized, and free Europe that it would help to create.[88]

The "common European home" initiative that Gorbachev described in his July 6 address to the Council of Europe strongly resembled European peace activists' vision of a denuclearized, reunified, and free Europe. Gorbachev had previously presented the "common European home" as a concept that guided Soviet policy toward Europe, an ideal of a peaceful continent in which East-West cooperation on security, environmental, economic, and cultural issues broke down the blocs in Europe.[89] In his speech in Strasbourg, how-ever, Gorbachev portrayed the "common European home" as an extension of the Helsinki process. He declared, "It is up to all of us, all the participants in the [CSCE] European process, to make the best possible use of the ground-work laid down through our common efforts. Our idea of a common Euro-pean home serves the same purpose too." Gorbachev proposed that a "second Helsinki-type meeting" be held within the next eighteen to twenty-four months so that leaders could discuss both "the most immediate issues" and "how they contemplate future stages of progress towards a European Com-munity of the twenty-first century."[90] Gorbachev clearly shared European peace activists' view that a reunified Europe could be built on a revitalized and expanded Helsinki process.

While Gorbachev had long insisted that the Soviet Union belonged in Europe, he argued in Strasbourg that the United States also had a place in the "common European home." The Soviet leader declared that "the realities of today and the prospects for the foreseeable future are obvious: the Soviet Union and the United States are a natural part of the European international and political structure. Their involvement in its evolution is not only justified, but also historically conditioned. No other approach is acceptable. In fact, it will even be counterproductive."[91] Gorbachev's statements fit in with Prague 88 activists' recognition that Europe had indelible links to the United States and the Soviet Union.

In his address to the Council of Europe, Gorbachev explained that his "common European home" was built on a "foundation" of disarmament with its "bearing frame" consisting of East-West cooperation on economic, environmental, and humanitarian issues. The disarmament proposals set forth by Gorbachev mirrored those of European peace activists, including the opening of tactical nuclear arms reduction negotiations, the elimination of nuclear weapons by 2000, the reduction of conventional forces to a level of reasonable sufficiency, the withdrawal of foreign troops from other countries, and the dissolution of the blocs in Europe. Gorbachev's ideas for economic, environmental, and humanitarian cooperation between the two halves of Europe also echoed European peace activists' proposals. As part of the effort to establish a "common European economic dimension," the Soviet leader called for better relations between countries in the EEC, CMEA, and European Free Trade Association. He advocated the creation of "an all-European institute for ecological research and assessment," among other cooperative environmental protection measures. Gorbachev's suggestions for cultural cooperation included the establishment of "an ad hoc working group or a kind of European institute for comparative humanitarian law," as well as initiatives to promote the study of European languages and transnational film projects.[92]

In discussing the humanitarian dimension of the "common European home," Gorbachev also endorsed European activists' concept of the indivisibility of peace and human rights. "A world where military arsenals would be reduced but where human rights would be violated would not be a safe place," Gorbachev contended. "We have come to this conclusion ourselves once and for all."[93] Although Soviet citizens still did not enjoy many civil or political rights in July 1989, Gorbachev's affirmation of the idea that respect for human rights was a prerequisite for international peace was a hopeful sign that he would continue to pursue the political liberalization of the Soviet Union.

The work of END activists like Mary Kaldor and E. P. Thompson provided inspiration for Gorbachev's security policy, so it is unsurprising that his address to the Council of Europe on the "common European home" echoed European activists' appeals for a peaceful, united, and free Europe.[94] Thompson even acknowledged the similarity between the proposals set forth by END and Gorbachev. In the spring of 1990, he reflected, "To our surprise, after 1985 our own words started to come back to us—from Moscow. It was Gorbachev now who took our lines, who spoke of ridding Europe of nuclear weapons 'from the Atlantic to the Urals,' who proposed a practical agenda for the dissolution of both blocs and advocated the withdrawal of Soviet and U.S. troops within their own borders by the year 2000."[95]

Yet Gorbachev and European peace activists were not the only ones setting forth a vision for Europe's future in 1989. Bush administration officials wanted to craft a vision for Europe that would counter Gorbachev's concept of a nuclear-free "common European home," in which there would be respect for different systems and the United States might not have a clear place. U.S. officials believed that the United States and NATO allies should offer a vision of Europe's future based on "the common values, culture, and heritage, amounting to a 'Western experience,' shared by the United States and Europe, including Eastern Europe, but not by the Soviet Union." Under this concept, Europe would be reunified by East European countries adopting political and economic reforms with Western assistance. The United States would endorse continued West European integration and keep its nuclear weapons and ground and air forces in Europe to maintain European security. Although the United States would applaud Soviet reforms that fostered freedom and peace, the Soviet Union would be outside of Europe because it did not support the "Western" principles that bound together the United States, Western Europe, and Eastern Europe.[96]

Bush's most famous expression of his vision for Europe's future came in his May 31 speech to the West German citizens of Mainz. The interagency Deputies Committee had proposed that Bush use his trip to Western Europe in May to "offer a positive political agenda for the future of Europe to compete with, and go beyond, Gorbachev's 'common European home.'"[97] In his address in Mainz, Bush called for a Europe "whole and free." Noting that "the Cold War began with the division of Europe," Bush argued that "it can only end when Europe is whole." In his view, the key to the reunification of Europe was the spread of freedom and democracy to Eastern Europe. Bush declared that the Eastern bloc's experiment with socialism had failed, and he vowed to "help open the closed societies of the East." Proposing a revitalization of the Helsinki process to "promote free elections and political pluralism in Eastern Europe," Bush urged Western political parties to offer advice and support to East Europeans trying to form new political parties in their countries. He called on the United States and Western Europe to provide technology and training to East Europeans so that they could better tackle environmental problems. Declaring that the Berlin Wall "must come down," Bush advocated "mak[ing] all Berlin a center of commerce between East and West." He held up West European integration as a model for Eastern Europe, hailing the fact that "this process of integration, a subtle weaving of shared interests, which is so nearly complete in Western Europe, has now finally begun in the East." Arguing that "a strong Western defense is the best road to peace," Bush set forth conventional arms control proposals that would require the Warsaw Pact to engage in far steeper reductions than NATO.[98]

In this speech, Bush also explicitly criticized Gorbachev's concept of a "common European home" and presented his vision of a Europe "whole and free" as a superior alternative. He believed that Gorbachev's idea of a "common European home," which called for respect for different sociopolitical systems in Europe, would not include sufficient protections for individual freedom. Noting that many East Europeans still faced government repression and had difficulty traveling abroad, Bush declared, "There cannot be a common European home until all within it are free to move from room to room." Bush also believed that Gorbachev's "common European home" concept was too restricted, proclaiming that "the path of freedom leads to a larger home, a home where West meets East, a democratic home, the commonwealth of free nations." Bush feared that the United States might be excluded from Gorbachev's "common European home" on geographical grounds. Trying to cement the bond between the United States and Europe rhetorically, Bush spoke of what "we, the nations of Western Europe," could teach East Europeans, namely that security in Europe "is built on shared values and agreements that link free peoples."[99]

*   *   *

Although Poland and Hungary were undergoing dramatic political changes during the first half of 1989, the GDR and Czechoslovakia lagged woefully behind in undertaking reform. In May 1989, Honecker boasted, "We took power in order to keep it forever."[100] That same month, however, Hungary began ripping the Iron Curtain by dismantling the barbed-wire fence along its border with Austria. Desperate to escape Honecker's regime, over thirty thousand East Germans had fled to the West through Hungary by late September.[101]

Despite this exodus, prominent East German peace activists stayed in the GDR and established new opposition groups. On September 9, Bärbel Bohley, who had been a member of Women for Peace and the Initiative for Peace and Human Rights, cofounded New Forum, which became the largest opposition group in the GDR. Recognizing that the mass emigration from the GDR signified that "communication between state and society is clearly not functioning properly," New Forum sought a "restructuring" of the GDR. Its founding statement declared that it aimed to promote policies "based on the desire for justice, democracy, and peace, and for the protection and preservation of nature." Unlike activists in Poland and Hungary, where economic conditions were worse than in the GDR, New Forum members wanted to reform, not abandon, socialism. They also sought modifications to the GDR's election laws that would permit independent candidates to run for office. By November 6, New Forum had more than one hundred thousand members.[102]

On September 12, East German peace activist Ulrike Poppe cofounded Democracy Now. Inspired by Gorbachev's reforms in the Soviet Union and noting that changes were underway in Poland and Hungary, Democracy Now activists called for the end of state socialism and the introduction of democratic socialism in the GDR. They also sought respect for human rights, environmental protection measures, a reduction in the size of the East German military, and the introduction of alternative civilian service. Affirming the indivisibility of peace and human rights, Democracy Now declared, "The purpose of our proposals is to achieve internal peace in our country and thereby simultaneously to serve the cause of international peace."[103]

Like Democracy Now, Democratic Awakening also advocated a more democratic form of socialism in the GDR. Democratic Awakening, however, put more emphasis on disarmament and the establishment of a "European peace order" than the other new East German opposition groups did. Cofounded on October 2 by East German anti-nuclear activist Rainer Eppelmann, Democratic Awakening proclaimed, "The political demands and action program of Democratic Awakening are rooted in the great hope of the creation of a Common European Home, a European peace order, and a more just world." Yet Democratic Awakening activists' concept of a "common

European home" was more limited than Gorbachev's vision, as they did not advocate the dissolution of the military alliances.[104]

As veterans of the East German peace movement established new opposition groups in September and early October, thousands took to the streets of Leipzig and East Berlin to demand freedom and democracy in the GDR.[105] Amid these protests, Gorbachev traveled to the GDR for a celebration of its fortieth anniversary on October 7. During this visit, Gorbachev warned the members of the East German Politburo that people would not support socialism without reforms to improve their living standards and open up society. Although he did not mention Honecker by name, Gorbachev encouraged the Politburo to make a leadership change so that it could better address the problems plaguing the GDR.[106] On October 18, Egon Krenz replaced Honecker as general secretary of the Socialist Unity Party (SED).

Yet mass protests only increased after Honecker's departure, as Krenz proved to be uninterested in genuine reform. On November 4, five hundred thousand rallied in East Berlin, while almost a million people demonstrated across the GDR two days later. These protesters called for free and fair elections and an end to travel restrictions.[107] Meanwhile, tens of thousands of East Germans fled to the West through Czechoslovakia in early November. Fearful that East German refugees were emboldening Czechoslovak dissidents, Czechoslovak leaders threatened to close the border with the GDR.[108]

Against this backdrop of mass demonstrations in East German cities and rising anger among Czechoslovak officials, the SED Central Committee hastily endorsed new rules for foreign travel and emigration on November 9. East Germans would still need to obtain permission to leave the GDR, but they no longer had to satisfy strict eligibility requirements to apply for personal foreign travel. The new rules also stated that "permanent emigration may take place over all border crossings between the GDR and FRG and Berlin (West)." These new regulations would take effect "right away," but their announcement was initially set for 4:00 a.m. on November 10. Krenz, however, told SED spokesman Günter Schabowski to unveil the new rules at a televised press conference on the evening of November 9.[109]

Schabowski's botched presentation of the new travel rules had momentous, unintended consequences. He read excerpts of the new regulations at rapid speed, glossing over the provisions that allowed authorities to reject travel and emigration requests. In response to a question about when the new rules would take effect, Schabowski frantically scanned his papers before answering "'right away.'" Journalists soon began reporting that the GDR had opened its borders. When tens of thousands of East Germans congregated at the checkpoints along the Berlin Wall demanding to cross into West Berlin in accordance with the new travel rules, the East German border officials opened the gates. Elated Berliners soon climbed atop the Wall before beginning to tear it down.[110] The most visible symbol of the Cold War would soon lay in pieces on the ground.

Rather than trying to stop the fall of the Wall, Soviet officials praised the course of events in the GDR. In a message to Krenz, Gorbachev declared, "All has been accomplished in the correct fashion, continue energetically and resolutely in the same direction." A spokesman for Shevardnadze proclaimed, "These are changes in the right direction. We are evolving from a divided post-war Europe toward the common European home."[111] Writing in his diary on November 10, Chernyaev hailed the fall of the Wall, suggesting that it signified the end of Europe's division. The fall of the Berlin Wall "has to do not only with 'socialism,' but with the shift in the world balance of forces. This is the end of Yalta, the Stalinist legacy, and 'the defeat of Hitlerite Germany,'" he wrote. Chernyaev also lauded Gorbachev for allowing the Wall to come down, writing, "That is what Gorbachev has done. And he has indeed turned out to be a great leader. He has sensed the pace of history and helped history to find a natural channel."[112]

Gorbachev did not use force to halt the dramatic events in the GDR because he recognized that it would undermine his "common European home" initiative, which Soviet officials pursued enthusiastically in the fall of 1989. In an October 14 memorandum to Gorbachev, Georgy Shakhnazarov, one of the Soviet leader's top aides, set forth a plan for the de-blocking of Europe by 2000. Adopting a series of proposals long touted by European peace activists, Shakhnazarov called for the dissolution of the NATO and Warsaw Pact military organizations, Soviet troop withdrawal from Eastern Europe, and the elimination of all foreign military bases in Europe by the end of the century. He contended that this plan for "military détente in Europe" would go a long way toward the realization of Gorbachev's "common European home" concept. "Similar ideas literally fill the air," Shakhnazarov wrote. "One can have no doubt that this proposal will find a positive response, and will define clear timelines in the future development of the European process."[113] Gorbachev continued to call for the revitalization of the Helsinki process to facilitate the creation of the "common European home." During an October 25 meeting with Finnish president Mauno Koivisto, for example, Gorbachev repeated the proposal that he had made in Strasbourg to convene another Helsinki

Conference to determine "what the possibilities for building the common European home are."[114]

Gorbachev knew that the use of force in the GDR would make his appeals for a "common European home" appear hypocritical and would prompt an outpouring of opposition toward the Soviet Union and his idea of a denuclearized, reunified, and free Europe. During his first meeting with a non-communist East European leader, Gorbachev explained to Mazowiecki, "Our policy is to provide a solution to complex international problems. As difficult as the problems of Eastern Europe are, we must maintain a pan-European process. For this to happen, all its members must exhibit a very mature approach."[115]

Gorbachev decided to maintain his "common European home" initiative at the expense of preserving communist regimes in Eastern Europe because he believed that the security, economic, and environmental benefits of the "common European home" outweighed the disadvantages of losing the Soviet empire in Eastern Europe. Recognizing that Europe "bristles with weapons, both nuclear and conventional," Gorbachev contended in 1987 that the establishment of a "common European home" was essential to ensure that war did not break out in Europe.[116] By 1989, the Soviet leadership envisioned the creation of pan-European security structures that would make NATO and Warsaw Pact military structures obsolete and reduce tension in Europe.[117]

In addition to security, the "common European home" promised desperately needed economic benefits for the Soviet Union and Eastern Europe. In explaining the origins of the "common European home" concept to the Council of Europe on July 6, 1989, Gorbachev noted, "The idea is linked with our domestic, economic and political perestroika which called for new relations above all in that part of the world [Europe] to which we, the Soviet Union, belong, and with which we have been tied most closely over the centuries."[118] Sergei Karaganov, the deputy director of the Institute of Europe, wrote that the "unprecedented concurrence of Eastern and Western economic interests" made 1989 a fitting year to begin moving toward the pan-European economic integration of the "common European home." "We in the Soviet Union are badly in need of funds, of talent, of people who could help with the restructuring and modernization and humanization of our economy," he acknowledged. Western Europe was a promising source of the loans, investment, and experts who could help the Soviets jump-start their economy. Since it would take time to establish European-wide economic integration, Karaganov urged the Europeans and Americans to immediately "consider seriously the possibility of increasing economic exchange with the Soviet Union; that is, to remove the discriminating controls which do nothing to promote the security of any country but only hinder the process of *rapprochement* between East and West in the economic field."[119]

Gorbachev also likely viewed the "common European home" as a way to ensure that the ongoing economic integration of Western Europe did not have negative ramifications for the Soviet Union and Eastern Europe. The Single European Act, which was signed in 1986 and ratified in 1987, set the European Community a target date of 1992 to create a single market. Karaganov wrote in 1989 that the economic integration of Western Europe would make it "an even more interesting trading partner to its socialist neighbours" and could "serve as a pilot project for the future development of all-European economic integration." Yet he also noted, "Many people in the East fear that 1992 might serve to strengthen the economic divide of Europe and thus make it even more difficult for them to break into the European market-place and to adjust to the changing conditions."[120] The "common European home," with its promise of pan-European economic integration, would prevent Eastern bloc countries from being disadvantaged by the formation of a single market within the European Community.

Gorbachev also recognized that Europe was facing a host of environmental challenges and believed that cooperation through the "common European home" was essential to address these problems. "Europe is one of the most industrialized regions of the world. Its industry and transport have developed to a point where their danger to the environment is close to being critical. This problem has crossed far beyond national borders, and is now shared by all of Europe," he wrote in 1987.[121] In his address to the Council of Europe, the Soviet leader advocated the development of a "long-term continental ecological program," the establishment of a European center for environmental monitoring, the launch of "an all-European institute for ecological research and assessment," and the creation of a supranational body with "binding authority" over the environmental policies of European countries, among other measures. Gorbachev was hopeful that "it is in this [environmental] direction, which is indeed a priority direction, that the all-European process will advance most rapidly."[122] The Soviet leader believed that if he intervened in Eastern Europe to halt the 1989 revolutions and thereby undermined the "common European home," he would be consigning Europe to environmental ruin.

In fact, the East European revolutions actually intensified Gorbachev's resolve to pursue the "common European home" initiative. Although Gorbachev respected East Europeans' right to choose their form of government, he feared that the events of 1989 might lead to instability in Eastern Europe. The fall of the Berlin Wall on November 9 raised the specter of German reunification, which particularly worried Gorbachev.[123] His concern about German reunification was driven largely by his childhood memories of the Second World War, during which the Nazis had occupied his hometown and arrested his grandmother. Gorbachev had gone into hiding during the war after rumors began circulating that the Nazis were planning to massacre communist families in his hometown. His most indelible wartime memory, however, was his discovery of Red Army soldiers' remains while walking with his friends in the forest in 1943. In his memoir, Gorbachev acknowledged that the Second World War had a lasting effect on his "view of the world."[124] Would a reunified Germany generate instability as it had done during the two world wars? Gorbachev initially shared his predecessors' view that the division of Germany was necessary to safeguard the Soviet Union, yet he slowly recognized that German reunification was unavoidable.[125]

The "common European home" offered a vehicle for containing any instability that arose as a result of the revolutions in Eastern Europe, particularly in the GDR. Gorbachev believed that it would enable the countries of Europe to oversee a gradual and orderly reunification of Germany.[126] In discussing the prospects for German reunification on November 21, 1989, Gorbachev told Canadian prime minister Brian Mulroney, "I am not a prophet but at some stage, in the framework of the new Europe toward which we are moving now, there could be some changes that would involve the two German states."[127] Shevardnadze recalled that although the fall of the Berlin Wall was "unambiguously positive, changes of such magnitude and rapid pace undoubtedly had a destabilizing effect, which no sane person could desire. The new danger that the process just begun would wipe out existing boundaries and bring chaos and collapse to this vital region, forced us to act, to look for the correct formula, which could not be other than this: dynamism within a framework of stability." Soviet officials believed that the "common European home" provided such a formula. Shevardnadze noted that Soviet foreign policy in the year following the Berlin Wall's collapse was motivated by "the desire to determine the forms of a common European order that would be rational, viable, and above all, secure."[128]

Gorbachev's determination to pursue his "common European home" initiative also explains his unwillingness to intervene in Czechoslovakia's Velvet Revolution. The spark that set off this revolution was the Czechoslovak authorities' violent suppression of an officially sanctioned student demonstration in Prague on November 17, 1989.[129] Two days later, Václav Havel and a group of activists from Charter 77 and other Czechoslovak organizations founded Civic Forum, which condemned the suppression of the student demonstration and called for negotiations with the government to implement reforms.[130] As demonstrations and strikes engulfed Czechoslovakia, Civic Forum set forth a list of goals on the eve of a planned November 27 general strike. In addition to demanding protections for human rights and the environment, a democratic political system, a free-market economy, and artistic and academic freedom, Civic Forum advocated Czechoslovakia's participation in the "common European home" initiative. "We are striving for our country to once again occupy a worthy place in Europe and in the world," the activists wrote. "We are counting on inclusion into European integration. We want to subordinate our policy toward our partners in the Warsaw Pact and COMECON to the idea of the 'Common European home.'"[131] How could Gorbachev use force against an opposition group that shared his goal of creating a "common European home"?

After talks and roundtable negotiations between Civic Forum and the government, President Gustáv Husák installed a new cabinet in which noncommunists held the majority on December 10. He then resigned the presidency. Nineteen days later, the Federal Assembly elected Havel the new president of Czechoslovakia.[132] Jiří Dienstbier, a former Charter 77 spokesperson who had issued the Prague Appeal and played a major role in the Prague 88 meeting, became Czechoslovakia's foreign minister.[133]

*   *   *

In the midst of this upheaval, Bush and Gorbachev prepared for their first summit off the coast of Malta on December 2 and 3, 1989. In late July, Bush proposed that the two leaders meet for an "unstructured informal meeting." His aim for this meeting with Gorbachev was to "reduce the chances there could be misunderstandings between us" and "to get our relationship on a more personal basis."[134]

Although this may have sounded similar to Gorbachev's proposal for "a quick one-on-one meeting" with Reagan in Reykjavik in 1986, Bush did not seek a dramatic breakthrough on nuclear arms reduction in Malta.[135] Rather, he repeatedly stated that he would not negotiate arms reduction with Gorbachev during the summit. "As you know, we are working hard to ensure that this does not become an arms control meeting," Bush told Mitterrand two days before the summit opened. "We will not be drawn into the details of ongoing negotiations, and we certainly will not make any unilateral deals over the heads of our allies." Rather than discuss the specifics of arms reduction proposals with Gorbachev, Bush intended "to talk with him about our general approach and philosophy." He wanted to focus on conventional force reductions, rather than nuclear weapons cuts.[136] As they had explained throughout 1989, Bush and his top advisors believed that U.S. nuclear weapons were an essential means of compensating for Soviet conventional superiority. Yet Bush did plan to express his interest in making progress on START, the Threshold Test Ban Treaty and Peaceful Nuclear Explosions Treaty verification protocols, and an "open skies" verification regime in the next year.[137]

Mindful of Gorbachev's record of offering "surprise" proposals during summits and eager to be prepared for any new initiatives that he might unveil in Malta, Bush administration officials scripted responses to various points that Gorbachev might make during the upcoming meeting. The reply to a Soviet proposal to move toward minimum nuclear deterrence highlights the administration's continued opposition to sweeping nuclear arms reduction. Not only had nuclear weapons kept the peace in Europe for nearly forty-five years, but U.S. officials "do not think nuclear disarmament is a realistic or feasible goal. We do not think you can put the genie back in the bottle because the knowledge required to build the bomb cannot be unlearned. Indeed, that terrible knowledge is spreading." The response paper also noted that "the lower the number of forces on both sides, the less stable the balance can become because, at lower levels, small changes can have major impacts. I agree we should retain the minimum number of weapons necessary for a survivable, credible, and stabilizing deterrent, but at some point, smaller no longer is necessarily better." Rather than pursue radical nuclear disarmament, the superpowers should seek a START agreement that "would give us stabilizing cuts in the forces of both our countries."[138] Bush and Gorbachev's conversations about nuclear arms reduction in Malta promised to be far less dramatic than those in which Reagan and Gorbachev had engaged in Geneva, Reykjavik, Washington, and Moscow.

In addition to talking about the two sides' arms control approaches, Bush sought to "engage the Soviet leader in a broad discussion on the changes now underway in the world and the future of East-West relations." He planned to discuss *perestroika* in the Soviet Union, U.S.-Soviet economic relations, the East European revolutions, regional issues, and human rights. As with arms control, however, Bush administration officials did not "anticipate specific negotiations, nor do we envisage major agreements being concluded" on these issues.[139]

In preparation for the Malta summit, Bush received briefings from outside experts on Soviet domestic and foreign policy. These specialists hailed from universities and think tanks and were intended to "represent the range of opinion on the issues." Among those briefing Bush on East-West issues was Randall Forsberg, whose pamphlet *The Call to Halt the Nuclear Arms Race* had sparked the nuclear freeze movement nearly a decade before. She represented the Institute for Defense and Disarmament Studies, which was the think tank that she had founded in 1980.[140] Although the freeze movement's policy influence had evaporated by 1985, it had played an essential role in shifting the U.S. nuclear arms control paradigm from arms limitation to arms reduction during Reagan's first term. This was the first step toward reversing the superpower nuclear arms race and ending the Cold War. It was therefore fitting that a leader of the freeze movement was invited to the White House to help Bush prepare for the Cold War's final summit.

Taking place off Malta's coast on December 2 and 3, Bush and Gorbachev's first summit marked the end of the nearly forty-five-year Cold War. Deemed the "seasick summit" due to the bad weather that forced the two leaders to cancel some of their shipboard sessions, the Malta meeting nevertheless was a milestone in U.S.-Soviet relations.[141] During the first plenary session, Gorbachev asserted that the Cold War had ended and that the two sides needed to "evaluate the period of the Cold War" so that they did not try to resolve new problems using old Cold War–era approaches. He noted that the history of the Cold War had shown that "reliance on force, on military superiority, was wrong. It did not justify itself. The emphasis on confrontation based on our different ideologies is wrong. We had reached a dangerous point, and it is good that we stopped to reach an understanding."[142] By the second plenary session, Gorbachev pledged that "the Soviet Union will not under any circumstances initiate a war. This is so important that I wanted to repeat the announcement to you personally. Moreover, the USSR is prepared to cease considering the U.S. as an enemy and announce this openly. We are open to cooperation with America, including cooperation in the military sphere."[143]

In discussing the revolutionary events taking place in Eastern Europe, Gorbachev again linked his unwillingness to intervene in East European affairs to his "common European home" initiative, which he envisioned as the framework for a stable post–Cold War order. "Therefore, all of Europe is on the move, and it is moving in the direction of something new. We also consider ourselves Europeans, and we associate this movement with the idea of a common European home. I would like to ask E. A. Shevardnadze and Secretary of State Baker to discuss this idea in more depth, because I think it is in the interests of both the USSR and the U.S.," Gorbachev declared. He pressed Bush to support a revitalization of the Helsinki process as part of the effort to construct a "common European home." "We are convinced that we must work toward continuing and developing the Helsinki process, and by no means toward destroying what was created on the basis of it. After this, Helsinki II will be needed so that we can interpret the new situation and work out joint criteria and frameworks. It is understood that all the countries that signed the Helsinki Act, including of course the U.S. and Canada, must take part in this meeting," Gorbachev asserted.[144]

Although no agreements emerged from the Malta summit, both leaders vowed to continue cooperating on the full range of issues. They hoped to sign a START treaty and the Threshold Test Ban Treaty and Peaceful Nuclear Explosions Treaty verification protocols at a 1990 summit meeting in the United States. With the Iron Curtain in tatters and reform underway in the Soviet Union, the Cold War was at a close. The Soviet draft of Bush and Gorbachev's directives for their foreign ministers stated that the two leaders "came to a common conclusion that the period of cold war was over and that the emerging era of peace opened up unprecedented opportunities for multilateral and bilateral partnership."[145] In a press conference after the summit, Gorbachev affirmed that the world had entered the post–Cold War era, noting, "We stated, both of us, that the world leaves one epoch of cold war and enters another epoch. This is just the beginning. We're just at the very beginning of our long road to a long-lasting peaceful period." Bush declared that he was "optimistic that as the West works patiently together and increasingly cooperates with the Soviet Union, we can realize a lasting peace and transform the East-West relationship to one of enduring cooperation. And that is a future that's worthy of our peoples. And that's the future that I want to help in creating. And that's the future that Chairman Gorbachev and I began right here in Malta."[146]

The Bush administration's rejection of the goal of nuclear abolition prevented the superpowers from reaching dramatic nuclear arms reduction agreements as the Cold War came to an end. Recognizing that U.S. officials were unlikely to seek an agreement eliminating nuclear weapons in 1989, Gorbachev pursued European peace activists' vision for ending the Cold War through the reunification and denuclearization of an autonomous and free Europe. In line with European activists' calls for a nuclear-free Europe,

Gorbachev announced unilateral cuts in Soviet tactical nuclear weapons in Eastern Europe and proposed talks to eliminate these weapons from the continent. He also continued to advocate the creation of a "common European home," which was based on European activists' vision of a denuclearized, reunified, and free Europe. Understanding that the use of force in Eastern Europe would undermine his "common European home" proposal, Gorbachev refused to intervene militarily to stop the revolutions of 1989. He hoped in vain that the "common European home" would provide a framework for a stable and peaceful post–Cold War order.

Conclusion

"Now, 44 years after Winston Churchill's 'Iron Curtain' speech, the myth of monolithic communism has been shattered for all to see, the ideological conflict known as the Cold War is over, and the risk of global nuclear war being ignited in Europe is significantly diminished," declared an editorial in the April 1990 issue of the *Bulletin of the Atomic Scientists*. In response to the Cold War's end, the hands of the *Bulletin*'s famous Doomsday Clock were moved back to ten minutes to midnight. Yet the threat posed by nuclear weapons persisted. "Much remains to be done before the greatest short-term threat to the planet—the risk of nuclear war—is eliminated. Additional concrete actions that disarm the relations among nations are needed before the hands of the clock can be turned back further," the editorial warned. "Still, the termination of the Cold War has lifted a grim weight from the human psyche. It has returned to humanity its hope for a future, and the chance to create one."[1]

Although they did not achieve their goal of a nuclear-free world, grassroots and government nuclear abolitionists played a key role in ending the Cold War. Yet their inability to eliminate nuclear weapons has led scholars to overlook nuclear abolitionism's significance in the Cold War's endgame. In light of recently declassified documents that reveal the importance of nuclear abolitionism in the Cold War's conclusion, it is now clear that the end of the Cold War cannot be understood without taking into account nuclear abolitionists. Nuclear abolitionism was a diverse and global force that united political adversaries and reshaped political discourse and policy in the United States and the Eastern bloc during the 1980s. Grassroots and government nuclear abolitionists shifted U.S. and Soviet nuclear arms control paradigms from arms limitation to arms reduction. This new emphasis on nuclear arms reduction paved the way for the reversal of the superpower nuclear arms race, which began with the landmark 1987 INF Treaty. European peace activists' vision of a denuclearized, reunified, and free Europe shaped Gorbachev's "common European home" initiative, which he ultimately pursued as a framework for overcoming the Cold War and establishing a stable and peaceful post–Cold War order. Gorbachev refrained from intervening to halt the 1989 East European revolutions because he did not want to undermine this "common European home" concept. As revolutions swept across Eastern Europe, the Iron Curtain dividing Europe receded.

Why did nuclear abolitionism have such an impact on U.S. and Soviet security policy in the 1980s? After all, anti-nuclear sentiment was not a new phenomenon during this decade. In the wake of the U.S. atomic bombings of Hiroshima and Nagasaki in August 1945, grassroots anti-nuclear weapons movements burst forth across the globe.[2] They flourished again from the mid-1950s through the mid-1960s in response to the development of the hydrogen bomb and widespread atmospheric nuclear testing.[3] Like Reagan, Jimmy Carter was a nuclear abolitionist who vowed in his 1977 inaugural address to pursue arms control negotiations as "a step toward our ultimate goal—the elimination of all nuclear weapons from this Earth."[4] Yet these earlier grassroots and government nuclear abolitionists were unable to reshape U.S. and Soviet policies in a way that ended the Cold War. Why were grassroots and government nuclear abolitionists in the 1980s able to do what their forerunners could not?

Nuclear abolitionists were so influential in the 1980s because they counted the leaders of the two superpowers and large numbers of ordinary individuals among their number. Gorbachev, Reagan, and grassroots anti-nuclear activists played crucial roles in ending the Cold War. In the U.S. case, both Reagan and grassroots activists were essential in shifting the U.S. nuclear arms control paradigm from arms limitation to arms reduction. This was the first step toward reversing the superpower nuclear arms race and ending the Cold War. Shortly after entering the White House, Reagan's budding nuclear abolitionism led him to declare that his administration would pursue nuclear arms reduction rather than mere arms limitation. Pressure from U.S. and West European anti-nuclear activists, however, accelerated the Reagan administration's timetable for beginning nuclear arms reduction negotiations with the Soviets. U.S. and West European anti-nuclear activists were particularly vital in prompting Reagan's advisors, who were not nuclear abolitionists, to support the opening of talks aimed at reducing U.S. and Soviet nuclear weapons.

Gorbachev took power with a moral opposition to nuclear weapons that made him want to end the Cold War to reduce the risk of nuclear conflict. Facing an inordinately militarized economy, Gorbachev also sought to end the Cold War so that he could pursue much-needed economic and political reforms in the Soviet Union. Gorbachev's nuclear abolitionism led him initially to try to end the Cold War by concluding nuclear disarmament agreements. He also advocated a nuclear-free "common European home," which he prioritized in 1987 as it became evident that he and Reagan were unlikely to sign a treaty eliminating their nuclear weapons.

Yet grassroots anti-nuclear and peace activists had an important influence on the substance of Gorbachev's nuclear arms reduction and "common European home" initiatives. Gorbachev incorporated END activists' proposals into his January 15, 1986, initiative for the elimination of nuclear weapons by 2000. Anti-nuclear activists also influenced Gorbachev's February 1987 decision to pursue an INF treaty separately from agreements on START and strategic defenses. This was a crucial decision, as it removed the major obstacle blocking the conclusion of an INF treaty. European peace activists' appeals for a denuclearized, reunified, and free Europe shaped Gorbachev's vision of a nuclear-free "common European home," in which there would be pan-European security structures, economic integration, and cooperation on environmental and humanitarian issues. Gorbachev also adopted European activists' proposals for how to overcome the division of Europe, embracing in particular their appeals for the revitalization of the Helsinki process.

Given the importance of nuclear abolitionists in the Cold War's endgame, it is a great irony that the Cold War ended on the watch of a U.S. president who rejected nuclear abolitionism. George H. W. Bush and his top advisors viewed nuclear weapons as an essential means of compensating for Soviet conventional superiority. Yet it was Reagan and Gorbachev's pursuit of nuclear abolition that enabled Bush to preside over a Cold War victory for the West during his first year in office. Reagan and Gorbachev's efforts to eliminate nuclear weapons over the previous four years reduced superpower tensions, yielded the landmark INF Treaty, and produced a framework for a START agreement. Gorbachev also played a far more significant role in the Cold War's endgame in 1989 than Bush did. The Soviet leader refused to intervene to stop the 1989 East European revolutions because he believed that the use of force would undermine support for his nuclear-free "common European home" initiative. These revolutions tore the fabric of the Iron Curtain, as they swept communist governments from power and paved the way for the reunification of Germany.

The events of 1989 also underscore that nuclear abolitionism was most influential when grassroots and government actors were pursuing it on a global scale. Although the Cold War ended in 1989 with the lifting of the Iron Curtain, there was also a missed opportunity for the United States and the Soviet Union to eliminate or at least drastically cut their nuclear arsenals.

This book contends that Bush bears the primary responsibility for this missed opportunity to achieve more dramatic nuclear arms reduction as the Cold War drew to a close. Abandoning Reagan's goal of nuclear abolition, the Bush administration was in no hurry to achieve nuclear arms control agreements with the Soviets. In fact, Bush thwarted Gorbachev's efforts to achieve sweeping nuclear arms reduction in 1989. He repeatedly rejected Soviet proposals to reduce or eliminate tactical nuclear weapons and made little effort to conclude a START agreement.

Bush clearly did not share Reagan's nuclear abolitionism. He also did not face the same pressure from U.S. anti-nuclear activists that Reagan had confronted during his first term. The U.S. nuclear freeze movement had been unable to adapt in the face of a series of setbacks between late 1983 and early 1985. These included Senate rejection of the freeze resolution in October 1983, congressional appropriation of MX missile funding in November 1983, Reagan's reelection in November 1984, and the resumption of U.S.-Soviet nuclear arms reduction negotiations without the implementation of a freeze in March 1985. Boosted by his landslide victory in the 1984 presidential election, Reagan continued to reject the freeze movement's disarmament strategy, preferring instead to negotiate arms reduction from a position of strength and pursue SDI. Although the Freeze Campaign and older anti-nuclear organizations like SANE continued to be active after 1985, they no longer influenced U.S. arms control policy as they once had.

In the midst of financial difficulties and national staff cuts, the Freeze Campaign decided in late 1986 to merge with SANE the following year. SANE pulled in more than $4 million of revenue in 1987, meaning that it was in a far better financial situation than the Freeze Campaign, which only had $570,000 of revenue during the same year. While the Freeze Campaign benefited from merging with a more financially stable organization, SANE gained access to the Freeze Campaign's vast network of state and local grassroots freeze groups.[5] At its first national congress in November 1987, the new SANE/FREEZE organization adopted a broad set of political goals that included the implementation of a bilateral nuclear freeze, nuclear abolition, the demilitarization of space, conventional force reductions, military spending cuts, economic conversion, and the enactment of "new foreign and military policies which exclude military intervention, protect human rights, and promote social and economic development."[6]

Yet the merger and the broadening of its goals did not enable the freeze movement to regain the strength and policy influence that it had exerted in the early 1980s. Membership in SANE/FREEZE declined as the Cold War came to an end and Americans became less concerned about the nuclear arms race. After the merger, SANE/FREEZE boasted more than 170,000 members who were part of over 270 state and local groups. In the fall of 1990, there were 130,000 members in 250 state and local groups. Two and a half years later, only 100,000 members in 200 state and local groups remained.[7]

By the time of the Malta summit in December 1989, the European peace movement had also weakened considerably. Following Reagan and Gorbachev's signing of the INF Treaty in December 1987, a sense of complacency began to set in among European peace activists that ultimately gave way to apathy after the East European revolutions and the end of the Cold War. After all, many of the European peace activists' goals had been achieved by the end of 1989. An entire class of nuclear weapons in Europe had been eliminated. The Berlin Wall, the most infamous dividing line in Europe, lay in pieces on the ground. East Europeans were reclaiming their political and civil rights. The Cold War was over.

Months before the fall of the Berlin Wall, Czechoslovakia's Velvet Revolution, and the Malta summit, Mary Kaldor lamented in an *END Journal* editorial that "it is a difficult time for the peace movement. Gorbachev's reforms, the INF Treaty, the enthusiasm even of Right-wing leaders for détente, let us feel we can sit back and relax." She noted that a recent cartoon on the cover of the Italian Peace Association's magazine epitomized this sentiment. "I'm taking a nap for peace," it proclaimed. Although she contended that "there is more than ever to do," many END activists seemed satisfied with what they already had achieved.[8] In the spring of 1989, END published its last issue of the *END Journal* due to financial difficulties. Although END planned to raise money to relaunch the journal as a monthly magazine that addressed North-South issues in addition to East-West relations and the nuclear arms race, the funding never materialized for this new publication.[9]

The transnational END Conventions fared better than END did in the late 1980s and early 1990s. More than one thousand people attended the 1988 END Convention in Lund, which was the first one held after the signing of the INF Treaty. Not only was this one of the largest END Conventions, but it also drew record attendance from Poland and Hungary, as both independent activists and delegates from official peace committees in these countries participated in the conference for the first time. During one of the conference sessions, END cofounder E. P. Thompson welcomed Solidarity activist Jacek Kuroń to his first END Convention, proudly proclaiming, "At last, after eight years, we have put peace and freedom together." This comment was a tribute to East European dissidents' influence on the agenda of the broader European peace movement, and conference attendees cheered as Kuroń hugged Thompson.[10] With increasing participation from independent East European activists, the END Liaison Committee held conventions in Vitoria in 1989, Helsinki and Tallinn in 1990, and Moscow in 1991.[11]

Although END Conventions continued to take place into the early 1990s, their sessions increasingly focused on issues other than nuclear disarmament. Even at the 1988 END Convention in Lund, Kaldor reflected that "so great was the interest in issues of democracy, civil society, ecology etc., that I began to wonder if anyone is still concerned about the arms race."[12] With the U.S. and European anti-nuclear movements declining by the end of 1989, there was no groundswell of public sentiment to pressure U.S. and Soviet leaders to abolish nuclear weapons during the early years of the post–Cold War era.

As of 2021, the *Bulletin's* Doomsday Clock stands at one hundred seconds to midnight, which is "the closest it has ever been to civilization-ending apocalypse." This clock setting reflects not only the risk of nuclear war, but also the problem of climate change. In unveiling the Doomsday Clock setting in January 2021, the *Bulletin* lamented that "the potential for the world to stumble into nuclear war—an ever-present danger over the last 75 years—increased in 2020." The United States, Russia, China, North Korea, India, and Pakistan are modernizing (and, in some cases, expanding) their nuclear forces while nuclear arms control efforts languish. The INF Treaty, a major milestone in the Cold War's endgame, is no longer in force following the Trump administration's withdrawal from the agreement in 2019. The only remaining U.S.-Russian nuclear arms control accord is the New START Treaty, which U.S. president Joseph Biden and Russian president Vladimir Putin extended for five years in January 2021. Biden, however, is finding it difficult to revive the Iran nuclear deal, which Trump exited in 2018. Meanwhile, Iran is on the verge of producing the fuel for a nuclear bomb. The prospects for resurrecting U.S.-North Korean disarmament negotiations look bleak as 2021 draws to a close.[13]

Climate change is also putting humanity in grave danger. The *Bulletin* warned that "global greenhouse gas concentrations in the atmosphere have hit a record high, and 2020 was essentially tied with 2016 as the warmest year on record." The effects of climate change are already evident in a surge of weather disasters ranging from wildfires to hurricanes. The compromise Glasgow Climate Pact urges governments to devise plans in 2022 for steeper cuts in emissions and to offer more assistance to countries most affected by climate change. Yet this COP26 deal fails to ensure that the world does not warm more than 1.5 degrees Celsius, which is a key provision of the 2015 Paris Agreement. Meanwhile, the spread of disinformation online makes it harder to combat both climate change and the ongoing COVID-19 pandemic.[14]

All is not lost, however, as even the *Bulletin* acknowledges.[15] The Cold War's final decade shows that positive transformations can occur in perilous circumstances and ordinary individuals can help facilitate global change. In 1979, as Soviet SS-20 missile deployments proceeded, SALT II languished in the U.S. Senate, NATO decided to install INF missiles in Europe, and the Soviets invaded Afghanistan, almost no one would have predicted that the Cold War would be over ten years later. During the 1980s, however, grassroots and government nuclear abolitionists shifted U.S. and Soviet nuclear arms control paradigms from arms limitation to arms reduction and reshaped the Soviet approach to Eastern Europe. This paved the way for the reversal of the U.S.-Soviet nuclear arms race and the lifting of the Iron Curtain dividing Europe.

Grassroots anti-nuclear and peace activists were able to help end the Cold War partly because they formed large, broad-based movements in the West and transnational connections across the Cold War divide. During the 1980s, anti-nuclear rallies in Belgium, the FRG, the Netherlands, and the United States set records for the largest demonstration in each country's history.[16] These U.S. and West European movements attracted not only veteran peace protesters but also individuals who were new to political activism. The size and composition of these movements made them difficult for politicians to ignore, even if these officials did not always adopt the specific proposals that activists advocated.

Transnational connections enabled the West European peace movement to lend a powerful voice to the arguments of Eastern bloc activists, who were unable to form mass movements due to government persecution. By publishing East European proposals for a denuclearized, reunified, autonomous, and free Europe and advocating them in correspondence and meetings with Soviet officials and academicians, West European activists enabled East European ideas to reach audiences that they never would have reached otherwise. There is great irony in the oppression of Eastern bloc dissidents who advocated nuclear disarmament, the dissolution of the blocs, European autonomy, and human rights. For Gorbachev incorporated East European proposals in his "common European home" initiative after West European peace activists presented them.

Grassroots anti-nuclear activists also wielded such policy influence in the 1980s because Gorbachev and Reagan shared their goal of eliminating nuclear weapons. The two leaders were therefore uniquely attuned to the activists' concerns and proposals. During the 1980s, nuclear abolitionism made for strange bedfellows, as it united political adversaries who disagreed on many issues but had a common desire for nuclear disarmament. Although they were at odds over human rights and the viability of socialism, Gorbachev and Eastern bloc dissidents pursued the shared aim of a nuclear-free world. Similarly, Reagan and U.S. and West European anti-nuclear activists sought nuclear abolition, although their contrasting views on the utility of military strength in negotiations and the threshold of danger in the nuclear age led them to advance starkly different disarmament strategies. Reagan and the activists actually had an adversarial relationship, as each viewed the other's disarmament strategy as dangerous. Nevertheless, Gorbachev, Reagan, and grassroots anti-nuclear activists played vital roles in the Cold War's endgame. Grassroots and government nuclear abolitionists needed one another to bring the Cold War to a close.

Individuals concerned about nuclear weapons and climate change in the twenty-first century should take a page from the 1980s. The mobilization of large, broad-based coalitions and the formation of transnational ties increase the likelihood of policy influence. Yet it is also essential to have allies in government. This means that citizens living in democracies must prioritize nuclear issues and climate change when voting for political candidates. For their part, government officials should consider nonstate actors' proposals for averting climate catastrophe and reducing nuclear weapons.

Despite their inability to eliminate nuclear weapons, grassroots and government nuclear abolitionists deserve credit for playing a pivotal role in ending the Cold War. This was truly a monumental achievement, as the Cold War had dominated international affairs for nearly half a century. Grassroots and government nuclear abolitionists in the 1980s also provide a model for enacting dramatic, positive change in a peaceful manner. As the world faces the threat of climate change and a renewed nuclear arms race, we would be wise to remember and follow their example.

NOTES

Introduction

1. Randall Forsberg, WGBH Educational Foundation interview, November 9, 1987, https://openvault.wgbh.org/catalog/V_F6CC542AF94B434FBC7E1DBE45F07024.

2. *The Call to Halt the Nuclear Arms Race*, p. 1, reprinted in *Security Dialogue* 12, no. 4 (October 1981): 417–21.

3. Tony Benn, *Conflicts of Interest: Diaries, 1977–1980* (London: Hutchinson, 1990), 591.

4. "Appeal for European Nuclear Disarmament, launched on 28 April 1980," reprinted in *Protest and Survive*, ed. E. P. Thompson and Dan Smith (Harmondsworth: Penguin, 1980), 223–26, 224.

5. For a list of individuals from outside of the United Kingdom who had signed the END Appeal by September 1980, see Ken Coates, *European Nuclear Disarmament: No Cruise Missiles, No SS20's* (Nottingham: Bertrand Russell Peace Foundation, 1980), Wilson Center History and Public Policy Program Digital Archive (henceforth WCDA), https://digitalarchive.wilsoncenter.org/document/110907.

6. Letter, Ronald Reagan to Charles Burton Marshall, April 8, 1980, in *Reagan: A Life in Letters*, ed. Kiron K. Skinner, Annelise Anderson, and Martin Anderson (New York: Free Press, 2003), 398–99.

7. Minutes of National Security Council meeting, November 12, 1981, p. 4, folder "NSC 00025 12 Nov 1981 [Theater Nuclear Forces, NATO, Strategic Forces]," Box 3, Executive Secretariat (henceforth ES), NSC: Meeting Files, Ronald Reagan Presidential Library (henceforth RRPL).

8. Ronald Reagan, *An American Life: The Autobiography* (New York: Simon and Schuster, 1990), 550; Ronald Reagan White House diary, December 3, 1981, https://www.reaganfoundation.org/ronald-reagan/white-house-diaries/diary-entry-12031981/.

9. This book is not the first to present Reagan as a nuclear abolitionist, although it uses newly available evidence to illuminate Reagan's desire to eliminate nuclear weapons. Other works that highlight Reagan's nuclear abolitionism during the early years of his presidency include James Graham Wilson, *The Triumph of Improvisation: Gorbachev's Adaptability, Reagan's Engagement, and the End of the Cold War* (Ithaca: Cornell University Press, 2014); Melvyn P. Leffler, *For the Soul of Mankind: The United States, the Soviet Union, and the Cold War* (New York: Hill and Wang, 2007); Paul Lettow, *Ronald Reagan and His Quest to Abolish Nuclear Weapons* (New York: Random House, 2005); Hal Brands, *Making the Unipolar Moment: U.S. Foreign Policy and the Rise of the Post–Cold War Order* (Ithaca: Cornell University Press, 2016); and Robert Service, *The End of the Cold War, 1985–1991* (New York: PublicAffairs, 2015).

10. Letter, Reagan to Marshall, April 8, 1980, 399.

11. "Record of the Meeting Between the Prime Minister and Mr. M.S. Gorbachev, Member of the Politburo and Secretary of the Central Committee of the CPSU, at Chequers on Sunday 16 December at 3.00 pm," pp. 5–6, The National Archives of the UK (TNA): PREM/19/1394.

12. "Excerpts from Speech by Gorbachev," *New York Times*, December 19, 1984.

13. See, for example, Peter Schweizer, *Victory: The Reagan Administration's Secret Strategy That Hastened the Collapse of the Soviet Union* (New York: Atlantic Monthly Press, 1994); Peter Schweizer, *Reagan's War: The Epic Story of His Forty-Year Struggle and Final Triumph over Communism* (New York: Doubleday, 2002); and Francis H. Marlo, *Planning Reagan's War: Conservative Strategists and America's Cold War Victory* (Washington, DC: Potomac Books, 2012). In analyzing the end of the Cold War, John Lewis Gaddis has emphasized the importance of Reagan's grand strategy of "exploiting Soviet weaknesses and asserting western strengths." Gaddis, however, does not give Reagan full credit for the end of the Cold War and does acknowledge his nuclear abolitionism. See Gaddis, *The Cold War: A New History* (New York: Penguin, 2005), quote at 222.

14. See, for example, Archie Brown, *The Gorbachev Factor* (New York: Oxford University Press, 1996); Robert D. English, *Russia and the Idea of the West: Gorbachev, Intellectuals, and the End of the Cold War* (New York: Columbia University Press, 2000); Vladislav M. Zubok, *A Failed Empire: The Soviet Union in the Cold War from Stalin to Gorbachev* (Chapel Hill: University of North Carolina Press, 2009); and William Taubman, *Gorbachev: His Life and Times* (New York: W. W. Norton, 2017). One key tenet of "new thinking" was that neither a nuclear arms race nor a nuclear war could be won.

15. Michael Cotey Morgan has argued that the principles of the Helsinki Final Act influenced Gorbachev's policies and helped precipitate the 1989 East European revolutions. See Morgan, *The Final Act: The Helsinki Accords and the Transformation of the Cold War* (Princeton: Princeton University Press, 2018). Daniel C. Thomas has advanced a similar argument, although he focuses specifically on the impact of the human rights norms established by the Helsinki Final Act. See Thomas, *The Helsinki Effect: International Norms, Human Rights, and the Demise of Communism* (Princeton: Princeton University Press, 2001). Sarah B. Snyder has emphasized the importance of the transnational network of human rights advocates that emerged in the wake of the Helsinki Final Act. See Snyder, *Human Rights Activism and the End of the Cold War: A Transnational History of the Helsinki Network* (Cambridge: Cambridge University Press, 2011).

16. See, for example, Stephen G. Brooks and William C. Wohlforth, "Power, Globalization, and the End of the Cold War: Reevaluating a Landmark Case of Ideas," *International Security* 25, no. 3 (Winter 2000/2001): 5–53; and Odd Arne Westad, *The Cold War: A World History* (New York: Basic Books, 2017). For an analysis of the "interplay" between structural changes and U.S. grand strategy in the Cold War's endgame, see Brands, *Making the Unipolar Moment*. On the importance of structural factors and U.S. and Soviet grand strategies in shaping the "beginning of the end of the Cold War" (1980–85), see Simon Miles, *Engaging the Evil Empire: Washington, Moscow, and the Beginning of the End of the Cold War* (Ithaca: Cornell University Press, 2020).

17. Memorandum of conversation, final meeting, October 12, 1986, 3:25–4:30 and 5:30–6:50 p.m., p. 5, National Security Archive Electronic Briefing Book (henceforth NSAEBB) No. 203, "The Reykjavik File," https://nsarchive2.gwu.edu/NSAEBB/NSAEBB203/Document15.pdf.

18. See Matthew Evangelista, *Unarmed Forces: The Transnational Movement to End the Cold War* (Ithaca: Cornell University Press, 1999). This book also considers anti-nuclear activists' influence on Gorbachev's missile defense policy, but it reveals new and wider channels through which activists were able to shape Soviet initiatives.

19. See, for example, Leffler, *For the Soul of Mankind*; Wilson, *The Triumph of Improvisation*; and Beth A. Fischer, "The United States and the Transformation of the Cold War," in *The Last Decade of the Cold War: From Conflict Escalation to Conflict Transformation*, ed. Olav Njølstad (London: Frank Cass, 2004), 226–40.

20. Ronald Reagan, "The President's News Conference," January 29, 1981, American Presidency Project, University of California at Santa Barbara (henceforth APP), https://www.presidency.ucsb.edu/documents/the-presidents-news-conference-992; Ronald Reagan, "Remarks of the President and Prime Minister Margaret Thatcher of the United Kingdom Following Their Meetings," February 26, 1981, APP, https://www.presidency.ucsb.edu/documents/remarks-the-president-and-prime-minister-margaret-thatcher-the-united-kingdom-following-0.

21. On Reagan's dislike of confrontation with his aides, see Lou Cannon, *President Reagan: The Role of a Lifetime* (New York: Simon and Schuster, 1991), 176–78.

22. See, for example, Alexander M. Haig Jr., *Caveat: Realism, Reagan, and Foreign Policy* (New York: Macmillan, 1984), 228.

23. See, for example, Reagan, "Remarks of the President and Prime Minister Margaret Thatcher."

24. Ronald Reagan, "Remarks to Members of the National Press Club on Arms Reduction and Nuclear Weapons," November 18, 1981, APP, https://www.presidency.ucsb.edu/documents/remarks-members-the-national-press-club-arms-reduction-and-nuclear-weapons; "Treaty Between the United States of America and the Union of Soviet Socialist Republics on the Elimination of Their Intermediate-Range and Shorter-Range Missiles," signed December 8, 1987, APP, https://www.presidency.ucsb.edu/documents/treaty-between-the-united-states-america-and-the-union-soviet-socialist-republics-the.

25. National Security Decision Directive (NSDD) 33, May 14, 1982, https://reaganlibrary.archives.gov/archives/reference/Scanned%20NSDDS/NSDD33.pdf; NSDD 44, July 10, 1982, https://reaganlibrary.archives.gov/archives/reference/Scanned%20NSDDS/NSDD44.pdf; "Treaty Between the United States of America and the Union of Soviet Socialist Republics on Further Reduction and Limitation of Strategic Offensive Arms (START I)," signed July 31, 1991, https://www.nti.org/wp-content/uploads/2021/09/start_1_treaty.pdf.

26. Memorandum of conversation, final meeting, October 12, 1986.

27. Andrei Grachev, *Gorbachev's Gamble: Soviet Foreign Policy and the End of the Cold War* (Cambridge: Polity, 2008), 66.

28. See, for example, "Soviet Package in Nuclear and Space Talks," October 1, 1985, folder "Geneva-Soviet Proposal/Assessment-Sep/Oct 1985 [1 of 2]," Box 90719, Sven Kraemer Files, RRPL; Gorbachev statement on disarmament, January 16, 1986, Foreign Broadcast Information Service (FBIS) translation, folder "NSDD 214/NSDD 210 (Part 1)—Reacting to Gorbachev January 1986 Proposal–February 1986 (6 of 12)," RAC Box 8, Robert E. Linhard Files, RRPL; Memorandum of conversation, first meeting, October 11, 1986, 10:40 a.m.–12:30 p.m., pp. 4–5, 3, NSAEBB No. 203, https://nsarchive2.gwu.edu/NSAEBB/NSAEBB203/Document09.pdf.

29. For an early statement on the "common European home," see Mikhail Gorbachev, "Address to French Parliamentarians," October 3, 1985, in Mikhail S. Gorbachev, *A Time for Peace* (New York: Richardson and Steirman, 1985), 270–74.

30. For a recent examination of the East German uprising, the Hungarian Revolution, and the Prague Spring, see Westad, *The Cold War*, 192–94, 201–6, 373–76.

31. Memorandum of conversation, final meeting, October 12, 1986.

32. Both John Lewis Gaddis and Archie Brown have considered the counterfactual in which John Hinckley's assassination attempt on Reagan was successful and George H. W. Bush became president in March 1981. For their contrasting views on whether the Cold War still would have ended when and how it did, see Archie Brown, *The Human Factor: Gorbachev, Reagan, and Thatcher, and the End of the Cold War* (New York: Oxford University Press, 2020), 308; and Gaddis, *The Cold War*, 222.

33. Books that have lauded the Bush administration's management of the end of the Cold War include Jeffrey A. Engel, *When the World Seemed New: George H. W. Bush and the End of the Cold War* (New York: Houghton Mifflin Harcourt, 2017); Wilson, *The Triumph of Improvisation*; Philip Zelikow and Condoleezza Rice, *To Build a Better World: Choices to End the Cold War and Create a Global Commonwealth* (New York: Twelve, 2019); and Christopher Maynard, *Out of the Shadow: George H. W. Bush and the End of the Cold War* (College Station: Texas A&M University Press, 2008). Drawing on newly available evidence, this book builds on Thomas Blanton's argument that the Bush administration's skepticism of Gorbachev led to missed opportunities for more dramatically reducing nuclear weapons as the Cold War ended. See Blanton, "U.S. Policy and the Revolutions of 1989," in *Masterpieces of History: The Peaceful End of the Cold War in Europe, 1989*, ed. Svetlana Savranskaya, Thomas Blanton, and Vladislav Zubok (Budapest: Central European University Press, 2010), 49–98.

34. See, for example, Henry Richard Maar III, *Freeze! The Grassroots Movement to Halt the Arms Race and End the Cold War* (Ithaca: Cornell University Press, 2022); Aaron Donaghy, *The Second Cold War: Carter, Reagan, and the Politics of Foreign Policy* (Cambridge: Cambridge University Press, 2021); Angela Santese, "Ronald Reagan, the Nuclear Weapons Freeze Campaign and the Nuclear Scare of the 1980s," *International History Review* 39, no. 3 (2017): 496–520; William M. Knoblauch, *Nuclear Freeze in a Cold War: The Reagan Administration, Cultural Activism, and the End of the Arms Race* (Amherst: University of Massachusetts Press, 2017); Lawrence S. Wittner, *Toward Nuclear Abolition: A History of the World Nuclear Disarmament Movement, 1971 to the Present*, vol. 3 of *The Struggle Against the Bomb* (Stanford: Stanford University Press, 2003); Jeffrey W. Knopf, *Domestic Society and International Cooperation: The Impact of Protest on U.S. Arms Control Policy* (Cambridge: Cambridge University Press, 1998); David S. Meyer, *A Winter of Discontent: The Nuclear Freeze and American Politics* (New York: Praeger, 1990); David Cortright, *Peace Works: The Citizen's Role in Ending the Cold War* (Boulder: Westview Press, 1993); Robert Kleidman, *Organizing for Peace: Neutrality, the Test Ban, and the Freeze* (Syracuse: Syracuse University Press, 1993); Douglas C. Waller, *Congress and the Nuclear Freeze: An Inside Look at the Politics of a Mass Movement* (Amherst: University of Massachusetts Press, 1987); and Bradford Martin, *The Other Eighties: A Secret History of America in the Age of Reagan* (New York: Hill and Wang, 2011). Relatedly, Marilena Gala and Andrea Chiampan have contended that West European governments pressured the Reagan administration to begin INF negotiations in 1981 and shaped the substance of U.S. INF proposals. While Gala and Chiampan note that West European governments were facing increasingly anti-nuclear publics in the early 1980s, their focus remains on West European government officials rather than anti-nuclear activists. See Gala, "'The Essential Weaknesses of the December 1979 "Agreement"': The White House and the Implementing of the Dual-Track Decision," *Cold War History* 19, no. 1 (2019): 21–38; and Chiampan, "The Reagan Administration and the INF Controversy, 1981–83," *Diplomatic History* 44, no. 5 (November 2020): 860–84.

35. See, for example, Lettow, *Ronald Reagan and His Quest to Abolish Nuclear Weapons*; and Martin Anderson and Annelise Anderson, *Reagan's Secret War: The Untold Story of His Fight to Save the World from Nuclear Disaster* (New York: Crown, 2009).

36. Some scholars have argued that East European dissidents convinced West European anti-nuclear activists to put more emphasis on human rights concerns by explaining the concept of the indivisibility of peace and human rights. These scholars, however, overlook East Europeans' influence on West European activists' thinking about the elimination of the blocs in Europe and European autonomy. See, for example, Wittner, *Toward Nuclear Abolition*, esp. 238–40; Patrick Burke, "A Transcontinental Movement of Citizens? Strategic Debates in the 1980s Western Peace Movement," in *Transnational Moments of Change: Europe 1945, 1968, 1989*, ed. Gerd-Rainer Horn and Padraic Kenney (Lanham: Rowman and Littlefield, 2004), 189–206; Kacper Szulecki, "Hijacked Ideas: Human Rights, Peace, and Environmentalism in Czechoslovak and Polish Dissident Discourses," *East European Politics and Societies* 25, no. 2 (May 2011): 272–95; and Christian Philip Peterson, "Changing the World from 'Below': U.S. Peace Activists and the Transnational Struggle for Peace and Détente in the 1980s," *Journal of Cold War Studies* 22, no. 3 (Summer 2020): 180–224. This book demonstrates that East European and ultimately West European activists viewed nuclear disarmament, the elimination of the blocs, European autonomy, and human rights as interconnected.

37. Mikhail Gorbachev, *Memoirs* (New York: Doubleday, 1995), 419.

Chapter 1

1. Bernard T. Feld, "The Hands Move Closer to Midnight," *Bulletin of the Atomic Scientists* 37, no. 1 (January 1981): 1.

2. Ibid.

3. On the U.S. anti-nuclear movement in the 1970s, see Meyer, *A Winter of Discontent*, 137–55; Kyle Harvey, *American Anti-Nuclear Activism, 1975–1990: The Challenge of Peace* (Basingstoke: Palgrave Macmillan, 2014), 14–27; and Wittner, *Toward Nuclear Abolition*, 9–11, 25–31.

4. On the campaign against the B-1 bomber, see Wittner, *Toward Nuclear Abolition*, 28; and Meyer, *A Winter of Discontent*, 144. On Carter's decision to cancel the B-1 bomber, see Matthew J. Ambrose, *The Control Agenda: A History of the Strategic Arms Limitation Talks* (Ithaca: Cornell University Press, 2018), 116–17.

5. Harvey, *American Anti-Nuclear Activism*, 14–16, 24–25; Meyer, *A Winter of Discontent*, 144–46; Wittner, *Toward Nuclear Abolition*, 29.

6. Meyer, *A Winter of Discontent*, 147–49; Harvey, *American Anti-Nuclear Activism*, 18–19, 20–23; Wittner, *Toward Nuclear Abolition*, 30.

7. Meyer, *A Winter of Discontent*, 160.

8. Lyndon B. Johnson, "Message to the 18-Nation Disarmament Conference in Geneva," January 21, 1964, APP, https://www.presidency.ucsb.edu/documents/message-the-18-nation-disarmament-conference-geneva.

9. On Johnson's unsuccessful attempts to garner Soviet interest in a nuclear freeze, see James Cameron, *The Double Game: The Demise of America's First Missile Defense System and the Rise of Strategic Arms Limitation* (New York: Oxford University Press, 2018), 79–106.

10. On Nixon and Kissinger's pursuit of an offensive freeze during the SALT I negotiations, see Cameron, *The Double Game*, 136–60. On U.S. and Soviet proposals during the SALT II negotiations, see Ambrose, *The Control Agenda*, 55–144. On Soviet calls for a nuclear freeze outside of the SALT II negotiations, see Meyer, *A Winter of Discontent*, 159.

11. Cameron, *The Double Game*, 157–59; Ambrose, *The Control Agenda*, 56–57.

12. Ambrose, *The Control Agenda*, 143.

13. Arms Control Association, "U.S.-Russian Nuclear Arms Control Agreements at a Glance," April 2020, https://www.armscontrol.org/factsheets/USRussiaNuclearAgreements.

14. "Treaty Between the United States of America and the Union of Soviet Socialist Republics on the Limitation of Strategic Offensive Arms, Together with Agreed Statements and Common Understandings Regarding the Treaty," June 18, 1979, https://fas.org/nuke/control/salt2/text/salt2-2.htm.

15. Senator Mark Hatfield, 96th Cong., 1st sess., *Congressional Record* 125 (June 26, 1979): S16577–78.

16. Randy Kehler, WGBH Educational Foundation interview, November 10, 1987, https://openvault.wgbh.org/catalog/V_3645177E51414C2687960DD1E63C9881.

17. "Background on Randy Kehler," Randy Kehler Papers, University of Massachusetts Amherst Libraries Special Collections and University Archives, http://scua.library.umass.edu/umarmot/kehler-randy/.

18. Daniel Ellsberg, *Secrets: A Memoir of Vietnam and the Pentagon Papers* (New York: Viking Penguin, 2002), 270–73.

19. "Background on Randy Kehler."

20. Wittner, *Toward Nuclear Abolition*, 29.

21. "Background on Randy Kehler"; Kehler, WGBH interview.

22. Kehler, WGBH interview.

23. Meyer, *A Winter of Discontent*, 160.

24. Forsberg, WGBH interview, November 9, 1987; George Sommaripa and Randall Forsberg, "Strategy for a Concerted National Effort to Halt the Nuclear Arms Race—First Draft," August 25, 1980, p. 3, folder "Freeze, 1980–1981," Box 50, Series G: Records of the National Office of SANE (Washington, DC), 1971–87, SANE, Inc. Collection, Swarthmore College Peace Collection (henceforth SCPC).

25. Forsberg, WGBH interview, November 9, 1987.

26. Randall Forsberg, WGBH Educational Foundation interview, March 3, 1988, https://openvault.wgbh.org/catalog/V_F4ABF4A779CE4613BDBF7A73CC019CAC; Benjamin Redekop, "'Physicians to a Dying Planet': Helen Caldicott, Randall Forsberg, and the Anti-Nuclear Weapons Movement of the Early 1980s," *Leadership Quarterly* 21, no. 2 (April 2010): 280, 282.

27. Forsberg, WGBH interview, November 9, 1987.

28. *The Call to Halt the Nuclear Arms Race*, p. 1.

29. Forsberg, WGBH interview, November 9, 1987.

30. *The Call to Halt the Nuclear Arms Race*, p. 3; Treaty on the Non-Proliferation of Nuclear Weapons (NPT), July 1, 1968, https://www.un.org/disarmament/wmd/nuclear/npt/text.

31. Forsberg, WGBH interview, November 9, 1987.

32. Terry Provance, "Strategy Discussion Paper Nuclear Moratorium," August 21, 1980, folder "Freeze, 1980–1981," Box 50, Series G, SANE, Inc. Collection, SCPC; Memorandum, Carol Jensen, Human Security Program Coordinator, Clergy and Laity Concerned to Ad Hoc Committee for a Nuclear Weapons Freeze, Mobilization for Survival National Coordinating Committee, Clergy and Laity Concerned National Assembly, and others, July 14, 1980, folder "Freeze, 1980–1981," Box 50, Series G, SANE, Inc. Collection, SCPC.

33. For a list of interim steering committee members, see "Proposed Structure for Nuclear Freeze Campaign," p. 3, folder "Freeze, 1980–1981," Box 50, Series G, SANE, Inc. Collection, SCPC.

34. Provance, "Strategy Discussion Paper Nuclear Moratorium," p. 3; Sommaripa and Forsberg, "Strategy for a Concerted National Effort to Halt the Nuclear Arms Race—First Draft," p. 6.

35. Provance, "Strategy Discussion Paper Nuclear Moratorium," pp. 3, 2, 4.

36. Letter, David Cortright to Carol Jensen, August 11, 1980, p. 1, folder "Freeze, 1980–1981," Box 50, Series G, SANE, Inc. Collection, SCPC.

37. David Cortright, "I Never Expected to Protest the Vietnam War While on Active Duty," *New York Times*, November 8, 2019.

38. David Cortright, Kroc Institute for International Peace Studies, University of Notre Dame, https://kroc.nd.edu/faculty-and-staff/david-cortright/.

39. Letter, Cortright to Jensen, p. 2.

40. Memorandum, Jensen to Ad Hoc Committee for a Nuclear Weapons Freeze et al., p. 2; Provance, "Strategy Discussion Paper Nuclear Moratorium," p. 5.

41. Letter, Cortright to Jensen, p. 2.

42. Sommaripa and Forsberg, "Strategy for a Concerted National Effort to Halt the Nuclear Arms Race—First Draft," pp. 1, 2.

43. *The Call to Halt the Nuclear Arms Race*, p. 4.

44. "Public Programs Spur Local Freeze Activity," *Freeze Newsletter* 1, no. 1 (March 1981): 5; "Advertisements in Newspapers," *Freeze Newsletter* 1, no. 1 (March 1981): 4; "Petition Campaigns," *Freeze Newsletter* 1, no. 1 (March 1981): 4. On local freeze work, see also Sommaripa and Forsberg, "Strategy for a Concerted National Effort to Halt the Nuclear Arms Race—First Draft," p. 4.

45. "Arms Race Referendum in Western Massachusetts: Summary of Results," folder "Freeze, 1980–1981," Box 50, Series G, SANE, Inc. Collection, SCPC.

46. Forsberg, WGBH interview, November 9, 1987.

47. "State and Local Initiatives: Western Mass. Districts, Vermont Towns Vote for Freeze," *Freeze Newsletter* 1, no. 1 (March 1981): 3.

48. See, for example, "Nine Congressional Reps. Endorse 'Call,'" *Freeze Newsletter* 1, no. 1 (March 1981): 9.

49. Michael Bess, *Realism, Utopia, and the Mushroom Cloud: Four Activist Intellectuals and Their Strategies for Peace, 1945–1989: Louise Weiss, France, Leo Szilard, USA, E. P. Thompson, England, Danilo Dolci, Italy* (Chicago: University of Chicago Press, 1993), 126, 94–117.

50. Ibid., 111.

51. Lawrence S. Wittner, *Resisting the Bomb: A History of the World Nuclear Disarmament Movement, 1954–1970*, vol. 2 of *The Struggle Against the Bomb* (Stanford: Stanford University Press, 1997), 44–51.

52. Bess, *Realism, Utopia, and the Mushroom Cloud*, 113–14.

53. Ibid., 107–24; Edward Palmer Thompson, WGBH Educational Foundation interview, October 15, 1987, https://openvault.wgbh.org/catalog/V_30B5C742B3FF4FAFB5B4A282CC0C1644.

54. Thompson, WGBH interview.

55. In 1981, the Reagan administration began referring to TNF as INF. In this book, I use the acronym that U.S. policymakers employed at the time. I also adopt the definitions of INF and shorter-range missiles set forth in the 1987 INF Treaty. According to this agreement, INF have a range capability between 1,000 and 5,500 kilometers, while shorter-range missiles have a range capability between 500 and 1,000 kilometers.

56. NATO, "Special Meeting of Foreign and Defence Ministers (The 'Double-Track' Decision on Theatre Nuclear Forces)," December 12, 1979, https://www.nato.int/cps/en/natolive/official_texts_27040.htm. For an excellent overview of the Euromissile Crisis from the first Soviet SS-20 deployments through the signing of the INF Treaty, see Leopoldo Nuti, Frédéric Bozo, Marie-Pierre Rey, and Bernd Rother, eds., *The Euromissile Crisis and the End of the Cold*

War (Stanford: Stanford University Press, 2015). On the Soviet decision to deploy SS-20 missiles, see also Raymond L. Garthoff, *Détente and Confrontation: American-Soviet Relations from Nixon to Carter*, rev. ed. (Washington, DC: Brookings Institution, 1994), 958–74; and Jonathan Haslam, *The Soviet Union and the Politics of Nuclear Weapons in Europe, 1969–87* (Ithaca: Cornell University Press, 1990). On NATO's formulation of the dual-track decision, see also Stephanie Freeman, "The Making of an Accidental Crisis: The United States and the NATO Dual-Track Decision of 1979," *Diplomacy and Statecraft* 25, no. 2 (June 2014): 331–55; Kristina Spohr Readman, "Conflict and Cooperation in Intra-Alliance Nuclear Politics: Western Europe, the United States, and the Genesis of NATO's Dual-Track Decision, 1977–1979," *Journal of Cold War Studies* 13, no. 2 (Spring 2011): 39–89; and Leopoldo Nuti, "The Origins of the 1979 Dual Track Decision—A Survey," in *The Crisis of Détente in Europe: From Helsinki to Gorbachev, 1975–1985*, ed. Leopoldo Nuti (London: Routledge, 2009), 57–71.

57. Thompson, WGBH interview.

58. Edward Thompson, "Resurgence in Europe, and the Role of END," in *The CND Story: The First 25 Years of CND in the Words of the People Involved*, ed. John Minnion and Philip Bolsover (London: Allison and Busby, 1983), 80–84, 81.

59. John Palmer, "Ken Coates Obituary: Politician, Activist and Writer of the Left," *Guardian*, June 29, 2010.

60. Ken Coates, "Memorandum on the Possibility of an Appeal for a Nuclear-Free Zone in Europe," January 24, 1980, END/1/1, Folder 1, European Nuclear Disarmament (henceforth END) Collection, London School of Economics Library (henceforth LSEL).

61. Ken Coates, "For a Nuclear-Free Europe," in Thompson and Smith, *Protest and Survive*, 227–45, 235–38, 232–33.

62. Olof Palme, "Shadows Across Europe," *END Bulletin* 1 (1980): 9–11.

63. Coates, "For a Nuclear-Free Europe," 235.

64. Letter, Ken Coates to Mary [Kaldor], January 29, 1980, END/1/1, Folder 1, END Collection, LSEL.

65. Melinda Rankin, *The Political Life of Mary Kaldor: Ideas and Action in International Relations* (Boulder: Lynne Rienner, 2017), 19, 21–26, 30–34.

66. Ibid., 17–19, 21, 27–30, 44.

67. Letter, Ken Coates to Bruce [Kent], February 12, 1980, END/1/1, Folder 1, END Collection, LSEL.

68. "NWFZ Appeal Meeting," March 8, 1980, END/1/1, Folder 1, END Collection, LSEL; Richard Winkler, "END Comes to the UK," *New Statesman*, March 14, 1980, END/1/1, Folder 1, END Collection, LSEL.

69. Thompson, "Resurgence in Europe," 81–83.

70. Benn, *Conflicts of Interest*, 591.

71. "Appeal for European Nuclear Disarmament," 223.

72. Ibid., 224–25.

73. Ibid., 226, 225.

74. Coates, "For a Nuclear-Free Europe," 244–45; Thompson, "Resurgence in Europe," 84.

75. Edward Thompson, "Notes on Exterminism, the Last Stage of Civilization," *New Left Review*, no. 121 (May 1, 1980): 30.

76. "For a Nuclear-Free Zone in All Europe," *END Bulletin* 1 (1980): 3.

77. Letter, Ken Coates to "Dear Friend," March 14, 1980, END/1/1, Folder 1, END Collection, LSEL; Letter, Ken Coates to Mary Kaldor, April 16, 1980, END/1/1, Folder 1, END

Collection, LSEL. For lists of some of the most well-known British and foreign individuals who had signed the END Appeal by mid-April 1980, see "Writers . . . ," END/1/1, Folder 1, END Collection, LSEL; "Foreign Signatories," END/1/1, Folder 1, END Collection, LSEL.

78. Coates, *European Nuclear Disarmament.*

79. Patrick Burke, "European Nuclear Disarmament: Transnational Peace Campaigning in the 1980s," in *Nuclear Threats, Nuclear Fear, and the Cold War of the 1980s,* ed. Eckart Conze, Martin Klimke, and Jeremy Varon (New York: Cambridge University Press, 2017), 227–50, 234.

80. Fear that a world war might occur in the next ten years dramatically increased among West Europeans between 1977 and 1980. In 1977, a little more than 10 percent of West Europeans believed that the outbreak of a third world war within a decade was probable. By 1980, nearly 40 percent of West Europeans thought that another world war would take place in the next ten years. Thomas R. Rochon, *Mobilizing for Peace: The Antinuclear Movements in Western Europe* (Princeton: Princeton University Press, 1988), 46–49.

81. For articles about non-British anti-nuclear organizations that appeared in *END Bulletin* in 1980 and early 1981, see, for example, Pax Christi, "'Not in Our 'Theatre'" Say Dutch and Belgians," *END Bulletin* 2 (1980): 6; Jon Grepstad, "Norway's Fight Against New European Nuclear Weapons," *END Bulletin* 2 (1980): 19–20; and "The Netherlands Against Nuclear Weapons," *END Bulletin* 4 (February 1981): 5–9. For announcements of upcoming anti-nuclear events in 1980 and early 1981, see, for example, "Calendar of Events," *END Bulletin* 1 (1980): 15; and Graham Carey, "Easter 1981," *END Bulletin* 4 (February 1981): 15.

82. For an example from 1980, see Albert de Smaele, "Disarmament in Europe: A Belgian Initiative," *END Bulletin* 1 (1980): 16–17.

83. "Editorial: An Idea Whose Time Has Come," *END Bulletin* 6 (Autumn 1981): 2.

84. Tony Simpson, "Peace Activists Convene in London," *END Bulletin* 3 (1980): 20.

85. European Nuclear Disarmament, "Report of the Consultative Meeting Held at Haus Der Jugend, Frankfurt, Germany from 6–8 March 1981," END/15/1, Folder 1, END Collection, LSEL.

86. Wittner, *Resisting the Bomb,* 450–62; "Treaty Banning Nuclear Weapon Tests in the Atmosphere, in Outer Space, and Under Water," August 5, 1963, https://fas.org/nuke/control /ltbt/text/ltbt2.htm.

87. Cathy Ashton, "The End of the '70s—the Beginning of the Revival," in Minnion and Bolsover, *The CND Story,* 75–77, 75–76; Walter Pincus, "Neutron Killer Warhead Buried in ERDA Budget," *Washington Post,* June 6, 1977.

88. Ashton, "The End of the '70s," 75. On Carter's decision to defer production of the neutron bomb, see Jimmy Carter, *Keeping Faith: Memoirs of a President* (New York: Bantam Books, 1982), 225–28.

89. Bruce Kent, WGBH Educational Foundation interview, November 26, 1987, https:// openvault.wgbh.org/catalog/V_D6186A06D99F4F4F8FDFEF367B48E6D7.

90. Ibid.; John Minnion and Philip Bolsover, "Introduction," in Minnion and Bolsover, *The CND Story,* 9–41, 34.

91. *Protect and Survive,* prepared for the Home Office by the Central Office of Information, 1980, WCDA, https://digitalarchive.wilsoncenter.org/document/110193.

92. Philip Bolsover, "A Victory—and a New Development," in Minnion and Bolsover, *The CND Story,* 89–93, 89. See also Kent, WGBH interview.

93. On the false alarms, see Richard Burt, "False Nuclear Alarms Spur Urgent Effort to Find Flaws," *New York Times,* June 13, 1980; and "That Nuclear Alarm Wasn't False," *New York Times,*

June 30, 1980. On the contribution of these false alarms to the growth of British anti-nuclear activism, see Kent, WGBH interview; and Minnion and Bolsover, "Introduction," 35.

94. "50,000 in London Nuclear Protest," *New York Times*, October 27, 1980.

95. Tony Simpson, "Protest and Survive: October 1980, London," *END Bulletin* 4 (February 1981): 14.

96. Carey, "Easter 1981," 15.

97. "Interchurch Peace Council (IKV) Internal Paper," January 1972, pp. 1, 5, 3–4, WCDA, https://digitalarchive.wilsoncenter.org/document/122387. On IKV as the leading force in the Dutch peace movement, see Sebastian Kalden, "A Case of 'Hollanditis': The Interchurch Peace Council in the Netherlands and the Christian Peace Movement in Western Europe," in Conze et al., *Nuclear Threats, Nuclear Fear, and the Cold War of the 1980s*, 251–67, 252.

98. IKV, "Concept for Peace Week and Peace Paper 1977," March 8, 1977, p. 1, WCDA, https://digitalarchive.wilsoncenter.org/document/122407; IKV, "IKV Messages 1976/77—No. 4," June 1977, p. 3, WCDA, https://digitalarchive.wilsoncenter.org/document/122416.

99. IKV, "IKV Messages 1976/77—No. 4," pp. 4, 1.

100. Ruud van Dijk, "'A Mass Psychosis': The Netherlands and NATO's Dual-Track Decision, 1978–1979," *Cold War History* 12, no. 3 (August 2012): 384; Giles Scott-Smith, "The Netherlands Between East and West: Dutch Politics, Dual Track, and Cruise Missiles," in Nuti et al., *The Euromissile Crisis and the End of the Cold War*, 251–68, 252–53.

101. Wittner, *Toward Nuclear Abolition*, 67.

102. Van Dijk, "'A Mass Psychosis,'" esp. 385, 392, 388, 390, 396–98.

103. Ibid.

104. On Belgian prime minister Wilfried Martens's concern about Flemish socialists' opposition to U.S. TNF deployments, see ibid., 397.

105. Wittner, *Toward Nuclear Abolition*, 67–68.

106. Flora Lewis, "NATO Approves Plan to Install Missiles and Promote Talks," *New York Times*, December 13, 1979.

107. On the protests at Wyhl and their impact on West German politics and society, see Stephen Milder, "The 'Example of Wyhl': How Grassroots Protest in the Rhine Valley Shaped West Germany's Antinuclear Movement," in Conze et al., *Nuclear Threats, Nuclear Fear, and the Cold War of the 1980s*, 167–85.

108. On the importance of the West German environmental movement's support for the peace movement, see Christoph Becker-Schaum, "The Institutional Organization of the Peace Movement," in *The Nuclear Crisis: The Arms Race, Cold War Anxiety, and the German Peace Movement of the 1980s*, ed. Christoph Becker-Schaum, Philipp Gassert, Martin Klimke, Wilfried Mausbach, and Marianne Zepp (New York: Berghahn Books, 2016), 154–72, 160–61. See also Silke Mende and Birgit Metzger, "Eco-pacifism: The Environmental Movement as a Source for the Peace Movement," in Becker-Schaum et al., *The Nuclear Crisis*, 119–37.

109. Sebastian Kalden and Jan Ole Wiechmann, "The Churches," in Becker-Schaum et al., *The Nuclear Crisis*, 242–57, 242–44.

110. Kalden and Wiechmann, "The Churches," 243–44; Kalden, "A Case of 'Hollanditis,'" 256–57.

111. Krefeld Appeal, November 1980, German Historical Institute, Washington, DC, https://ghdi.ghi-dc.org/sub_document.cfm?document_id=1129.

112. Saskia Richter, "The Protagonists of the Peace Movement," in Becker-Schaum et al., *The Nuclear Crisis*, 189–206, 190.

113. Ibid. Richter accepts Bastian's statement that he was the author of the Krefeld Appeal.

114. Gerhard Wettig, "The Last Soviet Offensive in the Cold War: Emergence and Development of the Campaign Against NATO Euromissiles, 1979–1983," *Cold War History* 9, no. 1 (February 2009): 91–92. For the view that the Krefeld Appeal was a communist initiative, see also Becker-Schaum, "The Institutional Organization of the Peace Movement," 162–63.

115. Richter, "The Protagonists of the Peace Movement," 190.

116. Edmund Morris, *Dutch: A Memoir of Ronald Reagan* (New York: Random House, 1999), 221.

117. Stephen Vaughn, *Ronald Reagan in Hollywood: Movies and Politics* (Cambridge: Cambridge University Press, 1994), 121–22; Lettow, *Ronald Reagan and His Quest to Abolish Nuclear Weapons*, 3–5.

118. Reagan, *An American Life*, 105–15. See also Cannon, *President Reagan*, 282–87.

119. Reagan, *An American Life*, 126–30, 132–36.

120. Ibid., 138–45.

121. Cannon, *President Reagan*, 287–91.

122. Ronald Reagan, "Address Accepting the Presidential Nomination at the Republican National Convention in Detroit," July 17, 1980, APP, https://www.presidency.ucsb.edu /documents/address-accepting-the-presidential-nomination-the-republican-national-convention -detroit.

123. On Carter's nuclear modernization program, see Brian J. Auten, *Carter's Conversion: The Hardening of American Defense Policy* (Columbia: University of Missouri Press, 2008).

124. Transcript of the Carter-Reagan presidential debate, October 28, 1980, Commission on Presidential Debates, https://www.debates.org/voter-education/debate-transcripts/october -28-1980-debate-transcript/.

125. Ronald Reagan, "Televised Address by Governor Ronald Reagan, 'A Strategy for Peace in the 80s,'" October 19, 1980, APP, https://www.presidency.ucsb.edu/documents/televised -address-governor-ronald-reagan-strategy-for-peace-the-80s.

126. Transcript of the Carter-Reagan presidential debate, October 28, 1980.

127. In early 1982, Reagan's own administration would admit that the United States and the Soviet Union had a rough parity in strategic ballistic missile warheads. See minutes of National Security Council meeting, April 21, 1982, p. 2, folder "NSC 00046 21 Apr 82 (2/5)," Box 5, ES, NSC: Meeting Files, RRPL; Ronald Reagan, "The President's News Conference," May 13, 1982, APP, https://www.presidency.ucsb.edu/documents/the-presidents-news-conference-999.

128. Lettow, *Ronald Reagan and His Quest to Abolish Nuclear Weapons*, 23, 30–31.

129. Reagan, "Televised Address by Governor Ronald Reagan, 'A Strategy for Peace in the 80s.'"

130. In describing Reagan's firing of him in 1987, chief of staff Donald Regan wrote that the president "dislikes confrontations more than any man I have ever known." Donald T. Regan, *For the Record: From Wall Street to Washington* (San Diego: Harcourt Brace Jovanovich, 1988), 98.

131. Cannon, *President Reagan*, 80. For Haig's account of the meeting with Reagan, see Haig, *Caveat*, 4–7.

132. Cannon, *President Reagan*, 73–79.

133. Haig, *Caveat*, 219, 220.

134. Cannon, *President Reagan*, 84.

135. Caspar Weinberger, interview by Stephen Knott and Russell L. Riley, Miller Center Ronald Reagan Oral History Project, November 19, 2002, https://millercenter.org/the-presidency /presidential-oral-histories/caspar-weinberger-oral-history.

136. Cannon, *President Reagan*, 84.

137. See, for example, Ronald Reagan, "Remarks at the International Business Council in Chicago," September 9, 1980, APP, https://www.presidency.ucsb.edu/documents/remarks-the -international-business-council-chicago.

138. Colin L. Powell, with Joseph E. Persico, *My American Journey* (New York: Random House, 1995), 258–59.

139. *Foreign Relations of the United States*, 1981–1988, vol. 3, Soviet Union, January 1981– January 1983, ed. James Graham Wilson (Washington, DC: Government Publishing Office, 2016), Document 15.

140. "Common Sense and the Common Danger," November 11, 1976, in *Alerting America: The Papers of the Committee on the Present Danger*, ed. Charles Tyroler II (Washington, DC: Pergamon-Brassey's, 1984), 3–5.

141. Richard Allen, interview by Stephen F. Knott, Russell L. Riley, and James Sterling Young, Miller Center Ronald Reagan Oral History Project, May 28, 2002, https://millercenter .org/the-presidency/presidential-oral-histories/richard-allen-oral-history.

142. Nuclear Freeze Steering Committee minutes, November 5, 1980, p. 1, folder "Freeze, 1980–1981," Box 50, Series G, SANE, Inc. Collection, SCPC.

143. Thompson, WGBH interview.

144. Krefeld Appeal.

Chapter 2

1. U.S. Congress, Senate, Committee on Foreign Relations, *Nomination of Eugene V. Rostow: Hearings Before the Committee on Foreign Relations, United States Senate, Ninety-Seventh Congress, First Session, on Nomination of Eugene V. Rostow, to Be Director, Arms Control and Disarmament Agency (ACDA), June 22 and 23, 1981* (Washington, DC: U.S. Government Printing Office, 1981), 49.

2. Reagan, *An American Life*, 550.

3. U.S. Congress, *Nomination of Eugene V. Rostow*, 50, 52–53.

4. Reagan, "The President's News Conference," January 29, 1981.

5. "Republican Party Platform of 1980," July 15, 1980, APP, https://www.presidency.ucsb .edu/documents/republican-party-platform-1980; "Transcript of Reagan News Conference with Bush on Plans for Administration," *New York Times*, November 7, 1980.

6. For public statements that strategic arms reduction negotiations could begin before the completion of U.S. nuclear modernization, see, for example, U.S. Congress, Senate, Committee on Armed Services, *Nomination of Caspar W. Weinberger to Be Secretary of Defense: Hearing Before the Committee on Armed Services, United States Senate, Ninety-Seventh Congress, First Session, on Nomination of Caspar W. Weinberger to Be Secretary of Defense, January 6, 1981* (Washington, DC: U.S. Government Printing Office, 1981), 24; U.S. Congress, Senate, Committee on Foreign Relations, *Nomination of Alexander M. Haig, Jr: Hearings Before the Committee on Foreign Relations, United States Senate, Ninety-Seventh Congress, First Session, on the Nomination of Alexander M. Haig, Jr. to Be Secretary of State, January 9, 10, 12, 13, 14, 15, 1981* (Washington, DC: U.S. Government Printing Office, 1981), 153; Ronald Reagan, "Excerpts from

an Interview with Walter Cronkite of CBS News," March 3, 1981, APP, https://www.presidency .ucsb.edu/documents/excerpts-from-interview-with-walter-cronkite-cbs-news.

7. Haig, *Caveat*, 228.

8. See, for example, Reagan, "The President's News Conference," January 29, 1981; Ronald Reagan, "Remarks During a White House Briefing on the Program for Economic Recovery," February 24, 1981, APP, https://www.presidency.ucsb.edu/documents/remarks-during-white -house-briefing-the-program-for-economic-recovery.

9. Reagan, "The President's News Conference," January 29, 1981.

10. "Russia Answers Reagan Blast," *Los Angeles Times*, January 30, 1981.

11. Reagan, "Remarks of the President and Prime Minister Margaret Thatcher."

12. "Summary Record of the SCG Meeting, 31 March," p. 3, TNA: FCO/46/2700.

13. Reagan, *An American Life*, 269–70.

14. Ibid., 270.

15. Cannon, *President Reagan*, 301.

16. *Foreign Relations of the United States*, 1981–1988, vol. 3, Document 47.

17. Reagan, *An American Life*, 271–73.

18. European Nuclear Disarmament, "Report of the Consultative Meeting Held at Haus Der Jugend, Frankfurt, Germany from 6–8 March 1981," p. 2; "TNF Modernisation and the Netherlands," April 1981, END/20/8, Folder 2, END Collection, LSEL.

19. "World News; Belgian Parties Agree on Forming a Government," *New York Times*, May 12, 1980; "Around the World; Belgian Missile Deployment Is Tied to U.S.-Soviet Talks," *New York Times*, September 20, 1980.

20. Bielefeld Appeal, December 1980, German Historical Institute, Washington, DC, https://ghdi.ghi-dc.org/sub_document.cfm?document_id=1130. See also Jan Hansen, "Political Parties," in Becker-Schaum et al., *The Nuclear Crisis*, 104–18, 105, 108–9; Tim Geiger and Jan Hansen, "Did Protest Matter? The Influence of the Peace Movement on the West German Government and the Social Democratic Party, 1977–1983," in Conze et al., *Nuclear Threats, Nuclear Fear and the Cold War of the 1980s*, 290–315, 302.

21. Bielefeld Appeal; Krefeld Appeal.

22. Richard Halloran, "Weinberger Exhorts Allies to Share Burden of Defense," *New York Times*, April 8, 1981.

23. "Summary Record of the SCG Meeting, 31 March," pp. 2–3.

24. Telegram number 291 of 24 April, April 24, 1981, TNA: FCO/46/2701.

25. Memorandum, Robert Schweitzer, Sven Kraemer, and Chris Shoemaker to Richard Allen, April 29, 1981, p. 3, folder "NSC 00008 30 Apr 81 1/3," Box 1, ES, NSC: Meeting Files, RRPL.

26. Minutes of National Security Council meeting, April 30, 1981, pp. 2–5, folder "NSC 00008 30 Apr 81 2/3," Box 1, ES, NSC: Meeting Files, RRPL.

27. Ibid., p. 7.

28. Ronald Reagan White House diary, April 30, 1981, https://www.reaganfoundation.org /ronald-reagan/white-house-diaries/diary-entry-04301981/.

29. NATO, Final Communiqué—North Atlantic Council Ministerial Session, Rome, May 4–5, 1981, https://www.nato.int/docu/comm/49-95/c810504a.htm.

30. "Strategy for Stopping the Nuclear Arms Race," Freeze Strategy Drafting Committee, March 1981, p. 8, END/19/17, END Collection, LSEL.

31. Pam Solo, *From Protest to Policy: Beyond the Freeze to Common Security* (Cambridge: Ballinger, 1988), 63.

32. "Coming Up . . . Freeze Strategy Conference," *Freeze Newsletter* 1, no. 1 (March 1981): 2.

33. "First Annual Freeze Conference, March 20–22, 1981," folder "Freeze, 1980–1981," Box 50, Series G, SANE, Inc. Collection, SCPC.

34. "Strategy for Stopping the Nuclear Arms Race," pp. 11–15.

35. "First Annual Freeze Conference, March 20–22, 1981," pp. 1, 3.

36. "Nuclear Weapon Freeze Campaign Update," *Freeze Newsletter* 1, no. 1 (March 1981).

37. "Petition Campaigns in 17 States; Connecticut Delivers 22,500 Signatures," *Freeze Newsletter* 1, no. 2 (July 1981): 3, 14.

38. Ibid.

39. "20 New Eng. Towns Freeze," *Freeze Newsletter* 1, no. 2 (July 1981): 14.

40. Mary Ellen Donovan, "Plainfield, N.H., 1981: Against the Arms Race," *New York Times*, March 28, 1981.

41. Forsberg, WGBH interview, March 3, 1988.

42. George Gallup, "Worldwide Nuclear Arms Vote Favored," *Sunday Oregonian*, June 21, 1981.

43. George Gallup, "Wide Support Found for World Referendum," *Freeze Newsletter* 1, no. 2 (July 1981): 15.

44. "Mothers' Day Rallies in 20 Cities," *Freeze Newsletter* 1, no. 2 (July 1981): 10.

45. "Barnstorming Through South Dakota and Oregon," *Freeze Newsletter* 1, no. 2 (July 1981): 11.

46. Patti Davis, *The Way I See It: An Autobiography* (New York: G. P. Putnam's Sons, 1992), 246–47.

47. Program, "Survival Sunday 4," June 14, 1981, folder "Survival Sunday, 1981 and 1982," Box 2, David Cortright Papers, SCPC; Davis, *The Way I See It*, 277, 280–81.

48. "Reagan Daughter Hailed at Rally of 18,000 Opposing Atom Power," UPI, June 16, 1981.

49. Davis, *The Way I See It*, 267–68, 277–79.

50. Ibid., 281–82.

51. Ronald Reagan White House diary, December 6, 1982, https://www.reaganfoundation.org/ronald-reagan/white-house-diaries/diary-entry-12061982/.

52. "Remarks of EVR at National Security Council Meeting at Los Angeles, August 17, 1981, on Strategic Weapons Systems, (Somewhat Edited)," pp. 1–2, folder "NSC 00020 17 Aug 1981 [East-West Trade, Central America, Strategic Forces]," Box 2, ES, NSC: Meeting Files, RRPL; U.S. Congress, *Nomination of Eugene V. Rostow*, 50.

53. "Remarks of EVR at National Security Council Meeting at Los Angeles," p. 2.

54. Ronald Reagan, "Remarks and a Question-and-Answer Session with Reporters on the Announcement of the United States Strategic Weapons," October 2, 1981, APP, https://www.presidency.ucsb.edu/documents/remarks-and-question-and-answer-session-with-reporters-the-announcement-the-united-states.

55. Ronald Reagan, "Remarks and a Question-and-Answer Session at a Working Luncheon with Out-of-Town Editors," October 16, 1981, APP, https://www.presidency.ucsb.edu/documents/remarks-and-question-and-answer-session-working-luncheon-with-out-town-editors.

56. SANE Statement on the Reagan Nuclear Arms Plan, October 5, 1981, folder "SANE Statement on Reagan Nuclear Arms Plan, Oct. 5, 1981," Box 71, Series G, SANE, Inc. Collection, SCPC.

57. Leslie H. Gelb, "Reagan Orders Production of 2 Types of Neutron Arms for Stockpiling in the U.S.," *New York Times*, August 9, 1981.

58. "A Solution in Search of a Problem," *END Bulletin* 7 (Winter 1981/82): 2–3.

59. Reagan, "Remarks and a Question-and-Answer Session at a Working Luncheon with Out-of-Town Editors."

60. William Borders, "150,000 in London Rally Against Bomb," *New York Times*, October 25, 1981.

61. "100,000 Protest U.S. Rockets in Europe," UPI, June 20, 1981; Kalden and Wiechmann, "The Churches," 244–46.

62. Becker-Schaum, "The Institutional Organization of the Peace Movement," 163–65; Kalden and Wiechmann, "The Churches," 246.

63. Wittner, *Toward Nuclear Abolition*, 144; "Message from Europe," *END Bulletin* 10 (July–August 1982): 3.

64. Thompson, WGBH interview; Kent, WGBH interview.

65. Thompson, WBGH interview; Borders, "150,000 in London Rally Against Bomb."

66. Mary Kaldor and Dan Smith, "European Nuclear Disarmament—Report of the Research Conference, Amsterdam, May 29–31, 1981," June 1981, pp. 1–2, 4–5, END/15/1, Folder 2, END Collection, LSEL.

67. Ibid., pp. 2, 6.

68. Stephen Tunnicliffe, "International Peace Conference, Copenhagen 5–6 September," *END Bulletin* 7 (Winter 1981/82): 17.

69. For more on the IPCC, see Wittner, *Toward Nuclear Abolition*, 233–34.

70. Ken Coates, "Rome END Consultation: Preparing for the European Convention," *END Bulletin* 7 (Winter 1981/82): 7.

71. Ken Coates, "After the Demo's . . . Forward to the END Convention," *END Bulletin* 8 (Spring 1982): 18–19.

72. Ibid., 19.

73. "Whose Zero Option?," *END Bulletin* 8 (Spring 1982): 2.

74. Wittner, *Toward Nuclear Abolition*, 144, 143, 131, 159, 140. For firsthand accounts of these protests, see Tony Simpson, "Two Million on the Street," *END Bulletin* 8 (Spring 1982): 14–16.

75. "Whose Zero Option?," 2.

76. See, for example, Petra Karin Kelly, "The Position of the Green Party and the German Peace Movement as Regards the NATO Decision of 12 December 1979," July 1982, pp. 5–6, 8, 10, END/20/15, END Collection, LSEL.

77. Petra Kelly, WGBH Educational Foundation interview, December 16, 1986, https://openvault.wgbh.org/catalog/V_1BDBA12B806E409FB7545AFDCF19CDA1#at_280.957_s; Simpson, "Two Million on the Street," 14.

78. Ronald Reagan, "Remarks on Signing the Economic Recovery Tax Act of 1981 and the Omnibus Budget Reconciliation Act of 1981, and a Question-and-Answer Session with Reporters," August 13, 1981, APP, https://www.presidency.ucsb.edu/documents/remarks-signing-the-economic-recovery-tax-act-1981-and-the-omnibus-budget-reconciliation.

79. Reagan, "Remarks and a Question-and-Answer Session at a Working Luncheon with Out-of-Town Editors." Some scholars have echoed Reagan's claims about Soviet influence in West European peace movements, particularly the West German movement. See, for example, Wettig, "The Last Soviet Offensive in the Cold War." For a persuasive critique of Wettig's

argument, see Holger Nehring and Benjamin Ziemann, "Do All Paths Lead to Moscow? The NATO Dual-Track Decision and the Peace Movement—A Critique," *Cold War History* 12, no. 1 (February 2012): 1–24.

80. "Appeal for European Nuclear Disarmament," 223–26.

81. "European Nuclear Disarmament Steering Committee—Minutes of a Meeting Held on 4th June 1980 in House of Commons Committee Room at 11.30 a.m.," p. 2, END/1/1, Folder 2, END Collection, LSEL.

82. Letter from Yuri Zhukov, December 2, 1982, END/14/21, END Collection, LSEL.

83. Thompson, WGBH interview.

84. For Reagan publicly touting allied governments' support for U.S. INF deployments, see Reagan, "Remarks and a Question-and-Answer Session at a Working Luncheon with Out-of-Town Editors."

85. "Record of a Meeting Between the Secretary of State for Foreign and Commonwealth Affairs and the United States Secretary of State: State Department, Washington, Friday 17 July 1981," TNA: FCO/46/2703.

86. FRG paper for 27/8 meeting—Non-paper, "Preparation of LRTNF Negotiations," pp. 2–3, TNA: FCO/46/2703.

87. Marilena Gala, "The Euromissile Crisis and the Centrality of the 'Zero Option,'" in Nuti et al., *The Euromissile Crisis and the End of the Cold War*, 158–75, 159–60.

88. D. H. Gillmore to Private Secretary, "TNF Arms Control: Public Handling of Western Position During Negotiations," September 1, 1981, p. 1, TNA: FCO/46/2703; FRG paper for 27/8 meeting, pp. 2–3.

89. Telegram number 2776 of 18 September 1981, p. 1, TNA: FCO/46/2704.

90. Telegram number 694 of 15 September, September 15, 1981, p. 2, TNA: FCO/46/2704.

91. "UK Summary Record of the Special Consultative Group Meeting in Brussels, 16 September 1981," pp. 2, 3, TNA: FCO/46/2704.

92. Ibid., pp. 3, 4.

93. D. H. Gillmore to PS/PUS et al., September 30, 1981, pp. 2–3, TNA: FCO/46/2704.

94. NSC Briefing Paper on TNF, p. 3, folder "NSC 00022 13 Oct 81," Box 3, ES, NSC: Meeting Files, RRPL.

95. US non-paper handed out by Gompert 13/10—Non-paper, "Public Document on TNF Arms Control," p. 4, TNA: FCO/46/2705.

96. NSC Briefing Paper on TNF, pp. 3–4.

97. Minutes of National Security Council meeting, October 13, 1981, p. 3, folder "NSC 00022, 13 Oct 81," Box 3, ES, NSC: Meeting Files, RRPL.

98. Ibid., p. 5.

99. Ibid., pp. 5, 7, 6.

100. Ibid., pp. 2–7.

101. "NPG Ministerial Communiqué—Zero Option," TNA: FCO/46/2705.

102. NATO, Final Communiqué—Nuclear Planning Group, Gleneagles, October 20–21, 1981, https://www.nato.int/docu/comm/49-95/c811020a.htm.

103. "UK Record of SCG Meeting: Brussels, 26 October 1981," p. 8, TNA: FCO/46/2706.

104. NSC Briefing Paper on Theater Nuclear Forces, pp. 2, 4–5, folder "NSC 00025 12 Nov 1981 [Theater Nuclear Forces, NATO, Strategic Forces]," Box 3, ES, NSC: Meeting Files, RRPL.

105. Ibid., pp. 2–3.

106. Minutes of National Security Council meeting, November 12, 1981, pp. 4, 7.

107. Ibid., p. 2.

108. Ibid., pp. 5, 6, 7, 9.

109. Reagan, "Remarks to Members of the National Press Club on Arms Reduction and Nuclear Weapons."

110. Foreign policy speech, composite draft, November 14, 1981, 8:30 pm, p. 10, folder 35 (11/16/81–11/18/81), Box 2, Series III: Presidential Speeches, Presidential Handwriting File, RRPL.

111. Foreign policy speech, revised draft, November 17, 1981, 8:00 am, p. 6, folder 35 (11/16/81–11/18/81), Box 2, Series III: Presidential Speeches, Presidential Handwriting File, RRPL.

112. Reagan, "Remarks to Members of the National Press Club on Arms Reduction and Nuclear Weapons."

113. END press release for December 8, 1981, December 6, 1981, END/6/2, Folder 2, END Collection, LSEL.

114. Kelly was playing off of George H. W. Bush's characterization of Reagan's economic proposals as "voodoo economics" during the 1980 Republican primaries. See Robert Shogan, "Bush Ends His Waiting Game, Attacks Reagan," *Los Angeles Times*, April 14, 1980.

115. Kelly, "The Position of the Green Party," p. 8.

116. "The Rally of November 21st 1981," and "Position of the New Dutch Government on Nuclear Weapons," in Cooperation Group Stop the Neutron Bomb Stop the Nuclear Arms Race International Newsletter, No. 10, March 1982, END/20/8, Folder 3, END Collection, LSEL.

117. Mary Kaldor, Randy Kehler, and Mient Jan Faber, "Learning from Each Other," *END Journal* 2 (February–March 1983): 22.

118. Kehler, WGBH interview.

119. Meyer, *A Winter of Discontent*, 181.

120. Kehler, WGBH interview.

121. Cortright, *Peace Works*, 17–20; Barbara Atlas et al., "Can We the People, Prevent the Nuclear War in Preparation?," folder "Freeze, 1980–1981," Box 50, Series G, SANE, Inc. Collection, SCPC.

122. John Herbers, "Widespread Vote Urges Nuclear Freeze," *New York Times*, November 4, 1982.

123. Ronald Reagan, "Interview in Oklahoma City with Reporters from the *Daily Oklahoman*," March 16, 1982, APP, https://www.presidency.ucsb.edu/documents/interview-oklahoma-city-with-reporters-from-the-daily-oklahoman.

124. Ronald Reagan, "Interview in New York City with Members of the Editorial Board of the *New York Post*," March 23, 1982, APP, https://www.presidency.ucsb.edu/documents/interview-new-york-city-with-members-the-editorial-board-the-new-york-post.

125. Ronald Reagan, "Address at the Republican National Convention in Kansas City," August 19, 1976, APP, https://www.presidency.ucsb.edu/documents/address-the-republican-national-convention-kansas-city-missouri.

126. Reagan, *An American Life*, 550. Reagan heard this statistic at an NSC meeting on December 3, 1981. See Reagan White House diary, December 3, 1981.

127. Reagan, *An American Life*, 548–50.

128. Ibid., 550.

129. Cannon, *President Reagan*, 180, 182, 176–78.

130. Martin Anderson, *Revolution: The Reagan Legacy* (Stanford: Hoover Institution Press, 1990), 309.

131. Opening statement for news conference on nuclear arms reduction, March 30, 1982, 2:45 p.m. draft, p. 3, folder "Nuclear [Freeze] (3 of 8)," Box OA 9422, David Gergen Files, RRPL.

132. See Ronald Reagan, "The President's News Conference," March 31, 1982, APP, https://www.presidency.ucsb.edu/documents/the-presidents-news-conference-1001.

133. "Opening Remarks for Drafting Session on 'The Freeze,'" folder "Nuclear Freeze/Nuclear Policy (2)," RAC Box 12, John Poindexter Files, RRPL. Interestingly, one of Reagan's handwritten drafts of the statement declares that the United States could consider freezing the production of nuclear weapons after the superpowers had enacted deep reductions in their nuclear arsenals. "President's Draft, 30 Mar 82," p. 1, folder "Nuclear Freeze/Nuclear Policy (1)," RAC Box 12, John Poindexter Files, RRPL.

134. "Minutes of the December 21, 1981, Meeting of the US Government Contacts Task Force of the National Nuclear Weapons Freeze Campaign, 1:00 to 3:00 pm," folder "U.S. Government Relations Task Force, May 1981–Mar. 1982," Box 8, National Nuclear Weapons Freeze Campaign (henceforth NNWFC) Records, State Historical Society of Missouri at St. Louis (henceforth SHSM-SL).

135. "Strategy for Stopping the Nuclear Arms Race," pp. 13–15.

136. Solo, *From Protest to Policy*, 74. See also Kehler, WGBH interview.

137. Kehler, WGBH interview.

138. For the text of the resolution, see S.J.Res. 163, 97th Cong. (1982); H.J. Res. 434, 97th Cong. (1982). See also Waller, *Congress and the Nuclear Freeze*, 60–66.

139. Knopf, *Domestic Society and International Cooperation*, 214–15.

140. Judith Miller, "Arms Control Drive to Open," *New York Times*, April 18, 1982; Robert G. Kaiser, "Ground Zero Week, Despite Fizzles, Calls Attention to A-War Risk," *Washington Post*, April 25, 1982.

141. Memorandum, William Clark to Edwin Meese III, James A. Baker III, and Michael Deaver, April 22, 1982, pp. 1–3, folder "Nuclear [Freeze] (1 of 8)," Box OA 9422, David Gergen Files, RRPL.

142. Ibid., p. 3.

143. Minutes of National Security Council meeting, April 21, 1982, p. 8.

144. Letter, Ronald Reagan to Miss Virginia F. Adams, April 21, 1982, in Skinner et al., *Reagan: A Life in Letters*, 401–2.

145. State Department Views, p. 1, folder "NSC 00046 21 Apr 82 (1/5)," Box 5, ES, NSC: Meeting Files, RRPL.

146. Minutes of National Security Council meeting, April 21, 1982, p. 7.

147. Memorandum, Alexander M. Haig Jr. to the president, May 1, 1982, p. 1, folder "NSC 00049 03 May 82 (1/2)," Box 6, ES, NSC: Meeting Files, RRPL.

148. "NSC, START, 21 Apr 1982," p. 3, folder "NSC 00046 21 Apr 82 (1/5)," Box 5, ES, NSC: Meeting Files, RRPL.

149. Reagan's handwritten note is at the bottom of a memo that Clark had sent him. Memorandum, William P. Clark to the president, March 27, 1982, folder "Nuclear Freeze (03/23/1982–04/05/1982)," Box 20, ES, NSC: Subject File-N, RRPL.

150. "NSC, 5/3/82, START," pp. 2, 3, 5–6, folder "NSC 00049 03 May 82 (1/2)," Box 6, ES, NSC: Meeting Files, RRPL.

151. Strobe Talbott, *Deadly Gambits: The Reagan Administration and the Stalemate in Nuclear Arms Control* (New York: Knopf, 1984), 263–68.

152. NSDD 33; NSDD 44.

153. Ronald Reagan, "Address at Commencement Exercises at Eureka College in Illinois," May 9, 1982, APP, https://www.presidency.ucsb.edu/documents/address-commencement -exercises-eureka-college-illinois.

154. Edward F. Snyder, "A Commentary on President Reagan's 'START' Proposal," May 11, 1982, folder "Reagan, 1980–1984," Box 6, NNWFC Records, SHSM-SL; Press Release, "U.S. and U.S.S.R. Urged to Suspend Nuclear Arms During START Talks," folder "U.S. Govt. Relations Task Force, Apr.–Jul. 1982," Box 8, NNWFC Records, SHSM-SL; "Reagan Letter," folder "U.S. Govt. Relations Task Force, Apr.–Jul. 1982," Box 8, NNWFC Records, SHSM-SL.

155. Reagan, "The President's News Conference," May 13, 1982.

156. Ronald Reagan, "Remarks and a Question-and-Answer Session with the Student Body of Providence-St. Mel High School in Chicago, Illinois," May 10, 1982, APP, https://www .presidency.ucsb.edu/documents/remarks-and-question-and-answer-session-with-the-student -body-providence-st-mel-high.

157. On the magnitude of Reagan's proposed START reductions, see Reagan, "The President's News Conference," May 13, 1982.

158. Ronald Reagan, "Radio Address to the Nation on Nuclear Weapons," April 17, 1982, APP, https://www.presidency.ucsb.edu/documents/radio-address-the-nation-nuclear -weapons-0.

159. See, for example, Ronald Reagan, "Remarks and a Question-and-Answer Session in Los Angeles at a Meeting with Editors and Broadcasters from Western States," July 1, 1982, APP, https://www.presidency.ucsb.edu/documents/remarks-and-question-and-answer-session-los -angeles-meeting-with-editors-and-broadcasters.

160. See, for example, Ronald Reagan, "Remarks in Columbus to Members of Ohio Veterans Organizations," October 4, 1982, APP, https://www.presidency.ucsb.edu/documents /remarks-columbus-members-ohio-veterans-organizations.

161. See, for example, Ronald Reagan, "Remarks at the Centennial Meeting of the Supreme Council of the Knights of Columbus in Hartford, Connecticut," August 3, 1982, APP, https:// www.presidency.ucsb.edu/documents/remarks-the-centennial-meeting-the-supreme-council -the-knights-columbus-hartford.

162. "And Little Children Shall Lead Them in N.Y. March," *Los Angeles Times*, June 12, 1982; Robert D. McFadden, "A Spectrum of Humanity Represented at the Rally," *New York Times*, June 13, 1982; Anna Quindlen, "About New York: Earnestness and Whimsy in a Colorful Panorama," *New York Times*, June 13, 1982; Paul L. Montgomery, "Throngs Fill Manhattan to Protest Nuclear Weapons," *New York Times*, June 13, 1982.

Chapter 3

1. Reagan, *An American Life*, 566; Helen Broinowski Caldicott, *A Desperate Passion: An Autobiography* (New York: Norton, 1996), 259–60.

2. Letter, Ronald Reagan to Patti (Reagan) Davis, December 1982, in Skinner et al., *Reagan: A Life in Letters*, 64.

3. Caldicott, *A Desperate Passion*, 261–64.

4. Reagan White House diary, December 6, 1982.

5. Caldicott, *A Desperate Passion*, 265.

6. Caldicott, *A Desperate Passion*, 260–66; Reagan, *An American Life*, 566, 562.

7. NBC News, "Poll Results #77," April 13, 1982, p. 1, folder "Nuclear Freeze (January 1982– June 1982) (2 of 6)," Box 40, Elizabeth Dole Files, RRPL.

8. Memorandum, Red Cavaney to Michael Deaver, April 16, 1982, folder "Nuclear Freeze (January 1982–June 1982) (2 of 6)," Box 40, Elizabeth Dole Files, RRPL; Memorandum, Eugene Rostow to the assistant to the president for national security affairs, folder "Nuclear Freeze (04/08/1982–04/15/1982)," Box 20, ES, NSC: Subject File-N, RRPL.

9. Memorandum, William P. Clark to the president, folder "Arms Control/Nuclear Freeze (Public/Legislative Meetings, etc.) (1)," RAC Box 1, Robert C. "Bud" McFarlane Files, RRPL; Memorandum, Clark to Meese, Baker, and Deaver, April 22, 1982.

10. Memorandum, Clark to Meese, Baker, and Deaver, April 22, 1982.

11. Memorandum, Clark to the president.

12. Memorandum, William P. Clark (for the president) to the secretary of state; secretary of defense; director, Arms Control and Disarmament Agency; and director, International Communication Agency, April 26, 1982, folder "Nuclear Freeze (04/08/1982–04/15/1982)," Box 20, ES, NSC: Subject File-N, RRPL.

13. Memorandum, William P. Clark to the secretary of state; secretary of defense; director of central intelligence; chairman, Joint Chiefs of Staff; director, Arms Control and Disarmament Agency; and director, International Communication Agency, May 10, 1982, pp. 1, 4, folder "Arms Control/Nuclear Freeze (Public/Legislative Meetings, etc.) (3)," RAC Box 1, Robert C. "Bud" McFarlane Files, RRPL.

14. Robert C. McFarlane with Zofia Smardz, *Special Trust* (New York: Cadell and Davies, 1994), 133–45, 150, 168, 196–97.

15. Judith Miller, "House Foreign Affairs Panel Seeks Nuclear Freeze," *New York Times*, June 24, 1982; Waller, *Congress and the Nuclear Freeze*, 110–29.

16. Solo, *From Protest to Policy*, 88–89.

17. Waller, *Congress and the Nuclear Freeze*, 135–37.

18. Memorandum, Robert Linhard/Sven Kraemer through Richard T. Boverie to William P. Clark, June 29, 1982, folder "[Nuclear Policy Issues-Public Diplomacy/Information Policy; Congressional Distribution of Arms Control Material; Q/A Freeze, April–May 1982] (6)," Box 90213, Sven Kraemer Files, RRPL.

19. United States Department of State, "The Nuclear Freeze," April 1982, pp. 2–3, 6, folder "[Nuclear Policy Issues-Public Diplomacy/Information Policy; Congressional Distribution of Arms Control Material; Q/A Freeze, April–May 1982] (7)," Box 90213, Sven Kraemer Files, RRPL.

20. Memorandum, L. Paul Bremer III to William P. Clark, August 3, 1982, folder "Nuclear Freeze (7/12/82–8/12/82)," Box 20, ES, NSC: Subject File-N, RRPL; Ronald Reagan White House diary, August 5, 1982, https://www.reaganfoundation.org/ronald-reagan/white-house-diaries /diary-entry-08051982/; "Draft Talking Points," folder "Nuclear Freeze (7/12/82–8/12/82)," Box 20, ES, NSC: Subject File-N, RRPL.

21. Waller, *Congress and the Nuclear Freeze*, 138.

22. Reagan White House diary, August 5, 1982.

23. On the House floor debate on the Zablocki freeze resolution, see Waller, *Congress and the Nuclear Freeze*, 142–58.

24. Kehler, WGBH interview.

25. Waller, *Congress and the Nuclear Freeze*, 158.

26. "Minutes of the Executive Committee Meeting," August 13, 1982, p. 1, folder "Executive Committee Meetings, June–December 1982," Box 2, NNWFC Records, SHSM-SL.

27. Wisconsin Nuclear Weapons Freeze Campaign, "Vote Yes Freeze the Nuclear Arms Race-Sept 14," folder "Nuclear Freeze (6)," Box 15, Morton Blackwell Files, RRPL. On the 1982 economic recession, see H. W. Brands, *Reagan: The Life* (New York: Doubleday, 2015), 317–19.

28. Memorandum, ACDA/CPA–Thomas Graham Jr. to State/PM–Mr. Robert Dean, deputy director, August 17, 1982, folder "Nuclear Freeze (8/18/82)," Box 20, ES, NSC: Subject File-N, RRPL.

29. Memorandum, William P. Clark to James A. Baker III, August 16, 1982, p. 1, folder "Nuclear Freeze (7/12/82–8/12/82)," Box 20, ES, NSC: Subject File-N, RRPL; Memorandum, Dave Gergen to administration spokesmen, August 6, 1982, folder "Nuclear Freeze/Arms Control," Box OA 11222, Michael Baroody Files, RRPL. See also Solo, *From Protest to Policy*, 97.

30. "Draft Speech Material," folder "Nuclear Freeze/Arms Control," Box OA 11222, Michael Baroody Files, RRPL.

31. Andrew H. Malcolm, "2 Familiar Names Win Wisconsin Races," *New York Times*, September 16, 1982.

32. "Minutes of the Executive Committee Meeting," September 28, 1982, p. 4, folder "Executive Committee Meetings, June–December 1982," Box 2, NNWFC Records, SHSM-SL.

33. Kathryn Buxton, "Personalities," *Washington Post*, October 30, 1982.

34. Guidance attached to memorandum, Dave Gergen to Jim Baker, September 9, 1982, folder "Nuclear Freeze (7)," Box OA 9422, David Gergen Files, RRPL. For the text of the Wisconsin referendum, see Wisconsin Nuclear Weapons Freeze Campaign, "Vote Yes Freeze the Nuclear Arms Race-Sept 14."

35. See, for example, Richard T. Boverie, memorandum for the record, October 18, 1982, folder "Nuclear Freeze (8)," Box OA 9422, David Gergen Files, RRPL.

36. Reagan, "Remarks in Columbus to Members of Ohio Veterans Organizations."

37. Ronald Reagan, "The President's News Conference," November 11, 1982, APP, https://www.presidency.ucsb.edu/documents/the-presidents-news-conference-1003.

38. Ronald Reagan, "Remarks and a Question-and-Answer Session with Reporters on Production of the MX Missile," December 10, 1982, APP, https://www.presidency.ucsb.edu/documents/remarks-and-question-and-answer-session-with-reporters-production-the-mx-missile.

39. Reagan quoted Barron's article in his meeting with Caldicott in December 1982. Caldicott, *A Desperate Passion*, 264.

40. Herbers, "Widespread Vote Urges Nuclear Freeze."

41. "Incumbents Opposed to Nuclear Weapons Freeze Who Lost on November 2, 1982 and Their Successful Opponents," folder "U.S. Govt. Relations Task Force, Aug.–Dec. 1982," Box 8, NNWFC Records, SHSM-SL.

42. Sommaripa and Forsberg, "Strategy for a Concerted National Effort to Halt the Nuclear Arms Race—First Draft," p. 4.

43. Jim Castelli, *The Bishops and the Bomb: Waging Peace in a Nuclear Age* (Garden City: Image Books, 1983), 60, 85.

44. See, for example, Castelli, *The Bishops and the Bomb*, 82–83; Letter, Lawrence Eagleburger to Archbishop Bernardin, June 5, 1982, folder "Nuclear Freeze (11/82)," Box 20, ES, NSC: Subject File-N, RRPL; Letter, William P. Clark to Clare Boothe Luce, July 30, 1982, folder "Nuclear Freeze (11/82)," Box 20, ES, NSC: Subject File-N, RRPL; Letter, Caspar Weinberger to Archbishop Bernardin, September 13, 1982, folder "Arms Control, Nuclear (Bishops' Letter) (11/16/1982–11/22/1982)," Box 1, Robert Sims Files, RRPL.

45. Richard Halloran, "Minuet with Catholic Bishops over Nuclear War," *New York Times*, December 16, 1982.

46. See, for example, letter, William P. Clark to Archbishop Bernardin, November 16, 1982, p. 4, folder "Arms Control, Nuclear (Bishops' Letter) (11/16/1982–11/22/1982)," Box 1, Robert Sims Files, RRPL.

47. A. James Reichley, "Religion and Political Realignment," *Brookings Review* 3, no. 1 (Fall 1984): 32; Memorandum, Elizabeth H. Dole to James A. Baker III, November 23, 1982, folder "Nuclear Freeze (July–December 1982) [1 of 2]," Box 40, Elizabeth Dole Files, RRPL.

48. Castelli, *The Bishops and the Bomb*, 87–94, 100–5.

49. Letter, Clark to Bernardin, November 16, 1982; "Text of Administration's Letter to U.S. Catholic Bishops on Nuclear Policies," *New York Times*, November 17, 1982.

50. Halloran, "Minuet with Catholic Bishops over Nuclear War"; Note, John [Poindexter] to Bud [McFarlane], December 20, 1982, folder "Nuclear Freeze (12/82)," Box 20, ES, NSC: Subject File-N, RRPL.

51. Castelli, *The Bishops and the Bomb*, 118, 117.

52. "Catholic Bishops Pastoral Letter on War and Peace," December 6, 1982, folder "Arms Control, Nuclear (Bishops' Letter) (11/23/1982–12/27/1982)," Box 1, Robert Sims Files, RRPL. Jared McBrady has argued that the Vatican had some success in moderating the pastoral letter's criticism of U.S. nuclear policy in early 1983. Reagan's relationship with Pope John Paul II played a key role in motivating the Vatican's efforts. Jared McBrady, "The Challenge of Peace: Ronald Reagan, John Paul II, and the American Bishops," *Journal of Cold War Studies* 17, no. 1 (Winter 2015): 129–52.

53. Richard Halloran, "House, 245–176, Votes Down $988 Million for MX Missile; Setback for Reagan Policy," *New York Times*, December 8, 1982.

54. On the composition of the anti-MX coalition and its strategy for stopping the MX, see Cortright, *Peace Works*, 141–43, 144–46; and John D. Isaacs and Katherine Magraw, "The Lobbyist and the MX," *Bulletin of the Atomic Scientists* 39, no. 2 (February 1983): 56–57.

55. Coalition for a New Foreign and Military Policy, "Budget Bulletin #8—How (and What) We Won on the MX," December 20, 1982, p. 2, folder "Defense appropriation, FY 83, 1982–1983," Box 21, Series K: MX Files—Records of SANE and of the National Campaign to Stop the MX, 1976–85, SANE, Inc. Collection, SCPC.

56. "Estimated Number of Citizens Alerted to Support the Addabbo Anti-MX Amendment Through SANE's Grass-roots Lobbying Campaign, November 3–December 7, 1982," folder "FY 83 appropriations and continuing resolution, 1982–1983," Box 29, Series K, SANE, Inc. Collection, SCPC.

57. Letter, Henry Kendall to the Honorable Joseph Addabbo, August 26, 1982, folder "Defense appropriation, FY 83, 1982–1983," Box 21, Series K, SANE, Inc. Collection, SCPC. This letter was sent to each member of the House Appropriations Committee. See also letter, Diane D. Aronson to the Honorable Joseph Addabbo, September 2, 1982, folder "Defense appropriation, FY 83, 1982–1983," Box 21, Series K, SANE, Inc. Collection, SCPC.

58. See, for example, letter, Charles A. Monfort to the Honorable Joseph R. Biden, October 15, 1982, folder "Defense appropriation, FY 83, 1982–1983," Box 21, Series K, SANE, Inc. Collection, SCPC; Union of Concerned Scientists, "Dense Pack—How Much Will It Cost?," folder "Defense appropriation, FY 83, 1982–1983," Box 21, Series K, SANE, Inc. Collection, SCPC; Union of Concerned Scientists, "Questions About Dense Pack," folder "Defense appropriation, FY 83, 1982–1983," Box 21, Series K, SANE, Inc. Collection, SCPC.

59. "Notes from Visits—Week of September 13–17," pp. 1, 2, folder "Defense appropriation, FY 83, 1982–1983," Box 21, Series K, SANE, Inc. Collection, SCPC.

60. "Whip Calls Made Approx. Nov. 18, 1982," folder "FY 83 appropriations and continuing resolution, 1982–1983," Box 29, Series K, SANE, Inc. Collection, SCPC.

61. Senator William Proxmire, "Who Will End Up on Top with the MX, Doves or Hawks?" 97th Cong., 2nd sess., *Congressional Record* 128 (November 29, 1982): S27669.

62. Representative Les AuCoin, 97th Cong., 2nd sess., *Congressional Record* 128 (December 7, 1982): H29071.

63. Representative Edward Markey, 97th Cong., 2nd sess., *Congressional Record* 128 (December 7, 1982): H29052; Representative Patricia Schroeder, 97th Cong., 2nd sess., *Congressional Record* 128 (December 7, 1982): H29073; Representative Harold Ford, 97th Cong., 2nd sess., *Congressional Record* 128 (December 7, 1982): H29091.

64. See AuCoin, *Congressional Record* 128: H29070–71; Markey, *Congressional Record* 128: H29052–53; Schroeder, *Congressional Record* 128: H29073; Harold Ford, *Congressional Record* 128: H29090–91.

65. George C. Wilson and David Hoffman, "Joint Chiefs Had Counseled Reagan Against 'Dense Pack,'" *Washington Post*, December 9, 1982.

66. Halloran, "House, 245–176, Votes Down $988 Million for MX Missile."

67. Wilson, *The Triumph of Improvisation*, 67.

68. Letter, David Cortright to Senator, December 13, 1982, folder "FY 83 appropriations and continuing resolution, 1982–1983," Box 29, Series K, SANE, Inc. Collection, SCPC; Letter, Robert Tiller to Senator, December 13, 1982, folder "FY 83 appropriations and continuing resolution, 1982–1983," Box 29, Series K, SANE, Inc. Collection, SCPC; Letter, Henry W. Kendall to Senator, December 13, 1982, folder "FY 83 appropriations and continuing resolution, 1982–1983," Box 29, Series K, SANE, Inc. Collection, SCPC.

69. "SANE Calls for Senate to Defeat MX," December 8, 1982, folder "FY 83 appropriations and continuing resolution, 1982–1983," Box 29, Series K, SANE, Inc. Collection, SCPC.

70. Coalition for a New Foreign and Military Policy, "Budget Bulletin #8," p. 2.

71. Senator Alan Cranston, 97th Cong., 2nd sess., *Congressional Record* 128 (December 16, 1982): S31342.

72. Helen Dewar and Bill Peterson, "Conferees Drop Jobs Plan, Defy Reagan on MX," *Washington Post*, December 20, 1982.

73. "Treaty Between the United States of America and the Union of Soviet Socialist Republics on the Limitation of Anti-Ballistic Missile Systems (ABM Treaty)," signed May 26, 1972, https://2009-2017.state.gov/t/avc/trty/101888.htm. On the ABM Treaty negotiations, see Cameron, *The Double Game*.

74. On the role of strategic defenses in Reagan's strategic modernization program, see "Strategic Study Package," p. 10, folder "Reagan announcement on strategic systems, Oct. 2, 1982," Box 71, Series G, SANE, Inc. Collection, SCPC.

75. Letter, Edward Teller to Ronald Reagan, July 23, 1982, folder "Nuclear Freeze," CFOA 415, Edwin Meese Files, RRPL.

76. On Reagan's desire to develop nonnuclear missile defenses, see minutes of National Security Planning Group meeting, December 17, 1984, p. 7, folder "NSPG 0104 17 Dec 1984," Box 3, ES, NSC: NSPG Files, RRPL. Reagan's handwritten note to Clark is at the top of a memo from Jay Keyworth to the president on Teller's letter. See memorandum, Jay Keyworth to the president, July 29, 1982, p. 1, folder "Nuclear Freeze," CFOA 415, Edwin Meese Files, RRPL.

77. Donald R. Baucom, *The Origins of SDI, 1944–1983* (Lawrence: University Press of Kansas, 1992), 183.

78. McFarlane, *Special Trust*, 224–26; Baucom, *The Origins of SDI*, 181.

79. Cannon, *President Reagan*, 326.

80. Baucom, *The Origins of SDI*, 183.

81. Ibid., 185–88.

82. Ibid., 188–91.

83. McFarlane, *Special Trust*, 229–30; Caspar W. Weinberger, *Fighting for Peace: Seven Critical Years in the Pentagon* (New York: Warner Books, 1990), 304.

84. Ronald Reagan White House diary, February 11, 1983, https://www.reaganfoundation.org/ronald-reagan/white-house-diaries/diary-entry-02111983/.

85. "Decisions Made by the Third National Conference of the Nuclear Weapons Freeze Campaign, St. Louis, Missouri, February 4–6, 1983," pp. 1–3, folder "National Conference (3rd Annual), Feb.–Mar. 1983," Box 4, NNWFC Records, SHSM-SL; Michael Wright, Caroline Rand Herron, and Carlyle C. Douglas, "'Freeze' Prepares for '84 Contests," *New York Times*, February 13, 1983.

86. Howell Raines, "Hart Enters Presidential Race, Stressing New Ideas," *New York Times*, February 18, 1983; Adam Clymer, "Mondale Begins His '84 Campaign," *New York Times*, February 22, 1983.

87. Adam Clymer, "Cranston Enters Presidential Race," *New York Times*, February 3, 1983.

88. Minutes of National Security Council meeting, February 25, 1983, p. 2, http://www.thereaganfiles.com/19830225nsc75minutes.pdf. Reagan was likely referring to the 1982 documentary *If You Love This Planet*.

89. Ronald Reagan, "Remarks at the Annual Convention of the National Association of Evangelicals in Orlando, Florida," March 8, 1983, APP, https://www.presidency.ucsb.edu/documents/remarks-the-annual-convention-the-national-association-evangelicals-orlando-florida.

90. Reagan, *An American Life*, 568.

91. Baucom, *The Origins of SDI*, 192–93.

92. McFarlane, *Special Trust*, 230–31.

93. George P. Shultz, *Turmoil and Triumph: My Years as Secretary of State* (New York: Charles Scribner's Sons, 1993), 249.

94. Weinberger, *Fighting for Peace*, 306–7.

95. Cannon, *President Reagan*, 331.

96. McFarlane, *Special Trust*, 231–32.

97. Ronald Reagan, "Address to the Nation on Defense and National Security," March 23, 1983, APP, https://www.presidency.ucsb.edu/documents/address-the-nation-defense-and-national-security.

98. Ronald Reagan, "Question-and-Answer Session with Reporters on Domestic and Foreign Policy Issues," March 29, 1983, APP, https://www.presidency.ucsb.edu/documents/question-and-answer-session-with-reporters-domestic-and-foreign-policy-issues-0.

99. Anthony Lewis, "Abroad at Home; the President's Fantasy," *New York Times*, March 27, 1983.

100. George W. Rathjens and Jack Ruina, "100% Defense? Hardly," *New York Times*, March 27, 1983.

101. Francis X. Clines, "Democrats Assert Reagan Is Using 'Star Wars' Scare to Hide Blunders," *New York Times*, March 25, 1983.

102. Marta Daniels, "What's Wrong with President Reagan's Plans for a 'Defensive' Missile System?," March 28, 1983, folder "Reagan, 1980–1984," Box 6, NNWFC Records, SHSM-SL.

103. Kehler, WGBH interview.

104. Forsberg, WGBH interview, November 9, 1987.

105. Editorial, *END Bulletin* 10 (July/August 1982): 2; "Message from Europe," 3.

106. Bill Howard, "Sunday June 6," *END Bulletin* 9 (May/June 1982): 9; "Europe Demands a Future," *END Bulletin* 10 (July/August 1982): 16–17.

107. "Message from Europe," 3.

108. Editorial, *END Bulletin* 9 (May/June 1982): 2.

109. For attendance figures, see Paulo Gentiloni, "Green, Red and Rainbow-Coloured," trans. Peter Wright, *END Bulletin* 11 (1982): 7.

110. For the reports of these affinity groups and thematic workshops, see "END Convention Brussels 1982, Workshop Round-up," *END Bulletin* 11 (1982): 12–19.

111. Gentiloni, "Green, Red and Rainbow-Coloured," 9.

112. "END Convention Brussels 1982, Workshop Round-up," 14.

113. On the transnational movement for grassroots nuclear-free zones in the 1970s and 1980s, see Susanne Schregel, "Global Micropolitics: Toward a Transnational History of Grassroots Nuclear-Free Zones," in Conze et al., *Nuclear Threats, Nuclear Fear and the Cold War of the 1980s*, 206–26.

114. Gentiloni, "Green, Red and Rainbow-Coloured," 9.

115. Wittner, *Toward Nuclear Abolition*, 133–34, 160–61.

116. "END Convention Brussels 1982, Workshop Round-up," 15.

117. Gentiloni, "Green, Red and Rainbow-Coloured," 9.

118. John Mepham, "END Supporters Conference—Links with Europe," *END Bulletin* 10 (July/August 1982): 22.

119. Stuart Holland and Tony Simpson, "Editorial," *END Bulletin* 11 (1982): 2.

120. Maynard W. Glitman, *The Last Battle of the Cold War: An Inside Account of Negotiating the Intermediate Range Nuclear Forces Treaty* (New York: Palgrave Macmillan, 2006), 73–74.

121. Paul H. Nitze with Ann M. Smith and Steven L. Rearden, *From Hiroshima to Glasnost: At the Center of Decision, A Memoir* (New York: Grove Weidenfeld, 1989), 373.

122. Ibid., 374–85.

123. For Shultz's account of attending this play, see Shultz, *Turmoil and Triumph*, 1085.

124. Shultz, *Turmoil and Triumph*, 121; Weinberger, *Fighting for Peace*, 344.

125. Nitze, *From Hiroshima to Glasnost*, 388–89.

126. Martin Klimke and Laura Stapane, "From Artists for Peace to the Green Caterpillar: Cultural Activism and Electoral Politics in 1980s West Germany," in Conze et al., *Nuclear Threats, Nuclear Fear and the Cold War of the 1980s*, 116–41,122–24; Philipp Baur, "Nuclear Doomsday Scenarios in Film, Literature, and Music," in Becker-Schaum et al., *The Nuclear Crisis*, 322–37, 329–30.

127. Hansen, "Political Parties," 105–6, 112–13; Kristina Spohr, *The Global Chancellor: Helmut Schmidt and the Reshaping of the International Order* (Oxford: Oxford University Press, 2016), 129.

128. Spohr, *The Global Chancellor*, 129–30.

129. James M. Markham, "Bonn Parliament Votes Out Schmidt and Elects Kohl," *New York Times*, October 2, 1982.

130. Leslie H. Gelb, "White House Pleased by Bonn's Conservative Turn," *New York Times*, October 2, 1982.

131. Wittner, *Toward Nuclear Abolition*, 142, 143–44.

132. Memorandum, Paul H. Nitze to Kenneth W. Dam, December 10, 1982, folder "Nuclear-Intermediate Range Nuclear Forces (INF) October 1982–December 1982," Box 21, ES, NSC: Subject File-N, RRPL.

133. "NSPG Meeting, 13 Jan 1983," pp. 1, 7, folder "NSPG 0050 13 Jan 1983 [Arms Control/INF]," Box 1, ES, NSC: NSPG Files, RRPL.

134. State Department, "INF Arms Control," folder "NSPG 0049 10 Jan 1983 [US/Soviet Relations] (2 of 2)," Box 1, ES, NSC: NSPG Files, RRPL.

135. Shultz, *Turmoil and Triumph*, 159.

136. *Foreign Relations of the United States*, 1981–1988, vol. 4, Soviet Union, January 1983–March 1985, ed. Elizabeth C. Charles (Washington, DC: Government Publishing Office, 2021), Document 1; Shultz, *Turmoil and Triumph*, 162.

137. On Haig's departure, see Cannon, *President Reagan*, 193–205.

138. Shultz, *Turmoil and Triumph*, 117–19.

139. Ibid., 161; State Department, "INF Arms Control," p. 1.

140. "NSPG Meeting, 13 Jan 1983," esp. pp. 2, 3.

141. Ibid., p. 2.

142. "Our Future Course in the Intermediate Nuclear Force Negotiations," pp. 3–4, folder "NSPG 0049 10 Jan 1983 [US/Soviet Relations] (2 of 2)," Box 1, ES, NSC: NSPG Files, RRPL.

143. "Nuclear Issues Text of Briefing for the Prime Minister at Chequers: 30 January 1983," p. 5, TNA: PREM/19/973.

144. Ronald Reagan White House diary, January 13, 1983, https://www.reaganfoundation.org/ronald-reagan/white-house-diaries/diary-entry-01131983/.

145. Telegram number 074 of 08 Feb 83, p. 1, TNA: PREM/19/973.

146. Telegram number Misc 066 dated 18 February 1983, p. 1, TNA: CAB/164/1664.

147. Letter, Ronald Reagan to Margaret Thatcher, February 16, 1983, TNA: CAB/164/1664; Telegram number Misc 066 dated 18 February 1983; Letter, Ronald Reagan to Margaret Thatcher, February 22, 1983, TNA: CAB/164/1664.

148. On British anti-nuclear music, see William M. Knoblauch, "'Will You Sing About the Missiles?' British Antinuclear Protest Music of the 1980s," in Conze et al., *Nuclear Threats, Nuclear Fear and the Cold War of the 1980s*, 101–15.

149. Baur, "Nuclear Doomsday Scenarios," 325.

150. On West German anti-nuclear music, see Klimke and Stapane, "From Artists for Peace to the Green Caterpillar," 118–22; and Baur, "Nuclear Doomsday Scenarios," 329–33.

151. On nuclear war in West German literature of the 1980s, see Baur, "Nuclear Doomsday Scenarios," 326–29.

152. Klimke and Stapane, "From Artists for Peace to the Green Caterpillar," 119, 121; Baur, "Nuclear Doomsday Scenarios," 330–32.

153. James M. Markham, "Kohl and His Coalition Win Decisively in West Germany; U.S. Aides Feel Reassurance," *New York Times*, March 7, 1983; Hansen, "Political Parties," 111.

154. "Next Steps in INF," pp. 2–3, folder "NSPG 0059 18 Mar 1983 [INF, Lebanon]," Box 1, ES, NSC: NSPG Files, RRPL.

155. See, for example, memorandum, R. B. Bone to A. J. Coles, February 9, 1983, p. 1, TNA: PREM/19/973; Telegram Number 074 of 08 Feb 83, p. 2.

156. "Note of a discussion at Chequers on Sunday 30th January 1983 at 10.30 am, Nuclear Defence Policy—Arms Control," February 1, 1983, p. 2, TNA: PREM/19/973.

157. Ronald Reagan, "Remarks Announcing a Proposed Interim Intermediate-Range Nuclear Force Reduction Agreement," March 30, 1983, APP, https://www.presidency.ucsb.edu/documents/remarks-announcing-proposed-interim-intermediate-range-nuclear-force-reduction-agreement.

158. Letter, Margaret Thatcher to Ronald Reagan, March 24, 1983, p. 2, TNA: CAB/164/1664.

159. Memorandum, R. B. Bone to A. J. Coles, "INF," March 29, 1983, TNA: CAB/164/1664.

160. Tony Judt, *Postwar: A History of Europe Since 1945* (New York: Penguin, 2005), 545–46; William I. Hitchcock, *The Struggle for Europe: The Turbulent History of a Divided Continent, 1945–Present* (New York: Anchor Books, 2004), 324–25, 331.

161. James Hinton, *Protests and Visions: Peace Politics in Twentieth-Century Britain* (London: Hutchinson Radius, 1989), 191.

162. On Craxi's support for the NATO dual-track decision as prime minister, see Leopoldo Nuti, "The Nuclear Debate in Italian Politics in the Late 1970s and the Early 1980s," in Nuti et al., *The Euromissile Crisis and the End of the Cold War*, 231–50, 242–44.

163. Mary Kaldor, "Calling the Negotiators' Bluff," *END Journal* 5 (August–September 1983): 2.

164. West Europeans staged speaking tours in the United States and attended Freeze Campaign National Conferences, while freeze activists gave talks in Western Europe and appeared at the transnational END Conventions. See, for example, Dan Smith, "American 'Freeze' Helping to Thaw Cold War," *END Bulletin* 10 (July–August 1982): 27–28; Mike Jendrzejczyk, "Letter from America—Freeze: A Mandate to Stop the Nuclear Arms Race," *END Journal* 3 (April–May 1983): 6; "Minutes, National Committee Meeting, December 3–5, 1982, San Francisco, California," p. 1, folder "National Committee, Sept.–Dec. 1982," Box 5, NNWFC Records, SHSM-SL; "A Meeting of Minds," *END Journal* 4 (June–July 1983): 5.

165. Memorandum, Randy Kehler to the executive committee, September 27, 1982, pp. 4, 3, folder "Executive Committee Meetings, June–Dec. 1982," Box 2, NNWFC Records, SHSM-SL.

166. E. P. Thompson, *Beyond the Cold War: A New Approach to the Arms Race and Nuclear Annihilation* (New York: Pantheon, 1982), 130–31.

167. "Decisions Made by the Third National Conference of the Nuclear Weapons Freeze Campaign," p. 2.

168. Solo, *From Protest to Policy*, 121, 127, 130–32.

169. "Euromissile Actions: Washington Focus," folder "Euromissiles, Nov. 1983–June 1984," Box 2, NNWFC Records, SHSM-SL.

170. Jane Dibblin, "An Outpouring of Protest—Peaceful and Determined," *END Journal* 7 (December 1983–January 1984): 10–12, 17.

171. Steven Erlanger, "Cruise Missiles Backed in British Vote, 362–218," *Boston Globe*, November 1, 1983.

172. "Italians Approve Plan on Missiles," *New York Times*, November 17, 1983.

173. James M. Markham, "Bonn Parliament Votes to Deploy New U.S. Missiles," *New York Times*, November 23, 1983.

174. *Report of the President's Commission on Strategic Forces* (Washington, DC: The Commission, 1983), 14–18.

175. Ibid., 22–24.

176. Memorandum, William P. Clark to the president, May 7, 1983, p. 1, folder "NSC 00079 10 May 83 [START] [1/2]," Box 8, ES, NSC: Meeting Files, RRPL. The members of Congress who expressed this sentiment to the White House included Senators William Cohen, Charles Percy, and Sam Nunn and Representatives Norman Dicks and Al Gore.

177. Letter, William S. Cohen, Sam Nunn, and Charles H. Percy to the president, April 29, 1983, Box 60, Folder 6, Series 6: Chief of Staff, James A. Baker III Papers, Public Policy Papers, Department of Rare Books and Special Collections, Princeton University Library.

178. "Congress to Vote Soon on U.S.-Soviet Nuclear Weapons Freeze," January 28, 1983, folder "National Conference (3rd Annual, Feb. 4–6, 1983), Dec. 1982–Jan. 1983," Box 4, NNWFC Records, SHSM-SL; "Decisions Made by the Third National Conference of the Nuclear Weapons Freeze Campaign," p. 1.

179. "Congress to Vote Soon on U.S.-Soviet Nuclear Weapons Freeze."

180. Letter, Randy Kehler to national conference participant, February 4, 1983, folder "National Conference (3rd Annual, Feb. 4–6, 1983), Dec. 1982–Jan. 1983," Box 4, NNWFC Records, SHSM-SL.

181. Gary Geipel, "5,000 Rally in Capital to Urge Nuclear Freeze," *Los Angeles Times*, March 9, 1983; Margot Hornblower, "5,000 Supporters of Freeze Pour In as Hill Action Nears," *Washington Post*, March 8, 1983.

182. Waller, *Congress and the Nuclear Freeze*, 186.

183. Ibid., 185.

184. For a firsthand account of the House debate on the freeze resolution, see ibid., 181–285.

185. H.J.Res. 13, 98th Cong. (1983).

186. Kehler, WGBH interview.

187. Knopf, *Domestic Society and International Cooperation*, 220.

188. Meyer, *A Winter of Discontent*, 231.

189. Lou Cannon and George C. Wilson, "Reagan Reassures Congress, Is Rewarded with MX Vote," *Washington Post*, May 12, 1983; Lou Cannon and George C. Wilson, "President Backs Arms Build-Down," *Washington Post*, May 13, 1983.

190. Hedrick Smith, *The Power Game: How Washington Works* (New York: Random House, 1988), 545–49.

191. Ronald Reagan, "Remarks Announcing Changes in the United States Position at the Strategic Arms Reduction Talks," June 8, 1983, APP, https://www.presidency.ucsb.edu/documents/remarks-announcing-changes-the-united-states-position-the-strategic-arms-reduction-talks.

192. Ronald Reagan, "Remarks to Reporters Announcing New United States Initiatives in the Strategic Arms Reduction Talks," October 4, 1983, APP, https://www.presidency.ucsb.edu/documents/remarks-reporters-announcing-new-united-states-initiatives-the-strategic-arms-reduction; "Changes in Original U.S. START Position," folder "Nuclear-Intermediate Range Nuclear Forces (INF) February 1984–June 1984," Box 22, ES, NSC: Subject File-N, RRPL.

193. Shultz, *Turmoil and Triumph*, 360. Clark convinced Reagan to delete this reference to nuclear abolition from the final letter.

194. Memorandum, William P. Clark to the president, September 29, 1983, p. 1, folder "NSPG 0071 29 Sep 1983 [START]," Box 2, ES, NSC: NSPG Files, RRPL.

195. Reagan, "Remarks to Reporters Announcing New United States Initiatives in the Strategic Arms Reduction Talks."

196. "Public Diplomacy Action Plan for START and the Nuclear Freeze," September 1, 1983, p. 2, folder "[Public Diplomacy Action Plan for START and the Nuclear Freeze]," Box 90213, Sven Kraemer Files, RRPL.

197. Baur, "Nuclear Doomsday Scenarios," 323–24.

198. One hundred million viewers amounted to half of American adults. For viewing numbers, see ibid., 322.

199. Memorandum, Pam McIntyre to local freeze supporters, "The Viewing of the Film, 'The Day After,'" folder "The Day After, Aug.–Oct. 1983," Box 2, NNWFC Records, SHSM-SL.

200. "'The Day After' Project Sponsored by the Freeze and SANE," folder "The Day After, Aug.–Oct. 1983," Box 2, NNWFC Records, SHSM-SL.

201. Ronald Reagan White House diary, November 18, 1983, https://www.reaganfoundation .org/ronald-reagan/white-house-diaries/diary-entry-11181983/.

202. Knoblauch, *Nuclear Freeze in a Cold War*, 68–69; Ronald Reagan, "Address Before the Japanese Diet in Tokyo," November 11, 1983, APP, https://www.presidency.ucsb.edu/documents /address-before-the-japanese-diet-tokyo.

203. Knoblauch, *Nuclear Freeze in a Cold War*, 69, 73.

204. Shultz, *Turmoil and Triumph*, 373–74.

205. Ronald Reagan, "Remarks to Reporters on the Soviet Attack on a Korean Civilian Airliner," September 2, 1983, APP, https://www.presidency.ucsb.edu/documents/remarks-reporters -the-soviet-attack-korean-civilian-airliner.

206. Reagan, *An American Life*, 584.

207. Ronald Reagan White House diary, October 10, 1983, https://www.reaganfoundation .org/ronald-reagan/white-house-diaries/diary-entry-10101983/.

208. Cannon, *President Reagan*, 56–64.

209. Reagan White House diary, November 18, 1983; Reagan, *An American Life*, 585–86.

210. See, for example, Simon Miles, "The War Scare That Wasn't: Able Archer 83 and the Myths of the Second Cold War," *Journal of Cold War Studies* 22, no. 3 (Summer 2020): 86–118; Miles, *Engaging the Evil Empire*, 80–82. For the conventional view, see, for example, Nate Jones, ed., *Able Archer 83: The Secret History of the NATO Exercise That Almost Triggered Nuclear War* (New York: New Press, 2016), 1–59; Hal Brands, *What Good Is Grand Strategy? Power and Purpose in American Statecraft from Harry S. Truman to George W. Bush* (Ithaca: Cornell University Press, 2014), 104, 124; Wilson, *The Triumph of Improvisation*, 78; Don Oberdorfer, *From the Cold War to a New Era: The United States and the Soviet Union, 1983–1991* (Baltimore: Johns Hopkins University Press, 1998), 65–67; and Beth A. Fischer, *The Reagan Reversal: Foreign Policy and the End of the Cold War* (Columbia: University of Missouri Press, 1997), 123–31.

211. Miles, "The War Scare That Wasn't," 86–118; Miles, *Engaging the Evil Empire*, 80–82.

212. Reagan White House diary, November 18, 1983.

213. Ronald Reagan, "Statement on Soviet Union Withdrawal from the Intermediate-Range Nuclear Force Negotiations," November 23, 1983, APP, https://www.presidency.ucsb.edu /documents/statement-soviet-union-withdrawal-from-the-intermediate-range-nuclear-force -negotiations; Ronald Reagan, "Remarks and a Question-and-Answer Session with Reporters on Strategic Arms Reduction Talks," December 8, 1983, APP, https://www.presidency.ucsb .edu/documents/remarks-and-question-and-answer-session-with-reporters-strategic-arms -reduction-talks.

Chapter 4

1. Barton Gellman, "Weinberger Victorious in Oxford Debate," *Washington Post*, February 28, 1984; "The Oxford Debate That Weinberger Won," *Washington Post*, March 6, 1984. On the controversy surrounding the cancelled May 1983 debate, see also R. W. Apple Jr., "Weinberger Drops Debate at Oxford," *New York Times*, April 20, 1983.

2. "The Oxford Debate That Weinberger Won."

3. Ibid. Margaret Thatcher personally called Weinberger with the results of the vote the next morning. Weinberger, *Fighting for Peace*, 170.

4. This chapter challenges the view that Reagan shifted U.S. policy toward the Soviet Union in a conciliatory direction in 1983–84. For this "Reagan reversal" argument, see Fischer, *The Reagan Reversal*; and Donaghy, *The Second Cold War*.

5. Ray Moseley, "Nation/World: New Missile Protests in Britain: Parliament Blocked; Defense Minister Sprayed," *Chicago Tribune*, November 16, 1983.

6. Tyler Marshall, "Missile Parts Arrive at U.S. Base in Germany Despite Protesters," *Los Angeles Times*, November 27, 1983.

7. Kate Soper, "Re: New END 'Appeal,'" March 23, 1984, p. 2, END/1/12, END Collection, LSEL.

8. Editorial, *END Journal* 7 (December 1983–January 1984): 2.

9. "Transcription of Tape Recordings of E.N.D. Discussion at a Meeting in Hampstead Friends' Meeting House, 17th March, 1984, Tape One-Political Discussion, 10–12 a.m.," pp. 7, 12–13, END/1/10, Folder 1-Quarterly meetings, 1984, END Collection, LSEL.

10. Ibid., pp. 8–11.

11. Edward Thompson, "'Freeze and Withdraw': Does It Need a Political Dimension?," END/1/10, Folder 1, END Collection, LSEL. See also "Transcription of Tape Recordings of E.N.D. Discussion at a Meeting in Hampstead Friends' Meeting House, 17th March, 1984," pp. 3–6.

12. Thompson, "'Freeze and Withdraw.'"

13. "Transcription of Tape Recordings of E.N.D. Discussion at a Meeting in Hampstead Friends' Meeting House, 17th March, 1984," p. 30.

14. See, for example, Soper, "Re: New END 'Appeal,'" p. 1.

15. "Minutes Policy Group," April 13, 1984, END/1/12, END Collection, LSEL.

16. "Notes on Contributors," in *Voices from Prague: Documents on Czechoslovakia and the Peace Movement*, ed. Jan Kavan and Zdena Tomin (London: END and Palach Press, 1983), 75.

17. Charter 77, "Declaration of Charter 77," January 1, 1977, https://chnm.gmu.edu/1989/files/download/899/fullsize; Jan Kavan and Zdena Tomin, "Introduction," in Kavan and Tomin, *Voices from Prague*, 4; "Notes on Contributors," 75.

18. Dr. Jaroslav Šabata, "Letter to E. P. Thompson," April 1983, in Kavan and Tomin, *Voices from Prague*, 53, 56, 60, 67–68.

19. "Transcription of Tape Recordings of E.N.D. Discussion at a Meeting in Hampstead Friends' Meeting House, 17th March, 1984," pp. 25, 30.

20. "European Declaration of Peace," pp. 1–2, END/1/12, END Collection, LSEL.

21. "Appeal for European Nuclear Disarmament," 223–26.

22. "European Declaration of Peace," p. 3.

23. Šabata, "Letter to E. P. Thompson," April 1983, 61; "European Declaration of Peace," pp. 3–4.

24. Patrick D. M. Burke, "European Nuclear Disarmament: A Study of Transnational Social Movement Strategy" (PhD diss., University of Westminster, 2004), 80.

25. See, for example, "The END Hungary Working Group," October 1984, END/12/1, END Collection, LSEL.

26. "European Nuclear Disarmament Steering Committee—Minutes of a Meeting held on 4th June 1980," p. 2.

27. Kavan and Tomin, "Introduction," 6.

28. "Charter 77," *END Bulletin* 8 (Spring 1982): 20.

29. Bedřich Placák, Václav Malý, and Jiří Hájek, "Statement on West European Peace Movements," November 15, 1981, in Kavan and Tomin, *Voices from Prague*, 22–23.

30. Radim Palouš, Anna Marvanová, and Ladislav Lis, "Open Letter to Peace Movements," March 29, 1982, in Kavan and Tomin, *Voices from Prague*, 24, 25; Radim Palouš, Anna Marvanová, and Ladislav Lis, "Open Letter from Charter 77 to the Dutch Interchurch Peace Council (IKV)," August 27, 1982, in Kavan and Tomin, *Voices from Prague*, 26, 27.

31. Palouš, Marvanová, and Lis, "Open Letter from Charter 77," 27.

32. "Letter to the Peace and Anti-Nuclear Movements in Western Europe from the Committee of Social Resistance, Poland," May 9, 1983, reprinted in "Talking Politics with Poland," *END Journal* 7 (December 1983–January 1984): 8–9.

33. "Talking Politics with Poland," 8; "END Briefing Sheet Poland," p. 2, END/13/5, END Collection, LSEL.

34. "Peace Is Indivisible—A Statement by the Committee for Social Resistance KOS," October 20, 1983, END/13/10, Folder 1, END Collection, LSEL.

35. Ibid.

36. John Sandford, *The Sword and the Ploughshare: Autonomous Peace Initiatives in East Germany* (London: Merlin Press / European Nuclear Disarmament, 1983), 58–59, 61–62; Ken Coates and Michael Meacher, ". . . But Independent Voices Remain," *END Bulletin* 10 (July/August 1982): 20.

37. "The Berlin Appeal—Peace Without Weapons," January 25, 1982, END/11/1, Folder 1, END Collection, LSEL.

38. Sandford, *The Sword and the Ploughshare*, 58, 67.

39. Ibid., 33; "The 'Women's Letter,'" October 1982, in Sandford, *The Sword and the Ploughshare*, 97–99.

40. Jan Williams and Barbara Einhorn, "Report on the Visit to W. Berlin/E. Berlin 7–14 November 1982," END/11/1, Folder 1, END Collection, LSEL.

41. B. Einhorn, "Report on My Recent Visit to Berlin," January 5, 1984, END/11/1, Folder 1, END Collection, LSEL.

42. "Imprisoned Peace Women Released—Charges Dropped," *END Journal* 8 (February–March 1984): 5.

43. On the Soviet counterdeployments, see Dusko Doder, "Moscow to Deploy Missiles Westward," *Washington Post*, October 25, 1983.

44. Einhorn, "Report on My Recent Visit to Berlin," p. 5.

45. Edward Thompson, "European Declaration," May 18, 1984, END/1/12, END Collection, LSEL.

46. "END Declaration of Peace," *END Journal* 12 (October–November 1984): 30.

47. Letter, Václav Benda, Jiří Ruml, and Jana Sternová (spokespersons of Charter 77) to END Convention in Perugia, reprinted in *END Journal* 12 (October–November 1984): 31–32.

48. Letter, END (European Nuclear Disarmament) to Charter 77, March 1985, p. 2, END/10/1, END Collection, LSEL.

49. KOS, CODENE, Legambiente, "Beyond Yalta," July 1984, END/13/10, Folder 1, END Collection, LSEL.

50. Letter, END (European Nuclear Disarmament) to Charter 77 spokespersons Václav Benda, Jiří Ruml, Jana Sternová, November 9, 1984, END/10/1, END Collection, LSEL.

51. Letter from Peter Crampton (chair of END), January 17, 1985, END/10/1, END Collection, LSEL; "Joint Declaration of Independent Peace Defenders in the German Democratic Republic and Czechoslovakia," November 22, 1984, END/10/2, END Collection, LSEL.

52. "Demands Presented by Representatives of the European and US Peace Movements at the Start of the Geneva Talks, 12 March 1985," p. 2, folder "Geneva arms control talks, March 1985," Box 80, Series G, SANE, Inc. Collection, SCPC.

53. "Decisions Made by the Fourth National Conference of the Nuclear Weapons Freeze Campaign, December 2–4, 1983," pp. 1–2, folder "National Conference (4th Annual, Dec. 2–4, 1983), Sept.–Nov. 1983," Box 4, NNWFC Records, SHSM-SL.

54. Kehler, WGBH interview.

55. Solo, *From Protest to Policy*, 162–64; H.R.5571, 98th Cong. (1984); S.2634, 98th Cong. (1984).

56. Solo, *From Protest to Policy*, 148.

57. Ibid., 147–49.

58. "The Freeze Voter '84 Plan of Action," September 6, 1984, folder "Freeze Voter '84 program," Box 3, Series D, Freeze Voter Records, SCPC; "Freeze Voter '84 Targeting Policy and Criteria," folder "Freeze Voter '84 program," Box 3, Series D, Freeze Voter Records, SCPC.

59. David Cortright, "Where Do We Go from Here: Next Steps for the Freeze/Peace Movement," December 1, 1983, folder "Cortright, David: Strategy papers, 1982–1987," Box 75, Series G, SANE, Inc. Collection, SCPC.

60. Memorandum, Caspar Weinberger to the president, March 23, 1984, pp. 2–5, folder "NSC 00104 27 March 1984 (1/3)," Box 11, ES, NSC: Meeting Files, RRPL.

61. Memorandum, Robert C. McFarlane to the president, March 27, 1984, folder "NSC 00104 27 March 1984 (3/3)," Box 11, ES, NSC: Meeting Files, RRPL.

62. Minutes of National Security Planning Group meeting, March 27, 1984, p. 5, folder "NSC 00104 27 March 1984 (3/3)," Box 11, ES, NSC: Meeting Files, RRPL.

63. See, for example, Reagan White House diary, January 13, 1983.

64. "Mr. Minister," September 23, 1984, in *Reagan, in His Own Hand: The Writings of Ronald Reagan That Reveal His Revolutionary Vision for America*, ed. Kiron K. Skinner, Annelise Anderson, and Martin Anderson (New York: Free Press, 2001), 496–98.

65. Shultz, *Turmoil and Triumph*, 484.

66. Anatoly Dobrynin, *In Confidence: Moscow's Ambassador to America's Six Cold War Presidents (1962–1986)* (New York: Times Books, 1995), 556.

67. Shultz, *Turmoil and Triumph*, 484.

68. Bernard Gwertzman, "Gromyko Meetings End with Accord on Further Talks," *New York Times*, September 30, 1984.

69. Forsberg, WGBH interview, November 9, 1987.

70. See, for example, letter, Randall Forsberg to Walter Mondale, March 2, 1984, pp. 1–2, folder "Freeze Voter '84 program," Box 3, Series D, Freeze Voter Records, SCPC.

71. Meyer, *A Winter of Discontent*, 247–49.

72. Solo, *From Protest to Policy*, 164.

73. Meyer, *A Winter of Discontent*, 244.

74. "History of Freeze Voter '84," folder "Freeze Voter '84 program," Box 3, Series D, Freeze Voter Records, SCPC; Meyer, *A Winter of Discontent*, 245–46.

75. "Freeze Voter '84 . . . Congressional Changes 98th to 99th Congress," p. 2, folder "Freeze Voter '84 program," Box 3, Series D, Freeze Voter Records, SCPC.

76. Ronald Reagan White House diary, November 7, 1984, https://www.reaganfoundation.org/ronald-reagan/white-house-diaries/diary-entry-11071984/.

77. *Foreign Relations of the United States*, 1981–1988, vol. 4, attachment to Document 310.

78. On Chernenko's time in power, see Miles, *Engaging the Evil Empire*, 90–105, 107–8. On the "death watch," see memorandum, James W. Lucas to Robert C. McFarlane, August 30, 1984, folder "Chernenko, Konstantin Ustinovich (elected 02/13/1984) died 03/10/1985 8:30 p.m. (3)," Box 21, Jack F. Matlock Files, RRPL.

79. Ronald Reagan White House diary, November 28, 1984, https://www.reaganfoundation .org/ronald-reagan/white-house-diaries/diary-entry-11281984/.

80. Minutes of National Security Planning Group meeting, December 5, 1984, p. 3, folder "NSPG 0101 5 Dec 1984 [Arms Control]," Box 3, ES, NSC: NSPG Files, RRPL.

81. Ibid., pp. 2–4, 5.

82. Minutes of National Security Planning Group meeting, December 10, 1984, p. 2, folder "NSPG 0102 10 Dec 1984 [Arms Control] (1 of 2)," Box 3, ES, NSC: NSPG Files, RRPL.

83. NSDD 153, January 1, 1985, https://www.reaganlibrary.gov/public/archives/reference /scanned-nsdds/nsdd153.pdf.

84. Bernard Gwertzman, "U.S. and Soviet Set Talks on Missiles and Arms in Space," *New York Times*, January 9, 1985.

85. Shultz, *Turmoil and Triumph*, 523.

86. Nuclear Weapons Freeze Campaign, "1985 Strategy Paper," December 1984, pp. 3–4, 5, folder "Strategy Committee, Dec. 1984," Box 7, NNWFC Records, SHSM-SL.

87. Nuclear Weapons Freeze Campaign, "1985 Strategy Paper," pp. 6, 13–14; "Decisions Made by the Fifth National Conference of the Nuclear Weapons Freeze Campaign," December 7–9, 1984, folder "National Conference (5th Annual, Dec. 7–9, 1984), Dec. 7–9, 1984," Box 5, NNWFC Records, SHSM-SL.

88. Nuclear Weapons Freeze Campaign, "1985 Strategy Paper," pp. 4–5.

89. David Treadwell, "U.S.-Soviet Arms Talks Will Be Wide-Ranging: Gromyko, Shultz to Meet in Geneva Jan. 7–8; No Conditions Set on Nuclear and Space Issues," *Los Angeles Times*, November 23, 1984.

90. Nuclear Weapons Freeze Campaign, "1985 Strategy Paper," pp. 8–9.

91. Memorandum, Bob Stein on behalf of Illinois Freeze Campaign to Pat Harmon, Barbara Roche, January 28, 1985, p. 1, folder "Strategy Committee, 1985," Box 7, NNWFC Records, SHSM-SL.

92. Memorandum, Stein to Harmon, Roche; Letter, Randy Kehler to Bob Stein, February 5, 1985, folder "Strategy Committee, 1985," Box 7, NNWFC Records, SHSM-SL; Memorandum, Bob Stein to executive committee of National Freeze Campaign, February 8, 1985, folder "Strategy Committee, 1985," Box 7, NNWFC Records, SHSM-SL.

93. Letter, Dr. Jane Gruenebaum to George Shultz and Andrei Gromyko, March 8, 1985, folder "Geneva arms control talks, March 1985," Box 80, Series G, SANE, Inc. Collection, SCPC.

94. "Demands Presented by Representatives of the European and US Peace Movements at the Start of the Geneva Talks, 12 March 1985."

95. Draft, "Stop While We Talk: A Proposal for a National Campaign," March 21, 1985, pp. 1, 2, folder "Strategy Committee, 1985," Box 7, NNWFC Records, SHSM-SL.

96. David Foglesong has noted that freeze activists participated in U.S.-Soviet citizen exchange programs in the late 1980s, which he argued helped to reduce U.S.-Soviet hostility and end the Cold War. David Scott Foglesong, "When the Russians Really Were Coming: Citizen Diplomacy and the End of Cold War Enmity in America," *Cold War History* 20, no. 4 (2020): 419–40.

97. *Foreign Relations of the United States*, 1981–1988, vol. 5, Soviet Union, March 1985–October 1986, ed. Elizabeth C. Charles (Washington, DC: Government Publishing Office, 2020), Document 1.

98. Reagan, *An American Life*, 611.

99. Gorbachev, *Memoirs*, 28–34.

100. Mikhail Gorbachev and Zdeněk Mlynář, *Conversations with Gorbachev: On Perestroika, the Prague Spring, and the Crossroads of Socialism*, trans. George Shriver (New York: Columbia University Press, 2002), 15.

101. Gorbachev and Mlynář, *Conversations with Gorbachev*, 47–48; Gorbachev, *Memoirs*, 77–78, 102–3.

102. Gorbachev, *Memoirs*, 95–97, 165.

103. Mikhail Gorbachev, *On My Country and the World*, trans. George Shriver (New York: Columbia University Press, 2000), 177–78, 180.

104. "Record of the Meeting Between the Prime Minister and Mr. M.S. Gorbachev at Chequers on Sunday 16 December at 3.00 pm," pp. 5–6, 7.

105. "Excerpts from Speech by Gorbachev," December 19, 1984.

106. Zubok, *A Failed Empire*, 283.

107. Gorbachev, *On My Country and the World*, 180.

108. Brooks and Wohlforth, "Power, Globalization, and the End of the Cold War," 14–16, 22–23.

109. On the far-reaching influence of the Soviet military-industrial complex, see Brown, *The Gorbachev Factor*, 212.

110. Gorbachev and Mlynář, *Conversations with Gorbachev*, 143.

111. "Excerpts from Speech by Gorbachev," December 19, 1984.

112. Gorbachev, *On My Country and the World*, 185.

113. Grachev, *Gorbachev's Gamble*, 66.

114. *Foreign Relations of the United States*, 1981–1988, vol. 5, attachment to Document 10; Zubok, *A Failed Empire*, 284.

115. See, for example, *Foreign Relations of the United States*, 1981–1988, vol. 5, Document 23; *Foreign Relations of the United States*, 1981–1988, vol. 5, attachment to Document 41.

116. On the Soviets' definition of "space-strike weapons," see Aleksandr G. Savelyev and Nikolai N. Detinov, *The Big Five: Arms Control Decision-Making in the Soviet Union*, ed. Gregory Varhall, trans. Dmitriy Trenin (Westport: Praeger, 1995), 85.

117. *Foreign Relations of the United States*, 1981–1988, vol. 5, Document 23.

118. William J. Eaton, "Gorbachev Agrees to Summit: Calls 7-Month Halt to Missile Deployment," *Los Angeles Times*, April 8, 1985.

119. Seth Mydans, "Soviet to Stop Atomic Tests; It Bids U.S. Do Same," *New York Times*, July 29, 1985.

120. Grachev, *Gorbachev's Gamble*, 56–57. Matthew Evangelista has argued that the Soviets' unilateral moratorium on nuclear tests, which they observed for nineteen months, was one of the key turning points in the end of the Cold War, because it showed that "the Soviet Union would not match every US step in the arms race." It also set a precedent for on-site verification of Soviet arms control initiatives. Matthew Evangelista, "Explaining the End of the Cold War: Turning Points in Soviet Security Policy," in Njølstad, *The Last Decade of the Cold War*, 118–34, 119–22. See also Evangelista, *Unarmed Forces*, 264–88.

121. "New Directions for the Peace Movement," pp. 4, 2, folder "Cortright, David: Strategy papers, 1982–1987," Box 75, Series G, SANE, Inc. Collection, SCPC.

122. Cortright, *Peace Works*, 168–69.

123. "SANE 1985 Program Report," pp. 2–3, folder "SANE Strategy and planning, 1986," Box 20a, Series G, SANE, Inc. Collection, SCPC; "An Appeal to World Leaders," folder "Summit petition, Pittsburgh, Oct. 1985," Box 80, Series G, SANE, Inc. Collection, SCPC.

124. Prague Appeal, March 11, 1985, END/10/1, END Collection, LSEL.

125. Ibid. On the creation of the CSCE and the negotiation of the Helsinki Final Act, see Morgan, *The Final Act*.

126. Letter to the Congress of the United States, "Initiative for a Sovereign Europe," April 1985, in *Voices from the GDR: Documents on Peace, Human Rights, Ecology* (London: END, July 1987), 17, END/11/10, END Collection, LSEL. West Berlin peace activists sent a similar letter to the Supreme Soviet of the Soviet Union.

127. "To the Signatories of the 'Prague Appeal,'" June 8, 1985, in *Voices from the GDR*, 49–50.

128. "Polish Peace Movement 'Freedom and Peace': A Conversation with Founding Member, Jacek Czaputowicz," *Uncensored Poland*, December 1985, p. 38, END/13/11, END Collection, LSEL; "Founding Declaration of the 'Freedom and Peace' Movement," April 14, 1985, END/13/1, END Collection, LSEL.

129. "Letter from the 'Freedom and Peace' Movement to Conference Participants in Amsterdam (July 1985)," END/13/9, END Collection, LSEL.

130. "Draft Statement on the Prague Appeal for CC 7th June 1985," END/10/3, END Collection, LSEL.

131. Many of these East European proposals were actually written as letters to the 1985 END Convention. See, for example, the Prague Appeal and WiP's letter to the convention.

132. Paul Anderson, "Notes of Two Meetings with Members of Independent Peace Groups, East Berlin," February 1985, END/11/2, END Collection, LSEL; Paul Anderson, "Report of Visit to Hungary," March 4, 1985, END/12/6, END Collection, LSEL; Clare Benjamin and Margaretta Jolly, "Notes from Visit to Budapest 27 March–8 April '85," END/12/6, END Collection, LSEL; Mary Kaldor, "Report on Hungary Trip," May 10, 1985, END/12/6, END Collection, LSEL; Mark Salter, "END Report on Visit to Poland September 1985," October 1985, END/13/6, END Collection, LSEL.

133. Anderson, "Report of Visit to Hungary," pp. 1–2.

134. "Letter from the 'Freedom and Peace' Movement to Conference Participants in Amsterdam (July 1985)."

135. Serge Schmemann, "Gromyko Made Soviet President by Gorbachev: Gromyko Made Soviet President as Gorbachev Forgoes the Title," *New York Times*, July 3, 1985.

136. Gorbachev, *Memoirs*, 179–80.

137. Eduard Shevardnadze, *The Future Belongs to Freedom*, trans. Catherine A. Fitzpatrick (New York: Free Press, 1991), 38.

138. Shevardnadze, *The Future Belongs to Freedom*, 23–26; Gorbachev, *Memoirs*, 180.

139. Reagan, *An American Life*, 635; Gorbachev, *Memoirs*, 405.

140. Memorandum of conversation, first private meeting, November 19, 1985, 10:20–11:20 a.m., pp. 2, 4, NSAEBB No. 172, "To the Geneva Summit," https://nsarchive2.gwu.edu/NSAEBB/NSAEBB172/Doc15.pdf.

141. Cortright, *Peace Works*, 170–72.

142. "Rough Notes of Meeting with Mikhail Gorbachev, Soviet Embassy, Geneva, November 19, 12:45–1:30 p.m.," folder "Geneva Summit: Rough Notes, Nov. 1985," Box 80, Series G, SANE, Inc. Collection, SCPC.

143. Cortright, *Peace Works*, 172–73.

144. Note, Bob McManis to Dr. Keyworth, October 18, 1985, folder "Nuclear Freeze (7)," RAC Box 10, George Keyworth Files, RRPL; Memorandum, Smith & Harroff, Inc. to our clients, October 15, 1985, folder, "Nuclear Freeze (7)," RAC Box 10, George Keyworth Files, RRPL.

145. Memorandum of conversation, second plenary meeting, November 19, 1985, 2:30–3:40 p.m., pp. 4–5, NSAEBB No. 172, https://nsarchive2.gwu.edu/NSAEBB/NSAEBB172/Doc17.pdf.

146. Memorandum of conversation, second private meeting, November 19, 1985, 3:40–4:45 p.m., pp. 5, 2, NSAEBB No. 172, https://nsarchive2.gwu.edu/NSAEBB/NSAEBB172/Doc19.pdf.

147. Memorandum of conversation, third plenary meeting, November 20, 1985, 11:30 a.m.–12:40 p.m., p. 6, NSAEBB No. 172, https://nsarchive2.gwu.edu/NSAEBB/NSAEBB172/Doc21.pdf.

148. Memorandum of conversation, second private meeting, November 19, 1985, p. 7.

149. Memorandum of conversation, dinner hosted by President and Mrs. Reagan, November 20, 1985, 8:00–10:30 p.m., pp. 3–4, NSAEBB No. 172, https://nsarchive2.gwu.edu/NSAEBB/NSAEBB172/Doc24.pdf.

150. "Joint Soviet–United States Statement on the Summit Meeting in Geneva," November 21, 1985, https://www.reaganlibrary.gov/archives/speech/joint-soviet-united-states-statement-summit-meeting-geneva.

Chapter 5

1. On Hofdi House, see Ken Adelman, *Reagan at Reykjavik: Forty-Eight Hours That Ended the Cold War* (New York: Broadside Books, 2014), 52–54.

2. *Foreign Relations of the United States*, 1981–1988, vol. 5, Document 280.

3. Memorandum of conversation, final meeting, October 12, 1986, p. 5.

4. The Soviets wanted to abolish "strategic offensive arms," meaning ICBMs, SLBMs, and strategic bombers. The Americans proposed eliminating "offensive ballistic missiles," which covered ICBMs, SLBMs, and short-range ballistic missiles. Both sides agreed that medium-range ballistic missiles would be eliminated under a separate INF Treaty. Ibid., pp. 9–11.

5. Ibid., p. 11.

6. Ibid., pp. 11–16.

7. Reagan, *An American Life*, 679.

8. Mary Kaldor, "Nice Smiles," *END Journal* 19 (December 1985–January 1986): 2, 27; Jamie Dettmer and Paul Anderson, "Little Joy at Geneva," *END Journal* 19 (December 1985–January 1986): 4–5.

9. Dettmer and Anderson, "Little Joy at Geneva," 4.

10. Ibid., 4–5.

11. John Tagliabue, "Upheaval in the East; Prague's Velvet Revolutionaries Recall John Lennon," *New York Times*, December 9, 1989.

12. Charter 77 Document No. 7/86: Space for the Younger Generation, March 6, 1986, p. 1, END/10/1, END Collection, LSEL; Milan Hauner, "Anti-militarism and the Independent Peace Movement in Czechoslovakia," in *In Search of Civil Society: Independent Peace Movements in the Soviet Bloc*, ed. Vladimir Tismaneanu (New York: Routledge, 1990), 88–117, 92.

13. Mary Kaldor, Bob Borosage, Mario Pianta, Judith Winther, Sheena Phillips, Pedro Vilanova, and Albert Statz, "How to Go Beyond Nato," *END Journal* 19 (December 1985–January 1986): 18–20.

14. See, for example, "Trust Group Faces KGB Harassment," *END Journal* 18 (October–November 1985): 3; "KGB Abducts Conscientious Objector," *END Journal* 19 (December 1985–January 1986): 12.

15. The Group to Establish Trust Between the USSR and the USA, "Appeal to the Governments and Publics of the USSR and the USA," June 4, 1982, END/14/2, END Collection, LSEL.

16. See, for example, "Polish Groups Risk Harassment," *END Journal* 19 (December 1985–January 1986): 11.

17. "Trust Group Faces KGB Harassment," 3.

18. Memorandum of conversation, dinner hosted by President and Mrs. Reagan, November 20, 1985, p. 3; *Foreign Relations of the United States*, 1981–1988, vol. 5, Document 166; *Foreign Relations of the United States*, 1981–1988, vol. 5, Document 172.

19. "Conference at the CC CPSU on preparation for the XXVII Congress of the CPSU," November 28, 1985, p. 1, NSAEBB No. 172, https://nsarchive2.gwu.edu/NSAEBB/NSAEBB172/Doc27.pdf.

20. John Newhouse, *War and Peace in the Nuclear Age* (New York: Knopf, 1989), 387.

21. Grachev, *Gorbachev's Gamble*, 66.

22. Gorbachev, *Memoirs*, 411.

23. Richard Rhodes, *Arsenals of Folly: The Making of the Nuclear Arms Race* (New York: Knopf, 2007), 213–14.

24. On the Big Five and the Little Five, see Savelyev and Detinov, *The Big Five*.

25. Dobrynin, *In Confidence*, 596.

26. Savelyev and Detinov, *The Big Five*, 92; Grachev, *Gorbachev's Gamble*, 68–69.

27. S. F. Akhromeyev and G. M. Kornienko, *Glazami marshala i diplomata: Kriticheskii vzgliad na vneshniuiu politiku SSSR do i posle 1985 goda* (Moscow: Mezhdunarodnye otnosheniia, 1992), 87–88.

28. Rhodes, *Arsenals of Folly*, 214.

29. Savelyev and Detinov, *The Big Five*, 92–93; Rhodes, *Arsenals of Folly*, 214–15.

30. *Foreign Relations of the United States*, 1981–1988, vol. 5, attachment to Document 177; Gorbachev statement on disarmament, January 16, 1986.

31. *Foreign Relations of the United States*, 1981–1988, vol. 5, attachment to Document 177.

32. Gorbachev statement on disarmament, January 16, 1986.

33. Ibid.

34. Ibid.

35. "Appeal for European Nuclear Disarmament," 224.

36. Editorial, *END Journal* 7, 2.

37. E. P. T., "There Appear Now to Be Three Lines of Approach to a New 'Appeal' or Programme," END/1/12, END Collection, LSEL.

38. Mary Kaldor, Pam Solo, and Eric Alfsen, "Freeze and Withdrawal," *END Journal* 13 (December 1984–January 1985): 32–33.

39. Tair Tairov, "From New Thinking to a Civic Peace," in *Europe from Below: An East-West Dialogue*, ed. Mary Kaldor (London: Verso, 1991), 43–48, 45.

40. Ibid., 45–46.

41. Letter from Yuri Zhukov, December 2, 1982, p. 4.

42. Letter, Meg Beresford (on behalf of the END Co-ordinating Committee) to Yuri Zhukov, January 1983, pp. 2, 1, END/14/23, Folder 3, END Collection, LSEL.

43. Mary Kaldor, "Impressions of Two Meetings with the Soviet Peace Committee," December 2, 1983, pp. 1, 3, END/14/2, END Collection, LSEL.

44. The Soviet Peace Committee representatives attended the END Convention as observers rather than delegates because they refused to sign the 1980 END Appeal, which contended that both the United States and the Soviet Union bore responsibility for the nuclear arms race. Wittner, *Toward Nuclear Abolition*, 250–51.

45. Tairov specifically singled out Zhukov and Soviet Peace Committee secretary Grigory Lokshin as viewing END this way. Tairov, "From New Thinking to a Civic Peace," 45.

46. "Excerpts from March 1986 Letters by Yury Medvedkov, Moscow," p. 6, END/14/3, Folder 2, END Collection, LSEL.

47. Alexei Pankin, "Soviet 'New Thinking,'" Ideas of 1989 Lecture Series (London School of Economics and Political Science, November 3, 1999).

48. "Statement by the Soviet Peace Committee," January 16, 1986, p. 1, END/14/18, END Collection, LSEL.

49. Letter from Yuri Zhukov, January 20, 1986, END/14/18, END Collection, LSEL.

50. Mary Kaldor, "An Offer We Can't Refuse?," *END Journal* 20 (February–March 1986): 7–8.

51. Memorandum, John M. Poindexter to the president, February 1, 1986, folder "NSDD 214/NSDD 210 (Part 1)—Reacting to Gorbachev January 1986 Proposal–February 1986 (5 of 12)," RAC Box 8, Robert E. Linhard Files, RRPL.

52. "Responding to Gorbachev's January Proposals," February 1, 1986, p. 2, folder "NSDD 214/NSDD 210 (Part 1)—Reacting to Gorbachev January 1986 Proposal–February 1986 (5 of 12)," RAC Box 8, Robert E. Linhard Files, RRPL.

53. Ronald Reagan White House diary, January 15, 1986, https://www.reaganfoundation.org/ronald-reagan/white-house-diaries/diary-entry-01151986/.

54. "Responding to Gorbachev's January Proposals."

55. Minutes of National Security Planning Group meeting, February 3, 1986, pp. 5, 3, 6, folder "NSPG 0127 02/03/1986 [Arms Control/Gorbachev] (2 of 2)," Box 4, ES, NSC: NSPG Files, RRPL.

56. NSDD 210, February 4, 1986, p. 2, https://www.reaganlibrary.gov/public/archives/reference/scanned-nsdds/nsdd210.pdf. Although NSDD 210 was issued prior to consultations with the allies on Gorbachev's proposals, NSDD 214 affirmed all of its decisions except those pertaining to INF. NSDD 214, February 21, 1986, p. 1, https://www.reaganlibrary.gov/public/archives/reference/scanned-nsdds/nsdd214.pdf.

57. NSDD 210, pp. 1–2.

58. On the mobility of SS-20s in Asia and U.S. officials' fear that they could be moved to target West European cities, see, for example, minutes of National Security Planning Group meeting, February 3, 1986, p. 2.

59. NSDD 214, p. 1.

60. Ronald Reagan, "Statement on the Soviet-United States Nuclear and Space Arms Negotiations," February 24, 1986, APP, https://www.presidency.ucsb.edu/documents/statement-the-soviet-united-states-nuclear-and-space-arms-negotiations-5.

61. On 1986 as the "International Year of Peace," see General Assembly resolution 37/16, *International Year of Peace*, A/RES/37/16 (November 16, 1982), https://undocs.org/en/A/RES/37/16.

62. Rainer Eppelmann, Peter Grimm, Ralf Hirsch, and Wolfgang Templin, "There Must Be Freedom of Movement for All Citizens," January 24, 1986, in *Voices from the GDR*, 5, 24–25.

63. "Introduction," in *Voices from the GDR*, 3.

64. "To the Party: Petition, 2/4/86 (Excerpt)," in *Voices from the GDR*, 4, 15.

65. Ibid., 15–16.

66. "GDR Peaceniks Demand Rights," *END Journal* 22–23 (Summer 1986): 5; "Notes on the Texts," in *Voices from the GDR*, 4.

67. Charter 77 Document No. 7/86: Space for the Younger Generation, pp. 1–3.

68. "END Briefing Sheet: Czechoslovakia and Peace," February 1987, pp. 4–5, END/10/1, END Collection, LSEL.

69. On the Jazz Section, see Peter Bugge, "Normalization and the Limits of the Law: The Case of the Czech Jazz Section," *East European Politics and Societies* 22, no. 2 (Spring 2008): 282–318.

70. Charter 77 Document No. 7/86: Space for the Younger Generation, p. 4.

71. Ibid., pp. 4–5.

72. Ibid., pp. 5–8.

73. Judith Eversley, "Meeting of the END Czech Working Group, Tuesday 3rd June 1986," June 4, 1986, p. 2, END/10/1, END Collection, LSEL.

74. See, for example, "Moscow Trust Group Faces Continuing Harassment," *END Journal* 20 (February–March 1986): 6; "Trust Group Under Pressure," *END Journal* 21 (April–May 1986): 5; "Shatravka Released—but Repression Continues," *END Journal* 22–23 (Summer 1986): 6.

75. "Polish Peaceniks Held," *END Journal* 21 (April–May 1986): 3.

76. "Shatravka Released," 6.

77. "Moscow Trust Group Faces Continuing Harassment," 6.

78. Jan Kavan, "Helsinki: An Assessment by East-West Independents—Introduction," *East European Reporter* 2, no. 1 (Spring 1986): 23–24.

79. "A Statement of Views of Some Signatories of Charter 77 Submitted to the Milan Forum," April 1986, *East European Reporter* 2, no. 1 (Spring 1986): 25–27.

80. "Excerpts from Speech by Gorbachev," December 19, 1984.

81. Marie-Pierre Rey, "'Europe Is Our Common Home': A Study of Gorbachev's Diplomatic Concept," *Cold War History* 4, no. 2 (January 2004): 34.

82. Mikhail Gorbachev, "Address on French Television," September 30, 1985, in Gorbachev, *A Time for Peace*, 248.

83. Gorbachev, "Address to French Parliamentarians," 270–74.

84. Ibid., 272.

85. Mikhail Gorbachev, "Joint Press Conference with François Mitterrand in Paris," October 4, 1985, in Gorbachev, *A Time for Peace*, 287; Gorbachev, "Address to French Parliamentarians," 272.

86. Gorbachev, "Address to French Parliamentarians," 272–74.

87. "Appeal for European Nuclear Disarmament," 224.

88. "Transcription of Tape Recordings of E.N.D. Discussion at a Meeting in Hampstead Friends' Meeting House, 17th March, 1984," pp. 8–9.

89. See, for example, Gorbachev, "Address on French Television," 248.

90. Ibid., 241–42.

91. Gorbachev, "Address to French Parliamentarians," 266.

92. Tairov, "From New Thinking to Civic Peace," 45, 44.

93. "Excerpts from March 1986 Letters by Yury Medvedkov, Moscow," p. 6.

94. Letter, END (European Nuclear Disarmament) to Charter 77, March 1985, p. 2.

95. Pankin, "Soviet 'New Thinking.'"

96. Gorbachev, "Address to French Parliamentarians," 275.

97. Rey, "'Europe Is Our Common Home,'" 51, 53.

98. "Political Report of the CPSU Central Committee to the 27th Congress of the Communist Party of the Soviet Union," delivered by Mikhail Gorbachev, general secretary of the CPSU Central Committee, February 25, 1986, in Mikhail S. Gorbachev, *Political Report of the CPSU Central Committee to the 27th Party Congress* (Moscow: Novosti Press Agency Publishing House, 1986), 88, 94–95.

99. Gorbachev, *Memoirs*, 428–29.

100. "Political Report of the CPSU Central Committee to the 27th Congress," 83, 26.

101. Speech by Mikhail Gorbachev to Ministry of Foreign Affairs, May 28, 1986, in Savranskaya et al., *Masterpieces of History*, 224.

102. Notes of CC CPSU Politburo session, July 3, 1986, in Savranskaya et al., *Masterpieces of History*, 234.

103. On Gorbachev's views on economic support for Eastern Europe and the CMEA in 1985–86, see Svetlana Savranskaya, "The Logic of 1989: The Soviet Peaceful Withdrawal from Eastern Europe," in Savranskaya et al., *Masterpieces of History*, 1–47, 14–16.

104. Speech by Mikhail Gorbachev to Ministry of Foreign Affairs, 224.

105. Savranskaya, "The Logic of 1989," 15, 16.

106. Notes of CC CPSU Politburo session, June 13, 1986, in Savranskaya et al., *Masterpieces of History*, 229.

107. Ibid., 228.

108. Memorandum from Mikhail Gorbachev to the CC CPSU Politburo on topical questions regarding collaboration with socialist countries, June 26, 1986, in Savranskaya et al., *Masterpieces of History*, 232–33.

109. Grachev, *Gorbachev's Gamble*, 66.

110. On the Chernobyl disaster, see Serhii Plokhy, *Chernobyl: The History of a Nuclear Catastrophe* (New York: Basic Books, 2018). See p. xii for quote. For the evacuation number, see Kate Brown, *Manual for Survival: A Chernobyl Guide to the Future* (New York: Norton, 2019), 7.

111. Brown, *Manual for Survival*, 310.

112. Grachev, *Gorbachev's Gamble*, 80–81.

113. *Foreign Relations of the United States*, 1981–1988, vol. 5, Document 280.

114. Shultz, *Turmoil and Triumph*, 728.

115. Gorbachev, *Memoirs*, 414.

116. Shultz, *Turmoil and Triumph*, 743.

117. "Statement by Secretary of State George P. Shultz and Remarks by the President on Soviet-United States Relations," September 30, 1986, APP, https://www.presidency.ucsb.edu/documents/statement-secretary-state-george-p-shultz-and-remarks-the-president-soviet-united-states.

118. Anatoly Chernyaev's notes, "Gorbachev's Instructions to the Reykjavik Preparation Group," October 4, 1986, p. 1, NSAEBB No. 203, https://nsarchive2.gwu.edu/NSAEBB/NSAEBB203/Document05.pdf.

119. "Osnovnyye pozitsii," p. 1, Box 4, folder 12 "Major issues for the meetings of the General Secretary of the CPSU Central Committee Mikhail Gorbachev with President of the

United States Ronald Reagan on the question of nuclear disarmament, 1986 October," Vitalii Leonidovich Kataev Papers, Hoover Institution Archives.

120. Anatoly Chernyaev's notes, "Gorbachev's Instructions to the Reykjavik Preparation Group," p. 4.

121. Ibid., p. 1.

122. See, for example, "Postanovleniye TsK KPSS o Vozmozhnykh Pozitsiyakh na Vstreche s Prezidentom Reyganom v Reyk'yavike," October 1986, Box 4, folder 11 "Thoughts for the meeting with Ronald Reagan, 1986 October," Vitalii Leonidovich Kataev Papers, Hoover Institution Archives.

123. Memorandum, George P. Shultz to the president, October 2, 1986, p. 1, NSAEBB No. 203, https://nsarchive2.gwu.edu/NSAEBB/NSAEBB203/Document04.pdf.

124. "Guidance for Reykjavik Preparatory Meeting to Help Focus Development of Briefing Material," folder "Reykjavik (4 of 4)," RAC Box 12, NSC: European and Soviet Affairs Directorate Records, RRPL.

125. For background on the U.S. and Soviet positions on START, INF, and defense and space on the eve of the Reykjavik summit, see "President Reagan's Trip to Reykjavik, October 10–12, 1986, Background Book," folder "Reykjavik (2 of 4)," RAC Box 12, NSC: European and Soviet Affairs Directorate Records, RRPL.

126. Minutes of National Security Planning Group meeting, June 6, 1986, p. 2, folder "NSPG 0134 06/06/1986 (2)," Box 4, ES, NSC: NSPG Files, RRPL.

127. Minutes of National Security Planning Group meeting, June 12, 1986, pp. 2, 3, folder "NSPG 0135 12 Jun 1986," Box 4, ES, NSC: NSPG Files, RRPL.

128. *Foreign Relations of the United States*, 1981–1988, vol. 5, Document 254.

129. Ronald Reagan White House diary, July 18, 1986, https://www.reaganfoundation.org/ronald-reagan/white-house-diaries/diary-entry-07181986/.

130. "Reagan-Gorbachev Preparatory Meeting—First Day," p. 1, folder "Reykjavik (3 of 4)," RAC Box 12, NSC: European and Soviet Affairs Directorate Records, RRPL.

131. Reagan, *An American Life*, 675.

132. Adelman, *Reagan at Reykjavik*, 1.

133. Memorandum of conversation, first meeting, October 11, 1986, pp. 4–5, 3, 5–6.

134. Shultz, *Turmoil and Triumph*, 760.

135. Memorandum of conversation, third meeting, October 12, 1986, 10:00 a.m.–1:35 p.m., pp. 7–8, NSAEBB No. 203, https://nsarchive2.gwu.edu/NSAEBB/NSAEBB203/Document13.pdf.

136. Memorandum of conversation, final meeting, October 12, 1986, pp. 1, 9–11.

137. Ibid., pp. 11–16.

138. "Transcript of Gorbachev-Reagan Reykjavik Talks: Part 4," October 12, 1986, published in FBIS-USR-93-121, September 20, 1993, p. 8, NSAEBB No. 203, https://nsarchive2.gwu.edu/NSAEBB/NSAEBB203/Document16.pdf.

139. "Update: Reagan Gorbachev Iceland Summit," NBC News, October 12, 1986, Vanderbilt Television News Archive, http://tvnews.vanderbilt.edu/program.pl?ID=891385; Frances Fitzgerald, *Way Out There in the Blue: Reagan, Star Wars, and the End of the Cold War* (New York: Simon and Schuster, 2000), 348.

140. Gorbachev, *Memoirs*, 419.

141. Mikhail Gorbachev, "Press Conference, Reykjavik, Iceland, October 12, 1986," in Mikhail S. Gorbachev, *Toward a Better World* (New York: Richardson and Steirman, 1987), 32, 35.

142. Gorbachev, *Memoirs*, 419.

Chapter 6

1. PBS, *American Experience*, "Reagan."

2. James Kuhn, interview by Stephen F. Knott and Darby Morrisroe, Miller Center Ronald Reagan Oral History Project, March 7, 2003, https://millercenter.org/the-presidency/presidential-oral-histories/james-kuhn-oral-history.

3. Ibid.

4. Ronald Reagan White House diary, October 12, 1986, https://www.reaganfoundation.org/ronald-reagan/white-house-diaries/diary-entry-10121986/.

5. Anatoly Chernyaev's notes, "Gorbachev's thoughts on Reykjavik (views expressed on the return flight, and upon arrival in Moscow)," October 12, 1986, NSAEBB No. 203, https://nsarchive2.gwu.edu/NSAEBB/NSAEBB203/Document19.pdf.

6. Jonathan Hunt and David Reynolds have also contended that Reagan's hardline advisors thwarted compromises on START and SDI after the Reykjavik summit, but they do not consider the impact that this had on Gorbachev's vision for ending the Cold War. Grassroots peace activists are not key players in their account of Reagan and Gorbachev's efforts to reduce superpower tensions. Jonathan Hunt and David Reynolds, "Geneva, Reykjavik, Washington, and Moscow, 1985–8," in *Transcending the Cold War: Summits, Statecraft, and the Dissolution of Bipolarity in Europe, 1970–1990*, ed. Kristina Spohr and David Reynolds (New York: Oxford University Press, 2016), 151–79.

7. "Press Briefing by Admiral John M. Poindexter, National Security Advisor," October 13, 1986, 4:05 p.m., folder "Reykjavik Briefings: Memo Eliminating Nuclear Weapons (1 of 5)," RAC Box 3, Alton Keel Files, RRPL; "Briefing by Mr. Richard N. Perle, ASD/ISP at the Pentagon," October 14, 1986, 11:30 a.m., folder "Reykjavik Briefings: Memo Eliminating Nuclear Weapons (2 of 5)," RAC Box 3, Alton Keel Files, RRPL; "Background Briefing by Senior Administration Officials (Brussels Enroute Andrews AFB)," October 13, 1986, pp. 12–15, folder "Summits-1986, Reykjavik, Iceland," Box I:161, Paul H. Nitze Papers, Manuscript Division, Library of Congress.

8. Ronald Reagan, "Good Evening, I'm Sure Most If Not All of You Know I'm Just Back from Iceland," pp. 4–5, Folder 496 (10/10/86–10/13/86), Box 25, Presidential Handwriting File Series III: Presidential Speeches 7/25/86–10/31/86, RRPL.

9. Ronald Reagan, "Address to the Nation on the Meetings with Soviet General Secretary Gorbachev in Iceland," October 13, 1986, APP, https://www.presidency.ucsb.edu/documents/address-the-nation-the-meetings-with-soviet-general-secretary-gorbachev-iceland.

10. Press briefing by Senators Robert Dole, Richard Lugar, Robert Byrd, Sam Nunn, and Congressman Robert Michel, October 14, 1986, p. 2, folder "[Reading File for Regan/Iceland Summit], 2 of 5," Box 5, Donald T. Regan Files, Series I: Subject File, RRPL.

11. Talking points on the question of whether Reagan proposed the elimination of all ballistic missiles or all nuclear weapons at Reykjavik, October 16, 1986, folder "[Reading File for Regan/Iceland Summit], 2 of 5," Box 5, Donald T. Regan Files, Series I: Subject File, RRPL. Emphasis added.

12. Memorandum, John M. Poindexter to the president, October 16, 1986, pp. 1, 3–6, folder "Reykjavik Briefings: Memo Eliminating Nuclear Weapons (4 of 5)," RAC Box 3, Alton Keel Files, RRPL.

13. NSDD 249, attachment 6—Defense and Space Instructions of October 27, 1986, p. 1, https://reaganlibrary.archives.gov/archives/reference/Scanned%20NSDDS/NSDD249.pdf.

14. Mikhail Gorbachev, "The Impact of the Meeting in Iceland with President Reagan, Moscow, October 22, 1986," in Gorbachev, *Toward a Better World*, 76.

15. Neil A. Lewis, "U.S. Says Russians Violate Diplomacy by Quoting Talks," *New York Times*, October 27, 1986.

16. Anatoly Chernyaev, "Notes from the Politburo Session," October 30, 1986, p. 4, NSAEBB No. 203, https://nsarchive2.gwu.edu/NSAEBB/NSAEBB203/Document23.pdf.

17. NSDD 250, November 3, 1986, p. 9, https://reaganlibrary.archives.gov/archives/reference/Scanned%20NSDDS/NSDD250.pdf.

18. Minutes of JCS meeting with the president, December 19, 1986, pp. 2–4, folder "JCS Response-NSDD 250, 12/19/1986 (1 of 4)," RAC Box 12, Robert Linhard Files, RRPL.

19. Ibid., pp. 3–4.

20. Memorandum, Alton Keel for the president to the secretary of defense and the chairman, Joint Chiefs of Staff, December 29, 1986, folder "JCS Response-NSDD 250, 12/19/1986 (1 of 4)," RAC Box 12, Robert Linhard Files, RRPL.

21. Memorandum, Robert M. Gates to the Honorable Frank C. Carlucci, January 15, 1987, folder "JCS Response to NSDD-250 Re: ICBMs (2)," Box 91729, Michael Donley Files, RRPL.

22. Executive summary, JCS response to NSDD 250, p. ES-1, ES-5, folder "JCS Response-NSDD 250, 12/19/1986 (1 of 4)," RAC Box 12, Robert Linhard Files, RRPL.

23. On the Iran-Contra scandal, see Malcolm Byrne, *Iran-Contra: Reagan's Scandal and the Unchecked Abuse of Presidential Power* (Lawrence: University Press of Kansas, 2014). For quotes, see Ronald Reagan, "Address to the Nation on the Iran Arms and Contra Aid Controversy," November 13, 1986, APP, https://www.presidency.ucsb.edu/documents/address-the-nation-the-iran-arms-and-contra-aid-controversy; and Ronald Reagan, "Remarks Announcing the Review of the National Security Council's Role in the Iran Arms and Contra Aid Controversy," November 25, 1986, APP, https://www.presidency.ucsb.edu/documents/remarks-announcing-the-review-the-national-security-councils-role-the-iran-arms-and-contra. On the war in Nicaragua, see Hal Brands, *Latin America's Cold War* (Cambridge: Harvard University Press, 2010), ch. 7; and Odd Arne Westad, *The Global Cold War: Third World Interventions and the Making of Our Times* (New York: Cambridge University Press, 2005), 339–48, 394–95.

24. Ronald Reagan, "Statement on the Special Review Board for the National Security Council," November 26, 1986, APP, https://www.presidency.ucsb.edu/documents/statement-the-special-review-board-for-the-national-security-council.

25. Byrne, *Iran-Contra*, 279–330.

26. "Excerpts from the Tower Commission's Report," February 26, 1987, APP, https://www.presidency.ucsb.edu/documents/excerpts-from-the-tower-commission-report.

27. On McFarlane's secret mission to Iran in May 1986, see Byrne, *Iran-Contra*, 194–207.

28. Anatoly Chernyaev, "Notes from the Conference with Politburo Members and Secretaries of the Central Committee," December 1, 1986, NSAEBB No. 203, https://nsarchive2.gwu.edu/NSAEBB/NSAEBB203/Document28.pdf.

29. "Campaign for Nuclear Disarmament, CND Working Visit to Moscow, 2–9 December 1986," pp. 1–3, END/14/3, Folder 1, END Collection, LSEL.

30. Joan Ruddock, "Visit to Moscow, Dec. 2nd–9th," *Sanity*, February 1987, p. 28, END/14/23, Folder 2, END Collection, LSEL.

31. "CND Working Visit to Moscow, 2–9 December 1986," pp. 5–6.

32. Ruddock, "Visit to Moscow, Dec. 2nd–9th," p. 28.

33. "CND Working Visit to Moscow, 2–9 December 1986," pp. 2–3, 4–5.

34. Mary Kaldor, "The Nearly Men," *END Journal* 25 (December 1986–January 1987): 2, 28.

35. Pankin, "Soviet 'New Thinking.'"

36. Andrei Sakharov, *Moscow and Beyond: 1986 to 1989*, trans. Antonia Bouis (New York: Knopf, 1991), 3.

37. Ibid., 15–17.

38. Dusko Doder and Louise Branson, *Gorbachev: Heretic in the Kremlin* (New York: Viking, 1990), 209–10.

39. Mikhail Gorbachev, *For the Sake of Preserving Human Civilization: Speech Before the Participants in the International Forum "For a Nuclear-Free World, for the Survival of Humanity,"* *Moscow, February 16, 1987* (Moscow: Novosti Press Agency Publishing House, 1987).

40. Sakharov, *Moscow and Beyond*, 21–24.

41. Evangelista, *Unarmed Forces*, 329. Evangelista has argued that the Moscow forum and Sakharov's statements played a vital role in convincing Gorbachev to pursue a separate INF agreement. As this book demonstrates, however, these were not the only channels through which peace activists pressed Soviet officials to untie the Reykjavik package.

42. Mikhail Gorbachev, *Perestroika: New Thinking for Our Country and the World* (New York: Harper and Row, 1987), 244–45.

43. Politburo session (excerpt), February 26, 1987, p. 1, NSAEBB No. 238, "The INF Treaty and the Washington Summit: 20 Years Later," https://nsarchive2.gwu.edu/NSAEBB /NSAEBB238/russian/Final1987-02-26%20Politburo.pdf.

44. Bill Keller, "Moscow, in Reversal, Urges Agreement 'Without Delay' to Limit Missiles in Europe," *New York Times*, March 1, 1987.

45. Politburo session (excerpt), February 26, 1987.

46. "For a Democratic Peace in Europe: A Memorandum to Citizens, Groups and Govern-ments of All CSCE Countries," *East European Reporter* 2, no. 2 (1986): 55.

47. Ibid., 54–59.

48. Ibid., 54–56.

49. Ibid., 59.

50. Politburo session (excerpt), February 26, 1987, p. 2.

51. Gorbachev, *Memoirs*, 437, 431.

52. Mikhail Gorbachev, *For a "Common European Home," for a New Way of Thinking: Speech by the General Secretary of the CPSU Central Committee at the Czechoslovak-Soviet Friendship Meeting, Prague, April 10, 1987* (Moscow: Novosti Press Agency Publishing House, 1987), 21–24. Tactical nuclear weapons, also known as short-range nuclear forces, typically have a range of less than five hundred kilometers.

53. Ibid., 28–30.

54. Ibid., 16–17.

55. Ibid., 24–26, 31.

56. Wilson, *The Triumph of Improvisation*, 117–18.

57. Chernyaev, "Notes from the Politburo Session," October 30, 1986, pp. 1–2.

58. Notes of CC CPSU Politburo session, January 29, 1987, in Savranskaya et al., *Master-pieces of History*, 242.

59. Notes of CC CPSU Politburo session, March 10, 1988, in Savranskaya et al., *Masterpieces of History*, 265–66.

60. Ibid., 265.

61. Shultz, *Turmoil and Triumph*, 890.

62. "Memorandum of Conversation between M. S. Gorbachev and U.S. Secretary of State George Shultz," April 14, 1987, pp. 1–3, NSAEBB No. 238, https://nsarchive2.gwu.edu/NSAEBB /NSAEBB238/russian/Final1987-04-14%20Gorbachev-Shultz.pdf.

63. Ibid., pp. 3–4.

64. Shultz, *Turmoil and Triumph*, 891.

65. "Memorandum of Conversation between M. S. Gorbachev and U.S. Secretary of State George Shultz," April 14, 1987, p. 4.

66. Ibid., pp. 6–7.

67. Shultz, *Turmoil and Triumph*, 894.

68. Politburo session, April 16, 1987, pp. 1–2, NSAEBB No. 238, https://nsarchive2.gwu.edu /NSAEBB/NSAEBB238/russian/Final1987-04-16%20Politburo.pdf.

69. NSDD 271, attachment 2, May 7, 1987, https://reaganlibrary.archives.gov/archives /reference/Scanned%20NSDDS/NSDD271.pdf.

70. NSDD 271, attachment 4, May 7, 1987, https://reaganlibrary.archives.gov/archives /reference/Scanned%20NSDDS/NSDD271.pdf.

71. NATO, "Statement on the Ministerial Meeting of the North Atlantic Council," Reykjavik, June 11–12, 1987, https://www.nato.int/docu/comm/49-95/c870612a.htm; Philip Taubman, "Americans Hopeful: Absence of Conditions in Remarks Said to Give Improved Outlook," *New York Times*, July 23, 1987.

72. *Foreign Relations of the United States*, 1981–1988, vol. 6, Soviet Union, October 1986– January 1989, ed. James Graham Wilson (Washington, DC: Government Publishing Office, 2016), Document 64.

73. Minutes of National Security Planning Group meeting, September 8, 1987, pp. 4–8, folder "NSPG 0165 09/08/1987 [Arms Control/Shevardnadze Visit]," Box 5, ES, NSC: NSPG Files, RRPL.

74. Ibid., p. 8.

75. Ibid., pp. 8–9.

76. Ibid., pp. 9–11.

77. "Joint Statement," September 18, 1987, folder "Shultz-Shevardnadze Meetings [09/18/1987] (2 of 2)," RAC Box 17, Robert Linhard Files, RRPL.

78. "Press Points Shevardnadze Visit," September 17, 1987, p. 4, folder "Shultz-Shevardnadze Meetings [09/17/1987]," RAC Box 17, Robert Linhard Files, RRPL.

79. Minutes of National Security Planning Group meeting, October 14, 1987, pp. 3, 6–7, folder "NSPG 0168 10/14/1987 [Shultz/Shevardnadze Moscow Meeting]," Box 5, ES, NSC: NSPG Files, RRPL.

80. "Memorandum of conversation between M. S. Gorbachev and U.S. Secretary of State G. Shultz. Excerpt," October 23, 1987, pp. 5–6, 10, 14, 15–16, NSAEBB No. 238, https://nsarchive2 .gwu.edu/NSAEBB/NSAEBB238/russian/Final1987-10-23%20Gorbachev-Shultz.pdf.

81. Shultz, *Turmoil and Triumph*, 999–1001.

82. Reagan, *An American Life*, 693–95.

83. See, for example, Senator Edward M. Kennedy, speaking on the nomination of Robert Bork, 100th Cong., 1st sess., *Congressional Record* 133 (July 1, 1987): S9188.

84. Reagan chronicled his phone calls and meetings with senators to advocate Bork's confirmation in his diary. See, for example, his entries on September 15, September 29, September 30, October 1, October 2, and October 7, 1987. Reagan also called Justice Powell on September 26 to ask if he would endorse Bork as his replacement. Ronald Reagan White House diary, September 26, 1987, https://www.reaganfoundation.org/ronald-reagan/white-house-diaries/diary-entry-09261987/.

85. Nina Totenberg, "Robert Bork's Supreme Court Nomination 'Changed Everything, Maybe Forever,'" *NPR*, December 19, 2012.

86. Reagan, *An American Life*, 695–97.

87. Letter, Mikhail Gorbachev to Ronald Reagan, October 28, 1987, p. 4, NSAEBB No. 238, https://nsarchive2.gwu.edu/NSAEBB/NSAEBB238/russian/Final1987-10-28%20Gorbachev%20Letter%20to%20Reagan.pdf; Ronald Reagan, "Remarks and a Question-and-Answer Session with Reporters on the Soviet-United States Summit Meeting," October 30, 1987, APP, https://www.presidency.ucsb.edu/documents/remarks-and-question-and-answer-session-with-reporters-the-soviet-united-states-summit.

88. Memorandum, E. Rowny to the national security advisor, November 6, 1987, pp. 1–2, folder "Summit Prep (General) 11/09/1987 (1 of 4)," RAC Box 19, Robert Linhard Files, RRPL.

89. Memorandum, Frank C. Carlucci to the president, "Scope Paper on December US-Soviet Summit," p. 2, folder "Summit Prep (General) 11/09/1987 (3 of 4)," RAC Box 19, Robert Linhard Files, RRPL.

90. Ibid., p. 4.

91. Untitled notes, folder "PRG (Policy Review Group), 11/04/1987, Summit Organization," RAC Box 19, Robert Linhard Files, RRPL.

92. Memorandum, Fritz W. Ermarth to Robert E. Linhard, November 13, 1987, folder "Summit Prep (General) 11/09/1987 (2 of 4)," RAC Box 19, Robert Linhard Files, RRPL.

93. "Remarks on Signing the Intermediate-Range Nuclear Forces Treaty," December 8, 1987, APP, https://www.presidency.ucsb.edu/documents/remarks-signing-the-intermediate-range-nuclear-forces-treaty.

94. Memorandum of conversation, December 9, 1987, 10:55 a.m.–12:35 p.m., pp. 6–8, 12, NSAEBB No. 238, https://nsarchive2.gwu.edu/NSAEBB/NSAEBB238/usdocs/Doc%2017%20 (Memcon%20Gorby%20Reagan%2012.09.87).pdf.

95. Memorandum of conversation, December 9, 1987, 10:35 a.m.–10:45 a.m., p. 1, NSAEBB No. 238, https://nsarchive2.gwu.edu/NSAEBB/NSAEBB238/usdocs/Doc%2016%20(Memcon%20Gorby%20Reagan%2012.09.87).pdf.

96. For a full list of the bilateral agreements signed during the Moscow summit, see information memorandum, M. James Wilkinson to Under Secretary Armacost, May 31, 1988, pp. 1–3, NSAEBB No. 251, "The Moscow Summit 20 Years Later," https://nsarchive2.gwu.edu/NSAEBB/NSAEBB251/22.pdf.

97. James Mann, *The Rebellion of Ronald Reagan: A History of the End of the Cold War* (New York: Viking, 2009), 304.

98. "The Gorbachev Interview: Text of Answers to the Written Questions—'It Is Essential to Continue Positive Contacts,'" *Washington Post*, May 22, 1988.

99. Speech by Mikhail Gorbachev at a dinner with Wojciech Jaruzelski, July 11, 1988, in Savranskaya et al., *Masterpieces of History*, 290–91. Although Gorbachev wanted to continue the Helsinki process, he also argued that "a number of problems extend beyond the framework of this process. We have to go further, to rethink the entire situation in Europe from the standpoint of the new political thinking."

100. William Taubman and Svetlana Savranskaya, "If a Wall Fell in Berlin and Moscow Hardly Noticed, Would It Still Make a Noise?" in *The Fall of the Berlin Wall: The Revolutionary Legacy of 1989*, ed. Jeffrey A. Engel (Oxford: Oxford University Press, 2009), 69–95, 79.

101. Anatoly S. Chernyaev, *My Six Years with Gorbachev*, trans. and ed. Robert D. English and Elizabeth Tucker (University Park: Pennsylvania State University Press, 2000), 105.

102. Jacques Lévesque, *The Enigma of 1989: The USSR and the Liberation of Eastern Europe* (Berkeley: University of California Press, 1997), 46.

103. Taubman and Savranskaya, "If a Wall Fell in Berlin and Moscow Hardly Noticed," 79.

104. Lévesque, *The Enigma of 1989*, 42.

105. Stephen Brown, "Cohabiting a 'Common Home,'" *END Journal* 37 (1989): 17.

106. Memorandum, Anatoly Dobrynin to Mikhail Gorbachev, September 18, 1988, NSAEBB No. 261 "Reagan, Gorbachev and Bush at Governors Island," https://nsarchive2.gwu .edu/NSAEBB/NSAEBB261/sov02.pdf.

107. Notes of a meeting between Mikhail Gorbachev and foreign policy advisors, October 31, 1988, in Savranskaya et al., *Masterpieces of History*, 311–12.

108. "Provisional Verbatim Record of the 72nd Meeting, Held at Headquarters, New York, on Wednesday, 7 December 1988: General Assembly, 43rd Session," A/43/PV.72, pp. 9–12, 26–28, https://digitallibrary.un.org/record/54974?ln=en.

109. "Gambler, Showman, Statesman," *New York Times*, December 8, 1988.

110. "Provisional Verbatim Record of the 72nd Meeting," pp. 33–35.

Chapter 7

1. George Bush and Brent Scowcroft, *A World Transformed* (New York: Knopf, 1998), 3.

2. Ronald Reagan White House diary, December 7, 1988, https://www.reaganfoundation .org/ronald-reagan/white-house-diaries/diary-entry-12071988/; "Provisional Verbatim Record of the 72nd Meeting," pp. 9–12, 26–28.

3. Bush and Scowcroft, *A World Transformed*, 6.

4. Memorandum of conversation, the president's private meeting with Gorbachev, December 7, 1988, 1:05–1:30 p.m., pp. 3–4, NSAEBB No. 261, https://nsarchive2.gwu.edu/NSAEBB /NSAEBB261/us08.pdf.

5. Reagan, *An American Life*, 721.

6. Gorbachev, *Memoirs*, 463.

7. Bush and Scowcroft, *A World Transformed*, 3.

8. Memorandum of conversation, the president's private meeting with Gorbachev, December 7, 1988, p. 4.

9. Gorbachev, *Memoirs*, 463.

10. Jon Meacham, *Destiny and Power: The American Odyssey of George Herbert Walker Bush* (New York: Random House, 2015).

11. Bush and Scowcroft, *A World Transformed*, 17; Robert Ajemian, "Where Is the Real George Bush?," *Time*, January 26, 1987.

12. Bush and Scowcroft, *A World Transformed*, 17, 12.

13. Hal Brands, *From Berlin to Baghdad: America's Search for Purpose in the Post–Cold War World* (Lexington: University Press of Kentucky, 2008), 14.

14. Bush and Scowcroft, *A World Transformed*, 12.

15. George Bush, "Address on Administration Goals Before a Joint Session of Congress," February 9, 1989, APP, https://www.presidency.ucsb.edu/documents/address-administration -goals-before-joint-session-congress.

16. National Security Review (NSR) 3, February 15, 1989, https://bush41library.tamu.edu /files/nsr/nsr3.pdf; NSR 4, February 15, 1989, https://bush41library.tamu.edu/files/nsr/nsr4.pdf; NSR 5, February 15, 1989, https://bush41library.tamu.edu/files/nsr/nsr5.pdf; NSR 12, March 3, 1989, https://bush41library.tamu.edu/files/nsr/nsr12.pdf; NSR 14, April 3, 1989, https:// bush41library.tamu.edu/files/nsr/nsr14.pdf.

17. Letter, George Bush to Mikhail Gorbachev, January 17, 1989, in Savranskaya et al., *Masterpieces of History*, 347.

18. Robert M. Gates, *From the Shadows: The Ultimate Insider's Story of Five Presidents and How They Won the Cold War* (New York: Simon and Schuster, 1996), 459–60.

19. NSR 12, pp. 1, 5–6, 8.

20. NSR 14, pp. 1–3.

21. Taubman and Savranskaya, "If a Wall Fell in Berlin and Moscow Hardly Noticed," 72–73.

22. Ibid., 72, 74; Ronald Grigor Suny, *The Soviet Experiment: Russia, the USSR, and the Successor States*, 2nd ed. (Oxford: Oxford University Press, 2011), 491.

23. Politburo session, December 27–28, 1988, p. 6, NSAEBB No. 261, https://nsarchive2 .gwu.edu/NSAEBB/NSAEBB261/sov10.pdf.

24. NSR 3, pp. 1–2.

25. NSR 4, pp. 2, 1.

26. Kristina Spohr, *Post Wall, Post Square: How Bush, Gorbachev, Kohl, and Deng Shaped the World After 1989* (New Haven: Yale University Press, 2020), 71–72. On Solidarity, see Timothy Garton Ash, *The Polish Revolution: Solidarity*, 3rd ed. (New Haven: Yale University Press, 2002).

27. On the Hungarian revolution, see Rudolf L. Tőkés, *Hungary's Negotiated Revolution: Economic Reform, Social Change, and Political Succession, 1957–1990* (Cambridge: Cambridge University Press, 1996).

28. NSR 4, pp. 1–2.

29. Letter, George Bush to Mikhail Gorbachev, January 17, 1989, 347–48.

30. Note, Bob [Gates] to Brent [Scowcroft], January 28, 1989, folder "USSR Collapse: U.S.-Soviet Relations Thru 1991 (January–April 1989)," OA/ID 91117-001, Brent Scowcroft Collection, George H. W. Bush Presidential Records (henceforth GHWBPR), George Bush Presidential Library (henceforth GBPL).

31. Memorandum, Brent Scowcroft to the president, March 1, 1989, pp. 2, 3, folder "USSR Collapse: U.S.-Soviet Relations Thru 1991 (January–April 1989)," OA/ID 91117-001, Brent Scowcroft Collection, GHWBPR, GBPL.

32. Memorandum of conversation, the secretary's meeting in Vienna with Soviet foreign minister Shevardnadze—plenary session, March 7, 1989, 11:05 a.m.–12:05 p.m., pp. 9, 10, folder "Vienna-Baker/Shevardnadze-March 1989," OA/ID CF00717-018, Condoleezza Rice Files, GHWBPR, GBPL.

33. James A. Baker III with Thomas M. DeFrank, *The Politics of Diplomacy: Revolution, War, and Peace, 1989–1992* (New York: G. P. Putnam's Sons, 1995), 68; Bush and Scowcroft, *A World Transformed*, 40; Gates, *From the Shadows*, 460.

34. Baker, *The Politics of Diplomacy*, 68.

35. Memorandum, Philip Zelikow/Condoleezza Rice through Robert D. Blackwill to Brent Scowcroft, March 2, 1989, folder "NSR-3-February 15, 1989-Comprehensive Review of U.S.-Soviet Relations [1]," OA/ID 90006-003, National Security Council H-Files-NSR Files, GHWBPR, GBPL.

36. Robert J. McCartney, "Soviets to Dismantle Some Tactical A-Arms: Shevardnadze Announces European Pullback," *Washington Post*, January 20, 1989.

37. Memorandum of conversation, the secretary's meeting in Vienna with Soviet foreign minister Shevardnadze—plenary session, March 7, 1989, p. 10.

38. Baker, *The Politics of Diplomacy*, 82; "Soviet Record of Conversation between M. S. Gorbachev and U.S. Secretary of State J. Baker," May 11, 1989, pp. 1–2, WCDA, https://digitalarchive .wilsoncenter.org/document/118702.

39. "Soviet Record of Conversation between M. S. Gorbachev and U.S. Secretary of State J. Baker," May 11, 1989, p. 2.

40. Ibid., pp. 1–3.

41. Memorandum, Brent Scowcroft to the president, "Short-Range Nuclear Forces and NATO's 'Comprehensive Concept,'" p. 1, folder "Soviet Power Collapse in Eastern Europe-SNF [Short-range Nuclear Forces]-April 1989 [1]," OA/ID 91120-002, Brent Scowcroft Collection, GHWBPR, GBPL.

42. NATO, "Declaration of the Heads of State and Government Participating in the Meeting of the North Atlantic Council," March 2–3, 1988, https://www.nato.int/docu/comm/49-95 /c880303a.htm.

43. Cable, USNATO 00703, February 7, 1989, p. 2, folder "Soviet Power Collapse in Eastern Europe-SNF [Short-range Nuclear Forces]-March 1989," OA/ID 91120-001, Brent Scowcroft Collection, GHWBPR, GBPL.

44. "Current Aspects of Arms Control: The Western European Position—Reply to the Annual Report of the Council: Report Submitted on Behalf of the Committee on Defence Questions and Armaments by Mr. de Beer, Rapporteur," April 25, 1989, pp. 95–96, Proceedings vol. 1, thirty-fifth session, first part, June 1989—Assembly document 1182, WEU-70.011, Assembly of Western European Union Fond, Historical Archives of the European Union.

45. "After INF: What Next?," *END Journal* 31 (December 1987–January 1988): 28.

46. Jonathan Steele, "Loosening the Superpower Bonds," *END Journal* 32 (February–March 1988): 2; Jonathan Steele, "Controlling the Arms Controllers," *END Journal* 33 (May–June 1988): 2; Mary Kaldor, "Past, Present, Future," *END Journal* 37 (1989): 2; Mary Kaldor, "The Legitimation Game," *END Journal* 37 (1989): 20.

47. Steele, "Controlling the Arms Controllers," 2.

48. Kaldor, "The Legitimation Game," 20–21.

49. Carole Tongue, "Playing a Positive Role," *END Journal* 37 (1989): 14.

50. "European Nuclear Disarmament Welcomes the Visit of President Gorbachev," END/14/23, Folder 2, END Collection, LSEL.

51. Pankin, "Soviet 'New Thinking.'"

52. Gorbachev statement on disarmament, January 16, 1986; Gorbachev, *For a "Common European Home," for a New Way of Thinking*, 23–24.

53. Tairov, "From New Thinking to a Civic Peace," 46.

54. On the Bush administration's opposition to SNF negotiations, see cable, USNATO 00703, February 7, 1989, pp. 2, 3; Proposed letter, George Bush to Helmut Kohl, folder "Soviet Power Collapse in Eastern Europe-SNF [Short-range Nuclear Forces]-March 1989," OA/ID 91120-001, Brent Scowcroft Collection, GHWBPR, GBPL; Memorandum, Brent Scowcroft to the president, "Short-Range Nuclear Forces and NATO's 'Comprehensive Concept,'" p. 2; Message, Brent Scowcroft to Peter Hartmann, April 18, 1989, folder "Soviet Power Collapse in Eastern Europe-SNF [Short-range Nuclear Forces]-April 1989 [1]," OA/ID 91120-002, Brent Scowcroft Collection, GHWBPR, GBPL; "Points to Be Made for Meeting with Norwegian Prime Minister Gro Harlem Brundtland," p. 1, folder "Soviet Power Collapse in Eastern Europe-SNF [Short-range Nuclear Forces]-May 1989 [1]," OA/ID 91120-004, Brent Scowcroft Collection, GHWBPR, GBPL.

55. "Soviet Record of Conversation between M. S. Gorbachev and U.S. Secretary of State J. Baker," May 11, 1989, pp. 4–5, 2.

56. Baker, *The Politics of Diplomacy*, 82.

57. David Hoffman, "Gorbachev 'Gambits' Challenged: White House Doubts Claim He Has Ended Nicaraguan Arms Aid," *Washington Post*, May 17, 1989.

58. See Gorbachev statement on disarmament, January 16, 1986; Gorbachev, *For a "Common European Home," for a New Way of Thinking*.

59. Lou Cannon, "Reagan Is Concerned About Bush's Indecision," *Washington Post*, May 6, 1989.

60. Chernyaev, *My Six Years with Gorbachev*, 215.

61. Gorbachev, *Memoirs*, 501.

62. Record of conversation between Aleksandr Yakovlev and Jack Matlock, July 20, 1989, in Savranskaya et al., *Masterpieces of History*, 506, 507, 508.

63. Ibid., 508-9.

64. "Press Conference, the Honorable James A. Baker III, Secretary of State," September 19, 1989, pp. 7, 6, folder "September 1989 Foreign Ministers," OA/ID CF01586-008, Richard A. Davis Files, GHWBPR, GBPL.

65. Overall joint statement, September 23, 1989, p. 1, folder "September 1989 Foreign Ministers," OA/ID CF01586-008, Richard A. Davis Files, GHWBPR, GBPL.

66. NSDD 307, May 27, 1988, p. 3, https://www.reaganlibrary.archives.gov/archives /reference/Scanned%20NSDDS/NSDD307.pdf.

67. Memorandum of conversation, the secretary's meeting in Vienna with Soviet foreign minister Shevardnadze—plenary session, March 7, 1989, p. 9.

68. Overall joint statement, September 23, 1989, p. 2.

69. "Record of Conversation Between President M. S. Gorbachev and Miklós Németh, Member of the HSWP CC Politburo, Chairman of the Council of Ministers of the People's Republic of Hungary," March 3, 1989, WCDA, https://digitalarchive.wilsoncenter.org/document /112492.

70. Record of conversation between Mikhail Gorbachev and Miklós Németh, March 3, 1989, in Savranskaya et al., *Masterpieces of History*, 412.

71. Spohr, *Post Wall, Post Square*, 75-78.

72. John Tagliabue, "Poland Sets Free Vote in June, First Since '45; Solidarity Reinstated," *New York Times*, April 6, 1989.

73. Spohr, *Post Wall, Post Square*, 66.

74. For an eyewitness account of the June 4 election and its immediate aftermath, see Timothy Garton Ash, *The Magic Lantern: The Revolution of '89 Witnessed in Warsaw, Budapest, Berlin, and Prague* (New York: Vintage Books, 1993), 25-46.

75. Spohr, *Post Wall, Post Square*, 103-5.

76. Wittner, *Toward Nuclear Abolition*, 415.

77. "Report on a Working Visit of Wojciech Jaruzelski to Moscow," May 9, 1989, p. 1, WCDA, https://digitalarchive.wilsoncenter.org/document/116226.

78. Paula Butturini, "Polish Party Yields After Talk with Gorbachev," *Chicago Tribune*, August 23, 1989.

79. William C. Wohlforth, ed., *Witnesses to the End of the Cold War* (Baltimore: Johns Hopkins University Press, 1996), 97.

80. Report from Mikhail Gorbachev to the CC CPSU Politburo regarding his meeting with the Trilateral Commission, January 21, 1989, in Savranskaya et al., *Masterpieces of History*, 350.

81. Mikhail Gorbachev, "Europe as a Common Home: Address Given by Mikhail Gorbachev to the Council of Europe," July 6, 1989, pp. 4, 2, https://chnm.gmu.edu/1989/archive/files/gorbachev-speech-7-6-89_e3ccb87237.pdf.

82. Ibid., p. 5.

83. Jan Kavan, "Prague '88 and Beyond," *East European Reporter* 3, no. 3 (Autumn 1988): 17.

84. Jiří Dienstbier, "The Helsinki Process 'from Below,'" insert for *END Journal* 37, March 1989, END/10/1, END Collection, LSEL.

85. Ibid.

86. For Kaldor's reflections on the Prague 88 meeting, see Mary Kaldor, "Welcome to Bad News," *END Journal* 36 (October 1988–January 1989): 17. For the signatories of the final proposal for a European Citizens' Assembly, see "Proposal for a Peace Parliament in Prague," *East European Reporter* 3, no. 3 (Autumn 1988): 20.

87. Kaldor, "Welcome to Bad News," 17; Kaldor, "Past, Present, Future," 2.

88. Advertisement, "An Alternative Vision of Europe," *END Journal* 37 (1989): 2.

89. See, for example, Gorbachev, "Address on French Television," 248; Gorbachev, "Address to French Parliamentarians," 270–74; Gorbachev, *For a "Common European Home," for a New Way of Thinking*, 28–31.

90. Gorbachev, "Europe as a Common Home," pp. 4, 8–9.

91. Ibid., p. 3.

92. Ibid., pp. 6–7, 10–13.

93. Ibid., p. 12.

94. Pankin, "Soviet 'New Thinking.'"

95. E. P. Thompson, "Ends and Histories," in Kaldor, *Europe from Below*, 7–25, 16–17.

96. Memorandum, Robert L. Hutchings through Robert D. Blackwill to Brent Scowcroft, April 3, 1989, pp. 2–3, folder "NSC0008a-April 04, 1989-U.S. Relations with Western Europe and Eastern Europe," OA/ID 90000-009, National Security Council H-Files-NSC Meeting Files, GHWBPR, GBPL. See also memorandum, Brent Scowcroft to the president, meeting with the National Security Council, April 4, 1989, pp. 1–2, folder "NSC0008a-April 04, 1989-U.S. Relations with Western Europe and Eastern Europe," OA/ID 90000-009, National Security Council H-Files-NSC Meeting Files, GHWBPR, GBPL.

97. Memorandum, Robert L. Hutchings through Robert D. Blackwill to Brent Scowcroft, April 3, 1989, p. 8.

98. George Bush, "Remarks to the Citizens in Mainz, Federal Republic of Germany," May 31, 1989, APP, https://www.presidency.ucsb.edu/documents/remarks-the-citizens-mainz-federal-republic-germany. On the unequal reductions in Bush's conventional arms control proposal, see Baker, *The Politics of Diplomacy*, 94.

99. Bush, "Remarks to the Citizens in Mainz, Federal Republic of Germany."

100. Leffler, *For the Soul of Mankind*, 430.

101. Spohr, *Post Wall, Post Square*, 108–16.

102. "New Forum Appeal," *East European Reporter* 4, no. 1 (Winter 1989/90): 14–15; "Interview with Bärbel Bohley," *East European Reporter* 4, no. 1 (Winter 1989/90): 15–17.

103. "Twelve Founders of a 'Citizens' Movement–"Democracy Now"': 'Appeal for Interference in Our Own Affairs' and 'Theses for a Democratic Transformation in the GDR,'" *East European Reporter* 4, no. 1 (Winter 1989/90): 19–21.

104. "Democratic Awakening—Social and Ecological," *East European Reporter* 4, no. 1 (Winter 1989/90): 22. Following the GDR's free elections in March 1990, Eppelmann became defense and disarmament minister. Wittner, *Toward Nuclear Abolition*, 415.

105. Spohr, *Post Wall, Post Square*, 135–36.

106. Record of conversation between Mikhail Gorbachev and members of the CC SED Politburo, October 7, 1989, in Savranskaya et al., *Masterpieces of History*, 545–46.

107. Spohr, *Post Wall, Post Square*, 138–43.

108. Mary Elise Sarotte, *The Collapse: The Accidental Opening of the Berlin Wall* (New York: Basic Books, 2014), 105–6.

109. Ibid., 106–15.

110. Sarotte, *The Collapse*, 116–19, 127–53; Spohr, *Post Wall, Post Square*, 144–47.

111. Lévesque, *The Enigma of 1989*, 159.

112. Diary of Anatoly Chernyaev regarding the fall of the Berlin Wall, November 10, 1989, in Savranskaya et al., *Masterpieces of History*, 586.

113. Memorandum from Georgy Shakhnazarov to Mikhail Gorbachev regarding military détente in Europe, October 14, 1989, in Savranskaya et al., *Masterpieces of History*, 555–56.

114. Record of conversation between Mikhail Gorbachev and Mauno Koivisto, October 25, 1989, in Savranskaya et al., *Masterpieces of History*, 562.

115. Record of conversation between Mikhail Gorbachev and Tadeusz Mazowiecki, November 24, 1989, in Savranskaya et al., *Masterpieces of History*, 606.

116. Gorbachev, *Perestroika*, 195–96.

117. Shevardnadze, *The Future Belongs to Freedom*, 130; Sergei A. Karaganov, "Towards a New Security System in Europe," in *Gorbachev and Europe*, ed. Vilho Harle and Jyrki Iivonen (London: Pinter Publishers, 1990), 40–50, 46.

118. Gorbachev, "Europe as a Common Home," p. 4.

119. Karaganov, "Towards a New Security System in Europe," 43, 49.

120. Ibid., 44, 45.

121. Gorbachev, *Perestroika*, 196.

122. Gorbachev, "Europe as a Common Home," p. 11.

123. Gorbachev repeatedly expressed his concerns about German reunification to foreign leaders in the weeks after the fall of the Berlin Wall. See, for example, record of telephone conversation between Mikhail Gorbachev and François Mitterrand, November 14, 1989, in Savranskaya et al., *Masterpieces of History*, 593–94; Record of conversation between Mikhail Gorbachev and Brian Mulroney, November 21, 1989, in Savranskaya et al., *Masterpieces of History*, 600–1; and Soviet transcript of the Malta summit, December 2–3, 1989, first private session, December 2, 1989, pp. 18–19, NSAEBB No. 298 "Bush and Gorbachev at Malta," https://nsarchive2.gwu.edu/NSAEBB/NSAEBB298/Document%2010.pdf.

124. Gorbachev, *Memoirs*, 28–34.

125. Ibid., 517, 528.

126. Mary Sarotte has argued that Gorbachev envisioned the "common European home" as a model for German reunification that would contain a neutral Germany. She refers to the "common European home" as the "heroic model" of reunification. Yet she does not address the longer history of the "common European home" concept, suggesting that it arose only in 1989. Mary Elise Sarotte, *1989: The Struggle to Create Post–Cold War Europe* (Princeton: Princeton University Press, 2009), esp. 105–6.

127. Record of conversation between Mikhail Gorbachev and Brian Mulroney, November 21, 1989, 601.

128. Shevardnadze, *The Future Belongs to Freedom*, 127–28.

129. For an eyewitness account of the Velvet Revolution, see Garton Ash, *The Magic Lantern*, 78–130.

130. "Proclamation on the Establishment of Civic Forum 19 November 1989," November 19, 1989, WCDA, https://digitalarchive.wilsoncenter.org/document/117216.

131. "List of Goals by the Civic Forum, 26 November 1989," November 26, 1989, WCDA, https://digitalarchive.wilsoncenter.org/document/117217.

132. Spohr, *Post Wall, Post Square*, 188.

133. Wittner, *Toward Nuclear Abolition*, 415.

134. Letter, George Bush to Mikhail Gorbachev, July 21, 1989, in George Bush, *All the Best, George Bush: My Life in Letters and Other Writings* (New York: Scribner, 1999), 433–34.

135. *Foreign Relations of the United States*, 1981–1988, vol. 5, Document 280.

136. "Points to Be Made for Telephone Conversation with President Mitterrand," p. 4, folder "USSR Collapse: U.S.-Soviet Relations Thru 1991 (November 1989)," OA/ID 91117-007, Brent Scowcroft Collection, GHWBPR, GBPL.

137. "Points to Be Made in NSC Meeting on Your Discussion with Gorbachev," p. 6, NSAEBB No. 298, https://nsarchive2.gwu.edu/NSAEBB/NSAEBB298/Document%207.pdf. See also "Draft Presidential Message to Allied Leaders on Malta Meeting," p. 5, folder "Summit (Malta)-November 1989 ['5]," OA/ID CF00770-022, Arnold Kanter Files, GHWBPR, GBPL.

138. "Gorbachev Presentation on Minimum Nuclear Deterrence" and "President's Response," folder "Summit (Malta)-November 1989 [3]," OA/ID CF00770-020, Arnold Kanter Files, GHWBPR, GBPL.

139. "Draft Presidential Message to Allied Leaders on Malta Meeting." See also "Points to Be Made in NSC Meeting on Your Discussion with Gorbachev."

140. Memorandum, Brent Scowcroft to the president, "Meetings on the Soviet Union," pp. 1, 2, folder "Summit at Malta December 1989: Malta Memcons [2]," OA/ID CF00718-007, Condoleezza Rice Files, GHWBPR, GBPL.

141. See, for example, Michael Dobbs, "The Seasick Summit," *Washington Post*, December 3, 1989.

142. Memorandum of conversation, first expanded bilateral session with Chairman Gorbachev of the Soviet Union, December 2, 1989, 10:00–11:55 a.m., p. 7, folder "Malta Summit-December 89," OA/ID CF00769-005, Arnold Kanter Files, GHWBPR, GBPL.

143. Soviet transcript of the Malta summit, December 2–3, 1989, third meeting between Gorbachev and Bush (plenary session), December 3, 1989, pp. 21–22, NSAEBB No. 298, https://nsarchive2.gwu.edu/NSAEBB/NSAEBB298/Document%2010.pdf.

144. Ibid., pp. 28, 29.

145. Soviet draft, "Directives for the Ministers of Foreign Affairs of the USSR and the United States," December 3, 1989, NSAEBB No. 298, https://nsarchive2.gwu.edu/NSAEBB/NSAEBB298/Document%2011.pdf.

146. "Remarks of the President and Soviet Chairman Gorbachev and a Question-and-Answer Session with Reporters in Malta," December 3, 1989, pp. 3, 2, https://chnm.gmu.edu/1989/archive/files/bush-interview-12-3-89_43aefd5a82.pdf.

Conclusion

1. "Ten Minutes to Midnight," *Bulletin of the Atomic Scientists* 46, no. 3 (April 1990): 3.

2. See Lawrence S. Wittner, *One World or None: A History of the World Nuclear Disarmament Movement Through 1953*, vol. 1 of *The Struggle Against the Bomb* (Stanford: Stanford University Press, 1993).

3. See Wittner, *Resisting the Bomb*.

4. Jimmy Carter, "Inaugural Address," January 20, 1977, APP, https://www.presidency.ucsb.edu/documents/inaugural-address-0. On Carter's nuclear abolitionism, see Auten, *Carter's Conversion*, 95.

5. Kleidman, *Organizing for Peace*, 164.

6. "Summary: SANE/FREEZE 1988 Strategy," p. 1, folder "Strategy and goals, 1987," Box 1, Series D: Programmatic Efforts, Peace Action Records, SCPC.

7. Kleidman, *Organizing for Peace*, 167–68.

8. Kaldor, "Past, Present, Future," 2.

9. "To Our Readers," *END Journal* 36 (October 1988–January 1989): 23; Kaldor, "Past, Present, Future," 2.

10. Mary Kaldor, "From Gloom to Surprise," *END Journal* 36 (October 1988–January 1989): 21.

11. On East Europeans' increasing participation in the END Conventions, see Wittner, *Toward Nuclear Abolition*, 416–17.

12. Kaldor, "From Gloom to Surprise," 21.

13. Science and Security Board of the *Bulletin of the Atomic Scientists*, "This Is Your COVID Wake-Up Call: It Is 100 Seconds to Midnight," January 27, 2021, https://thebulletin.org/doomsday-clock/current-time/; Katie Rogers and Rick Gladstone, "Biden Suggests Nuclear Talks with Iran May Resume," *New York Times*, October 30, 2021; Choe Sang-Hun, "North Korea Displays Large Missile Arsenal amid Stalled Talks," *New York Times*, October 12, 2021.

14. Science and Security Board, "This Is Your COVID Wake-Up Call"; Steven Mufson and Annabelle Timsit, "'It Is Not Enough': World Leaders React to COP26 Climate Agreement," *Washington Post*, November 14, 2021.

15. Science and Security Board, "This Is Your COVID Wake-Up Call."

16. Wittner, *Toward Nuclear Abolition*, 143, 144–45, 140, 176.

INDEX

ACKNOWLEDGMENTS

I am grateful to a number of institutions and individuals for generously supporting this project. For research funding, I am indebted to the John Sloan Dickey Center for International Understanding at Dartmouth College, the Mellon Foundation/American Council of Learned Societies, the University of Virginia Graduate School of Arts and Sciences, the Thomas Jefferson Memorial Foundation and the Institute of the Humanities and Global Cultures at the University of Virginia, and the Lynde and Harry Bradley Foundation. I benefited greatly from a Mellon/ACLS Dissertation Completion Fellowship and postdoctoral fellowships from the Dickey Center at Dartmouth and the Belfer Center for Science and International Affairs at the Harvard Kennedy School, which enabled me to focus intensively on researching and writing this book. The vibrant intellectual communities at Dartmouth and Harvard also pushed me to refine my thinking in ways that greatly improved this book. I also thank Mississippi State University for providing a new intellectual home and a semester of leave during this project's final stage.

I am particularly indebted to the scholarly community at the University of Virginia, where I began this project. I am especially grateful to my advisor, William Hitchcock, for his mentorship and invaluable feedback on multiple drafts of this manuscript. I owe a special thanks to Melvyn Leffler for his tireless support and incisive comments on my work throughout graduate school. Will and Mel are model scholars and teachers, and I am fortunate to have had the opportunity to work with them. I also benefited from the guidance and feedback of Brian Balogh and Allen Lynch, and I deeply appreciate their support. Thomas Schwartz has been a wonderful mentor since my undergraduate days at Vanderbilt University, and he kindly read an early draft of this manuscript.

For especially helpful comments on portions of this book, I am grateful to David Allen, Mary Barton, Paul Behringer, Max Edelson, Alexandra Evans, Udi Greenberg, Alexander Keyssar, Edward Miller, Jennifer Miller,

Nicholas Miller, Aroop Mukharji, Shannon Nix, Odd Arne Westad, William Wohlforth, and George Yin. I also benefited from presenting my research at conferences and workshops hosted by the Wilson Center's Nuclear Proliferation International History Project, the Society for Historians of American Foreign Relations, the Clements Center for National Security at the University of Texas at Austin, Dartmouth College, the Harvard Kennedy School, and LSE IDEAS. I thank the commentators and participants in those events, especially Patrick Burke, Matthew Evangelista, Frank Gavin, Petra Goedde, Mary Sarotte, and James Wilson.

Excerpts from this book appeared in my chapter, "Ronald Reagan and the Nuclear Freeze Movement," in the edited volume *The Reagan Moment: America and the World in the 1980s*. I am grateful to Cornell University Press for permission to reuse this material.

My editor at the University of Pennsylvania Press, Robert Lockhart, deserves special thanks. It has been a joy to work with Bob, whose insightful feedback has improved the final manuscript immeasurably. I am grateful to Christopher Dietrich for the opportunity to be included in the Power, Politics, and the World series. This book also benefited from the comments of the two anonymous reviewers. Any remaining shortcomings are my own.

My sincerest thanks go to my parents, Lynn and Patrick Freeman, to whom this book is dedicated. Their love and support have been unfailing and indispensable to the completion of this project. This book is also dedicated to the memory of my grandmother, Susan Parham. Her love and encouragement helped sustain me for twenty-three years, and her life continues to inspire me each day.